Elegance

THE GUIDE TO RELAIS & CHÂTEAUX IN FRANCE

Nathalie Gaume

Introduction
1. The Art of Living at Relais & Châteaux
- The History of Relais & Châteaux
- Principles and Values
- The Unique Experience

Chapter 1: Relais & Châteaux in Île-de-France
1. General Presentation of the Region
- History and Heritage
- Gastronomy and Wine
2. Addresses and Descriptions
- The Château de Montvillargenne
- Le Relais Christine
- The Queen's Pavilion

Chapter 2: Relais & Châteaux in Provence-Alpes-Côte d'Azur
1. General Presentation of the Region
- History and Heritage
- Gastronomy and Wine
2. Addresses and Descriptions
- The Bastide of Gordes
- Château de la Chèvre d'Or
- Villa Gallici

Chapter 3: Relais & Châteaux in Burgundy-Franche-Comté
1. General Presentation of the Region
- History and Heritage
- Gastronomy and Wine
2. Addresses and Descriptions
- Château de Gilly
- Le Relais Bernard Loiseau
- Hostellerie de Levernois

Chapter 4: Relais & Châteaux in New Aquitaine
1. General Presentation of the Region
- History and Heritage
- Gastronomy and Wine
2. Addresses and Descriptions
- Les Prés d'Eugénie - Maison Guérard
- Château Cordeillan-Bages
- Pavia Hotel

Chapter 5: Relais & Châteaux in Auvergne-Rhône-Alpes
1. General Presentation of the Region
- History and Heritage
- Gastronomy and Wine
2. Addresses and Descriptions
- The Château de Bagnols
- Le Clos des Sens
- Hotel & Spa Le Doge

Chapter 6: Relais & Châteaux in Occitanie
1. General Presentation of the Region
- History and Heritage
- Gastronomy and Wine
2. Addresses and Descriptions
- Mercuès Castle
- Auriac Estate
- Old Castillon

Chapter 7: Relais & Châteaux in Normandy
1. General Presentation of the Region
- History and Heritage
- Gastronomy and Wine
2. Addresses and Descriptions
Chantore Castle
- La Ferme Saint-Siméon
- The Manor of the Impressionists

Chapter 8: Relais & Châteaux in Brittany
1. General Presentation of the Region
- History and Heritage
- Gastronomy and Wine
2. Addresses and Descriptions
- Castel Clara Thalasso & Spa
- Hotel Brittany & Spa
- The Castel Marie-Louise

Chapter 9: Relais & Châteaux in Pays de la Loire
1. General Presentation of the Region
- History and Heritage
- Gastronomy and Wine
2. Addresses and Descriptions
- Domaine de La Bretesche

- Château de Noirieux
- Relais de Chambord

Chapter 10: Relais & Châteaux in the Grand Est
1. General Presentation of the Region
- History and Heritage
- Gastronomy and Wine
2. Addresses and Descriptions
Adoménil Castle
- Le Chambard
- Hostellerie La Cheneaudière

Chapter 11: Relais & Châteaux in Hauts-de-France
1. General Presentation of the Region
- History and Heritage
- Gastronomy and Wine
2. Addresses and Descriptions
- Montreuil Castle
- The Chartreuse du Val Saint Esprit
- Beaulieu Castle

Chapter 12: Relais & Châteaux in Corsica
1. General Presentation of the Region
- History and Heritage
- Gastronomy and Wine
2. Addresses and Descriptions
- Hôtel & Spa des Pecheurs
- Casadelmar
- Murtoli Estate

Conclusion
1. The Future of Relais & Châteaux
- New Trends
- Innovations and Developments
- The Role of Sustainability

Introduction

1. The Art of Living at Relais & Châteaux

Introduction

Relais & Châteaux are much more than just luxury hotels; they embody the very essence of the French art of living. Founded in 1954, these exceptional establishments offer a unique experience, combining warm hospitality, refined gastronomy and an exceptional setting. In this introduction, we will explore the history of Relais & Châteaux, their principles and values, and the unrivaled experience they offer.

The History of Relais & Châteaux

Relais & Châteaux has its origins in France, in the mid-20th century, when seven passionate hoteliers came together to create an association dedicated to promoting excellence in the hotel and restaurant industry. Their goal was to provide unique experiences, where every customer would be treated like an honored guest. In 1954, this vision became reality with the creation of the Relais & Châteaux association.

From the start, the founders placed emphasis on the quality, authenticity and uniqueness of each establishment. Each hotel had to reflect the character and charm of its region, providing a truly local experience. Over the decades, the association grew, expanding beyond French borders to include properties around the world. Today, Relais & Châteaux has more than 500 establishments in nearly 60 countries, each proudly carrying the founding values of the association.

Principles and Values

Relais & Châteaux are based on a set of principles and values that guide every aspect of their operation. Among these, excellence, authenticity, respect for the environment and the promotion of local culture occupy a central place.

1. Excellence: Each Relais & Châteaux establishment is committed to offering impeccable service and high quality services. Attention to detail, professionalism of staff and constant search for improvement are at the heart of this quest for excellence.

2. Authenticity: Relais & Châteaux celebrate the cultural and architectural heritage of their region. Each property is unique and reflects the style and history of its surroundings. Whether it's a medieval castle, a Provençal villa or an Alpine chalet, each place tells a story.

3. Respect for the environment: Aware of their impact on the environment, Relais & Châteaux are committed to adopting sustainable practices. This includes reducing their carbon footprint, promoting organic farming and preserving natural resources.

4. Promotion of local culture: Relais & Châteaux play an important role in promoting local traditions. This is manifested through the gastronomy, architecture, art and activities offered to guests. By staying in a Relais & Châteaux, visitors discover the soul of the region.

The Unique Experience

Staying in a Relais & Châteaux is much more than just a night in a luxury hotel. It is an immersion in a universe where every detail is thought out to offer a memorable experience. Whether through the gastronomy, the welcome, the setting or the activities, each aspect of the stay is designed to delight the senses and create unforgettable memories.

Gastronomy

Gastronomy plays a central role in the Relais & Châteaux experience. Many establishments are home to Michelin-starred restaurants, where renowned chefs create culinary masterpieces using local and seasonal produce. The tasting menus offer a taste journey, where each dish is a discovery.

In addition to gourmet restaurants, Relais & Châteaux often offer cooking classes, allowing guests to learn culinary techniques and discover the chefs' secrets. These interactive experiences strengthen the link between customers and local culture, immersing them in the world of regional gastronomy.

Home

The welcome in a Relais & Châteaux is marked by personal and warm attention. From the moment they arrive, customers are treated like honored guests. The staff, often multilingual and highly qualified, is happy to respond to each request with courtesy and efficiency.

Every detail is thought of to ensure the comfort and well-being of customers. The rooms are tastefully decorated, combining elegance and modern comfort. The services offered, such as the spa, concierge and tailor-made activities, add a touch of luxury and personalization to the experience.

The framework

Relais & Châteaux are often located in exceptional locations, whether in the peaceful countryside, the Mediterranean coast or in the heart of historic towns. Each establishment is chosen for its unique setting, offering stunning views, a magnificent garden or proximity to cultural and natural sites of interest.

The properties themselves are often historic or architectural landmarks, carefully restored to preserve their old-world charm while providing modern comforts. Guests can stay in castles, manors, villas or chalets, each offering a distinct atmosphere and its own charm.

Activities

Relais & Châteaux offer a range of activities to enrich guests' stay. Whether it's guided tours of the region, wine tastings, cooking classes, hiking or wellness activities, each establishment offers unique experiences tailored to its guests.

These activities allow visitors to discover the local culture, relax and fully enjoy their surroundings. For example, a stay at a Relais & Châteaux in Provence could include a visit to the lavender fields, an olive oil tasting and a local pottery workshop.

Conclusion

Relais & Châteaux embody the very essence of the French art of living. Each establishment, with its history, its setting and its welcome, offers a unique and memorable experience. By celebrating excellence, authenticity, respect for the environment and the promotion of local culture, Relais & Châteaux continue to appeal to travelers from around the world.

In this book, we will explore the different Relais & Châteaux establishments in France, region by region, to discover the hidden gems and unforgettable experiences they offer. From Île-de-France to Provence, via Burgundy and Brittany, each chapter will take you on an extraordinary journey through one of the most beautiful countries in the world. Prepare to be amazed by the beauty, luxury and hospitality of Relais & Châteaux de France.

- The History of Relais & Châteaux

Introduction

Relais & Châteaux today represent excellence in luxury hospitality, harmoniously combining comfort, gastronomy and heritage. To understand the appeal and importance of these establishments, it is essential to return to the origins of this prestigious association, follow its evolution and discover how it has shaped and influenced the hospitality industry over the decades. This chapter explores the fascinating history of Relais & Châteaux, from its humble beginnings to its international fame.

The Origins: The Road to Happiness

The story of Relais & Châteaux begins in 1954, a time when road trips across France were increasingly popular. Road trips allowed travelers to discover the country's varied landscapes and hidden treasures at their own pace. It is in this context that seven visionary hoteliers decided to create an association to promote their establishments located between Paris and Nice.

Under the name "Route of Happiness", these pioneers wanted to offer travelers a series of stages where they could stop, rest and enjoy the local cuisine. Each hotelier brought their own personal touch, ensuring a unique experience at every stage of the journey. The idea was simple but revolutionary: to offer high-quality hospitality, rooted in local traditions and friendliness.

The Birth of Relais & Châteaux

The Route du Bonheur quickly gained popularity, and in 1954, the Relais & Châteaux association was officially founded. The seven founding hoteliers – Marcel and Nelly Tilloy, Bernard Naegelen , Francis and Paulette Olivier, Louis Gineste, and André Daguin – implemented a strict set of criteria to ensure that each member establishment offered a high level of quality.

From the outset, Relais & Châteaux have stood out for their unique approach to hospitality. Unlike large, standardized hotel chains, each member establishment had to reflect the character and spirit of its region. Whether through architecture, decoration, cuisine or service, each Relais & Châteaux had to offer an authentic and personalized experience.

The 1960s and 1970s: Expansion and Recognition

During the 1960s and 1970s, Relais & Châteaux experienced significant expansion. The association has attracted new members, not only in France, but also in other European countries. This international expansion has diversified the offering and strengthened the reputation of Relais & Châteaux as a synonym for luxury and excellence.

One of the defining moments of this period was the adoption of the slogan "Everywhere, unique in the world", reflecting the association's philosophy that each establishment should be exceptional and inimitable. This slogan has become a promise of quality and authenticity, attracting discerning travelers from around the world.

During this period, Relais & Châteaux also began to make a name for themselves in the world of gastronomy. Many talented chefs have joined the association, bringing with them their culinary skills and passion for local produce. The Relais & Châteaux restaurants quickly earned Michelin stars, thus consolidating the association's gastronomic reputation.

The 1980s and 1990s: Diversification and Modernization

The 1980s and 1990s were marked by continued diversification and modernization of Relais & Châteaux. The association has expanded its admissions criteria to include a wider variety of establishments, from boutique hotels and country inns to historic villas and castles.

This diversification has allowed Relais & Châteaux to offer a wider range of experiences to their guests, while remaining faithful to their fundamental principles of authenticity, quality and conviviality. At the same time, the association invested in training and professional development initiatives for its members, ensuring that each establishment maintained high standards of service and hospitality.

The modernization of Relais & Châteaux has also involved the adoption of new technologies to improve the guest experience. From online reservation systems to loyalty programs, Relais & Châteaux have successfully integrated technological advances while preserving their charm and unique character.

The 2000s: A Strengthened Commitment to Sustainability

At the turn of the millennium, Relais & Châteaux made a strong commitment to sustainability and environmental responsibility. Aware of their impact on the environment, the members of the association have adopted eco-responsible practices to minimize their ecological footprint and preserve natural resources.

This commitment has translated into several concrete initiatives, such as using organic and local products in kitchens, reducing energy and water consumption, and promoting sustainable modes of transportation for customers. Many establishments have also invested in programs to preserve biodiversity and support local communities.

In 2014, on the occasion of its 60th anniversary, Relais & Châteaux published a 20-point manifesto, affirming its commitment to excellence, authenticity and sustainability. This manifesto has become a roadmap for the future of the association, guiding its actions and decisions in a constantly changing world.

Contemporary Challenges and New Perspectives

Today, Relais & Châteaux continue to develop and evolve in the face of contemporary challenges. The COVID-19 pandemic has had a significant impact on the hospitality industry, forcing establishments to quickly adapt to new health and economic realities. Despite these challenges, Relais & Châteaux has demonstrated resilience and innovation, implementing strict safety protocols and exploring new forms of hospitality, such as virtual experiences and gourmet delivery services.

At the same time, the association continues its international expansion, with new members regularly joining its ranks. Relais & Châteaux strive to remain at the forefront of innovation, while preserving the values and traditions that have made them successful. The future of Relais & Châteaux looks promising, with numerous projects and initiatives underway to continue to offer unique and memorable experiences to their guests.

Conclusion

The history of Relais & Châteaux is one of passion, vision and commitment to excellence. From its modest beginnings on the Road to Happiness to its international reputation, the association has remained faithful to its fundamental principles while evolving and adapting to the challenges and opportunities of each era. Relais & Châteaux are not just places to stay, but destinations in themselves, where every detail is thought of to offer an unparalleled experience.

By celebrating the art of living, gastronomy, authenticity and sustainability, Relais & Châteaux continue to inspire and seduce travelers from around the world. This book invites you to discover these exceptional establishments, through their stories, their traditions and the unique experiences they offer. Prepare to embark on an extraordinary journey to the heart of the Relais & Châteaux de France, where each page will reveal the hidden treasures of French hospitality and gastronomy.

- Principles and Values

Introduction

Relais & Châteaux represents much more than a simple association of luxury hotels and restaurants; they embody a true art of living, a deep commitment to excellence, authenticity, sustainability and the promotion of local cultures. These principles and core values are at the heart of every member property, guiding their daily practices and creating unique guest experiences. This chapter explores in depth the principles and values that define Relais & Châteaux, revealing how they are integrated into every aspect of hospitality, gastronomy and environmental management.

Excellency

Excellence is one of the cornerstones of Relais & Châteaux. It manifests itself through every detail of the customer experience, from the warm welcome to the high-quality services. The members of the association are committed to offering impeccable service, marked by attention to detail, professionalism and a constant search for improvement.

A Personalized Service

Excellence in Relais & Châteaux begins with personalized service. Each client is welcomed as an honored guest, with tailor-made services that meet their specific needs and preferences. Staff are often trained to anticipate customer desires, providing services that go beyond expectations. Whether by organizing a special activity, preparing a personalized meal or creating a special ambiance in the room, every detail is carefully thought out to guarantee an unforgettable experience.

High Standing Facilities

The Relais & Châteaux facilities also reflect this commitment to excellence. Each property invests in high-quality amenities and amenities, from luxurious rooms to world-renowned spas to elegantly decorated common areas. Rooms are often furnished with exceptional attention to detail, offering ultimate comfort and a refined aesthetic. Spas offer a range of treatments and therapies aimed at providing optimal relaxation and well-being.

The formation continues

To maintain these high standards, Relais & Châteaux invest in the continuing training of their staff. Regular training programs are organized to enhance the skills of employees and keep them updated with the latest trends and innovations in the hospitality industry. This ongoing training ensures that each staff member is capable of providing superior service, contributing to the overall guest experience.

Authenticity

Authenticity is another central value of Relais & Châteaux. Each member property strives to reflect the character and spirit of its region, providing a truly local experience. This authenticity is manifested through the architecture, decoration, cuisine and activities offered to customers.

Architecture and Decoration

Relais & Châteaux are often located in exceptional historic or architectural buildings. Whether a medieval castle, a Provençal villa or an Alpine chalet, each establishment tells a story and reflects the heritage of its region. The owners are investing in the restoration and preservation of these buildings, respecting their historic character while integrating elements of modern comfort.

The interior decoration is also carefully chosen to reflect the authenticity and charm of the place. Antique furniture, local artwork and traditional materials are often used to create a warm and authentic atmosphere. Each piece thus becomes a testimony to the history and culture of the region.

Local Gastronomy

Gastronomy is a key element of the authenticity of Relais & Châteaux. Each chef strives to highlight local and seasonal produce, creating dishes that celebrate the richness and diversity of regional cuisine. The menus are often inspired by local culinary traditions, but revisited with a touch of modernity and innovation.

Relais & Châteaux chefs work in close collaboration with local producers, thus promoting a local and sustainable economy. This approach not only guarantees the freshness and quality of the ingredients, but also contributes to the preservation of the region's agricultural and culinary traditions.

Local Activities and Experiences

To provide an authentic experience, Relais & Châteaux offer a range of activities and experiences that allow guests to discover local culture. Guided tours of historic sites, craft workshops, wine tastings and nature excursions are often organized to immerse guests in the local environment.

These activities allow guests to better understand and appreciate the culture and heritage of the region, while creating unique memories. For example, a stay at a Relais & Châteaux in Tuscany could include a visit to the local vineyards, an Italian cooking lesson and a walk through the olive groves.

Sustainability

Sustainability is an essential value for Relais & Châteaux, which are committed to adopting eco-responsible practices and minimizing their impact on the environment. This commitment is reflected in several initiatives aimed at preserving natural resources, reducing carbon emissions and promoting responsible tourism.

Resource Management

Relais & Châteaux implement sustainable management practices for natural resources, particularly water and energy. Many establishments have invested in water management systems to reduce consumption and optimize the use of available resources. Technologies such as rainwater harvesting systems and water-saving devices are commonly used.

To reduce their carbon footprint, Relais & Châteaux favor renewable energy sources, such as solar panels and geothermal heating systems. The use of energy-efficient technologies, such as LED bulbs and energy-efficient appliances, is also encouraged.

Sustainable Food

Sustainability also requires responsible eating. Relais & Châteaux are committed to using products from organic and sustainable farming. Chefs favor local and seasonal ingredients, reducing the need for transport and promoting a circular economy.

Many establishments have set up vegetable gardens and organic gardens to produce their own fruits, vegetables and herbs. These initiatives not only ensure the freshness and quality of ingredients, but also raise customer awareness of the importance of sustainable food.

Waste Reduction

Reducing waste is another crucial aspect of Relais & Châteaux's sustainable commitment. Facilities implement recycling and composting programs to minimize the amount of waste sent to landfills. Reducing the use of single-use plastic and promoting recyclable and biodegradable materials are also priorities.

Some Relais & Châteaux have adopted innovative practices to transform waste into resources. For example, food scraps can be used to produce compost, which enriches the soil in the facility's gardens.

Promotion of Local Culture

Relais & Châteaux play an important role in the promotion and preservation of local cultures. This commitment is manifested through several initiatives aimed at promoting cultural heritage, artisanal traditions and local communities.

Support for Local Artisans

Relais & Châteaux often collaborate with local artisans to promote and preserve traditional know-how. Establishments can organize workshops and demonstrations to allow customers to discover artisanal crafts such as pottery, basketry, soap making or tapestry.

By supporting local artisans, Relais & Châteaux contribute to the sustainability of artisanal traditions and the economic viability of local communities. These collaborations also reinforce the authenticity of the customer experience, providing a direct link to the culture and heritage of the region.

Valorization of Cultural Heritage

Promoting cultural heritage is a priority for Relais & Châteaux. The establishments are committed to preserving and promoting historic sites, monuments and local traditions. Partnerships with museums, archaeological sites and cultural institutions enrich the cultural offering for customers.

Relais & Châteaux can also organize cultural events, such as concerts, art exhibitions and festivals, to celebrate and promote local culture. These initiatives help raise customer awareness of the importance of cultural heritage and strengthen the connection between the establishment and the local community.

Social and Community Engagement

Social and community engagement is an important dimension of the Relais & Châteaux approach. Establishments are actively involved in local communities, supporting social, educational and charitable initiatives. This may include training and apprenticeship programs for young people, collaborations with charities and community development projects.

By engaging in these initiatives, Relais & Châteaux contribute to strengthening the social fabric and improving the quality of life of local communities. This commitment reflects the values of solidarity, sharing and social responsibility which are at the heart of the association.

Conclusion

The principles and values of

Relais & Châteaux are the pillars that support the excellence and authenticity of each member establishment. The commitment to excellence is demonstrated through personalized service, high-quality facilities and ongoing staff training. Authenticity is celebrated through architecture, decor, gastronomy and local activities, providing guests with a truly unique experience.

Sustainability is a priority for Relais & Châteaux, which adopt eco-responsible practices to preserve natural resources and promote sustainable eating. Waste reduction and resource management are crucial aspects of this commitment. Finally, the promotion of local culture, support for artisans and social and community engagement strengthen the link between establishments and local communities, while offering customers an authentic immersion in regional culture.

These principles and values make Relais & Châteaux much more than places to stay; they are destinations in themselves, where every detail is thought of to offer an unforgettable and enriching experience. This book invites you to discover these exceptional establishments, through their stories, their traditions and the unique experiences they offer. Prepare to be amazed by the beauty, luxury and hospitality of Relais & Châteaux de France, where each page will reveal the hidden treasures of French hospitality and gastronomy.

- The Unique Experience

Introduction

Relais & Châteaux represent a harmonious fusion of luxurious comfort, refined gastronomy and cultural heritage. More than just a stay, each visit to a Relais & Châteaux establishment is a sensory and emotional adventure that leaves lasting memories. This chapter explores the multiple facets of the unique experience that these establishments offer their guests, from exceptional gastronomy to personalized welcome, including enchanting settings and exclusive activities.

Gastronomy: A Culinary Journey

Star Chefs and their Creations

Gastronomy is at the heart of the Relais & Châteaux experience. Many establishments are home to Michelin-starred restaurants, where renowned chefs display their talents to create culinary works of art. Each meal is a celebration of flavors, textures and aromas, carefully orchestrated to delight the senses.

Relais & Châteaux chefs are artists passionate about local and seasonal products. They maintain close relationships with regional producers, thus guaranteeing the freshness and quality of the ingredients. This approach allows us to create menus that reflect the terroir, while incorporating innovative and personal touches.

Tasting Menus

The tasting menus are an emblematic Relais & Châteaux experience. These multi-stage meals allow guests to enjoy a variety of dishes, each designed to offer a new taste discovery. Each bite tells a story, showcasing the chef's ingenuity and the richness of local produce.

Tasting menus are often accompanied by wine selections carefully chosen by expert sommeliers. Each food and wine pairing is designed to enhance the flavors and create perfect harmony, thus offering a complete and memorable culinary experience.

Cooking Classes

For food lovers, many Relais & Châteaux offer cooking classes. These interactive workshops allow customers to learn the chefs' techniques and discover the secrets of local cuisine. From lessons on preparing traditional dishes to tips for successful modern recipes, each class is an opportunity to immerse yourself in the establishment's culinary world.

Cooking classes are often accompanied by visits to local markets, where participants can select the fresh ingredients that will be used during the lesson. This immersive experience strengthens the connection between guests and the region's food culture, creating lasting and enriching memories.

The Welcome: Personalized Warmth

A Tailored Service

The welcome at Relais & Châteaux is characterized by personalized and warm attention. Every detail is carefully orchestrated to ensure the comfort and well-being of guests. Upon arrival, guests are greeted by dedicated staff, ready to respond to every request with courtesy and efficiency.

The tailor-made service is a hallmark of Relais & Châteaux. Whether by organizing a special activity, preparing a personalized meal or creating a special ambiance in the room, every aspect of the stay is designed to satisfy the guests' desires. Staff are often multilingual and trained to anticipate needs, ensuring a seamless experience.

Elegant and Comfortable Rooms

The Relais & Châteaux rooms are havens of peace, combining elegance and modern comfort. Each room is tastefully decorated, mixing traditional and contemporary elements to create a welcoming and refined atmosphere. High-quality materials, period furniture and local artwork add a touch of authenticity and luxury.

Room amenities are designed to provide optimal comfort. From plush beds with Egyptian cotton sheets to luxurious bathrooms equipped with premium toiletries, every detail is thought of to ensure guests' well-being. Additional services, such as 24-hour room service, pillow menus and concierge services, add a touch of personalization that makes each stay unique.

Friendly Common Spaces

The common areas of Relais & Châteaux are designed to promote relaxation and conviviality. Elegantly decorated lounges, comfortable libraries and peaceful gardens provide places where guests can relax and socialize. Establishments often host events and social activities, such as wine tastings, musical evenings and literary readings, to enrich the guest experience.

Spas and wellness centers are also key elements of the Relais & Châteaux experience. Offering a range of treatments and therapies, from massages to facials, these spaces are sanctuaries of relaxation and rejuvenation. Wellness facilities, such as swimming pools, saunas and hot tubs, allow guests to relax and rejuvenate in luxurious surroundings.

The Setting: Exceptional Places

Historical and Architectural Sites

Relais & Châteaux are often located in exceptional historic or architectural buildings. Whether a medieval castle, a Provençal villa, an 18th century manor house or an Alpine chalet, each establishment tells a unique story and reflects the heritage of its region.

These historic buildings are carefully restored to preserve their original character and charm, while incorporating elements of modern comfort. The owners invest in the conservation of architectural features, such as stone facades, wooden beams, period fireplaces and wall frescoes, offering guests an immersion in local history and culture.

Enchanting Landscapes

The Relais & Châteaux are located in exceptional locations, offering breathtaking views of the surrounding landscapes. Whether in the heart of peaceful countryside, overlooking the Mediterranean coast, nestled in the mountains or in the center of historic towns, each establishment is chosen for its unique and enchanting setting.

The gardens and parks of Relais & Châteaux are often works of art in themselves, carefully designed to provide spaces for relaxation and contemplation. Guests can wander through formal gardens, fruit orchards, vineyards and forests, discovering the natural beauty and biodiversity of the area.

Access to Cultural and Natural Sites

The Relais & Châteaux are ideally located to provide easy access to cultural and natural sites of interest. Guests can explore picturesque villages, historic castles, art museums and archaeological sites, discovering the cultural richness of the region.

Establishments often offer guided tours and excursions to allow guests to discover the region's hidden gems. Whether it's a hike in the mountains, a boat ride on a lake, a visit to a wine cellar or a hot air balloon trip, each activity is designed to provide a unique and memorable experience.

Activities: Unique Experiences

Cultural and Craft Activities

To enrich their guests' experience, Relais & Châteaux offer a range of cultural and artisanal activities. Guests can participate in craft workshops, pottery classes, soap-making demonstrations, painting lessons or sewing workshops. These activities allow guests to discover local traditions and know-how, while creating unique memories.

The establishments also organize cultural events, such as concerts, art exhibitions, film screenings and conferences, offering guests an immersion in the cultural life of the region. These events are often hosted by local artists and experts, strengthening the connection between guests and the local community.

Outdoor and Well-Being Activities

Relais & Châteaux offer a variety of outdoor and wellness activities to allow guests to relax and recharge. Guided hikes, horseback rides, bike rides, kayak tours and outdoor yoga sessions are often organized to provide guests with an immersive nature experience.

Relais & Châteaux spas and wellness centers offer a range of treatments and therapies to promote relaxation and well-being. From massages to facials, mud baths to aromatherapy sessions, each treatment is designed to provide deep relaxation and rejuvenation. Wellness facilities, such as swimming pools, saunas, steam rooms and hot tubs, provide luxurious relaxation spaces where guests can recharge and revitalize.

Educational and Fun Experiences

Relais & Châteaux also offer educational and fun experiences for guests of all ages. Cooking workshops for children, wine tasting sessions for adults, visits to educational farms and family excursions are some of the activities offered to enrich guests' stay.

Establishments often host special programs for children, offering fun and educational activities such as scavenger hunts, gardening workshops, swimming lessons and puppet shows. These programs allow children to discover the culture and nature of the region, while having fun and making new friends.

Conclusion

The unique Relais & Châteaux experience is a celebration of the art of living, gastronomy, authenticity and sustainability. Each establishment, with its enchanting setting, warm welcome, exceptional gastronomy and enriching activities, offers a memorable and immersive experience. By staying in a Relais & Châteaux, guests discover not only an exceptional place, but also a way of living that celebrates beauty, quality and authenticity.

This chapter explored the multiple facets of the unique Relais & Châteaux experience, revealing how every detail is carefully orchestrated to deliver an unforgettable stay. Whether through gastronomy, hospitality, setting or activities, every aspect of the stay is designed to delight the senses and create lasting memories. As you discover these exceptional establishments, you will be transported to a world where luxury and authenticity meet, offering a truly unique and enriching experience.

Chapter 1: Relais & Châteaux in Île-de-France

1. General Presentation of the Region

Île-de-France, the beating heart of France, is much more than the region housing the capital Paris. It is the reflection of centuries of history, a rich and varied culture, and an economic and social dynamism which continues to shape the country. This chapter explores Île-de-France in depth, its hidden treasures, its contrasts, and why it is the perfect setting for Relais & Châteaux.

History and Heritage

Origins and Antiquity

Île-de-France, of which Paris is the central jewel, has deep historical roots dating back to Antiquity. Initially populated by the Parisii , a Gallic tribe, the region was conquered by the Romans in the 1st century BCE. Roman Lutetia, the ancestor of Paris, developed into an important center of Roman Gaul. The remains of this era, such as the thermal baths of Cluny and the arenas of Lutetia, still bear witness to the importance of this region in the Roman Empire.

The Middle Ages and the Renaissance

The Middle Ages saw Île-de-France transform into the political and religious heart of France. The construction of Notre-Dame de Paris Cathedral in the 12th century marks the beginning of the Gothic architectural boom. The region is also the birthplace of the French monarchy, with royal residences like the Château de Vincennes and the Bastille Fortress. The Renaissance brought an artistic and cultural outpouring, illustrated by the castles of Fontainebleau and Saint-Germain-en-Laye, where artists and intellectuals from all over Europe gathered.

Modern Times and the Contemporary Era

In the 17th and 18th centuries, under the reigns of Louis XIV and Louis XV, Île-de-France became the center of absolute power and French culture. The Palace of Versailles, with its French gardens, is the shining symbol of this era. The French Revolution shook the region, but it was reborn in the 19th century with the Haussmannian transformations of Paris, which modernized the city and prepared it for the 20th century.

Today, Île-de-France is a world metropolis. It is an international crossroads for business, culture and politics. Institutions like UNESCO and events like Paris Fashion Week put the region at the center of the global stage.

Geography and Landscapes

Urban and Rural Contrasts

Île-de-France is a region of contrasts, where the densely populated urban areas of Paris and its suburbs rub shoulders with peaceful rural spaces and majestic forests. The diversity of landscapes is one of the major assets of the region.

Paris the light city

Paris, the capital, is undoubtedly the most emblematic city in the world. Its famous monuments, such as the Eiffel Tower , the Louvre and Montmartre, attract millions of visitors each year. The Seine flows through the city, offering picturesque views and unforgettable walks. Historic neighborhoods, such as Le Marais and Saint-Germain-des-Prés, retain a timeless charm with their cobbled streets, cafes and boutiques.

The Little Crown and the Big Crown

The outlying areas of Paris, known as the Petite Couronne and Grande Couronne, offer a variety of landscapes and experiences. The Little Crown includes departments like Hauts-de-Seine, Seine-Saint-Denis and Val-de-Marne, where there are dynamic towns like Boulogne-Billancourt and Saint-Denis, with its historic basilica.

The Grande Couronne, which includes departments such as Seine-et-Marne, Essonne, Yvelines and Val-d'Oise, is marked by more preserved nature. Forests like Fontainebleau and Rambouillet offer green havens and playgrounds for outdoor enthusiasts. The historic castles and mansions, scattered throughout these regions, add a touch of grandeur and mystery.

Parks and Gardens

Île-de-France is also renowned for its numerous parks and gardens. The Jardin du Luxembourg, Jardin des Tuileries and Parc Monceau in Paris offer oases of calm in the heart of the city. Outside of Paris, the Parc de Sceaux, designed by Le Nôtre, and the gardens of Versailles are magnificent examples of French landscape architecture.

Green spaces are not limited to urban parks. The region is also home to nature reserves and protected forests, such as the Sénart forest and the Saint-Quentin-en-Yvelines nature reserve, which are valuable habitats for local flora and fauna.

Culture and Gastronomy

Cultural life

Île-de-France is a world-renowned cultural center. Paris, with its museums, theaters, art galleries and concert halls, is a true epicenter of cultural life. The Louvre Museum, Musée d'Orsay and Center Pompidou attract art lovers from around the world, while the Opéra Garnier and Opéra Bastille offer world-class performances.

There are also numerous festivals and cultural events. The Fête de la Musique, the Nuit Blanche and the Festival d'Automne are highlights of the Parisian cultural calendar. Outside of Paris, festivals like

Rock en Seine and Rencontres d'Arles (which, although located in Provence, attract many Parisians) add to the region's cultural richness.

Gastronomy

The gastronomy of Île-de-France is both rich and varied, reflecting regional and international influences. Paris is a global gastronomic capital, home to some of the world's most famous restaurants and most talented chefs. From Michelin stars to traditional bistros, the Parisian culinary scene is constantly evolving.

Parisian markets, such as Rungis, the world's largest fresh produce market, provide top-quality ingredients to restaurants and homes. Parisian bakeries, patisseries and chocolate shops are renowned for their delicious creations, from croissants to pain au chocolat to macaroons.

Local Products

Outside of Paris, Île-de-France also offers a variety of local products. Brie cheeses, notably Brie de Meaux and Brie de Melun, are specialties of the region. Fruits and vegetables grown in the rich agricultural lands of Seine-et-Marne and Essonne, as well as wines produced in the region's vineyards, add to the gastronomic richness.

Local markets, such as those in Versailles and Fontainebleau, are ideal places to discover and taste these regional products. The chefs at Relais & Châteaux in Île-de-France often source from these markets to create menus that highlight local and seasonal flavors.

Economy and Innovation

An International Economic Pole

Île-de-France is the economic engine of France and one of the main economic centers of Europe. Paris, in particular, is a hub for international business, finance, technology and the creative industry. The region is home to the La Défense district, the largest business district in Europe, home to many multinationals and financial institutions.

The technological sector of Île-de-France is booming, with innovation hubs like Station F, the largest startup campus in the world, and the Paris-Saclay cluster, which brings together universities, research and high-tech companies.

The Luxury Industry

Île-de-France is also a global center of the luxury industry. Paris is the capital of fashion and design, hosting prestigious events like Paris Fashion Week. Major French fashion houses, jewelers and perfumers, such as Chanel, Dior and Louis Vuitton, have their headquarters in the region, contributing to its international influence.

Relais & Châteaux in Île-de-France benefit from this proximity to the luxury industry, offering their clients exclusive shopping experiences and collaborations with prestigious brands. Relais & Châteaux spas and wellness centers often use high-quality beauty products from these renowned houses.

Tourism and Hospitality

Tourism is an essential pillar of the Île-de-France economy. Every year, millions of visitors flock to discover the treasures of Paris and its surroundings. Historical monuments, museums, restaurants and shops attract tourists from all over the world, making Île-de-France one of the most popular tourist destinations in the world.

Relais & Châteaux play a crucial role in the region's tourism industry, offering luxury accommodations and unique experiences that showcase the cultural and historical richness of Île-de-France. The association's establishments are destinations in themselves, attracting travelers looking for refinement, comfort and authenticity.

Relais & Châteaux in Île-de-France

Exceptional Establishments

The Relais & Châteaux in Île-de-France are among the most prestigious in the association. Each establishment offers a unique experience, combining elegance, comfort and gastronomic excellence. Whether in a historic castle, a country residence or a luxury hotel in the heart of Paris, each Relais & Châteaux in the region offers an exceptional setting and impeccable service.

The owners and managers of these establishments are often passionate about history and culture, investing in the preservation and restoration of their heritage. They work closely with local artisans, producers and artists to offer their customers an authentic immersion in the culture and heritage of Île-de-France.

The Relais & Châteaux Experience

Staying in a Relais & Châteaux in Île-de-France is much more than just a night in a luxury hotel. It is a complete experience that awakens the senses and creates unforgettable memories. Customers are welcomed as guests of honor, with personalized service that meets their every desire.

Relais & Châteaux establishments in the region offer a range of services and activities to enrich their guests' stay. From gourmet dining and guided tours of historic sites to spa treatments and nature excursions, every aspect of the stay is designed to provide a unique and memorable experience.

Excellence Gastronomy

Gastronomy is an essential pillar of the Relais & Châteaux experience in Île-de-France. The talented chefs who run the kitchens at these establishments are masters of French cuisine, using local and seasonal ingredients to create dishes that celebrate the richness and diversity of regional flavors.

The restaurants at Relais & Châteaux in Île-de-France are often Michelin-starred, offering unforgettable culinary experiences. Tasting menus, food and wine pairings and cooking classes allow guests to discover and appreciate local gastronomy, while learning the secrets of the chefs.

Conclusion

Île-de-France is a region of extraordinary richness and diversity. It combines history, culture, economy and nature in a unique way, providing an exceptional setting for Relais & Châteaux. These prestigious establishments take advantage of this wealth to offer their customers unparalleled experiences, marked by excellence, authenticity and refinement.

By discovering the Relais & Châteaux of Île-de-France, you will be transported into a world where every detail is designed to delight the senses and create lasting memories. From the splendor of Paris to the charms of the surrounding countryside, each stay in a Relais & Châteaux in the region is an invitation to discover the French art of living in all its splendor.

- History and Heritage

Île-de-France, a historic region that is home to the French capital, Paris, has been the birthplace of the French monarchy and the cultural and political heart of France for centuries. Its history is marked by a succession of significant events which have shaped not only the region but also the entire country. From Gallic tribes to medieval kings, from revolutions to modern transformations, each period has left an indelible mark on Île-de-France, creating a rich and diverse heritage.

The First Civilizations

The Parisii and Gaulish Lutetia

The first traces of civilization in Île-de-France date back to the time of the Parisii , a Gallic tribe who settled on the banks of the Seine. These trading people built the first version of Paris, then called Lutetia. Archaeological excavations have revealed remains from this period, including ceramic objects, weapons and jewelry that testify to the wealth and sophistication of this society.

Gallic Lutetia was an important commercial and cultural center. Its inhabitants lived from agriculture, fishing and river trade. Trade with other Gallic tribes and with the Roman Empire was frequent, bringing foreign influences and goods to Lutetia. The Parisii were also known for their skills in metalwork and craftsmanship, creating iron and bronze objects that were highly prized.

The Roman Conquest

In 52 BC, Julius Caesar conquered Gaul and integrated Lutetia into the Roman Empire. The city was renamed Lutetia and became an important administrative and military center. The Romans built iconic infrastructures there, such as baths, aqueducts, arenas and temples. The thermal baths of Cluny and the arenas of Lutetia are among the most remarkable remains of this era and bear witness to the prosperity of Lutetia under Roman domination.

Lutetia prospered under the Romans, benefiting from their expertise in engineering and town planning. The city became a strategic node on the Roman road which linked Gaul to Great Britain. The Romans also introduced new agricultural and artisanal practices, further enriching the local culture. The citizens of Lutetia enjoyed a sophisticated city life, with public baths, amphitheaters, and bustling markets.

The Middle Ages: The Emergence of Paris

The End of the Roman Empire and the Barbarian Invasions

The fall of the Roman Empire in the 5th century brought a period of turbulence for Lutetia. The city was invaded by Germanic tribes, notably the Franks, who renamed it Paris. This period of transition was marked by successive destructions and reconstructions, but Paris began to emerge as a center of power under the rule of the Merovingians.

The Franks, under the leadership of Clovis, made Paris the capital of their kingdom at the beginning of the 6th century. Clovis, the first Christian king of France, built numerous churches and monasteries, laying the foundations of an important religious center. Clovis's conversion to Christianity and his baptism in Reims marked the beginning of the Christian era in France, strengthening Paris's status as a religious center.

The Carolingians and the Foundation of the French Monarchy

Under the Carolingian dynasty, Paris continued to develop. Charlemagne, although he preferred Aachen as his primary residence, strengthened Paris as a political and military center. The Viking invasions of the 9th century threatened Paris, but the city managed to resist thanks to its robust fortifications and the determination of its defenders, notably Eudes, Count of Paris.

The importance of Paris grew under the reign of the first Capetians. Hugues Capet, crowned king of France in 987, made Paris the capital of his kingdom. The city became an administrative and judicial center, and the royal court was established there. The first Capetian kings consolidated their power and expanded their territory, making Paris the heart of the kingdom of France.

The Rise of Notre-Dame Cathedral

In the 12th century, Paris became a major center of Gothic art with the construction of Notre-Dame Cathedral. Begun in 1163 under Bishop Maurice de Sully, Notre-Dame became a symbol of Gothic architecture and a spiritual center for Christians across Europe. Its construction took place over nearly two centuries, involving hundreds of craftsmen and architects.

Notre-Dame Cathedral was not only an architectural feat, but also a center of power and culture. The kings of France were crowned and married there, and it became the seat of the Bishop of Paris. The cathedral also housed sacred relics, attracting pilgrims from all over the world. She played a central role in the religious and political life of medieval France.

The University of Paris and the Intellectual Golden Age

The 13th century marked the intellectual golden age of Paris with the founding of the University of Paris, also known as the Sorbonne. Founded by Robert de Sorbon in 1257, the university became a major center of theological and philosophical education in Europe. Renowned intellectuals, such as Thomas Aquinas and Albert the Great, taught there and helped make Paris a hotbed of knowledge and intellectual debate.

The University of Paris attracted students from across Europe, creating a cosmopolitan community of scholars and intellectuals. The theological and philosophical debates held there profoundly influenced medieval thought and scholasticism. The university also became a training center for clerics and civil servants, thus strengthening Paris' influence on royal and ecclesiastical administration.

The Renaissance and the Brilliance of the Monarchy

The Reign of Francis I and Italian Influence

The 16th century, under the reign of Francis I, was marked by a cultural and artistic renaissance. Francis I, an admirer of the Italian Renaissance, invited Italian artists and architects to his court, fostering a cultural exchange that enriched French heritage. Renaissance masterpieces, such as the Château de Fontainebleau, bear witness to this period of artistic excitement.

Fontainebleau became the symbol of the French Renaissance, with its elaborate frescoes, Italian gardens and sumptuous galleries. Francis I established his court there and made it a center of cultural and intellectual life. Artists like Leonardo da Vinci were invited to the court, and the king acquired many Italian works of art, thus enriching the royal collections.

Henry IV and the Modernization of Paris

The reign of Henry IV at the turn of the 17th century was a period of transformation for Paris. Henri IV undertook to modernize the city with ambitious projects, such as the construction of the Pont Neuf and the Place Royale (today Place des Vosges). These urban developments contributed to making Paris a modern and attractive city.

Henry IV also encouraged trade and industry, establishing factories and promoting the economic growth of Paris. Under his reign, the city experienced demographic expansion and economic diversification. New residential neighborhoods and public squares transformed the urban landscape, making Paris a modern metropolis.

Louis XIV and the Splendor of Versailles

Louis XIV, the Sun King, embodied the apogee of absolute monarchy. He transferred the court to Versailles, where he built the most sumptuous palace in Europe. Versailles became the center of France's political and cultural power, attracting nobles, artists and intellectuals from around the world.

The Palace of Versailles, with its formal gardens, richly decorated rooms and art galleries, symbolized the grandeur and opulence of the French monarchy. Louis XIV organized sumptuous parties, ballets and operas there, making Versailles the theater of aristocratic life. The king ruled with absolute authority, centralizing power and consolidating France's position as the dominant power in Europe.

The French Revolution and the Napoleonic Era

The Fall of the Monarchy

The end of the 18th century was marked by the French Revolution, a decisive turning point in the history of Île-de-France and of France as a whole. Taking the

Bastille on July 14, 1789 symbolized the start of the revolution. Paris became the scene of popular uprisings, political debates and radical transformations.

Revolutionaries overthrew the monarchy and proclaimed the Republic in 1792. The region experienced moments of terror and violence, but also of hope and change. New institutions were created, human rights proclaimed, and social and economic reforms implemented. Paris became the nerve center of these upheavals, with events such as the execution of Louis XVI and Marie Antoinette by guillotine.

Napoleon Bonaparte and the Restoration of the Empire

After the revolutionary period, Napoleon Bonaparte emerged as the undisputed leader of France. Crowned emperor in 1804, Napoleon set about reorganizing Paris and Île-de-France. He ordered the construction of iconic monuments, such as the Arc de Triomphe and the Vendôme Column, and renovated the city's infrastructure.

Napoleon centralized power and modernized the French administration. Under his reign, Paris was transformed into an imperial capital, with new bridges, roads and public buildings. Neoclassical architecture dominated this period, reflecting the Empire's ideals of grandeur and rationality. Napoleon also made Paris a center of culture and knowledge, founding institutions such as the Imperial University and the Louvre as a national museum.

Social and Economic Reforms

Napoleon introduced important reforms that transformed French society and the economy. The Civil Code, also known as the Napoleonic Code, established principles of civil law that are still in force today. These legal and administrative reforms brought new stability and coherence to France, strengthening the authority of the state and promoting meritocracy.

Napoleon's economic reforms encouraged industrialization and trade. It establishes banks and financial institutions to support economic development. Paris became a center of innovation and production, attracting entrepreneurs and workers from across Europe.

The 19th Century: Modernization and Transformation

Haussmann and the Metamorphosis of Paris

The 19th century was a period of radical transformation for Paris under the leadership of prefect Georges-Eugène Haussmann. Charged by Napoleon III with modernizing the city, Haussmann undertook large-scale works that redefined the urban landscape of Paris. He widened the boulevards, created new parks and gardens, constructed public buildings and modernized the city's infrastructure.

Haussmann's transformations brought air and light to a densely populated and often unsanitary city. Grand boulevards, such as the Champs-Élysées and Boulevard Saint-Germain, became bustling thoroughfares, lined with cafes, theaters and boutiques. The new parks, such as Parc Monceau and Parc des Buttes-Chaumont, provided spaces for relaxation and leisure for Parisians.

The good times

The Belle Époque, a period of prosperity and artistic creativity from the end of the 19th century until the start of the First World War, saw Paris shine as the world capital of art and culture. Art movements such as Impressionism, Post-Impressionism and Art Nouveau took off in the city.

Artists like Claude Monet, Edgar Degas and Henri de Toulouse-Lautrec captured Parisian life in their works, while writers like Émile Zola and Marcel Proust described the society of the time. Cabarets and cafés, such as the Moulin Rouge and the Café de Flore, became meeting places for artists, writers and intellectuals.

The Belle Époque was also a period of technological and scientific innovation. The universal exhibitions of 1889 and 1900, with the construction of the Eiffel Tower and the Grand Palais, showed the advances in science and industry. Paris became a symbol of modernity and progress, attracting visitors from all over the world.

The 20th Century: Wars, Reconstruction and Modernity

World Wars and their Consequences

The 20th century was marked by two world wars which had a profound impact on Île-de-France. During the First World War, Paris became a logistical and strategic center for the Allied forces. The city was spared direct combat, but suffered bombardments and shortages. The war left lasting scars on the region and the population.

The Second World War brought new challenges. Paris was occupied by Nazi forces from 1940 to 1944. The French Resistance, with iconic figures like Jean Moulin and General de Gaulle, played a crucial role in the liberation of Paris in August 1944. The city witnessed scenes of joy and celebration of liberation, but also of the destruction and suffering caused by war.

Reconstruction and Expansion

After the Second World War, Paris and Île-de-France undertook a period of reconstruction and modernization. The 1950s and 1960s saw the rise of suburbs and the construction of new housing to accommodate population growth. The region was transformed with industrialization and the expansion of transport infrastructure, notably the creation of the metro and the RER.

The region became a major economic center with the creation of industrial zones and business centers such as La Défense. Paris maintained its role as a cultural and intellectual center, attracting artists, writers and intellectuals from around the world. Art movements such as existentialism and the Nouveau Roman took root in the city, while film, music and theater festivals reinforced its status as a cultural capital.

Contemporary Transformations

The 20th century ended with a series of contemporary transformations which continue to shape Île-de-France. The region became a center of technological innovation and research, with hubs like Paris-Saclay attracting scientists and high-tech companies. The cultural diversity of Paris and its suburbs created a dynamic multicultural society, enriching the social and cultural life of the region.

Paris continued to evolve with ambitious architectural projects such as the construction of the National Library of France, the renovation of the Halles district and the modernization of transport infrastructure. The region is also committed to sustainability and ecological development initiatives, with projects aimed at reducing the carbon footprint and improving the quality of life of residents.

Conclusion

Île-de-France is a region of exceptional historical and heritage wealth. From the first Gallic tribes to modern revolutions and transformations, each period has left an indelible mark on the region. The historical remains, emblematic monuments and cultural institutions of Île-de-France bear witness to its central role in the history of France.

The Relais & Châteaux of Île-de-France fit perfectly into this rich and diverse heritage. Each property tells a unique story, providing guests with an immersive experience in the history and culture of the region. By discovering these exceptional places, you will be transported on a journey through time, discovering the hidden treasures and fascinating stories of Île-de-France.

- Gastronomy and Wine

Île-de-France, with Paris as the world capital of gastronomy, is a true paradise for food and wine lovers. The region is renowned for its rich culinary traditions, fresh produce markets, talented chefs and Michelin-starred restaurants. This chapter explores the Île-de-France gastronomic scene in depth, highlighting the historical influences, local products, great chefs, iconic restaurants and wines that make this region a culinary destination par excellence.

The Historical Roots of Ile-de-France Gastronomy

The Evolution of French Cuisine

French cuisine, as it is celebrated today, largely finds its roots in Île-de-France. The evolution of regional gastronomy reflects the political, social and cultural transformations of the region over the centuries.

At the court of the kings of France, gastronomy has always held a central place. Under Francis I, the influence of the Italian Renaissance introduced new techniques and ingredients to French cuisine. The sumptuous banquets organized at court were opportunities to demonstrate the wealth and power of the king. These feasts featured elaborate dishes, delicate pastries and artistic presentations.

In the 17th century, under Louis XIV, French cuisine evolved to become more refined and sophisticated. The creation of the kitchen brigade by François Pierre de La Varenne revolutionized the organization of royal kitchens, making it possible to serve more elaborate and structured meals. The court cuisine of Versailles, led by chefs like François Vatel, laid the foundations of French haute cuisine.

The 18th century saw the emergence of the first restaurants in Paris, offering quality cuisine accessible to a wider clientele. These establishments, like the Grand Véfour , helped popularize the culinary techniques and recipes of the royal court. The French Revolution democratized access to gastronomy, with royal chefs opening their own restaurants and sharing their know-how with the general public.

The Influence of Parisian Markets

Parisian markets have always been at the heart of the Île-de-France gastronomic scene. Iconic markets like the Halles de Paris, once nicknamed the "belly of Paris," have supplied the city with fresh produce for centuries. Today, markets like Marché d'Aligre, Marché des Enfants Rouges and Marché Raspail continue to provide quality ingredients to chefs and locals.

Markets play a crucial role in promoting local and seasonal products. Market gardeners, breeders and artisans sell their products there, offering an incredible diversity of fruits, vegetables, meats, cheeses, fish and pastries. The proximity of these markets allows chefs to source fresh ingredients every day, guaranteeing the quality and freshness of the dishes served in the restaurants.

Local Products and Regional Specialties

Cheeses

Île-de-France is famous for its cheeses, which are among the most popular in France. Brie, produced mainly in Seine-et-Marne, is undoubtedly the most emblematic cheese of the region. Brie de Meaux and Brie de Melun, two soft and bloomy rind varieties, are essential on cheese platters.

Coulommiers , another soft cheese, is often considered a cousin of Brie, although it is smaller and creamier. These cheeses are traditionally made from raw cow's milk and matured for several weeks to develop their rich, complex flavor.

Île-de-France cheeses are not limited to Brie and Coulommiers. Fontainebleau, a fresh and light cheese, is another regional specialty. Made from beaten white cheese and whipped cream, it is often served with fresh fruit or honey.

Cold cuts

Charcuterie is another specialty of Île-de-France, with products that reflect the traditional know-how of the region. Pâté en Croute, a meat terrine cooked in puff pastry, is a classic of French cuisine. It is often garnished with complex stuffings, including foie gras, game and pistachios, and served as a starter or main course.

Jambon de Paris, also known as white ham, is a tender and juicy cooked ham, often used in classic Parisian sandwiches like jambon-beurre. Made from high-quality pork, it is lightly seasoned and slow-cooked to retain its delicate flavor.

Pork Rillettes, another charcuterie delight, is made by slowly cooking pork in its own fat until it is tender and shredded. The rillettes are then potted and served with crusty bread, pickles and mustard.

Pastry and Desserts

Parisian pastry is recognized worldwide for its refinement and creativity. From classics like the croissant, pain au chocolat and mille-feuille to modern creations from renowned pastry chefs, Île-de-France desserts are a celebration of technique and taste.

Macarons, popularized by pastries like Ladurée and Pierre Hermé, are delicate meringues made from almond powder, topped with ganaches, creams or jams. These little colorful treats have become a symbol of French pastry, with a multitude of flavors ranging from classics like vanilla and raspberry to innovations like foie gras or wasabi.

Le Saint-Honoré, named in honor of the patron saint of bakers, is another Parisian classic. This complex cake combines a puff pastry base, cream puffs and a chiboust cream filling, all decorated with crunchy caramel.

Éclairs, Profiteroles and Tarte Tatins are other examples of the fine pastries found in the bakeries and tea rooms of Paris. Each pastry is a perfect balance of flavors, textures and artistic presentations.

Star Chefs and Restaurants

The Pioneers of Haute Cuisine

The Île-de-France gastronomic scene has been shaped by legendary chefs who revolutionized French cuisine. Auguste Escoffier, often considered the father of modern cuisine, set culinary standards that are still followed today. His techniques and recipes have influenced generations of chefs and contributed to the worldwide fame of French cuisine.

Fernand Point, another iconic figure, trained some of the greatest chefs in history, including Paul Bocuse, the Troisgros brothers and Alain Chapel. These chefs have perpetuated the tradition of haute cuisine while introducing innovations that have evolved French gastronomy.

Contemporary Chefs

Today, Île-de-France is home to many star chefs who continue to innovate and push the boundaries of cuisine. Alain Ducasse, with his restaurants in Paris and Versailles, is one of the most famous and influential chefs in the world. His culinary philosophy, based on the simplicity and purity of ingredients, is reflected in his refined and creative menus.

Anne-Sophie Pic, the only female chef in France to hold three Michelin stars, brings a feminine and innovative touch to French gastronomy. His restaurant in Paris, La Dame de Pic , is a tribute to his creativity and commitment to culinary excellence.

Yannick Alléno , with his restaurant Alléno Paris at Pavillon Ledoyen , is another example of culinary innovation in Île-de-France. Alléno is known for its modern, technical cuisine, which uses advanced methods to extract and intensify the flavors of ingredients.

Star Restaurants

Île-de-France is home to a multitude of Michelin-starred restaurants, each offering a unique gastronomic experience. Among the most renowned, we find Le Meurice, run by Alain Ducasse, which offers classic French cuisine revisited with a contemporary touch in a sumptuous setting.

Le Pré Catelan , led by chef Frédéric Anton, offers an exceptional culinary experience in the heart of the Bois de Boulogne. The restaurant, which holds three Michelin stars, is renowned for its elegant and refined dishes, as well as its impeccable service.

L'Arpège, run by Alain Passard , is another emblematic restaurant. Passard , pioneer of plant-based cuisine, offers menus that highlight vegetables from his own garden, prepared with incomparable mastery and creativity.

Wines of Île-de-France

The Ile-de-France Vineyard

Although Île-de-France is not as famous for its wines as regions like Burgundy or Bordeaux, it nevertheless has an ancient and respectable winemaking tradition. The once-thriving Ile-de-France region's vineyards have declined over the centuries, but recent efforts are aimed at revitalizing them.

The Suresnes vineyards, located on the slopes of the Seine, are among the oldest in the region. Suresnes wine, mainly produced from Chardonnay, is a fresh and fruity white wine, perfect to accompany seafood and light dishes.

The region also produces red and rosé wines, mainly from grape varieties such as Pinot Noir and Gamay. Ile-de-France wines, although modest in volume, are appreciated for their authenticity and unique character.

Wine Bars and Wine Shops

Paris is renowned for its wine bars and wine shops, which offer an impressive selection of French and international wines. Establishments like Le Barav , Le Verre Volé and La Cave des Papilles are favorite places for wine lovers, offering tastings, advice and a friendly atmosphere.

Parisian wine merchants, such as Lavinia and Nicolas, offer a varied range of wines, from grand crus to natural wines. These specialty boutiques also offer tasting classes and wine events, allowing customers to discover and appreciate the diversity of French wines.

Oenological Experiences

Relais & Châteaux in Île-de-France often offer unique wine experiences for their guests. From private tastings to vineyard tours, these experiences allow you to discover the region's wines and learn the secrets of winemaking.

Some properties, like Château de Ferrières, offer tasting workshops where guests can learn to identify the aromas and flavors of different wines. These workshops are often led by expert sommeliers, who share their passion and knowledge of wine.

Conclusion

The gastronomy and wines of Île-de-France are a celebration of the French art of living. The region, with its bustling markets, quality local produce, talented chefs and starred restaurants, offers an unrivaled culinary experience. Ile-de-France wines, although modest, add a touch of authentic terroir to this rich gastronomic tradition.

Relais & Châteaux in Île-de-France capture the essence of this region by offering their guests unique culinary and wine experiences. By staying in these exceptional establishments, visitors discover the richness and diversity of Ile-de-France gastronomy, while enjoying the hospitality and luxurious comfort of Relais & Châteaux. This chapter highlights the passion, know-how and innovation that make Île-de-France an essential destination for gourmets and wine lovers from around the world.

2. Addresses and Descriptions

Île-de-France is home to some of the most prestigious Relais & Châteaux, each offering a unique experience that combines luxury, comfort and historical heritage. In this chapter, we'll explore several of these establishments, detailing their history, architecture, culinary offerings, and activities available to visitors. These descriptions will help to understand why these places are essential for anyone wishing to discover Île-de-France at its best.

The Château de Montvillargenne

History and Architecture

The Château de Montvillargenne , located in Gouvieux in Oise, is a magnificent example of French architecture from the beginning of the 20th century. Built in 1900 by the Rothschild family, this castle was designed in an Anglo-Norman style, combining elegance and grandeur. The castle is surrounded by a vast six-hectare park, offering a peaceful and green setting.

The main castle building features stone facades with careful architectural details, such as turrets, wrought iron balconies and large arched windows. The interior of the castle is just as impressive, with wood-panelled lounges, marble fireplaces and painted ceilings.

Culinary Offers

Montvillargenne 's gourmet restaurant , "Le Vilargène ", offers refined French cuisine, highlighting local and seasonal products. The chef, renowned for his creativity and expertise, develops menus that combine tradition and innovation. The dishes are carefully presented, offering a culinary experience that is as aesthetic as it is tasteful.

The castle also has a cozy bar, where visitors can taste a selection of French wines, champagnes and cocktails, while enjoying the elegant atmosphere of the venue. Cooking classes and wine tasting workshops are regularly organized, allowing guests to discover the secrets of French gastronomy.

Activities and Services

The Château de Montvillargenne offers a range of activities for its guests. The spa, equipped with saunas, hammams and massage rooms, is the ideal place to relax and recharge your batteries. Sports enthusiasts can enjoy the fitness room, tennis courts and indoor swimming pool.

The castle grounds are perfect for leisurely walks, picnics or meditation sessions. Bicycles are available for guests to explore the surrounding area. The castle also organizes guided tours of local historic sites, gardening classes and craft workshops.

Le Relais Christine

History and Architecture

The Relais Christine, located in the heart of Paris, in the Saint-Germain-des-Prés district, is a charming hotel which occupies a former 13th century abbey. The hotel has managed to preserve the historic character of the building while offering modern and luxurious comfort. Stone walls, wooden beams and interior gardens create an intimate and peaceful atmosphere.

The hotel's architecture reflects its monastic past, with stone archways, cloisters and cobbled courtyards. The rooms and suites are tastefully decorated, mixing period furniture with contemporary elements. Each room is unique, offering a special charm and a view of the gardens or picturesque streets of Paris.

Culinary Offers

The Relais Christine does not have its own restaurant, but it offers a buffet breakfast service in an elegant dining room or in the comfort of the rooms. Breakfast offers a selection of fresh pastries, artisan breads, fruits, cheeses and cold cuts, as well as hot options upon request.

The hotel is ideally located close to many renowned Parisian restaurants and bistros. The hotel staff is happy to recommend local addresses and reserve tables for guests. Collaborations with local chefs also make it possible to organize private dinners in the hotel's suites or lounges.

Activities and Services

Le Relais Christine offers a range of services to make its guests' stay as pleasant as possible. The hotel's spa, located in vaulted cellars, offers relaxing treatments, massages and wellness sessions. A fitness room is also available to guests.

For those who want to explore Paris, the hotel offers electric bikes and boat rides on the Seine. The hotel concierge can arrange private tours of the city's museums, art galleries and historical monuments. Cooking workshops and wine tastings are also available for those who want to deepen their knowledge of Parisian culinary culture.

The Queen's Pavilion

History and Architecture

Le Pavillon de la Reine is a luxury boutique hotel located on Place des Vosges, one of the most historic and charming squares in Paris. The building, which dates from the 17th century, has been completely renovated to offer an elegant and refined setting while retaining its historic character. The hotel's name refers to Anne of Austria, Queen of France, who resided in this area.

The Pavillon de la Reine has a classic facade with wooden shutters and flowered balconies. The hotel's interior is decorated with antique furniture, artwork and sumptuous fabrics. The lounges, with their marble fireplaces and furnished bookcases, offer a cozy and sophisticated setting in which to relax.

Culinary Offers

Le Pavillon de la Reine offers a hearty buffet breakfast, served in an elegant dining room or in the interior courtyard. Breakfast includes a variety of fresh produce, pastries, fruits, yogurts, cereals and hot dishes.

The hotel also has a wine bar, where guests can enjoy a selection of French and international wines, accompanied by tapas and small plates. Staff are available to recommend restaurants and reserve tables at the area's best establishments, including Michelin-starred bistros and traditional brasseries.

Activities and Services

The Queen's Pavilion offers a range of services to make its guests' stay as comfortable as possible. The hotel spa, equipped with a jacuzzi, hammam and treatment rooms, is a haven of peace to relax after a day of sightseeing in Paris. A modern fitness room is also available to guests.

The hotel offers bicycles to explore the Marais and the surrounding area. The concierge can arrange private tours of the city's museums, galleries and historic monuments, as well as day trips to the surrounding areas of Paris, such as a visit to the Palace of Versailles or a day of wine tasting in Champagne .

The Domaine de Primard

History and Architecture

Le Domaine de Primard , located near Giverny, is an elegant country house which dates from the 18th century. Surrounded by formal gardens, orchards and meadows, the estate offers an idyllic setting for a romantic getaway or peaceful retreat. The main house, with its blue shutters and stone facades, has been carefully restored to preserve its old-world charm while offering modern comfort.

The interior of the estate is decorated with antique furniture, artwork and fine textiles. The rooms and suites are spacious and elegant, offering views of the gardens or surrounding countryside. The lounges, with their fireplaces and libraries, offer a cozy setting in which to relax and read.

Culinary Offers

The Domaine de Primard restaurant , led by a renowned chef, offers gourmet cuisine that highlights local and seasonal products. The menu changes regularly to reflect the ingredients available, with particular attention paid to presentation and flavors. Dishes are accompanied by a selection of regional wines, carefully chosen to complement each meal.

The estate also offers more casual dining options, such as garden picnics and al fresco dining. Guests can enjoy simple but delicious dishes, prepared with fresh ingredients from the estate's vegetable garden.

Activities and Services

Le Domaine de Primard offers a range of activities for its guests, from walks in the gardens to outdoor yoga classes. The estate's spa offers a variety of relaxing treatments, from massages to facials, in a peaceful and luxurious setting. A heated outdoor swimming pool is also available to relax and soak up the sun.

Nature lovers can explore the hiking trails around the estate, discover the local flora and fauna or visit Claude Monet's gardens in Giverny, located a few kilometers away. The estate also offers gardening workshops, cooking classes and wine tastings to enrich the guest experience.

The Château de Courcelles

History and Architecture

Château de Courcelles, located in Aisne, is a magnificent 17th century castle surrounded by French gardens and a moat. The castle, with its towers, mullioned windows and slate roofs, is a perfect example of classical French architecture. The interior of the castle is equally impressive, with woodwork, marble fireplaces and painted ceilings.

Château de Courcelles has a rich history, having hosted famous figures such as Jean Cocteau and Marcel Proust. Today, the castle has been transformed into a luxury hotel, offering an elegant and refined setting for unforgettable stays.

Culinary Offers

The Château de Courcelles gourmet restaurant offers refined French cuisine, highlighting local and seasonal products. The chef, recognized for his creativity and expertise, creates tasting menus that delight the taste buds. The dishes are carefully presented, and the service is impeccable.

The castle also has a wine bar, where guests can taste a selection of French and international wines, accompanied by cheeses and charcuterie. Cooking classes and wine tasting workshops are regularly organized to allow guests to discover the secrets of French gastronomy.

Activities and Services

Château de Courcelles offers a range of activities for its guests. The castle grounds are ideal for leisurely walks, picnics or meditation sessions. Bicycles are available for guests to explore the surrounding area, and guided tours of local historic sites can be arranged.

The castle also has an outdoor swimming pool, tennis court and spa. The spa offers a variety of relaxing treatments, from massages to facials, in a peaceful and luxurious setting. A fitness room is also available to guests.

The Castle of Villiers-le-Mahieu

History and Architecture

The Château de Villiers-le-Mahieu, located in Yvelines, is a 13th century castle surrounded by a moat and French gardens. The castle, with its turrets, battlements and mullioned windows, is a perfect example of French medieval architecture. The interior of the castle has been carefully restored to preserve its historic character while providing modern comfort.

The castle has a rich history, having been the residence of several noble families over the centuries. Today, it has been transformed into a luxury hotel, offering an elegant and refined setting for unforgettable stays.

Culinary Offers

The Château de Villiers-le-Mahieu restaurant offers refined French cuisine, highlighting local and seasonal products. The chef, recognized for his creativity and expertise, creates tasting menus that delight the taste buds. The dishes are carefully presented, and the service is impeccable.

The castle also has a wine bar, where guests can taste a selection of French and international wines, accompanied by cheeses and charcuterie. Cooking classes and wine tasting workshops are regularly organized to allow guests to discover the secrets of French gastronomy.

Activities and Services

The Château de Villiers-le-Mahieu offers a range of activities for its guests. The castle grounds are ideal for leisurely walks, picnics or meditation sessions. Bicycles are available for guests to explore the surrounding area, and guided tours of local historic sites can be arranged.

The castle also has an outdoor swimming pool, tennis court and spa. The spa offers a variety of relaxing treatments, from massages to facials, in a peaceful and luxurious setting. A fitness room is also available to guests.

Conclusion

The Relais & Châteaux in Île-de-France offer unique and unforgettable experiences, combining luxury, comfort and historical heritage. Each establishment, with its enchanting setting, warm welcome, exceptional gastronomy and enriching activities, offers total immersion in the French art of living. By discovering these exceptional places, you will be transported into a world where every detail is designed to delight the senses and create lasting memories. Whether for a romantic getaway, a peaceful retreat or a culinary exploration, Relais & Châteaux in Île-de-France are must-see destinations.

- The Château de Montvillargenne

The Château de Montvillargenne , located in Gouvieux in Oise, is one of the jewels of Relais & Châteaux in Île-de-France. With its rich history, impressive architecture, fine culinary offerings and a variety of activities and services, this castle offers an unforgettable experience to its visitors. In this chapter, we will explore in detail the history and architecture of the castle, its culinary offerings, the activities available and services offered, as well as the special events and unique experiences that can be had there.

History and Architecture

The Origins of the Castle

The Château de Montvillargenne was built at the beginning of the 20th century by the Rothschild family, one of the most influential and wealthy families in Europe. The architecture of the castle reflects the Anglo-Norman style, with a combination of grandeur and elegance that characterizes residences of this era. Situated in a six-hectare park, the castle offers an idyllic and peaceful setting, far from the hustle and bustle of city life.

The history of the castle is marked by several periods of transformation and renovation. Built in 1900, it was used as a private residence by the Rothschild family for several decades. During World War II, the castle was requisitioned by the German army, but it was returned to its owners after the war. In the 1980s, it was transformed into a luxury hotel, joining Relais & Châteaux in offering a unique experience of luxury and comfort.

The Architecture of the Castle

The architecture of the Château de Montvillargenne is a perfect example of the Anglo-Norman style, characterized by stone facades, slate roofs, turrets and wrought iron balconies. The large arched windows and careful architectural details add to the elegance of the building.

The interior of the castle is just as impressive, with wood-panelled lounges, marble fireplaces and painted ceilings. The castle's common areas, such as the entrance hall, lounges and library, are decorated with period furniture, tapestries and artwork, creating a warm and welcoming atmosphere.

The castle's rooms and suites are tastefully decorated, blending traditional and contemporary elements to provide modern comfort in a historic setting. Each room is unique, with views of the park or gardens, four-poster beds, solid wood furniture and luxurious fabrics. The bathrooms are fitted with marble bathtubs, walk-in showers and high-quality toiletries.

Culinary Offers

The Restaurant Le Vilargène

Montvillargenne 's gourmet restaurant , "Le Vilargène ", is a true culinary gem. Led by a renowned chef, the restaurant offers refined French cuisine, highlighting local and seasonal products. The chef, recognized for his creativity and expertise, develops menus that combine tradition and innovation, offering an exceptional culinary experience.

The restaurant's menu changes regularly to reflect the seasons and available ingredients. The dishes are carefully presented, with particular attention to detail and aesthetics. Guests can choose from a variety of tasting menus, each designed to provide a culinary journey through flavors and textures.

The Castle Bar

The bar at Château de Montvillargenne is a cozy and elegant place where guests can relax and enjoy a selection of French wines, champagnes and cocktails. The bar offers an intimate atmosphere, with comfortable seating, soft lighting and refined decoration.

The bar staff is highly trained and happy to recommend wines and spirits based on guest preferences. Wine tastings and mixology workshops are held regularly, allowing guests to discover new flavors and perfect their beverage knowledge.

Cooking Classes

For food lovers, the Château de Montvillargenne offers cooking classes led by the restaurant's chef. These interactive workshops allow customers to learn culinary techniques and discover the secrets of French cuisine. Classes are suitable for all levels, from beginners to experienced cooks.

Participants can choose from a variety of themes, such as baking, market cuisine, cooking techniques or wine pairings. Each class includes a practical demonstration, personalized advice from the chef and a tasting of the prepared dishes. Customers leave with recipes and tips that they can reproduce at home.

Activities and Services

The Château Spa

The Château de Montvillargenne spa is a haven of peace and relaxation. Equipped with saunas, hammams and massage rooms, the spa offers a variety of treatments for well-being and relaxation. Guests can choose from a range of massages, facials, body scrubs and wellness therapies, all carried out by professional therapists.

The spa uses high quality products from renowned brands to ensure optimal results and a luxurious experience. Guests can also enjoy the heated indoor swimming pool, jacuzzi and fitness room, which are at their disposal to complete their relaxation experience.

Outdoor activities

The six-hectare park surrounding the Château de Montvillargenne offers numerous opportunities for outdoor activities. Guests can stroll through the gardens, jog on the marked trails or enjoy picnics in picturesque spaces. Bicycles are also available to explore the surroundings in an ecological and active way.

For sports enthusiasts, the castle offers tennis courts, a pétanque court and organized outdoor activities, such as guided hikes, outdoor yoga sessions and meditation workshops. Guests can also play golf at the nearby courses, which offer magnificent views of the surrounding countryside.

Cultural Activities and Excursions

Château de Montvillargenne regularly organizes guided tours of local historic sites, day trips and cultural activities. Guests can discover the region's treasures, such as Chantilly Castle, Royaumont Abbey and the village of Senlis, with its medieval architecture and cobbled streets.

Local craft workshops, gardening classes and tastings of local products are also offered, allowing guests to immerse themselves in the culture and traditions of the region. The castle can arrange private tours and tailor-made experiences, tailored to guests' interests and preferences.

Special Events and Unique Experiences

Weddings and Receptions

Château de Montvillargenne is an ideal wedding venue, providing a romantic and elegant setting for ceremonies and receptions. The castle has several function rooms, each tastefully decorated and able to accommodate events of different sizes. The gardens and terraces provide stunning spaces for outdoor ceremonies, cocktails and photoshoots.

Chateau staff work closely with couples to create bespoke weddings, taking into account every detail from decoration to personalized menus. The castle's chefs create wedding menus that reflect the tastes and preferences of the bride and groom, using seasonal ingredients and local produce. The professional and attentive service teams ensure that every event goes off without a hitch.

Seminars and Business Meetings

The Château de Montvillargenne offers an exceptional setting for seminars, conferences and business meetings. The castle has several meeting rooms, equipped with the latest technology and offering flexible spaces for events of different sizes. Private lounges and terraces can also be used for more informal meetings or brainstorming sessions.

Hotel teams work with event organizers to create tailor-made programs, including coffee breaks, business lunches and dinners. Team-building activities and excursions can also be organized to strengthen team cohesion and provide moments of relaxation outside of work sessions.

Unique Experiences

Château de Montvillargenne offers unique experiences to make each stay memorable. These include private dinners in exclusive locations within the castle, such as the library or the gardens, offering an intimate and romantic atmosphere. Guests can also participate in wine tasting workshops, led by expert sommeliers, to discover the secrets of French wines.

Wellness getaways are also available, including personalized relaxation and relaxation programs, spa treatments, yoga and meditation sessions, as well as healthy and nutritious meals. These programs are designed to help clients recharge their batteries and regain physical and mental balance.

Conclusion

The Château de Montvillargenne is much more than just a luxury hotel; it is a destination in itself, offering a unique and unforgettable experience. With its rich history, impressive architecture, fine culinary offerings and a variety of activities and services, this castle is the ideal place to relax, recharge and discover the French art of living. Whether for a romantic getaway, a wellness retreat, a dream wedding or a business meeting, Château de Montvillargenne promises an exceptional experience, marked by luxury, comfort and elegance.

- Le Relais Christine

Located in the heart of Paris, in the historic district of Saint-Germain-des-Prés, the Relais Christine is a charming hotel which occupies a former 13th century abbey. This exceptional establishment is part of Relais & Châteaux and offers a unique experience that combines history, modern comfort and personalized service. In this chapter, we will explore in detail the history and architecture of Relais Christine, its culinary offerings, the activities available, the services offered as well as the special events and unique experiences that can be enjoyed there.

History and Architecture

The Origins of the Hotel

Relais Christine is located in a historic building that dates back to the 13th century, when the Grands-Augustins Abbey was founded on this location. The abbey, which played an important role in the religious and intellectual life of Paris, went through several centuries of transformation before becoming a charming hotel. The current building has preserved the historic character of the abbey while integrating modern elements to offer exceptional comfort.

The history of the abbey is rich and fascinating. It has welcomed many scholars and artists over the centuries, helping to make Saint-Germain-des-Prés an intellectual and cultural center. During the French Revolution, the abbey was largely destroyed, but some architectural elements were preserved and integrated into the current building. In the 1970s, the building was converted into a hotel, preserving its historic charm while adding modern conveniences.

The Architecture of Relais Christine

The architecture of Relais Christine reflects its monastic past, with medieval and classical elements that create a unique and welcoming atmosphere. The stone walls, wooden beams and interior gardens add to the charm of the place. The hotel's entrance, discreet and elegant, sets the tone for what awaits visitors inside.

The hotel's public areas are decorated with period furniture, artwork and sumptuous textiles. The entrance hall, lounges and library offer comfortable and refined settings in which to relax. Guests can enjoy the tranquility of the gardens, which are a true haven of peace in the heart of the city.

The rooms and suites at Relais Christine are tastefully decorated, mixing traditional and contemporary elements. Each room is unique, with views of the gardens or picturesque streets of Saint-Germain-des-Prés. Four-poster beds, solid wood furniture and luxurious fabrics create a cozy and elegant ambiance. The bathrooms, equipped with marble bathtubs and walk-in showers, offer modern comfort.

Culinary Offers

Breakfast

Although Relais Christine does not have its own restaurant, it offers a buffet breakfast service in an elegant dining room or in the comfort of the rooms. Breakfast offers a selection of fresh pastries, artisan breads, fruits, cheeses and cold cuts, as well as hot options upon request. Products are carefully selected for their quality and freshness, providing customers with a delicious and nourishing start to the day.

Breakfast can be served in the dining room, decorated with period furniture and artwork, or in the interior courtyard, offering a peaceful and relaxing ambiance. Guests can also choose to have breakfast in their room, where it is served on an elegant tray, with silver cutlery and fine china.

Collaborations with Local Chefs

For lunch and dinner, Relais Christine collaborates with local chefs and neighboring restaurants to provide guests with an exceptional culinary experience. The hotel staff is happy to recommend local addresses and reserve tables at renowned establishments. These collaborations allow customers to discover the richness of Parisian gastronomy, with options ranging from traditional bistros to Michelin-starred restaurants.

Relais Christine also organizes private dinners and special events in collaboration with local chefs. These events, which take place in the hotel's lounges or gardens, offer a unique and exclusive culinary experience. The menus are developed according to customer preferences, highlighting seasonal products and regional specialties.

The Wine Bar

Relais Christine has a cozy and elegant wine bar, where guests can enjoy a selection of French and international wines, accompanied by tapas and small plates. The bar offers an intimate atmosphere, with comfortable seating, soft lighting and refined decoration. The hotel's sommeliers are available to recommend wines based on guest preferences and to arrange private tastings.

Wine tasting workshops are regularly held at the bar, allowing guests to discover the secrets of French wines and learn to identify aromas and flavors. These workshops are led by expert sommeliers, who share their passion and knowledge of wine.

Activities and Services

The Relais Christine Spa

The Relais Christine spa, located in 13th century vaulted cellars, offers a unique setting to relax and recharge your batteries. The spa offers a variety of relaxing treatments, from massages to facials, performed by professional therapists. Customers can choose from a range of treatments using high quality products from renowned brands.

The spa also has a jacuzzi, hammam and fitness room, providing a complete space for well-being. Guests can enjoy these facilities at any time of the day, and private sessions can be booked for an even more exclusive experience.

Outdoor activities

Le Relais Christine offers electric bikes to its guests, allowing them to explore the picturesque streets of Saint-Germain-des-Prés and the surrounding area. Guests can stroll along the Seine, visit the Luxembourg Gardens or explore the historic districts of Paris at their own pace. The hotel concierge is available to provide maps, directions and recommendations for cycling tours.

For those who prefer to walk, private guided tours of the city's museums, art galleries and historical monuments can be arranged. These tours, led by expert guides, offer a unique perspective on the history and culture of Paris. Guests can also participate in themed walks, such as literary tours, street art tours or gastronomic explorations.

Cultural Activities and Experiences

Le Relais Christine regularly organizes cultural events and unique experiences for its guests. Private concerts, literary readings and art exhibitions are often held in the hotel lounges or gardens. These events offer immersion in the Parisian cultural scene and allow guests to meet artists, writers and musicians.

Guests can also participate in cooking workshops, baking classes and chocolate tastings, led by local chefs. These workshops provide an opportunity to learn French cooking techniques and taste delicious creations. Le Relais Christine also offers yoga and meditation classes, led by qualified instructors, in the hotel's gardens or wellness areas.

Special Events and Unique Experiences

Weddings and Receptions

Relais Christine is an ideal venue for intimate weddings and private receptions. The hotel's gardens and lounges provide a romantic and elegant setting for ceremonies and receptions. Hotel staff work closely with couples to create tailor-made events, taking into account every detail, from decor to personalized menus.

The hotel's chefs create wedding menus that reflect the tastes and preferences of the bride and groom, using seasonal ingredients and local produce. The professional and attentive service teams ensure that every event goes off without a hitch. Couples can also enjoy luxurious suites for their wedding night, with special services such as massages, in-room breakfasts and welcome gifts.

Seminars and Business Meetings

The Relais Christine offers an exceptional setting for seminars, conferences and business meetings. The hotel's private lounges, equipped with the latest technology, offer flexible spaces for events of different sizes. Hotel teams work with event organizers to create tailor-made programs, including coffee breaks, business lunches and dinners.

Team-building activities and excursions can also be organized to strengthen team cohesion and provide moments of relaxation outside of work sessions. Guests can take advantage of the hotel's

wellness facilities to unwind after a day of meetings, with spa treatments, yoga sessions and massages.

Unique Experiences

Le Relais Christine offers unique experiences to make each stay memorable. These include private dinners in exclusive locations within the hotel, such as the library or gardens, offering an intimate and romantic atmosphere. Guests can also participate in wine tasting workshops, led by expert sommeliers, to discover the secrets of French wines.

Wellness getaways are also available, including personalized relaxation and relaxation programs, spa treatments, yoga and meditation sessions, as well as healthy and nutritious meals. These programs are designed to help clients recharge their batteries and regain physical and mental balance.

Seasonal and Thematic Offers

Le Relais Christine regularly offers seasonal and thematic offers to enrich its customers' experience. At Christmas, the hotel is decked out in festive decorations and offers special menus, cookie decorating workshops and Christmas market visits. In summer, gourmet picnics can be organized in the Luxembourg gardens or on the banks of the Seine.

Romantic getaways are also offered, including candlelit dinners, duo massages and horse-drawn carriage rides through the streets of Paris. For culture lovers, special packages including tickets for exhibitions, shows and concerts are available, offering complete immersion in Parisian cultural life.

Conclusion

The Relais Christine is much more than just a charming hotel; it is a destination in itself, offering a unique and unforgettable experience in the heart of Paris. With its rich history, impressive architecture, refined culinary offerings and a variety of activities and services, this establishment is the ideal place to relax, recharge and discover the French art of living.

Whether for a romantic getaway, a wellness retreat, an intimate wedding or a business meeting, Relais Christine promises an exceptional experience, marked by luxury, comfort and elegance. Guests leave with unforgettable memories, enriched by the unique culture, gastronomy and hospitality of this iconic Saint-Germain-des-Prés hotel.

- The Queen's Pavilion

Located on the prestigious Place des Vosges in the historic Marais district of Paris, Le Pavillon de la Reine is a unique luxury hotel that combines the timeless elegance of French architecture with modern comfort and impeccable service. This establishment, a member of Relais & Châteaux, offers its guests an unforgettable experience, marked by historical charm, refined gastronomy, varied activities and first-rate services. In this chapter, we will explore in detail the history and architecture of the Pavillon de la Reine, its culinary offerings, the activities available, the services offered as well as the special events and unique experiences that can be enjoyed there.

History and Architecture

The Origins of the Queen's Pavilion

The Pavillon de la Reine owes its name to Anne of Austria, Queen of France and mother of Louis XIV, who resided in the district. The hotel is located in a historic 17th century building, built during the reign of Louis XIII, when the Place des Vosges was developed. This square, the oldest in Paris, is an emblematic example of Marais town planning, with its red brick facades, elegant arcades and slate roofs.

The building has been carefully restored to preserve its old-world charm while incorporating modern conveniences. The history of the Place des Vosges and the Marais district is rich and fascinating, marked by historical events, royal residences and architectural transformations. The Pavillon de la Reine fits perfectly into this historic setting, offering its guests a stay marked by elegance and refinement.

The Architecture of the Queen's Pavilion

The architecture of the Pavillon de la Reine reflects the classical French style of the 17th century, with red brick facades, mullioned windows and wrought iron balconies. The hotel entrance, discreet and elegant, gives access to a peaceful interior courtyard, lined with plants and flowers, offering a haven of peace in the heart of the city.

The interior of the hotel is tastefully decorated, mixing historical and contemporary elements. The lounges, with their marble fireplaces, woodwork and painted ceilings, offer a cozy and sophisticated setting in which to relax. The library, filled with old books and period furniture, is a place of tranquility and reflection.

The rooms and suites at the Pavillon de la Reine are carefully decorated, combining antique furniture, works of art and luxurious textiles. Each room is unique, with views of the interior courtyard or Place des Vosges. The bathrooms, equipped with marble bathtubs and walk-in showers, offer modern comfort. The suites, with their generous spaces and refined decorative touches, offer the ultimate luxury experience.

Culinary Offers

Breakfast

Le Pavillon de la Reine offers a hearty buffet breakfast, served in an elegant dining room or in the interior courtyard. Breakfast includes a variety of fresh produce, pastries, artisan breads, fruits, yogurts, cereals and hot dishes. Products are carefully selected for their quality and freshness, providing customers with a delicious and nourishing start to the day.

Breakfast can be served in the dining room, decorated with period furniture and artwork, or in the interior courtyard, offering a peaceful and relaxing ambiance. Guests can also choose to have breakfast in their room, where it is served on an elegant tray, with silver cutlery and fine china.

Collaborations with Local Chefs

Le Pavillon de la Reine does not have its own restaurant, but it collaborates with local chefs and neighboring restaurants to offer its guests an exceptional culinary experience. The hotel staff is happy to recommend local addresses and reserve tables at renowned establishments. These collaborations allow customers to discover the richness of Parisian gastronomy, with options ranging from traditional bistros to Michelin-starred restaurants.

The hotel also organizes private dinners and special events in collaboration with local chefs. These events, which take place in the hotel's lounges or gardens, offer a unique and exclusive culinary experience. The menus are developed according to customer preferences, highlighting seasonal products and regional specialties.

The Wine Bar

Le Pavillon de la Reine features a cozy and elegant wine bar, where guests can enjoy a selection of French and international wines, accompanied by tapas and small plates. The bar offers an intimate atmosphere, with comfortable seating, soft lighting and refined decoration. The hotel's sommeliers are available to recommend wines based on guest preferences and to arrange private tastings.

Wine tasting workshops are regularly held at the bar, allowing guests to discover the secrets of French wines and learn to identify aromas and flavors. These workshops are led by expert sommeliers, who share their passion and knowledge of wine.

Activities and Services

The Queen's Pavilion Spa

The Pavillon de la Reine spa is a haven of peace and relaxation. Equipped with saunas, hammams and massage rooms, the spa offers a variety of treatments for well-being and relaxation. Guests can choose from a range of massages, facials, body scrubs and wellness therapies, all carried out by professional therapists.

The spa uses high quality products from renowned brands to ensure optimal results and a luxurious experience. Guests can also take advantage of the fitness room, equipped with modern equipment, to maintain their wellness routine during their stay.

Outdoor activities

Le Pavillon de la Reine offers bicycles to its guests, allowing them to explore the Marais district and surrounding areas. Guests can stroll along the Seine, visit the Luxembourg Gardens or explore the historic districts of Paris at their own pace. The hotel concierge is available to provide maps, directions and recommendations for cycling tours.

For those who prefer to walk, private guided tours of the city's museums, art galleries and historical monuments can be arranged. These tours, led by expert guides, offer a unique perspective on the history and culture of Paris. Guests can also participate in themed walks, such as literary tours, street art tours or gastronomic explorations.

Cultural Activities and Experiences

The Pavillon de la Reine regularly organizes cultural events and unique experiences for its guests. Private concerts, literary readings and art exhibitions are often held in the hotel lounges or gardens. These events offer immersion in the Parisian cultural scene and allow guests to meet artists, writers and musicians.

Guests can also participate in cooking workshops, baking classes and chocolate tastings, led by local chefs. These workshops provide an opportunity to learn French cooking techniques and taste delicious creations. The Queen's Pavilion also offers yoga and meditation classes, led by qualified instructors, in the hotel's gardens or wellness areas.

Special Events and Unique Experiences

Weddings and Receptions

The Queen's Pavilion is an ideal venue for hosting intimate weddings and private receptions. The hotel's gardens and lounges provide a romantic and elegant setting for ceremonies and receptions. Hotel staff work closely with couples to create tailor-made events, taking into account every detail, from decor to personalized menus.

The hotel's chefs create wedding menus that reflect the tastes and preferences of the bride and groom, using seasonal ingredients and local produce. The professional and attentive service teams ensure that every event goes off without a hitch. Couples can also enjoy luxurious suites for their wedding night, with special services such as massages, in-room breakfasts and welcome gifts.

Seminars and Business Meetings

The Queen's Pavilion offers an exceptional setting for seminars, conferences and business meetings. The hotel's private lounges, equipped with the latest technology, offer flexible spaces for events of different sizes. Hotel teams work with event organizers to create tailor-made programs, including coffee breaks, business lunches and dinners.

Team-building activities and excursions can also be organized to strengthen team cohesion and provide moments of relaxation outside of work sessions. Guests can take advantage of the hotel's wellness facilities to unwind after a day of meetings, with spa treatments, yoga sessions and massages.

Unique Experiences

The Queen's Pavilion offers unique experiences to make every stay memorable. These include private dinners in exclusive locations within the hotel, such as the library or gardens, offering an intimate and romantic atmosphere. Guests can also participate in wine tasting workshops, led by expert sommeliers, to discover the secrets of French wines.

Wellness getaways are also available, including personalized relaxation and relaxation programs, spa treatments, yoga and meditation sessions, as well as healthy and nutritious meals. These programs are designed to help clients recharge their batteries and regain physical and mental balance.

Seasonal and Thematic Offers

The Pavillon de la Reine regularly offers seasonal and thematic offers to enrich its customers' experience. At Christmas, the hotel is decked out in festive decorations and offers special menus, cookie decorating workshops and Christmas market visits. In summer, gourmet picnics can be organized in the Luxembourg gardens or on the banks of the Seine.

Romantic getaways are also offered, including candlelit dinners, duo massages and horse-drawn carriage rides through the streets of Paris. For culture lovers, special packages including tickets for exhibitions, shows and concerts are available, offering complete immersion in Parisian cultural life.

Conclusion

The Queen's Pavilion is much more than just a luxury hotel; it is a destination in itself, offering a unique and unforgettable experience in the heart of Paris. With its rich history, impressive architecture, refined culinary offerings and a variety of activities and services, this establishment is the ideal place to relax, recharge and discover the French art of living.

Whether for a romantic getaway, a wellness retreat, an intimate wedding or a business meeting, the Pavillon de la Reine promises an exceptional experience, marked by luxury, comfort and elegance. Guests leave with unforgettable memories, enriched by the unique culture, gastronomy and hospitality of this emblematic hotel on Place des Vosges.

Chapter 2: Relais & Châteaux in Provence-Alpes-Côte d'Azur

1. General Presentation of the Region

The Provence-Alpes-Côte d'Azur (PACA) region is one of the most beautiful and diverse in France. Located in the southeast of the country, it is bordered by the Mediterranean to the south and the Alps to the north, offering an incredible variety of landscapes from sunny beaches to snow-capped mountains. This region, rich in history and culture, is also famous for its delicious cuisine, renowned wines and art of living. This chapter explores the PACA region in depth, highlighting its main geographical, historical, cultural and economic characteristics.

Geography and Landscapes

The Varied Landscapes of the Region

The PACA region is renowned for the diversity of its landscapes, which attract millions of visitors each year. The Côte d'Azur, with its sandy beaches, turquoise waters and glamorous seaside resorts like Nice, Cannes and Saint-Tropez, is a dream destination for sun and sea lovers. The coastal towns also offer a vibrant nightlife, luxury boutiques and Michelin-starred restaurants.

The Southern Alps, which extend to the Mediterranean, provide a striking contrast to the coast. This mountain range is a paradise for winter sports enthusiasts, with famous ski resorts like Serre Chevalier, Isola 2000 and Vars. In summer, the Southern Alps transform into a playground for hikers, cyclists and nature lovers, with marked trails, alpine lakes and breathtaking panoramas.

Provence, with its lavender fields, olive groves and hilltop villages, embodies the bucolic charm of the south of France. This region is famous for its picturesque landscapes, colorful markets and lively festivals. Historic cities like Avignon, Aix-en-Provence and Arles offer a rich cultural history, with ancient monuments, museums and art and music festivals.

Natural Parks

The PACA region is home to several protected natural parks which preserve its unique biodiversity and offer discovery opportunities for visitors. The Calanques National Park, located between Marseille and Cassis, is famous for its wild coves, limestone cliffs and crystal clear waters. It is a great place for hiking, climbing, kayaking and scuba diving.

The Mercantour National Park, in the Southern Alps, offers exceptional biodiversity, with snow-capped peaks, glacial lakes and green valleys. This park is a refuge for varied fauna and flora, including rare species such as the ibex, the wolf and the golden eagle. Hiking enthusiasts can explore well-marked trails, discover prehistoric cave paintings and admire stunning landscapes.

The Parc Naturel Régional du Luberon, in Provence, is another popular destination for its picturesque landscapes, charming villages and hiking trails. This park protects varied ecosystems, ranging from oak forests to scrubland hills, and offers opportunities for observing local flora and fauna.

History and Heritage

The Origins of the Region

The PACA region has a rich and complex history, marked by the influence of numerous civilizations. The first traces of human occupation date back to prehistoric times, with sites like the Vallée des Merveilles caves, which house rock carvings dating back to the Bronze Age. The Ligurians, an ancient Italic tribe, were among the first inhabitants of the region, followed by the Phocaeans, who founded the city of Massalia (now Marseille) in the 6th century BC.

The Romans left an indelible mark on the region, building towns, roads and monuments that still stand today. Sites like the ancient theater of Orange, the arenas of Arles and the Pont du Gard bear witness to the grandeur of the Roman Empire and its influence on the region. Provence was a prosperous Roman province, known for its production of wine, olive oil and ceramics.

The Middle Ages and the Renaissance

The Middle Ages saw the emergence of powerful city-states and lordships, which left behind castles, abbeys and fortified villages. The city of Avignon is famous for having been the seat of the papacy in the 14th century, with the Palais des Papes as a symbol of this ecclesiastical power. The crusades and religious wars also marked the region, leaving traces in local architecture and traditions.

The Renaissance brought artistic and cultural excitement, with emblematic figures such as the painter Paul Cézanne, originally from Aix-en-Provence. The region's towns prospered through trade, crafts, and agriculture. Markets and fairs played a central role in economic life, and exchanges with other regions and countries enriched local culture.

The Modern and Contemporary Era

The modern era has seen significant transformations in the PACA region, with the development of infrastructure, industrialization and the rise of tourism. The French Riviera became a popular destination for Europe's elite in the 19th century, attracting artists, writers and aristocrats in search of sun and beauty. Personalities like Coco Chanel, Pablo Picasso and Ernest Hemingway have contributed to the region's fame.

The 20th century brought rapid change, with the construction of roads, railways and airports, making access to the region easier. The seaside resorts of the French Riviera continued to develop, offering modern infrastructure and luxury services. Provence, for its part, has managed to preserve its rural charm, attracting visitors in search of authenticity and tranquility.

Today, the PACA region is a harmonious blend of tradition and modernity, with a diversified economy based on tourism, agriculture, industry and services. The region continues to attract visitors from all over the world, seduced by its natural beauty, its cultural richness and its art of living.

Culture and Traditions

Cultural life

The PACA region is a hotbed of creativity and cultural innovation, with a vibrant arts scene and a rich tradition of festivals and events. The city of Avignon is famous for its theater festival, one of the largest in the world, which attracts thousands of spectators and theater companies every year. The Cannes Film Festival, for its part, is a major event in the world of cinema, bringing together the biggest stars and internationally renowned directors.

The visual arts also occupy an important place in regional culture. The Maeght Foundation in Saint-Paul-de-Vence, the Matisse Museum in Nice and the Center d'Art Contemporain de Châteauvert are all places where you can admire modern and contemporary works of art. The region has been a source of inspiration for many artists, including Vincent Van Gogh, who created some of his most famous works in Arles.

Music is another essential component of cultural life in PACA. From classical music festivals, such as the Aix-en-Provence Festival, to jazz and contemporary music concerts, the region offers a varied and quality program. Local musical traditions, such as Provençal music and Occitan songs, are also preserved and celebrated during festivals and village fetes.

Gastronomy and Local Products

Gastronomy in Provence-Alpes-Côte d'Azur is a true art of living, highlighting local products and culinary traditions. Provençal cuisine is renowned for its Mediterranean flavors, with fresh, quality ingredients, such as olive oil, garlic, tomatoes, Provence herbs and sunny vegetables. Signature dishes include ratatouille, bouillabaisse, tapenade, aioli and pissaladière.

Local markets are essential places to discover the gastronomic richness of the region. The markets of Provence, such as those of Vaison-la-Romaine, Carpentras and Saint-Rémy-de-Provence, are full of fresh produce, fruits and vegetables, cheeses, charcuterie and artisanal products. Visitors can taste local specialties and meet producers, who share their passion and know-how.

Wine is another pride of the region, with renowned vineyards in appellations such as Côtes de Provence, Bandol, Châteauneuf

-du-Pape and Coteaux d'Aix-en-Provence. The region's wines, whether red, white or rosé, are appreciated for their quality and diversity. Cellars and wineries offer tastings and guided tours, allowing wine lovers to discover the secrets of Provençal viticulture.

Local Festivals and Traditions

The PACA region is rich in festivals and traditions, which bear witness to its history and culture. Village festivals, agricultural fairs and folk festivals are opportunities to celebrate local customs and continue traditions. The inhabitants of the region are attached to their roots and ensure that their cultural heritage is passed on to future generations.

The Nice Carnival is one of the region's most famous events, attracting thousands of visitors each year. This carnival, with its float parades, flower battles and street performances, is a joyful and colorful celebration of Nice culture. Costumes, masks and carnival traditions are passed down from generation to generation, making this event a highlight of the cultural life of the region.

Lavender festivals, like those of Sault and Valensole, celebrate the flowering of this emblematic plant of Provence. These festivals include parades, markets, distillation workshops and musical entertainment, offering an immersion in Provençal culture. The lavender harvest, traditionally carried out with a sickle, is also an important moment in rural life, marking the end of summer and the start of the harvest.

Economy and Innovation

Tourism

Tourism is one of the pillars of the PACA region's economy, attracting millions of visitors from all over the world each year. The diversity of landscapes, cultural richness and Mediterranean climate are all assets that make this region a popular destination. The seaside resorts of the French Riviera, the hilltop villages of Provence, the ski resorts of the Southern Alps and historic sites attract tourists with varied interests.

The region's tourist infrastructure is of high quality, with a diverse range of accommodation, starred restaurants, wellness centers and leisure activities. The international airports of Nice and Marseille, as well as rail and road links, facilitate access to the region. Sustainable and responsible tourism is also encouraged, with initiatives aimed at preserving the environment and promoting local heritage.

Agriculture and Local Products

Agriculture plays an essential role in the economy of the PACA region, with varied and quality production. The region is famous for its vineyards, olive groves, lavender fields and orchards. Agricultural products, such as wine, olive oil, honey, fruits and vegetables, are renowned for their excellence and diversity.

Farmers' markets, agricultural cooperatives and short circuits promote the marketing of local products and support the rural economy. Quality labels, such as the AOC (Appellation d'Origine Contrôlée) and the IGP (Protected Geographical Indication), guarantee the authenticity and quality of local products. Visitors can discover these products during tastings, farm tours and food festivals.

Industry and Innovation

The PACA region is also a center of innovation and industrial development, with varied sectors such as aeronautics, electronics, biotechnology and renewable energies. The Sophia Antipolis technology park, near Nice, is one of the main research and development centers in Europe, bringing together companies, universities and research laboratories.

Competitiveness clusters, such as Optitec (optics-photonics) and Safe Cluster (aeronautical and space security), promote innovation and collaboration between economic and scientific players.

Initiatives in favor of sustainable development and the energy transition are also encouraged, with projects aimed at reducing the carbon footprint and promoting renewable energies.

Transport infrastructure, such as the ports of Marseille and Toulon, motorways and high-speed train lines, supports the region's economic development. The proximity of Italy and Spain facilitates trade and international collaborations. The PACA region is a key player in the French economy, contributing to its dynamism and international influence.

Conclusion

The Provence-Alpes-Côte d'Azur region is an exceptional destination, rich in history, culture and varied landscapes. Whether enjoying the sunny beaches of the Côte d'Azur, exploring the picturesque villages of Provence, hitting the ski slopes of the Southern Alps or discovering the historical and cultural treasures of the region, there is something for everyone. tastes.

The Relais & Châteaux of the PACA region capture the essence of this diversity and offer their guests unforgettable experiences, combining luxury, comfort and authenticity. Each establishment, with its enchanting setting, its warm welcome, its exceptional gastronomy and its enriching activities, offers a total immersion in the Provençal art of living.

By discovering the Relais & Châteaux of Provence-Alpes-Côte d'Azur, you will be transported into a world where every detail is designed to delight the senses and create lasting memories. This chapter presented a detailed overview of the region, integrating geographical, historical, cultural and economic aspects to provide a comprehensive understanding of this unique destination.

- History and Heritage

The Provence-Alpes-Côte d'Azur (PACA) region is a land rich in history and heritage, shaped by millennia of successive civilizations. From the first prehistoric inhabitants to the splendor of the Roman era, from medieval dynasties to periods of artistic and cultural renaissance, each era has left its mark on this fascinating region. This chapter explores the history and heritage of PACA in detail, highlighting the key events, iconic monuments and cultural contributions that make this region a must-visit destination for history and heritage enthusiasts.

Origins and Antiquity

The First Traces of Civilization

The PACA region has been inhabited for millennia, as evidenced by the numerous archaeological sites scattered across the territory. The first traces of human occupation date back to the Paleolithic, with remains such as the cave paintings of the Vallée des Merveilles caves, located in the Mercantour National Park. These engravings, dating from the Bronze Age, depict human figures, animals and mysterious symbols, offering a fascinating insight into early human societies.

The Ligurians, an ancient Italic tribe, were among the first sedentary inhabitants of the region. They occupied the hills and mountains, living from agriculture and livestock. The Ligurians built fortified villages, called oppida, the remains of which can still be seen today. These oppida served as refuges in times of war and commercial centers for trade with neighboring tribes.

Greek and Roman Influence

In the 6th century BC, the Phocaeans, Greek colonists from Asia Minor, founded the city of Massalia (today Marseille). Massalia quickly became a thriving commercial and cultural center, establishing trade relations with indigenous peoples and other Greek colonies in the Mediterranean. The Greeks introduced new agricultural techniques, viticulture and artisanal practices which enriched the local culture.

The conquest of the region by the Romans in the 2nd century BC profoundly transformed the landscape and society. Provence became a prosperous Roman province, known as Provincia Romana, from which the current name Provence comes. The Romans built impressive infrastructure, such as roads, aqueducts, theaters, amphitheaters and temples.

Roman Monuments

The Roman remains are among the most impressive monuments in the PACA region. The ancient theater of Orange, a UNESCO World Heritage Site, is one of the best preserved Roman theaters in the world. Built in the 1st century, it could accommodate up to 10,000 spectators and served as a place of entertainment for the city's inhabitants.

The Arles Arena, another iconic site, is a testament to the grandeur of the Roman Empire. Built in the 1st century, the arenas could accommodate 20,000 spectators for gladiator fights, animal hunts and other spectacles. Today, they are still used for cultural events and historical reenactments.

The Pont du Gard, a Roman aqueduct near Nîmes, is an engineering masterpiece. Built in the 1st century, it was used to transport water from the Gardon river to the city of Nîmes. With its three levels of arches, it is one of the most visited and best preserved Roman monuments in France.

The Middle Ages: The Emergence of Provence

The Merovingian and Carolingian Dynasties

After the fall of the Roman Empire in the 5th century, the PACA region entered a period of turbulence, marked by barbarian invasions and power struggles. The Franks, under the Merovingian dynasty, established their domination over the region. The first Merovingian kings consolidated their power by building castles and fortifying towns.

Under the Carolingian dynasty, the region experienced a period of relative stability and prosperity. Charlemagne, crowned emperor in 800, strengthened the infrastructure and promoted the cultural and intellectual renaissance. Abbeys and monasteries, such as the Abbey of Saint-Victor in Marseille and the Abbey of Montmajour near Arles, became centers of knowledge and spirituality.

The Saracen and Viking Invasions

The 9th century was marked by Saracen and Viking invasions, which ravaged the region and disrupted daily life. The Saracens, coming from North Africa, settled in the mountains and carried out raids against towns and villages. The Vikings, for their part, sailed to the Mediterranean and attacked the coasts.

To defend against these invasions, local lords built fortifications and castles. The city of Nice, for example, was fortified to resist pirate attacks. People took refuge in the mountains and hills, building hilltop villages that provided natural protection against invaders.

The Counts of Provence

In the 11th century, the counts of Provence emerged as the main lords of the region. They consolidated their power by establishing matrimonial alliances and expanding their territory. Provence became a prosperous region, thanks to its agriculture, its crafts and its trade.

The counts of Provence built castles and palaces, such as the Palais des Comtes de Provence in Aix-en-Provence, which became the administrative and political center of the region. They also promote the development of towns and villages, granting charters and privileges to residents. Provence became a hotbed of culture and art, attracting troubadours, poets and artists.

The Palace of the Popes in Avignon

One of the most emblematic monuments of the PACA region is the Palais des Papes in Avignon. In the 14th century, Avignon became the seat of the papacy, under the leadership of Pope Clement V. The Palais des Papes, built between 1335 and 1364, is one of the largest and most important Gothic palaces in Europe.

This fortified palace, with its thick walls, imposing towers and ornately decorated rooms, reflects the power and wealth of the Catholic Church at that time. The Palace of the Popes served as the residence of the popes and the administrative center for Christianity. Today it is open to the public and hosts exhibitions, concerts and festivals.

The Renaissance and the Modern Era

The Renaissance in Provence

The Renaissance, which spanned from the 14th to the 16th century, was a period of artistic, intellectual and cultural renewal in Europe. In Provence, this period was marked by the rise of arts and letters, as well as architectural and urban transformations.

Aix-en-Provence, in particular, became an intellectual and artistic center. The city welcomed humanists, poets and artists, such as François Rabelais and Peter Paul Rubens. The private mansions and public buildings were built in a Renaissance style, with facades decorated with sculptures, frescoes and bas-reliefs.

The city of Nice, under the domination of the Dukes of Savoy, also experienced a period of prosperity and development. The dukes of Savoy favored town planning and architecture, building palaces, churches and fortifications. The Sainte- Réparate Cathedral and the Palais Lascaris are remarkable examples of Renaissance architecture in Nice.

The Wars of Religion

The 16th century was also marked by the wars of religion, which opposed Catholics and Protestants in France. Provence, like the rest of the country, was the scene of violent conflicts and persecution. Towns and villages were besieged, pillaged and burned.

Despite these troubles, the PACA region manages to preserve a certain stability and maintain its economic and cultural development. Cities like Marseille and Toulon continued to prosper thanks to maritime trade and trade with Mediterranean ports. The fortifications were reinforced to protect residents and property.

The Influence of Louis XIV

The 17th century was marked by the influence of Louis XIV, the Sun King, who centralized power and strengthened royal authority. The PACA region benefited from the king's policy of economic development and modernization. Infrastructure was improved, roads and bridges built, and ports expanded.

Marseille became a major trading port, linking France to the colonies and Mediterranean countries. The city grew rapidly, with the construction of new neighborhoods, public squares and monumental buildings. The Marseille Town Hall, built in the 17th century, is an example of classical architecture of that era.

Provence also experienced economic growth thanks to agriculture and crafts. Vine, olive and lavandin crops flourished, and local products, such as wine, olive oil and Marseille soap, became prized goods. Fairs and markets multiplied, promoting trade and relations with other regions.

Modern period

The French Revolution and the Napoleonic Empire

The French Revolution of 1789 had a profound impact on the PACA region, as on the rest of the country. The ideas of liberty, equality and fraternity spread quickly, and the population rose up against the old regime. The castles and properties of the aristocracy were confiscated and redistributed.

Cities in the region, such as Marseille and Toulon, played an active role in the Revolution. Marseille became a revolutionary stronghold, and its inhabitants, the Marseillais, participated in the storming of the Bastille. The song "La Marseillaise", which became the French national anthem, was composed by Claude Joseph Rouget de Lisle and popularized by Marseille volunteers.

Under the Napoleonic Empire, the PACA region experienced a period of stability and development. Napoleon Bonaparte, originally from Corsica, implemented administrative and judicial reforms that modernized the region. Infrastructure was improved, and the ports of Marseille and Toulon became strategic naval bases.

The 19th Century: The Industrial Era

The 19th century was a period of rapid transformation for the PACA region, with industrialization and urbanization. Railways and roads facilitated trade and travel, opening the region to the rest of France and Europe. Cities grew rapidly, with the construction of new neighborhoods, public buildings and monuments.

Marseille, in particular, became a major industrial and commercial center. The port of Marseille is expanding, welcoming commercial ships from around the world. The soap, textile, and metal industries prospered, attracting workers and entrepreneurs. The city acquired new infrastructures, such as the Palais de la Bourse and the Notre-Dame de la Garde Basilica.

The Côte d'Azur, for its part, became a popular destination for the European aristocracy. The cities of Nice, Cannes and Saint-Tropez attracted wealthy visitors in search of sun and relaxation. Luxury hotels, villas and casinos multiplied, creating a glamorous and cosmopolitan atmosphere. Artists and writers, such as F. Scott Fitzgerald and Ernest Hemingway, also found inspiration on the French Riviera.

The 20th Century: Wars and Reconstructions

The 20th century was marked by two world wars which had a profound impact on the PACA region. During the First World War, the region served as a rear base for troops and military operations. The port cities of Marseille and Toulon played a strategic role in the war effort, hosting warships and supply convoys.

The Second World War brought new challenges, with German occupation and Allied bombing. The PACA region was the scene of intense fighting, particularly during the Provence landings in August 1944. Allied forces, under the command of General de Lattre de Tassigny, quickly liberated the region, marking the end of the Nazi occupation.

After the war, the PACA region undertook a period of reconstruction and modernization. Infrastructure was rebuilt, cities renovated and industries revitalized. Tourism became a key sector of the economy, attracting visitors from all over the world. The Côte d'Azur, in particular, experienced spectacular growth, with the development of new seaside resorts and hotel complexes.

Recent Years: Sustainable Development and Innovation

In the 21st century, the PACA region continues to evolve, with an emphasis on sustainable development and innovation. Initiatives in favor of environmental protection, energy transition and the preservation of cultural heritage are encouraged. The region engages in sustainable development projects, such as promoting renewable energy, reducing carbon emissions and protecting biodiversity.

Technological and scientific innovation is also at the heart of the region's development. The Sophia Antipolis technology park, near Nice, is one of the main research and development centers in Europe, bringing together companies, universities and research laboratories. Competitiveness clusters, such as Optitec (optics-photonics) and Safe Cluster (aeronautical and space security), promote innovation and collaboration between economic and scientific players.

Initiatives in favor of culture and heritage are also encouraged, with restoration and enhancement projects for historic monuments. Festivals, exhibitions and cultural events help promote the richness and diversity of the region. Tourism, agriculture and industry continue to play a key role in the economy, supporting the development and prosperity of the region.

Monuments and Emblematic Sites

Historic monuments

The PACA region is rich in historical monuments, which bear witness to its glorious past and its cultural diversity. Among the most emblematic sites, we can cite:

- The Antique Theater of Orange: Listed as a UNESCO world heritage site, this Roman theater is one of the best preserved in the world. Every summer it hosts the Chorégies d'Orange, an opera and classical music festival.
- The Arena of Arles: This Roman monument, built in the 1st century, is a testimony to the greatness of the Roman Empire. Today it hosts cultural events and historical reenactments.
- The Palais des Papes in Avignon: This Gothic palace, built in the 14th century, was the seat of the papacy. It is now open to the public and hosts exhibitions and festivals.
- The Pont du Gard: This Roman aqueduct, built in the 1st century, is an engineering masterpiece. It is one of the most visited monuments in the region.

The Perched Villages

The hilltop villages of the PACA region are among the most beautiful in France, offering spectacular views and a picturesque atmosphere. These villages, often built on hills or mountains, offer an idyllic setting for walking and discovering the local heritage. Among the most famous, we can cite:

- Gordes: Located in the Luberon, this village is famous for its stone houses, its cobbled streets and its castle. It offers panoramic views of the valley and surrounding mountains.
- Eze: Perched on a hill overlooking the Mediterranean, this medieval village is a real gem. Its narrow streets, exotic gardens and breathtaking views make it a popular destination.
- Saint-Paul-de-Vence: This artists' village, located near Nice, is famous for its art galleries, boutiques and cafés. It attracted artists such as Marc Chagall, who lived and is buried there.
- Les Baux-de-Provence: This fortified village, perched on a rocky spur, offers spectacular views of the Alpilles. It is home to medieval ruins, museums and art exhibitions.

Natural Sites

The PACA region is also rich in natural sites, which offer breathtaking landscapes and opportunities for discovery. Among the most remarkable sites, we can cite:

- The Calanques of Marseille: This national park, located between Marseille and Cassis, is famous for its wild coves, limestone cliffs and crystal clear waters. It is a great place for hiking, climbing, kayaking and scuba diving.
- The Verdon: This canyon, nicknamed the "Grand Canyon of Provence", is one of the most spectacular in Europe. It offers stunning scenery, hiking trails and water activities.
- Mont Ventoux: This emblematic summit, nicknamed the "Giant of Provence", is a place of pilgrimage for cyclists and hikers. It offers panoramic views of the region and is home to varied flora and fauna.

- The Hyères Islands: These islands, located off the Var coast, are a paradise for lovers of nature and tranquility. They offer fine sandy beaches, hiking trails and diving sites.

Conclusion

The Provence-Alpes-Côte d'Azur region is a true treasure of history and heritage, offering unparalleled richness and diversity. From Roman remains to medieval castles, from hilltop villages to spectacular natural sites, every corner of the region tells a story and invites discovery.

The Relais & Châteaux of the PACA region capture the essence of this historical and cultural wealth, offering their guests unique and unforgettable experiences. Each establishment, with its enchanting setting, its warm welcome, its exceptional gastronomy and its enriching activities, offers a total immersion in the Provençal art of living.

By discovering the Relais & Châteaux of Provence-Alpes-Côte d'Azur, you will be transported into a world where every detail is designed to delight the senses and create lasting memories. This chapter explored the many facets of the region's history and heritage, revealing how each era helped shape this unique and fascinating destination.

- Gastronomy and Wine

The Provence-Alpes-Côte d'Azur (PACA) region is a paradise for food and wine lovers. With its colorful markets, its local products of exceptional quality, and its renowned vineyards, it offers an unrivaled culinary experience. Provençal cuisine, rich in flavors and traditions, is a pillar of the region's art of living. This chapter explores in depth the gastronomic aspects of the PACA region, detailing the local products, emblematic dishes, renowned chefs, starred restaurants and wines that make this region famous.

The Roots of Provençal Gastronomy

Mediterranean influence

The cuisine of the PACA region is deeply influenced by its Mediterranean environment. The sunny climate, fertile lands and proximity to the sea provide fresh and tasty ingredients that are at the heart of Provençal gastronomy. Olive oil, aromatic herbs (thyme, rosemary, basil), garlic, tomatoes, sunny vegetables and seafood are essential elements of this cuisine.

Meals in Provence are often simple but delicious, highlighting the quality of the products. Local markets play a central role, offering fresh, seasonal produce. The markets of Provence, such as those of Aix-en-Provence, Carpentras, Nice and Antibes, are essential places to discover local flavors and meet producers.

Local Products

Provençal local products are of exceptional quality and are used in a variety of traditional dishes. Among the most emblematic products, we find:

- Olive oil: Provence is one of the main olive oil producing regions in France. The olives are harvested by hand and cold pressed to produce high quality extra virgin olive oil. Olive oil from the Vallée des Baux-de-Provence and that from Nyons benefit from a protected designation of origin (AOP).
- Honey: The region produces a wide variety of honeys, including lavender honey, which is particularly prized for its delicate flavor and its therapeutic virtues. Honey is used in many recipes, from desserts to savory dishes.
- Herbes de Provence: A blend of aromatic herbs that includes thyme, rosemary, savory, marjoram and oregano. These herbs are used to flavor meats, fish, vegetables and sauces.
- Fruits and vegetables: The region is known for its sunny vegetables, such as tomatoes, zucchini, eggplants, peppers, as well as its fruits such as figs, apricots, melons and strawberries.

The Emblematic Dishes of Provençal Cuisine

The bouillabaisse

Bouillabaisse is undoubtedly the most emblematic dish of Provençal cuisine. Originally from Marseille, this fish soup is prepared with a variety of rock fish, shellfish and crustaceans, cooked in a broth flavored with Provence herbs, saffron, garlic and olive oil. Bouillabaisse is served with garlic-rubbed slices of toast and rouille sauce. Every family and restaurant has their own recipe, but the basic principle remains the same: use fresh, local fish to create a flavorful, comforting dish.

The ratatouille

Ratatouille is another emblematic dish of Provençal cuisine. This vegetable stew is prepared with tomatoes, zucchini, eggplant, peppers, onions and Provence herbs, slowly cooked in olive oil. Ratatouille can be served hot or cold, as an accompaniment to meat or fish, or as a main course with bread. It's a simple but delicious dish that highlights the natural flavors of vegetables.

Pissaladière

Pissaladière is a savory tart from Nice. It is prepared with bread dough, garnished with candied onions, anchovies and black olives. Pissaladière is often compared to pizza, but it has a distinct flavor thanks to the caramelized onions and salty anchovies. It is generally served as a starter or aperitif, accompanied by a glass of rosé wine from Provence.

Aioli

Aioli is a sauce made from garlic and olive oil, which is a mainstay of Provençal cuisine. It is often served with steamed vegetables, fish, shellfish and hard-boiled eggs. Aioli can also be used as a condiment to accompany grilled meats and sandwiches. The "aïoli garni" dish is a Provençal specialty that includes a variety of vegetables, fish and shellfish, served with a generous portion of aioli sauce.

The Tapenade

Tapenade is a spread made from olives, capers, anchovies and olive oil. It is often served as an aperitif, accompanied by toast or raw vegetables. Tapenade can be made with black or green olives, each offering a distinct flavor. It is a must for Provençal tables, appreciated for its simplicity and intense taste.

Star Chefs and Restaurants

The Pioneers of Provençal Haute Cuisine

The PACA region has always been a hotbed of culinary creativity, attracting talented chefs who have been able to highlight local products and culinary traditions. Pioneers of Provençal haute cuisine, such as Roger Vergé and Alain Ducasse, helped make the region a leading gastronomic destination.

Roger Vergé, chef of the famous restaurant Le Moulin de Mougins, is considered one of the founders of nouvelle cuisine. He revolutionized French cuisine by emphasizing the simplicity, lightness and natural flavors of ingredients. His approach influenced a generation of chefs and helped make Provençal cuisine a world standard.

Alain Ducasse, originally from the region, is one of the most famous and influential chefs in the world. With his numerous starred restaurants and his cookbooks, he has been able to promote French and Provençal gastronomy on an international scale. His restaurant Le Louis XV in Monte-Carlo is an example of the region's culinary excellence.

Contemporary Chefs

Today, the PACA region continues to attract renowned chefs, who perpetuate the tradition of haute cuisine while innovating and experimenting with new flavors. Among the most famous contemporary chefs, we find:

- Mauro Colagreco : Chef of the Mirazur restaurant in Menton, Mauro Colagreco was awarded three stars in the Michelin guide and his restaurant was ranked best restaurant in the world by the World's

50 Best Restaurants ranking in 2019. His cuisine, influenced by his Argentinian origins and his love for local products, is a harmonious blend of creativity and tradition.

- Gérald Passédat : Chef of the restaurant Le Petit Nice in Marseille, Gérald Passédat is known for his marine cuisine, highlighting fish and seafood from the Mediterranean. His restaurant has been awarded three Michelin stars, and he is recognized for his commitment to sustainability and responsible fishing.

- Arnaud Donckele : Chef of the La Vague d'Or restaurant in Saint-Tropez, Arnaud Donckele was also awarded three stars in the Michelin guide. Its cuisine, inspired by Provençal traditions and local products, is a tribute to the richness and diversity of the region.

Star Restaurants

The PACA region is home to numerous starred restaurants, each offering a unique and unforgettable culinary experience. Among the most famous, we find:

- Le Louis XV - Alain Ducasse in Monte-Carlo: This three-star restaurant, located in the Hôtel de Paris, is a temple of French gastronomy. Chef Alain Ducasse offers refined cuisine, highlighting products from the Mediterranean and Provence.

- Mirazur in Menton: Chef Mauro Colagreco offers inventive and elegant cuisine, inspired by local products and Mediterranean traditions. The restaurant offers stunning views of the sea and gardens, creating an exceptional dining experience.

- Le Petit Nice in Marseille: Chef Gérald Passédat offers exceptional marine cuisine, with dishes highlighting Mediterranean fish and seafood. The restaurant, located by the sea, offers a magnificent view of the bay of Marseille.

- La Vague d'Or in Saint-Tropez: Chef Arnaud Donckele offers inventive and refined cuisine, inspired by Provençal traditions and local products. The restaurant, located in the Résidence de la Pinède hotel, offers a breathtaking view of the sea and the gardens.

Wines of Provence

The Vineyards of the Region

The PACA region is also famous for its wines, particularly its rosés, which are appreciated for their freshness and elegance. The region's vineyards stretch from the hills of Provence to the steep slopes of the Alps, offering a great diversity of terroirs and grape varieties. Among the main appellations, we find:

- Côtes de Provence: This appellation, the largest in the region, produces quality rosé, red and white wines. Rosé wines, in particular, are renowned for their freshness, fruity aromas and lightness.

- Bandol: Located near the Mediterranean coast, this appellation is famous for its powerful and tannic red wines, made mainly from the Mourvèdre grape variety. Bandol wines are also known for their aging potential.

- Châteauneuf-du-Pape: Although this appellation is mainly associated with the Rhône valley, it is located on the border of the PACA region. Châteauneuf-du-Pape wines, whether red or white, are rich, complex and elegant.

- Coteaux d'Aix-en-Provence: This appellation produces rosé, red and white wines, appreciated for their freshness and balance. Rosé wines, in particular, are renowned for their aromas of red fruits and flowers.

Grape varieties

Provence wines are made from a wide variety of grape varieties, each bringing distinct characteristics to the wines. Among the most common grape varieties, we find:

- Grenache: This grape variety is one of the most widespread in Provence, used mainly for rosé and red wines. It brings aromas of red fruits, strawberry and cherry, as well as a soft and round texture.
- Mourvèdre: This grape variety is particularly important in the Bandol appellation, where it is used to produce powerful and tannic red wines. It brings aromas of black fruits, leather and spices, as well as aging potential.
- Syrah: Used mainly for red wines, this grape variety brings aromas of black fruits, pepper and violet, as well as a tannic structure.
- Cinsault: This grape variety is often used for rosé wines, providing aromas of red fruits, peach and melon, as well as a light and fresh texture.
- Vermentino : Also known as Rolle, this grape variety is used for white wines, providing aromas of white-fleshed fruit, lemon and flowers, as well as refreshing acidity.

Wine Estates

The PACA region is home to many renowned wine estates, each offering quality wines and a unique tasting experience. Among the most famous areas, we find:

- Château d' Eslans : Located in the Côtes de Provence appellation, this estate is famous for its prestigious rosé, Whispering Angel. The estate also produces quality red and white wines.
- Domaine Tempier : Located in the Bandol appellation, this estate is renowned for its powerful and tannic red wines, as well as its elegant rosé and white wines. Domaine Tempier wines are often considered among the best of the appellation.
- Château de Pibarnon : Also located in the Bandol appellation, this estate is famous for its rich and complex red wines, made mainly from the Mourvèdre grape variety. The estate also produces quality rosé and white wines.
- Domaine Ott: With several properties in Provence, including Château de Selle and Clos Mireille, Domaine Ott is renowned for its elegant and refined rosé wines. Domaine Ott wines are often considered among the best rosés in Provence.

Oenological Experiences

Relais & Châteaux in the PACA region often offer unique wine experiences for their guests. From private tastings to vineyard visits, these experiences allow you to discover the region's wines and learn the secrets of Provençal viticulture.

Customers can participate in tasting workshops, led by expert sommeliers, to learn how to identify the aromas and flavors of Provence wines. Guided tours of the wine estates allow you to discover the winemaking processes, meet the winemakers and taste wines directly from the source.

Relais & Châteaux also offer food and wine pairings, allowing you to savor Provence wines in harmony with local cuisine. These pairings highlight the flavors of the dishes and wines, providing a complete and unforgettable gastronomic experience.

Conclusion

The Provence-Alpes-Côte d'Azur region is a true land of gastronomy and wine, offering unparalleled richness and diversity. Provençal cuisine, with its Mediterranean flavors and quality local products, is a pillar of the region's art of living. The wines of Provence, renowned for their freshness and elegance, perfectly complement this culinary experience.

The Relais & Châteaux of the PACA region capture the essence of this gastronomic richness, offering their guests unique and unforgettable culinary and wine experiences. Each establishment, with its enchanting setting, its warm welcome, its exceptional gastronomy and its enriching activities, offers a total immersion in the Provençal art of living.

By discovering the Relais & Châteaux of Provence-Alpes-Côte d'Azur, you will be transported into a world where every detail is designed to delight the senses and create lasting memories. This chapter explored the multiple facets of the region's gastronomy and wines, revealing how each element contributes to making this destination a true oasis of flavors and culinary pleasures.

2. Addresses and Descriptions

The Provence-Alpes-Côte d'Azur (PACA) region is renowned for its spectacular landscapes, rich cultural heritage and exceptional gastronomy. The Relais & Châteaux in this region capture the essence of Provence, offering luxurious and memorable experiences. In this chapter, we will explore in detail some of the most prestigious establishments in the PACA region, highlighting their history, architecture, culinary offerings and activities on offer.

Château de la Chèvre d'Or

History and Architecture

The Château de la Chèvre d'Or is a luxury hotel located in Èze, a medieval village perched between Nice and Monaco. The hotel occupies several historic buildings in the village, some of which date from the Middle Ages. The castle takes its name from a local legend according to which a golden goat was hidden in the village by pirates.

The architecture of the Château de la Chèvre d'Or is a mixture of medieval and contemporary styles. Stone buildings, cobbled lanes and terraced gardens provide a picturesque and romantic setting. The rooms and suites are tastefully decorated, mixing traditional and modern elements. Each room is unique, offering spectacular views of the Mediterranean Sea or surrounding hills.

Culinary Offers

The Château de la Chèvre d'Or is home to several restaurants, including the gourmet restaurant La Chèvre d'Or, which has been awarded two stars in the Michelin guide. The chef offers creative and refined cuisine, highlighting local and seasonal products. The menu changes regularly to reflect the ingredients available, with particular attention paid to presentation and flavors.

The hotel also has several other dining options, including Les Remparts, a restaurant with panoramic sea views, and L'Apéro, a wine bar offering a selection of French and international wines. Guests can also enjoy alfresco dining in the terraced gardens, with menus specially designed for picnics and romantic dinners.

Activities and Services

Château de la Chèvre d'Or offers a range of activities for its guests, from relaxation to sport. The hotel's spa offers a variety of wellness treatments, from massages to facials, performed with high-quality products. Guests can also enjoy the heated outdoor swimming pool, jacuzzi and fitness room.

The terraced gardens are perfect for leisurely walks, meditation sessions or outdoor yoga sessions. The hotel also offers guided excursions to explore the medieval village of Èze, the surrounding hiking trails and the sights of the Côte d'Azur.

The Bastide of Gordes

History and Architecture

La Bastide de Gordes is a luxury hotel located in the village of Gordes, one of the most beautiful hilltop villages in Provence. The hotel is housed in a former 16th-century stately residence, which has been carefully restored to preserve its historic character whilst providing modern comfort.

The architecture of La Bastide de Gordes reflects its rich history, with stone facades, wooden shutters and terraces offering panoramic views of the Luberon valley. Rooms and suites are decorated with period furniture, artwork and fine textiles. Each room is unique, offering a cozy and elegant atmosphere.

Culinary Offers

La Bastide de Gordes offers several dining options, including the gourmet restaurant L'Orangerie, run by a Michelin-starred chef. The restaurant offers refined Provençal cuisine, highlighting local and seasonal products. The tasting menu offers an exceptional culinary experience, with creative and tasty dishes.

The hotel also has La Citadelle, a restaurant offering traditional Provençal cuisine, and Le Tigrr , an Asian restaurant with stunning views of the Luberon valley. Guests can also enjoy al fresco dining on the hotel's terraces, with menus specially designed for al fresco lunches and dinners.

Activities and Services

La Bastide de Gordes offers a range of activities for its guests, from relaxation to sport. The hotel's spa, located in a former vaulted cellar, offers a variety of wellness treatments, from massages to facials, performed with high-quality products. Guests can also enjoy the heated outdoor swimming pool, jacuzzi and fitness room.

The terraced gardens are perfect for leisurely walks, meditation sessions or outdoor yoga sessions. The hotel also offers guided excursions to explore the village of Gordes, the surrounding hiking trails and the sights of the Luberon region.

The Stone Mas

History and Architecture

Le Mas de Pierre is a luxury hotel located in Saint-Paul-de-Vence, an artists' village famous for its art galleries and picturesque streets. The hotel occupies several Provençal country houses, surrounded by lush gardens and orchards. Le Mas de Pierre combines the rustic charm of Provence with modern comfort, providing an idyllic setting for a romantic getaway or peaceful retreat.

The architecture of Mas de Pierre reflects the traditional Provençal style, with stone facades, tiled roofs and flower gardens. Rooms and suites are decorated with antique furniture, artwork and fine textiles. Each room offers views of the gardens, hills or the Mediterranean Sea.

Culinary Offers

Le Mas de Pierre offers several dining options, including the gourmet restaurant La Table de Pierre, run by a Michelin-starred chef. The restaurant offers inventive and refined cuisine, highlighting local and seasonal products. The tasting menu offers an exceptional culinary experience, with creative and tasty dishes.

The hotel also has Le Patio, a restaurant offering Mediterranean cuisine, and Le Bar, a cocktail bar offering a selection of French and international wines. Guests can also enjoy al fresco dining in the hotel gardens, with menus specially designed for picnics and romantic dinners.

Activities and Services

Le Mas de Pierre offers a range of activities for its guests, from relaxation to sport. The hotel's spa offers a variety of wellness treatments, from massages to facials, performed with high-quality products. Guests can also enjoy the heated outdoor swimming pool, jacuzzi and fitness room.

The lush gardens are perfect for leisurely walks, meditation sessions or outdoor yoga sessions. The hotel also offers guided excursions to explore the village of Saint-Paul-de-Vence, the surrounding hiking trails and the tourist sites of the French Riviera.

The Convent of the Minimes

History and Architecture

Le Couvent des Minimes is a luxury hotel located in Mane, a picturesque village in the Luberon. The hotel is housed in a former 17th-century convent, which has been carefully restored to preserve its historic character whilst providing modern comfort. Le Couvent des Minimes combines the elegance of the past with contemporary luxury, offering a peaceful and refined setting.

The architecture of the Couvent des Minimes reflects its rich history, with stone facades, stone vaults and terraced gardens. Rooms and suites are decorated with antique furniture, artwork and fine textiles. Each room offers a view of the gardens, hills or the village of Mane.

Culinary Offers

Le Couvent des Minimes offers several dining options, including the gourmet restaurant Le Cloître, run by a Michelin-starred chef. The restaurant offers inventive and refined cuisine, highlighting local and seasonal products. The tasting menu offers an exceptional culinary experience, with creative and tasty dishes.

The hotel also has Le Pesquier, a restaurant offering Provençal cuisine, and Le Bar, a cocktail bar offering a selection of French and international wines. Guests can also enjoy alfresco dining in the terraced gardens, with menus specially designed for picnics and romantic dinners.

Activities and Services

Le Couvent des Minimes offers a range of activities for its guests, from relaxation to sport. The hotel's spa offers a variety of wellness treatments, from massages to facials, performed with high-quality products. Guests can also enjoy the heated outdoor swimming pool, jacuzzi and fitness room.

The terraced gardens are perfect for leisurely walks, meditation sessions or outdoor yoga sessions. The hotel also offers guided excursions to explore the village of Mane, the surrounding hiking trails and the sights of the Luberon.

The Bastide of Capelongue

History and Architecture

La Bastide de Capelongue is a luxury hotel located in Bonnieux, a picturesque village in the Luberon. The hotel occupies an old Provençal bastide, surrounded by lush gardens and orchards. La Bastide de Capelongue combines the rustic charm of Provence with modern comfort, providing an idyllic setting for a romantic getaway or peaceful retreat.

The architecture of La Bastide de Capelongue reflects the traditional Provençal style, with stone facades, tiled roofs and flower gardens. Rooms and suites are decorated with antique furniture, artwork and fine textiles. Each room offers a view of the gardens, hills or the village of Bonnieux.

Culinary Offers

La Bastide de Capelongue offers several dining options, including the gourmet restaurant Edouard Loubet, run by the eponymous chef, which has been awarded two Michelin stars. The restaurant offers inventive and refined cuisine, highlighting local and seasonal products. The tasting menu offers an exceptional culinary experience, with creative and tasty dishes.

The hotel also has La Ferme, a restaurant offering traditional Provençal cuisine, and Le Bar, a cocktail bar offering a selection of French and international wines. Guests can also enjoy al fresco dining in the hotel gardens, with menus specially designed for picnics and romantic dinners.

Activities and Services

La Bastide de Capelongue offers a range of activities for its guests, from relaxation to sport. The hotel's spa offers a variety of wellness treatments, from massages to facials, performed with high-quality products. Guests can also enjoy the heated outdoor swimming pool, jacuzzi and fitness room.

The lush gardens are perfect for leisurely walks, meditation sessions or outdoor yoga sessions. The hotel also offers guided excursions to explore the village of Bonnieux, the surrounding hiking trails and the tourist sites of the Luberon.

Le Phébus & Spa

History and Architecture

Phébus & Spa is a luxury hotel located in Joucas, a picturesque village in the Luberon. The hotel occupies an old Provençal bastide, surrounded by lush gardens and orchards. Le Phébus & Spa combines the rustic charm of Provence with modern comfort, providing an idyllic setting for a romantic getaway or peaceful retreat.

The architecture of Phébus & Spa reflects the traditional Provençal style, with stone facades, tiled roofs and flower gardens. Rooms and suites are decorated with antique furniture, artwork and fine textiles. Each room offers a view of the gardens, hills or the village of Joucas.

Culinary Offers

Phébus & Spa offers several dining options, including the gourmet restaurant La Table de Xavier Mathieu, run by the eponymous chef, which has been awarded a Michelin star. The restaurant offers inventive and refined cuisine, highlighting local and seasonal products. The tasting menu offers an exceptional culinary experience, with creative and tasty dishes.

The hotel also has La Terrasse, a restaurant offering Mediterranean cuisine, and Le Bar, a cocktail bar offering a selection of French and international wines. Guests can also enjoy al fresco dining in the hotel gardens, with menus specially designed for picnics and romantic dinners.

Activities and Services

Le Phébus & Spa offers a range of activities for its guests, from relaxation to sport. The hotel's spa offers a variety of wellness treatments, from massages to facials, performed with high-quality products. Guests can also enjoy the heated outdoor swimming pool, jacuzzi and fitness room.

The lush gardens are perfect for leisurely walks, meditation sessions or outdoor yoga sessions. The hotel also offers guided excursions to explore the village of Joucas, the surrounding hiking trails and the tourist sites of the Luberon.

Conclusion

The Relais & Châteaux in Provence-Alpes-Côte d'Azur offer unique and unforgettable experiences, combining luxury, comfort and historical heritage. Each establishment, with its enchanting setting, its warm welcome, its exceptional gastronomy and its enriching activities, offers a total immersion in the Provençal art of living. Whether for a romantic getaway, a peaceful retreat or a cultural exploration, the Relais & Châteaux of the PACA region are must-see destinations.

By discovering these exceptional establishments, you will be transported to a world where every detail is designed to delight the senses and create lasting memories. This chapter has presented a detailed overview of some of the most prestigious Relais & Châteaux in the region, offering a glimpse of the unique experience that awaits you in each of these enchanting locations.

- The Bastide of Gordes

Located in the heart of the hilltop village of Gordes, one of the most beautiful villages in France, La Bastide de Gordes is a true pearl among the Relais & Châteaux of the Provence-Alpes-Côte d'Azur region. This prestigious establishment embodies elegance and refinement, offering its visitors a unique blend of historic charm and modern comfort. In this chapter, we will explore in detail the history and architecture of La Bastide de Gordes, its culinary offerings, the activities and services offered, as well as the special events and unique experiences that can be enjoyed there.

History and Architecture

A Rich and Fascinating History

The Bastide de Gordes is a former stately residence dating from the 16th century. The building has been carefully restored to preserve its historic character while providing top-notch modern comfort. The village of Gordes itself has a rich history, dating back to Roman times, and has always been a strategic location due to its hilltop position offering panoramic views over the Luberon valley.

Over the centuries, the bastide has hosted various personalities of the nobility and played an important role in local history. The recent restoration has retained period architectural elements, such as stone facades, stone vaults and majestic staircases, while integrating modern amenities for guest comfort.

Elegant and Authentic Architecture

The architecture of La Bastide de Gordes reflects the traditional Provençal style, with stone facades, wooden shutters and terraces offering panoramic views of the Luberon valley. The hotel's interiors are tastefully decorated, mixing historical and contemporary elements. Antique furniture, artwork and fine textiles create a cozy and elegant ambiance in each room and suite.

The rooms and suites at La Bastide de Gordes are unique, each offering personalized decoration and spectacular views of the surrounding area. The bathrooms, equipped with marble bathtubs and walk-in showers, offer modern and luxurious comfort. The hotel's common areas, such as the lounges, library and terraced gardens, are ideal places to relax and enjoy the enchanting surroundings.

Culinary Offers

L'Orangerie: Provençal Gastronomy

L'Orangerie is the gourmet restaurant of La Bastide de Gordes, run by a Michelin-starred chef. The restaurant offers refined Provençal cuisine, highlighting local and seasonal products. The chef, recognized for his creativity and expertise, creates tasting menus that delight the taste buds and offer an exceptional culinary experience.

L'Orangerie's menu changes regularly to reflect the seasons and available ingredients. The dishes are carefully presented, with particular attention to detail and flavors. Guests can choose from a variety of dishes, ranging from classics of Provençal cuisine to modern and innovative creations.

La Citadelle: Traditional Provençal Cuisine

La Citadelle is another restaurant in La Bastide de Gordes, offering traditional Provençal cuisine in an elegant and relaxed setting. The restaurant offers breathtaking views of the Luberon valley and the surrounding mountains, creating a peaceful and romantic ambiance.

The menu at La Citadelle highlights local products, such as sunny vegetables, aromatic herbs, olives, cheeses and local meats. The dishes are prepared with care and expertise, offering a true immersion in Provençal cuisine. Guests can enjoy dishes such as ratatouille, aioli, bouillabaisse and grilled meats, accompanied by carefully selected local wines.

Tigrr : Asian Flavors

Le Tigrr is the Asian restaurant at La Bastide de Gordes, offering a unique and exotic culinary experience. Located on a terrace with a panoramic view of the Luberon valley, Le Tigrr offers inventive and refined Asian cuisine, mixing Thai, Japanese and Chinese influences.

Tigrr's menu offers a variety of dishes, such as sushi, sashimi, sun sum, curries and vegetable stir-fries. The ingredients are fresh and of high quality, and the dishes are prepared with meticulous attention to detail and flavors. The restaurant also offers a selection of exotic cocktails and international wines to accompany meals.

The Bar: Relaxation and Refinement

The Bar at La Bastide de Gordes is a cozy and elegant venue where guests can relax and savor a selection of French and international wines, champagnes, cocktails and spirits. The bar offers an intimate atmosphere, with comfortable seating, soft lighting and refined decoration.

The bar staff is highly trained and happy to recommend drinks based on guest preferences. Wine tastings and mixology workshops are held regularly, allowing guests to discover new flavors and perfect their beverage knowledge.

Activities and Services

The Sisley Spa: Well-being and Relaxation

The Sisley Spa at La Bastide de Gordes is a haven of peace and relaxation, offering a variety of wellness treatments, from massages to facials, performed with high quality products. The spa, located in an old vaulted cellar, is a place of tranquility and serenity, perfect for recharging your batteries after a day of exploring the region.

The spa offers a range of personalized treatments, tailored to the needs of each guest. Professional therapists use advanced techniques and Sisley products to ensure optimal results and a luxurious experience. Guests can also enjoy the heated indoor swimming pool, jacuzzi, sauna and steam room to complete their relaxation experience.

Outdoor activities

La Bastide de Gordes is surrounded by magnificent terraced gardens, offering spectacular views of the Luberon valley and surrounding mountains. The gardens are perfect for leisurely walks, meditation sessions or outdoor yoga sessions. Guests can also enjoy the heated outdoor swimming pool, tennis court and fitness room.

The hotel also offers guided excursions to explore the village of Gordes, the surrounding hiking trails and the sights of the Luberon region. Guests can discover picturesque hilltop villages, lavender fields, vineyards and local markets. Electric bikes are also available to explore the region in an ecological and active way.

Cultural Activities and Experiences

La Bastide de Gordes regularly organizes cultural events and unique experiences for its guests. Private concerts, literary readings and art exhibitions are often held in the hotel lounges or gardens. These events offer immersion in the local cultural scene and allow guests to meet artists, writers and musicians.

Guests can also participate in cooking workshops, baking classes and chocolate tastings, led by local chefs. These workshops offer an opportunity to learn Provençal cooking techniques and taste delicious creations. La Bastide de Gordes also offers yoga and meditation classes, led by qualified instructors, in the hotel's gardens or wellness areas.

Special Events and Unique Experiences

Weddings and Receptions

La Bastide de Gordes is an ideal venue for organizing intimate weddings and private receptions. The hotel's gardens and lounges provide a romantic and elegant setting for ceremonies and receptions. Hotel staff work closely with couples to create tailor-made events, taking into account every detail, from decor to personalized menus.

The hotel's chefs create wedding menus that reflect the tastes and preferences of the bride and groom, using seasonal ingredients and local produce. The professional and attentive service teams ensure that every event goes off without a hitch. Couples can also enjoy luxurious suites for their wedding night, with special services such as massages, in-room breakfasts and welcome gifts.

Seminars and Business Meetings

La Bastide de Gordes offers an exceptional setting for seminars, conferences and business meetings. The hotel's private lounges, equipped with the latest technology, offer flexible spaces for events of different sizes. Hotel teams work with event organizers to create tailor-made programs, including coffee breaks, business lunches and dinners.

Team-building activities and excursions can also be organized to strengthen team cohesion and provide moments of relaxation outside of work sessions. Guests can take advantage of the hotel's wellness facilities to unwind after a day of meetings, with spa treatments, yoga sessions and massages.

Unique Experiences

La Bastide de Gordes offers unique experiences to make each stay memorable. These include private dinners in exclusive locations within the hotel, such as the library or gardens, offering an intimate and romantic atmosphere. Guests can also participate in wine tasting workshops, led by expert sommeliers, to discover the secrets of Provence wines.

Wellness getaways are also available, including personalized relaxation and relaxation programs, spa treatments, yoga and meditation sessions, as well as healthy and nutritious meals. These programs are designed to help clients recharge their batteries and regain physical and mental balance.

Seasonal and Thematic Offers

La Bastide de Gordes regularly offers seasonal and thematic offers to enrich its customers' experience. At Christmas, the hotel is decked out in festive decorations and offers special menus, cookie decorating workshops and Christmas market visits. In summer, gourmet picnics can be organized in the gardens or on the terraces.

Romantic getaways are also offered, including candlelit dinners, duo massages and horse-drawn carriage rides through the streets of Gordes. For culture lovers, special packages including tickets for exhibitions, shows and concerts are available, offering complete immersion in the cultural life of the region.

Conclusion

La Bastide de Gordes is much more than just a luxury hotel; it is a destination in itself, offering a unique and unforgettable experience in the heart of one of the most beautiful villages in France. With its rich history, impressive architecture, refined culinary offerings and a variety of activities and services, this establishment is the ideal place to relax, recharge your batteries and discover the Provençal art of living.

Whether for a romantic getaway, a wellness retreat, an intimate wedding or a business meeting, La Bastide de Gordes promises an exceptional experience, marked by luxury, comfort and elegance. Guests leave with unforgettable memories, enriched by the unique culture, gastronomy and hospitality of this iconic Gordes hotel.

- Château de la Chèvre d'Or

The Château de la Chèvre d'Or, located in the picturesque medieval village of Èze, is one of the most prestigious establishments in the Provence-Alpes-Côte d'Azur region. Nestled between Nice and Monaco, this luxury hotel offers a breathtaking view of the Mediterranean, an enchanting setting, and a unique experience combining history, elegance and modernity. In this chapter, we will explore in detail the history and architecture of Château de la Chèvre d'Or, its culinary offerings, the activities and services offered, as well as the special events and unique experiences that can be enjoyed there.

History and Architecture

A History Rooted in Legend

The Château de la Chèvre d'Or owes its name to a local legend according to which a golden goat was hidden in the village of Èze by pirates. This mystical story has spanned the centuries, adding a touch of mystery and romance to this extraordinary place.

The village of Èze, perched on a steep hill 427 meters above sea level, has a history dating back to ancient times. The Greeks, then the Romans, established colonies there. The current village has retained its medieval charm with its cobbled streets, stone houses and spectacular views. The castle itself was built in the 12th century and has been carefully restored over the years to preserve its historic character while incorporating modern amenities.

Majestic Architecture

The architecture of the Château de la Chèvre d'Or is a harmonious blend of medieval and contemporary styles. Stone buildings, winding lanes and terraced gardens provide a picturesque and romantic setting. The rooms and suites, scattered among several historic buildings in the village, are tastefully decorated, mixing traditional and modern elements. Each room is unique, offering spectacular views of the Mediterranean Sea or surrounding hills.

The hotel's interiors are decorated with antique furniture, artwork and fine textiles. The bathrooms, equipped with marble bathtubs and walk-in showers, offer modern and luxurious comfort. Common areas, such as lounges, terraces and gardens, are ideal places to relax and enjoy the enchanting surroundings.

Culinary Offers

La Chèvre d'Or: Starred Gastronomy

The gourmet restaurant La Chèvre d'Or, run by a Michelin-starred chef, is one of the establishment's jewels. The restaurant offers inventive and refined cuisine, highlighting local and seasonal products. The chef, recognized for his creativity and expertise, creates tasting menus that delight the taste buds and offer an exceptional culinary experience.

The menu at La Chèvre d'Or changes regularly to reflect the seasons and available ingredients. The dishes are carefully presented, with particular attention to detail and flavors. Guests can choose from a variety of dishes, ranging from French cuisine classics to modern and innovative creations.

Les Remparts: Mediterranean Cuisine

Les Remparts is another hotel restaurant, offering Mediterranean cuisine in an elegant and relaxed setting. The restaurant offers panoramic sea views, creating a peaceful and romantic ambiance. The menu highlights local products, such as seafood, sunny vegetables, aromatic herbs and local olive oils.

The dishes are prepared with care and expertise, offering a true immersion in Mediterranean cuisine. Guests can enjoy dishes such as bouillabaisse, seafood risotto, grilled fish and fresh salads, accompanied by carefully selected local wines.

L'Apéro: An Elegant Wine Bar

L'Apéro is the hotel's wine bar, offering a selection of French and international wines, champagnes and cocktails. The bar offers an intimate atmosphere, with comfortable seats, soft lighting and refined decoration. The bar staff is highly trained and happy to recommend drinks based on guest preferences.

Wine tastings and mixology workshops are held regularly, allowing guests to discover new flavors and perfect their beverage knowledge. Guests can also enjoy al fresco dining on the terraces, with menus specially designed for picnics and romantic dinners.

Activities and Services

The Spa: Well-being and Relaxation

The Château de la Chèvre d'Or spa is a haven of peace and relaxation, offering a variety of wellness treatments, from massages to facials, performed with high quality products. The spa, located in an old vaulted cellar, is a place of tranquility and serenity, perfect for recharging your batteries after a day of exploring the region.

The spa offers a range of personalized treatments, tailored to the needs of each guest. Professional therapists use advanced techniques and premium products to ensure optimal results and a luxurious experience. Guests can also enjoy the heated outdoor swimming pool, jacuzzi, sauna and steam room to complete their relaxation experience.

Outdoor activities

Château de la Chèvre d'Or is surrounded by magnificent terraced gardens, offering spectacular views of the Mediterranean Sea and the surrounding hills. The gardens are perfect for leisurely walks, meditation sessions or outdoor yoga sessions. Guests can also enjoy the heated outdoor swimming pool and fitness room.

The hotel also offers guided excursions to explore the medieval village of Èze, the surrounding hiking trails and the sights of the Côte d'Azur. Guests can discover picturesque hilltop villages, hidden beaches, vineyards and local markets. Electric bikes are also available to explore the region in an ecological and active way.

Cultural Activities and Experiences

Château de la Chèvre d'Or regularly organizes cultural events and unique experiences for its guests. Private concerts, literary readings and art exhibitions are often held in the hotel lounges or gardens. These events offer immersion in the local cultural scene and allow guests to meet artists, writers and musicians.

Guests can also participate in cooking workshops, baking classes and chocolate tastings, led by local chefs. These workshops offer an opportunity to learn Provençal cooking techniques and taste delicious creations. Château de la Chèvre d'Or also offers yoga and meditation classes, led by qualified instructors, in the hotel's gardens or wellness areas.

Special Events and Unique Experiences

Weddings and Receptions

Château de la Chèvre d'Or is an ideal venue for organizing intimate weddings and private receptions. The hotel's gardens and lounges provide a romantic and elegant setting for ceremonies and receptions. Hotel staff work closely with couples to create tailor-made events, taking into account every detail, from decor to personalized menus.

The hotel's chefs create wedding menus that reflect the tastes and preferences of the bride and groom, using seasonal ingredients and local produce. The professional and attentive service teams ensure that every event goes off without a hitch. Couples can also enjoy luxurious suites for their wedding night, with special services such as massages, in-room breakfasts and welcome gifts.

Seminars and Business Meetings

The Château de la Chèvre d'Or offers an exceptional setting for seminars, conferences and business meetings. The hotel's private lounges, equipped with the latest technology, offer flexible spaces for events of different sizes. Hotel teams work with event organizers to create tailor-made programs, including coffee breaks, business lunches and dinners.

Team-building activities and excursions can also be organized to strengthen team cohesion and provide moments of relaxation outside of work sessions. Guests can take advantage of the hotel's wellness facilities to unwind after a day of meetings, with spa treatments, yoga sessions and massages.

Unique Experiences

Château de la Chèvre d'Or offers unique experiences to make each stay memorable. These include private dinners in exclusive locations within the hotel, such as the library or gardens, offering an intimate and romantic atmosphere. Guests can also participate in wine tasting workshops, led by expert sommeliers, to discover the secrets of Provence wines.

Wellness getaways are also available, including personalized relaxation and relaxation programs, spa treatments, yoga and meditation sessions, as well as healthy and nutritious meals. These programs are designed to help clients recharge their batteries and regain physical and mental balance.

Seasonal and Thematic Offers

Château de la Chèvre d'Or regularly offers seasonal and thematic offers to enrich its customers' experience. At Christmas, the hotel is decked out in festive decorations and offers special menus, cookie decorating workshops and Christmas market visits. In summer, gourmet picnics can be organized in the gardens or on the terraces.

Romantic getaways are also offered, including candlelit dinners, couples massages and carriage rides through the streets of Èze. For culture lovers, special packages including tickets for exhibitions, shows and concerts are available, offering complete immersion in the cultural life of the region.

Conclusion

The Château de la Chèvre d'Or is much more than just a luxury hotel; it is a destination in itself, offering a unique and unforgettable experience in the heart of one of the most beautiful medieval villages on the French Riviera. With its rich history, impressive architecture, refined culinary offerings and a variety of activities and services, this establishment is the ideal place to relax, recharge your batteries and discover the Provençal art of living.

Whether for a romantic getaway, a wellness retreat, an intimate wedding or a business meeting, Château de la Chèvre d'Or promises an exceptional experience, marked by luxury, comfort and elegance. Guests leave with unforgettable memories, enriched by the unique culture, gastronomy and hospitality of this iconic Èze hotel.

-Villa Gallici

Villa Gallici is a sumptuous residence nestled in the city of Aix-en-Provence, renowned for its Provençal charm and elegant ambiance. This luxury hotel, a member of the prestigious Relais & Châteaux chain, offers a unique experience where the French art of living blends harmoniously with modern comfort. In this chapter, we will explore in detail the history and architecture of Villa Gallici , its culinary offerings, the activities and services offered, as well as the special events and unique experiences that can be had there.

History and Architecture

A Fascinating Story

Villa Gallici is located in Aix-en-Provence, a city rich in history and culture. Founded by the Romans, Aix-en-Provence is known for its thermal baths, its fountains and its avenues lined with plane trees. The city was an important cultural center during the Renaissance, attracting renowned artists and writers. Villa Gallici , built in the 18th century, embodies this historical and cultural heritage.

Formerly the residence of a wealthy Provençal family, the villa has been transformed into a luxury hotel while retaining its old-world charm. The owners have carefully restored the property, preserving the original architectural features and adding touches of contemporary luxury.

Elegant and Romantic Architecture

The architecture of Villa Gallici reflects classic Provençal style, with stone facades, wooden shutters and lush gardens. The hotel is surrounded by cypress trees, lavender and formal gardens, creating a serene and romantic ambiance. The villa's interiors are decorated with antique furniture, artwork and fine textiles, providing a warm and elegant atmosphere.

The rooms and suites at Villa Gallici are sumptuously appointed, each with a unique and personalized decoration. The walls are decorated with frescoes, hangings and gilded mirrors, while the bathrooms, fitted with marble and handcrafted ceramics, offer modern and luxurious comfort. The rooms also have private balconies or terraces, offering picturesque views of the gardens or the city of Aix-en-Provence.

Culinary Offers

The Villa Gallici Restaurant : Refined Cuisine

The Villa Gallici restaurant is a place where Provençal gastronomy is highlighted. The chef, recognized for his creativity and expertise, offers refined cuisine, using local and seasonal products. The menu changes regularly to reflect the ingredients available and offer an ever-changing dining experience.

The restaurant has an elegant dining room, decorated with crystal chandeliers, linen tablecloths and silver cutlery. Tables are arranged to provide optimal privacy and comfort. Guests can also choose to dine alfresco, on the shaded terrace, surrounded by lush gardens.

The tasting menu is a true symphony of flavors, with dishes such as ratatouille of sunny vegetables, fillet of beef Rossini, pan-fried scallops, and tarte Tatin with caramelized apples. Each dish is carefully prepared and artistically presented, providing an exceptional visual and taste experience.

The Wine Bar: Relaxation and Refinement

Gallici 's wine bar is a cozy and elegant venue where guests can relax and enjoy a selection of French and international wines, champagnes and cocktails. The bar offers an intimate atmosphere, with comfortable seats, soft lighting and refined decoration.

The bar staff is highly trained and happy to recommend drinks based on guest preferences. Wine tastings and mixology workshops are held regularly, allowing guests to discover new flavors and perfect their beverage knowledge. Guests can also enjoy light meals and tapas, prepared with fresh, high-quality ingredients.

Activities and Services

The Spa: Well-being and Relaxation

The Villa Gallici spa is a haven of peace and relaxation, offering a variety of wellness treatments, from massages to facials, performed with high quality products. The spa, located in an old vaulted cellar, is a place of tranquility and serenity, perfect for recharging your batteries after a day of exploring the region.

The spa offers a range of personalized treatments, tailored to the needs of each guest. Professional therapists use advanced techniques and luxury products to ensure optimal results and a luxurious experience. Guests can also enjoy the heated outdoor swimming pool, jacuzzi, sauna and steam room to complete their relaxation experience.

Outdoor activities

Villa Gallici is surrounded by magnificent French gardens, offering spectacular views of the surrounding hills and rooftops of Aix-en-Provence. The gardens are perfect for leisurely walks, meditation sessions or outdoor yoga sessions. Guests can also enjoy the heated outdoor swimming pool and fitness room.

The hotel also offers guided excursions to explore the city of Aix-en-Provence, the surrounding hiking trails and the region's tourist sites. Guests can discover picturesque villages, vineyards, local markets and historic sites. Electric bikes are also available to explore the region in an ecological and active way.

Cultural Activities and Experiences

Villa Gallici regularly organizes cultural events and unique experiences for its guests. Private concerts, literary readings and art exhibitions are often held in the hotel lounges or gardens. These events offer immersion in the local cultural scene and allow guests to meet artists, writers and musicians.

Guests can also participate in cooking workshops, baking classes and chocolate tastings, led by local chefs. These workshops offer an opportunity to learn Provençal cooking techniques and taste delicious creations. Villa Gallici also offers yoga and meditation classes, led by qualified instructors, in the hotel's gardens or wellness areas.

Special Events and Unique Experiences

Weddings and Receptions

Villa Gallici is an ideal venue for intimate weddings and private receptions. The hotel's gardens and lounges provide a romantic and elegant setting for ceremonies and receptions. Hotel staff work closely with couples to create tailor-made events, taking into account every detail, from decor to personalized menus.

The hotel's chefs create wedding menus that reflect the tastes and preferences of the bride and groom, using seasonal ingredients and local produce. The professional and attentive service teams ensure that every event goes off without a hitch. Couples can also enjoy luxurious suites for their wedding night, with special services such as massages, in-room breakfasts and welcome gifts.

Seminars and Business Meetings

Villa Gallici offers an exceptional setting for seminars, conferences and business meetings. The hotel's private lounges, equipped with the latest technology, offer flexible spaces for events of different sizes. Hotel teams work with event organizers to create tailor-made programs, including coffee breaks, business lunches and dinners.

Team-building activities and excursions can also be organized to strengthen team cohesion and provide moments of relaxation outside of work sessions. Guests can take advantage of the hotel's wellness facilities to unwind after a day of meetings, with spa treatments, yoga sessions and massages.

Unique Experiences

Villa Gallici offers unique experiences to make every stay memorable. These include private dinners in exclusive locations within the hotel, such as the library or gardens, offering an intimate and romantic atmosphere. Guests can also participate in wine tasting workshops, led by expert sommeliers, to discover the secrets of Provence wines.

Wellness getaways are also available, including personalized relaxation and relaxation programs, spa treatments, yoga and meditation sessions, as well as healthy and nutritious meals. These programs are designed to help clients recharge their batteries and regain physical and mental balance.

Seasonal and Thematic Offers

Villa Gallici regularly offers seasonal and thematic offers to enrich its guests' experience. At Christmas, the hotel is decked out in festive decorations and offers special menus, cookie decorating workshops and Christmas market visits. In summer, gourmet picnics can be organized in the gardens or on the terraces.

Romantic getaways are also offered, including candlelit dinners, couples massages and horse-drawn carriage rides through the streets of Aix-en-Provence. For culture lovers, special packages including tickets for exhibitions, shows and concerts are available, offering complete immersion in the cultural life of the region.

Conclusion

Villa Gallici is much more than just a luxury hotel; it is a destination in itself, offering a unique and unforgettable experience in the heart of the charming city of Aix-en-Provence. With its rich history, impressive architecture, refined culinary offerings and a variety of activities and services, this establishment is the ideal place to relax, recharge your batteries and discover the Provençal art of living.

Whether for a romantic getaway, a wellness retreat, an intimate wedding or a business meeting, Villa Gallici promises an exceptional experience, marked by luxury, comfort and elegance. Guests leave with unforgettable memories, enriched by the unique culture, gastronomy and hospitality of this iconic Aix-en-Provence hotel.

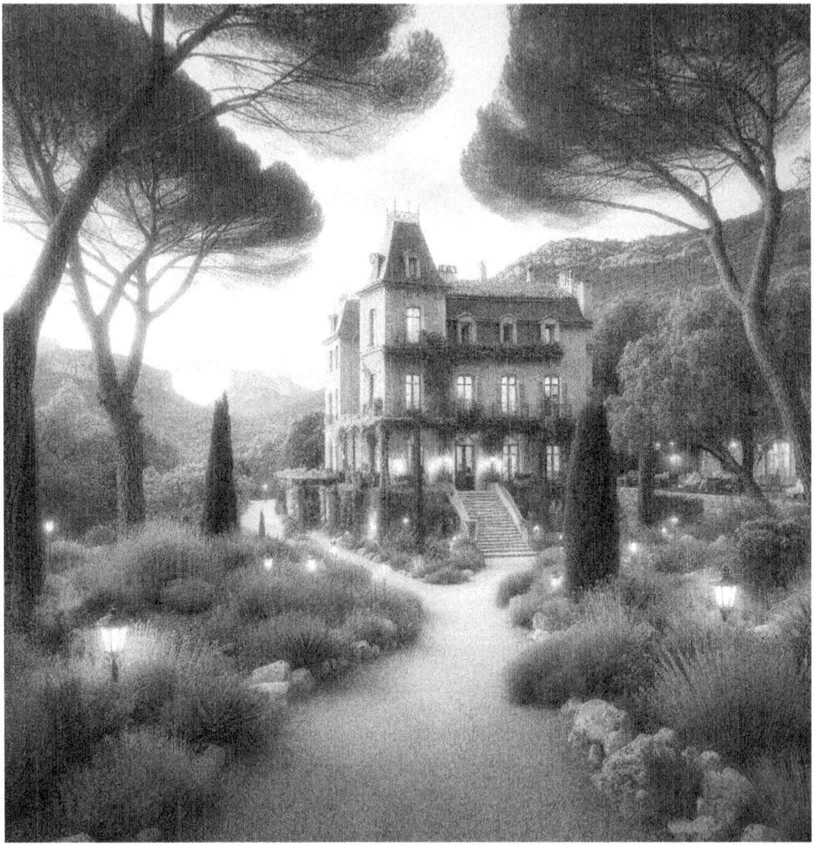

Chapter 3: Relais & Châteaux in Burgundy-Franche-Comté

1. General Presentation of the Region

The Burgundy-Franche-Comté region is one of the richest and most diverse in France, both in terms of its historical heritage and its varied landscapes and its renowned gastronomy. Located in the east of the country, this region is famous for its Burgundy wines, cheeses, historical monuments and natural sites. In this chapter, we will explore in detail the geographical, historical, cultural and economic characteristics of Burgundy-Franche-Comté.

Geography and Landscapes

A Diversity of Landscapes

Burgundy-Franche-Comté offers an incredible diversity of landscapes, from the rolling vineyards of Burgundy to the mountains of Jura, including the forests and lakes of Franche-Comté. This geographical variety makes the region an ideal place for lovers of nature and outdoor activities.

Burgundy's world-famous vineyards stretch over rolling hills and offer panoramic views of the surrounding countryside. Wine routes, such as the Route des Grands Crus, allow you to discover picturesque wine villages, prestigious wine estates and cellars where some of the best wines in the world are produced.

The Jura Mountains, with their rugged peaks, deep valleys and crystal-clear lakes, provide a spectacular setting for hiking, skiing, climbing and other outdoor activities. The Haut-Jura Regional Natural Park protects a large part of this region and is home to exceptional biodiversity, with rare species of flora and fauna.

Rivers and Lakes

The region is also crossed by several important rivers, including the Saône, the Doubs and the Yonne, which add to the beauty of the landscape and provide opportunities for boating, fishing and water activities. The Burgundy Canal, 242 kilometers long, connects the Saône to the Yonne and passes through magnificent landscapes, charming villages and historic sites. Canal river cruises are a pleasant way to explore the region at a leisurely pace.

The region's lakes, such as Lac de Chalain , Lac de Saint-Point and Lac des Settons, are popular destinations for swimming, sailing, fishing and picnicking. The glacial lakes of Jura, in particular, offer crystal clear waters and picturesque beaches, ideal for relaxing in summer.

History and Heritage

The Origins of the Region

Burgundy-Franche-Comté has a rich and complex history, marked by the influence of numerous civilizations. The first traces of human occupation date back to prehistory, with sites such as the Arcy-sur-Cure cave in Burgundy and the Osselle caves in Franche-Comté, which are home to cave paintings and archaeological remains.

The Celts, then the Romans, occupied the region and left numerous remains, such as the Roman theaters of Autun and the thermal baths of Luxeuil-les-Bains. The city of Besançon, formerly called Vesontio , was an important administrative and military center under the Roman Empire.

The Duchy of Burgundy

The Middle Ages was a period of great prosperity for Burgundy, particularly under the influence of the Dukes of Burgundy. The Duchy of Burgundy became one of the most powerful and influential in Europe, thanks to its wealth, its trade and its territorial expansion. The Dukes of Burgundy, such as Philip the Bold, John the Fearless and Charles the Bold, were patrons of arts and culture, contributing to the development of the region.

The Dukes of Burgundy resided primarily in Dijon, the duchy's capital, where they built palaces, churches and monuments that still stand today. The Palace of the Dukes of Burgundy, with its Philippe le Bon tower, is one of the city's most emblematic monuments. The Charterhouse of Champmol , founded by Philippe le Bold, is another important site, housing masterpieces of Gothic art.

Franche-Comté

Franche-Comté, for its part, was an independent region, successively attached to the Holy Roman Empire and the crown of Spain before being annexed to France in 1678 by the Treaty of Nijmegen. Besançon, the capital of Franche-Comté, is a remarkable fortified town, with fortifications designed by Vauban, Louis XIV's military engineer. The Citadel of Besançon, listed as a UNESCO World Heritage Site, is an exceptional example of 17th century military architecture.

The Franche-Comté region is also known for its abbeys and monasteries, such as the Fontenay Abbey, founded in the 12th century and listed as a UNESCO World Heritage Site, and the Baume-les-Messieurs Abbey, located in a spectacular natural site.

The Modern and Contemporary Era

Over the following centuries, Burgundy and Franche-Comté continued to develop and prosper. The French Revolution brought significant changes, with the creation of departments and the modernization of the administration. The industrialization of the 19th century stimulated the regional economy, with the development of the textile industry, metallurgy and the production of machine tools.

Today, the Burgundy-Franche-Comté region is a dynamic economic center, with varied sectors such as industry, agriculture, tourism and services. The main cities, such as Dijon, Besançon, Auxerre, Chalon-sur-Saône and Montbéliard, offer a mix of historical heritage and modernity, with modern infrastructure and a high quality of life.

Culture and Traditions

Cultural life

Burgundy-Franche-Comté is a hotbed of creativity and culture, with a vibrant arts scene and a rich tradition of festivals and events. Dijon, the regional capital, is known for its international film festival, Les Rencontres Cinematographics de Dijon, as well as its classical music festival, the Festival International d'Opéra Baroque.

Besançon hosts the Besançon Franche-Comté International Music Festival, one of the oldest and most prestigious classical music festivals in France. The festival features concerts, recitals and conducting competitions, attracting musicians and spectators from around the world.

The region is also famous for its tableware and crafts. Limoges porcelain, Nevers earthenware and Longwy enamels are examples of the region's artisanal know-how. Local markets, fairs and flea markets are opportunities to discover and purchase these unique artisanal products.

Gastronomy and Local Products

The gastronomy of Burgundy-Franche-Comté is one of the most renowned in France, highlighting local products and culinary traditions. The region is particularly famous for its wines, cheeses, meats and traditional dishes.

Burgundy wines are among the most prestigious in the world, with renowned appellations such as Chablis, Meursault, Pommard, Gevrey-Chambertin and Nuits-Saint-Georges. Red wines, mainly made from the Pinot Noir grape variety, and white wines, mainly made from the Chardonnay grape variety, are appreciated for their complexity, elegance and aging potential.

The region's cheeses, such as Comté, Morbier, Mont d'Or, Epoisses and Bleu de Gex, are also famous for their quality and diversity. Each cheese has its own history, manufacturing techniques and taste characteristics.

Traditional dishes from Burgundy-Franche-Comté include beef bourguignon, coq au vin, Burgundy escargot, Comtoise stew and Bresse chicken. The area's restaurants, ranging from bistros to Michelin-starred establishments, offer an exceptional dining experience, showcasing local produce and traditional recipes.

Local Festivals and Traditions

The Burgundy-Franche-Comté region is rich in festivals and traditions, which bear witness to its history and culture. Village festivals, agricultural fairs and folk festivals are opportunities to celebrate local customs and continue traditions.

The harvest, in particular, is a highlight of regional life. Every fall, the vineyards are filled with grape pickers, who harvest the grapes by hand. The harvest is followed by parties and celebrations, with wine tastings, festive meals and musical entertainment.

Christmas markets, such as those in Dijon, Besançon and Montbéliard, are also popular events, attracting visitors from across the region. The markets offer a variety of artisanal products, culinary specialties and gifts, creating a festive and warm atmosphere.

Economy and Innovation

Tourism

Tourism is one of the pillars of the economy of the Burgundy-Franche-Comté region, attracting millions of visitors from all over the world each year. The diversity of landscapes, cultural richness and historical heritage are all assets that make this region a popular destination.

The region's tourist infrastructure is of high quality, with a diverse range of accommodation, starred restaurants, wellness centers and leisure activities. The airports of Dijon and Dole, as well as rail and road links, facilitate access to the region. Sustainable and responsible tourism is also encouraged, with initiatives aimed at preserving the environment and promoting local heritage.

Agriculture and Local Products

Agriculture plays an essential role in the economy of the Burgundy-Franche-Comté region, with varied and quality production. Vineyards, cattle breeding, cereal crops and cheese production are among the main agricultural activities.

Agricultural products, such as wine, cheese, meat, cereals and fruits, are renowned for their excellence and diversity. Farmers' markets, agricultural cooperatives and short circuits promote the marketing of local products and support the rural economy.

Quality labels, such as the AOC (Appellation d'Origine Contrôlée) and the IGP (Protected Geographical Indication), guarantee the authenticity and quality of local products. Visitors can discover these products during tastings, farm tours and food festivals.

Industry and Innovation

The Burgundy-Franche-Comté region is also a hub of innovation and industrial development, with varied sectors such as agri-food, metallurgy, the pharmaceutical industry, aeronautics and renewable energies. Competitiveness clusters, such as Vitagora (taste-nutrition-health) and Nuclear Valley (nuclear industry), promote innovation and collaboration between economic and scientific players.

Transportation infrastructure, such as highways, high-speed train lines and river ports, supports the region's economic development. The proximity of Switzerland and Germany facilitates trade and international collaborations. The Burgundy-Franche-Comté region is a key player in the French economy, contributing to its dynamism and international influence.

Conclusion

The Burgundy-Franche-Comté region is an exceptional destination, rich in history, culture and varied landscapes. Whether enjoying the rolling vineyards of Burgundy, exploring the rugged Jura mountains, hitting the ski slopes, discovering historical and cultural treasures or savoring the renowned gastronomy, there is something for everyone.

The Relais & Châteaux of the Burgundy-Franche-Comté region capture the essence of this diversity and offer their guests unforgettable experiences, combining luxury, comfort and authenticity. Each establishment, with its enchanting setting, warm welcome, exceptional gastronomy and enriching activities, offers total immersion in the French art of living.

By discovering the Relais & Châteaux of Burgundy-Franche-Comté, you will be transported into a world where every detail is designed to delight the senses and create lasting memories. This chapter presented a detailed overview of the region, integrating geographical, historical, cultural and economic aspects to provide a comprehensive understanding of this unique destination.

- History and Heritage

The Burgundy-Franche-Comté region is a land rich in history and heritage, where each town, each village and each castle tells a unique story. From the Duchy of Burgundy to the fortifications of Franche-Comté, via medieval abbeys and historic vineyards, this region is a true treasure for lovers of history and culture. In this chapter, we will explore in detail key moments in the history of Burgundy-Franche-Comté, its iconic monuments and its cultural contributions.

The First Civilizations

Antiquity and the First Colonies

The Burgundy-Franche-Comté region has a history dating back to prehistory. The first traces of human occupation are visible in sites like the Arcy-sur-Cure caves in Burgundy and the Osselle caves in Franche-Comté, where cave paintings and archaeological remains have been discovered. These sites bear witness to the presence of human communities for millennia.

During the Celtic era, the region was inhabited by the tribes of the Aedui in Burgundy and the Séquanes in Franche-Comté. These Gallic tribes were known for their social organization and their trade with neighboring regions. They left important traces, notably in the form of oppida (Gallic fortifications) and religious sanctuaries.

With the arrival of the Romans in the 1st century BC, the region was integrated into the Roman Empire. The Romans built towns, roads, aqueducts and baths, some of which can still be seen today. Besançon, called Vesontio , became an important administrative and military center. Autun, known as Augustodunum , was founded by Emperor Augustus and became a prosperous town with a theater, amphitheater and thermal baths.

The Middle Ages: The Golden Age of Burgundy

The Duchy of Burgundy

The Middle Ages were a period of great prosperity for Burgundy, largely thanks to the Dukes of Burgundy. The Duchy of Burgundy, founded in the 9th century, became one of the most powerful and influential in Europe under the Valois dynasty. The Dukes of Burgundy, such as Philip the Bold, John the Fearless, Philip the Good and Charles the Bold, were patrons of arts and culture, contributing to the development of the region.

Philip the Bold, the first Valois duke, acquired the county of Flanders by marriage, which helped extend Burgundian influence in Europe. John the Fearless continued this policy of expansion, while Philip the Good and Charles the Bold made the court of Burgundy a center of cultural and artistic life. Burgundy became a hotbed of the Northern Renaissance, attracting artists, writers and thinkers from across Europe.

The Emblematic Monuments of the Duchy

The Palace of the Dukes of Burgundy in Dijon is one of the most emblematic monuments of this period. Originally built as a fortress in the 13th century, it was transformed into a sumptuous palace by the Valois dukes. The Philippe le Bon tower offers a breathtaking view of the city and its surroundings. Today, the palace houses the Musée des Beaux-Arts de Dijon, which has a rich collection of works of art, including the famous tombs of the Dukes of Burgundy.

The Charterhouse of Champmol , founded by Philippe le Bold in 1383, is another important site. Designed as a monastery for Carthusian monks, it is home to masterpieces of Gothic art, such as the Well of Moses, a monumental sculpture by Claus Sluter. Although partially destroyed over the centuries, the Chartreuse remains a testimony to the artistic grandeur of the Burgundian court.

The towns of Beaune and Cluny are also emblematic places of Burgundian medieval heritage. Beaune is famous for its Hospices de Beaune, a former medieval hospital founded in 1443 by Nicolas Rolin, chancellor of Philippe the Good. The building, with its colorful glazed tile roof, is a remarkable example of Burgundian Gothic architecture. Cluny, meanwhile, is famous for its abbey, founded in 910. Cluny Abbey was one of the largest and most influential abbeys in Europe, playing a key role in the monastic revival of the medieval era. .

Franche-Comté and the Holy Empire

While Burgundy prospered under the Valois dukes, Franche-Comté followed a different historical trajectory. Located on the border between France and the Holy Roman Empire, Franche-Comté was a strategic region disputed by several powers. It was part of the Holy Roman Empire and was later controlled by the House of Habsburg.

The city of Besançon, in particular, became an important administrative and military center. Its fortifications, designed by Vauban in the 17th century, bear witness to its strategic importance. The Citadel of Besançon, listed as a UNESCO World Heritage Site, is an exceptional example of military architecture from this era.

Luxeuil Abbey, founded in the 6th century by Saint Columbanus, is another important historical site. It became a major center of monastic and intellectual life in Europe during the Middle Ages. Baume-les-Messieurs Abbey, founded in the 9th century, is also notable for its architecture and spectacular natural setting.

The Renaissance and Modern Times

The Burgundian Renaissance

The Renaissance brought an artistic and cultural revival to Burgundy. Inspired by the humanist ideas and artistic innovations of the Italian Renaissance, Burgundian patrons encouraged the construction of castles, palaces, and churches in a Renaissance style.

The Château d'Ancy-le-Franc, built in the 16th century, is a perfect example of Renaissance architecture in Burgundy. Designed by Italian architect Sebastiano Serlio, the castle is famous for its frescoes, painted ceilings and formal gardens. The Château de Tanlay and the Château de Saint-Fargeau are other notable examples of Renaissance architecture in Burgundy.

The Reformation and the Wars of Religion

The 16th century was also marked by the Protestant Reformation and the Wars of Religion, which had a profound impact on Burgundy-Franche-Comté. The region, mainly Catholic, was the scene of violent conflicts between Catholics and Protestants. The cities of Besançon and Dijon were particularly affected by these unrest.

Despite these conflicts, the region continued to develop economically and culturally. Fairs and markets multiplied, and trade with other regions of Europe strengthened. Local artisans and artists flourished, contributing to the cultural richness of the region.

The Classical Age

In the 17th century, Burgundy-Franche-Comté was marked by the centralization of power under Louis XIV and the construction of fortifications to protect the borders of the kingdom. Louis XIV's military engineers, such as Vauban, built fortifications and citadels to strengthen the region's defense.

The Citadel of Besançon is one of the most impressive examples of military architecture from this era. Designed by Vauban between 1668 and 1711, the citadel dominates the city and offers spectacular views of the Doubs valley. Today it houses museums and exhibitions, offering insight into the military and cultural history of the region.

The French Revolution and the Industrial Era

French Revolution

The French Revolution of 1789 brought significant changes to Burgundy-Franche-Comté. Feudal structures were abolished, the property of the Church and the nobility was confiscated and redistributed, and departments were created to replace the old provinces.

Dijon became the prefecture of Côte-d'Or, Besançon that of Doubs, and other cities such as Auxerre, Mâcon and Lons-le-Saunier became important administrative centers. The Revolution also marked the beginning of the modernization of the region's administration and economy.

19th Century Industrialization

The 19th century was a period of rapid transformation for Burgundy-Franche-Comté, with industrialization and urbanization. Technological progress and the rise of the railways stimulated the economic development of the region.

Dijon became a major industrial and commercial center, with industries such as metallurgy, machine tool production, and food manufacturing. The town of Montbéliard, in Franche-Comté, became an important center of the automobile industry with the installation of the Peugeot factory.

Agriculture and viticulture continued to play a key role in the regional economy. Burgundy wines, in particular, gained international fame, and vineyards modernized to meet growing demand. Farmers' fairs and markets flourished, and regional products, such as cheeses and charcuterie, became popular specialties.

The 20th Century and the Contemporary Era

World Wars

The 20th century was marked by two world wars which had a profound impact on Burgundy-Franche-Comté. During the First World War, the region was an important production and logistics center for the war effort. Soldiers from the region participated in fighting on the Western Front, and many memorials were erected in their honor.

The Second World War brought new challenges, with the German occupation and the Resistance. The region was the scene of numerous acts of resistance, and heroic figures such as Lucie Aubrac and Jean Moulin played a crucial role in the fight against the occupier. The cities of Dijon and Besançon were bombed, and many historic buildings were damaged or destroyed.

Modern period

After the war, Burgundy-Franche-Comté undertook a period of reconstruction and modernization. Infrastructure was rebuilt, cities renovated and industries revitalized. Tourism became a key sector of the economy, attracting visitors from around the world to discover the historical and cultural treasures of the region.

Today, the Burgundy-Franche-Comté region is a dynamic economic center, with varied sectors such as industry, agriculture, tourism and services. The main cities, such as Dijon, Besançon, Auxerre,

Chalon-sur-Saône and Montbéliard, offer a mix of historical heritage and modernity, with modern infrastructure and a high quality of life.

The region continues to attract visitors for its historic sites, magnificent landscapes and renowned gastronomy. The region's Relais & Châteaux capture the essence of this rich heritage and offer their guests unforgettable experiences, combining luxury, comfort and authenticity.

Conclusion

Burgundy-Franche-Comté is a region rich in history and heritage, where every street corner, every village and every castle tells a unique story. From Roman remains to medieval fortifications, from Renaissance castles to 19th century industrial sites, the region offers an incredible diversity of monuments and historical sites.

The Relais & Châteaux of the Burgundy-Franche-Comté region capture the essence of this historical and cultural wealth, offering their guests unforgettable experiences. Each establishment, with its enchanting setting, warm welcome, exceptional gastronomy and enriching activities, offers total immersion in the history and heritage of the region.

By discovering the Relais & Châteaux of Burgundy-Franche-Comté, you will be transported into a world where every detail is designed to delight the senses and create lasting memories. This chapter explored the many facets of the region's history and heritage, revealing how each era helped shape this unique and fascinating destination.

- Gastronomy and Wine

The Burgundy-Franche-Comté region is world-renowned for its gastronomy and exceptional wines. Nestled in the heart of France, this region is a true paradise for lovers of good food and fine wines. With its quality local products, its ancestral culinary traditions and its legendary vineyards, Burgundy-Franche-Comté offers an unrivaled gastronomic experience. This chapter explores the gastronomic aspects of the region in detail, highlighting the local produce, iconic dishes, renowned chefs, starred restaurants and wines that this region is famous for.

The Roots of Burgundian and Franche-Comté Gastronomy

Local Products

Burgundy-Franche-Comté is a land rich in local products, which are the basis of its traditional cuisine. Among the most emblematic products, we find:

- Charolles Beef: An exceptional beef, renowned for its tenderness and delicate taste. This beef, raised outdoors in the meadows of Burgundy, is often used in dishes such as beef bourguignon.
- Burgundy Escargots: Traditionally prepared with butter, garlic and parsley, Burgundy snails are a staple of regional cuisine.
- Bresse Poultry: Bresse poultry is the only one to benefit from a controlled designation of origin (AOC). It is appreciated for its tender and tasty flesh.

- Parsley Ham: A typical Burgundy dish, parsley ham is prepared with ham, parsley and spices, and served in a terrine.
- Morels and Truffles: These precious mushrooms and tubers are used in many dishes for their unique aroma and intense flavor.

Cheeses

Burgundy-Franche-Comté is also renowned for its cheeses, each with its own character and manufacturing techniques. Among the most famous, we find:

- Comté: Originally from the Jura massif, Comté is a cooked pressed cheese, made from raw milk from Montbéliarde or French Simmental cows. It is appreciated for its firm texture and complex aromas.
- Époisses: This soft cheese, originally from Burgundy, is refined with Burgundy marc, which gives it a washed rind and a powerful flavor.
- Mont d'Or: Also called Vacherin du Haut-Doubs, Mont d'Or is a soft cheese made in the Jura. It is traditionally eaten hot, melted in its spruce box.
- Bleu de Gex: This blue cheese, made in the Jura massif, is appreciated for its creamy texture and slightly spicy taste.
- Morbier: Another Jura cheese, Morbier is recognizable by the line of ash that runs through its paste. It has a sweet and fruity flavor.

Burgundy Wines

Burgundy is world famous for its wines, which are among the most prestigious and sought-after in the world. Burgundy's vineyards cover approximately 28,000 hectares and are divided into several sub-regions, each with their own characteristics and appellations. Among the main appellations, we find:

- Chablis: Located in the north of Burgundy, the Chablis region is known for its dry white wines, made from the Chardonnay grape variety. Chablis wines are renowned for their minerality and freshness.
- Côte de Nuits: This sub-region, located south of Dijon, is famous for its great red wines, mainly made from the Pinot Noir grape variety. Côte de Nuits wines, such as Gevrey-Chambertin, Vosne-Romanée and Nuits-Saint-Georges, are appreciated for their complexity and aging potential.
- Côte de Beaune: Known for its white and red wines, Côte de Beaune produces some of Burgundy's greatest wines, such as Meursault, Puligny-Montrachet, Chassagne-Montrachet and Pommard. The white wines of the Côte de Beaune are renowned for their richness and elegance.
- Côte Chalonnaise: This sub-region produces quality white and red wines, as well as Crémants de Bourgogne. The best-known appellations are Mercurey, Givry and Rully.
- Mâconnais: Located in the south of Burgundy, the Mâconnais region is famous for its white wines, made mainly from the Chardonnay grape variety. The best-known appellations are Pouilly-Fuissé, Saint-Véran and Mâcon-Villages.

Franche-Comté Wines

Although less famous than Burgundy, Franche-Comté also produces quality wines, mainly in the Jura. Jura wines are known for their originality and diversity. Among the main appellations, we find:

- Arbois: The largest appellation in the Jura, Arbois produces red, white, rosé and yellow wines. White wines, made from the Savagnin grape variety, are particularly renowned for their unique character.
- Côtes du Jura: This appellation covers a large part of the Jura vineyards and produces a variety of wines, including white, red, rosé and sparkling wines.
- Château-Chalon: This small appellation is famous for its vin jaune, a dry and powerful white wine made from the Savagnin grape variety. The yellow wine is aged under veil for at least six years and three months, which gives it aromas of nuts and dried fruits.
- L'Étoile: This appellation mainly produces white wines, made from the Chardonnay, Savagnin and Poulsard grape varieties. Étoile wines are appreciated for their finesse and minerality.

Emblematic Dishes of Regional Cuisine

Beef Bourginon

Beef bourguignon is undoubtedly the most emblematic dish of Burgundian cuisine. This beef stew is prepared with Burgundy red wine, onions, carrots, mushrooms, bacon and aromatic herbs. The beef is slowly simmered in wine, giving it a tender texture and a rich, complex flavor. Beef bourguignon is often served with potatoes, pasta or bread.

Coq au vin

Coq au vin is another classic dish of Burgundian cuisine. The rooster is marinated then simmered in Burgundy red wine, with onions, mushrooms, bacon and aromatic herbs. Like beef bourguignon, coq au vin is a comforting and flavorful dish, perfect for winter meals.

Burgundy Snails

Burgundy snails, prepared with butter, garlic and parsley, are a popular regional specialty. Snails are generally served as a starter, in shells or small earthenware dishes. Garlic and parsley butter add a rich and delicious flavor to the snails.

La Gougere

Gougère is a savory pastry made from choux pastry and cheese. Originally from Burgundy, gougère is often served as an aperitif or starter. It is light and crispy, with a pronounced cheese flavor. Gougères can be made with different types of cheese, such as Comté, Gruyère or Emmental.

Comtoise Fondue

Comtoise fondue is a typical dish from Franche-Comté, prepared with melted Comté cheese, Jura white wine and garlic. Fondue is served with pieces of bread, potatoes and vegetables, which are dipped in melted cheese. It's a friendly and comforting dish, perfect for winter evenings.

Star Chefs and Restaurants

The Pioneers of Regional Haute Cuisine

Burgundy-Franche-Comté has always been a hotbed of culinary creativity, attracting talented chefs who have been able to highlight local products and culinary traditions. Pioneers of regional haute cuisine, such as Bernard Loiseau and Jacques Lameloise , helped make the region a leading gastronomic destination.

Bernard Loiseau, chef of the La Côte d'Or restaurant in Saulieu, was one of the most influential chefs of his generation. Its cuisine, inspired by local products and Burgundian traditions, has been awarded three stars in the Michelin guide. Jacques Lameloise , for his part, managed the Lameloise restaurant in Chagny, also three-starred, and is recognized for his refined and inventive cuisine.

Contemporary Chefs

Today, the Burgundy-Franche-Comté region continues to attract renowned chefs, who perpetuate the tradition of haute cuisine while innovating and experimenting with new flavors. Among the most famous contemporary chefs, we find:

- Jean-Michel Lorain : Chef of the La Côte Saint-Jacques restaurant in Joigny, Jean-Michel Lorain offers inventive and elegant cuisine, highlighting local and seasonal products. Its restaurant has been awarded two stars in the Michelin guide.
- Patrick Bertron : Chef of the Relais Bernard Loiseau restaurant in Saulieu, Patrick Bertron has been able to perpetuate the legacy of Bernard Loiseau while bringing his own creative touch to the cuisine. The restaurant has retained its two Michelin stars and is recognized for its inventive and refined cuisine.
- Éric Pras : Chef of the Lameloise restaurant in Chagny, Éric Pras offers elegant and creative cuisine, highlighting local and seasonal products. Its restaurant has retained its three stars in the Michelin guide.

Star Restaurants

The Burgundy-Franche-Comté region is home to numerous Michelin-starred restaurants, each offering a unique and unforgettable culinary experience. Among the most famous, we find:

- La Côte Saint-Jacques in Joigny: Chef Jean-Michel Lorain offers inventive and elegant cuisine, highlighting local and seasonal products. The restaurant has been awarded two stars in the Michelin guide.
- Relais Bernard Loiseau in Saulieu: Chef Patrick Bertron perpetuates the legacy of Bernard Loiseau with inventive and refined cuisine. The restaurant has been awarded two stars in the Michelin guide.
- Lameloise in Chagny: Chef Éric Pras offers elegant and creative cuisine, highlighting local and seasonal products. The restaurant has retained its three stars in the Michelin guide.

Oenological Experiences

Wine Tastings

Relais & Châteaux in the Burgundy-Franche-Comté region often offer unique wine experiences for their guests. From private tastings to vineyard visits, these experiences allow you to discover the region's wines and learn the secrets of Burgundian and Jura viticulture.

Customers can participate in tasting workshops, led by expert sommeliers, to learn how to identify the aromas and flavors of Burgundy and Jura wines. Guided tours of the wine estates allow you to discover the winemaking processes, meet the winemakers and taste wines directly from the source.

Food and Wine Pairings

Relais & Châteaux also offer food and wine pairings, allowing you to savor Burgundy and Franche-Comté wines in harmony with local cuisine. These pairings highlight the flavors of the dishes and wines, providing a complete and unforgettable gastronomic experience.

Chefs from Michelin-starred restaurants collaborate with sommeliers to create tasting menus that highlight the region's wines. Each dish is carefully paired with a wine, allowing guests to discover new combinations of flavors and textures.

Conclusion

The Burgundy-Franche-Comté region is a true land of gastronomy and wine, offering unparalleled richness and diversity. Burgundian and Franche-Comté cuisine, with its authentic flavors and quality local products, is a pillar of the region's art of living. Burgundy and Jura wines, renowned for their complexity and elegance, perfectly complement this culinary experience.

The Relais & Châteaux of the Burgundy-Franche-Comté region capture the essence of this gastronomic richness, offering their guests unique and unforgettable culinary and wine experiences. Each establishment, with its enchanting setting, warm welcome, exceptional gastronomy and enriching activities, offers total immersion in the French art of living.

By discovering the Relais & Châteaux of Burgundy-Franche-Comté, you will be transported into a world where every detail is designed to delight the senses and create lasting memories. This chapter explored the multiple facets of the region's gastronomy and wines, revealing how each element contributes to making this destination a true oasis of flavors and culinary pleasures.

2. Addresses and Descriptions

The Burgundy-Franche-Comté region is home to several prestigious Relais & Châteaux, each offering a unique and memorable experience. These establishments stand out for their enchanting setting, rich history, elegant architecture, exceptional cuisine and impeccable service. In this chapter, we'll explore some of the region's most notable Relais & Châteaux in detail, highlighting their distinctive features, culinary offerings and activities they offer.

Courcelles Castle

History and Architecture

The Château de Courcelles, located near Autun, is a magnificent example of classic French architecture. Built in the 18th century, this castle has been carefully restored to preserve its historic character while providing first-rate modern comfort. Surrounded by formal gardens and extensive grounds, the castle offers an idyllic setting for a romantic getaway or peaceful retreat.

The interiors of the castle are sumptuously decorated with antique furniture, artwork and fine textiles. The rooms and suites offer an elegant and warm atmosphere, with views of the gardens or the park. The bathrooms, equipped with marble bathtubs and walk-in showers, offer modern and luxurious comfort.

Culinary Offers

The Château de Courcelles gourmet restaurant is run by a Michelin-starred chef, who offers inventive and refined cuisine, highlighting local and seasonal products. The tasting menu offers an exceptional culinary experience, with creative and flavorful dishes, carefully presented to delight the eyes and taste buds.

The chateau also has an elegant wine bar, offering a selection of French and international wines, champagnes and cocktails. Customers can enjoy their favorite drinks in an intimate atmosphere, with comfortable seating and refined decoration.

Activities and Services

Château de Courcelles offers a range of activities for its guests, from relaxation to sport. The hotel's spa offers a variety of wellness treatments, from massages to facials, performed with high-quality products. Guests can also enjoy the heated outdoor swimming pool, jacuzzi and fitness room.

The castle's gardens and grounds are perfect for leisurely walks, meditation sessions or outdoor yoga sessions. The castle also offers guided excursions to explore the town of Autun, the surrounding hiking trails and the region's tourist sites.

Hostellerie de Levernois

History and Architecture

The Hostellerie de Levernois is located a few kilometers from Beaune, in the heart of the Burgundian vineyards. This 18th-century residence, surrounded by lush gardens and vineyards, offers an elegant and peaceful setting. The architecture of the Hostellerie de Levernois reflects the charm of the Burgundian countryside, with stone facades, wooden shutters and flower gardens.

The interiors of the hostelry are decorated with antique furniture, works of art and refined textiles, offering a warm and elegant ambiance. The rooms and suites are spacious and comfortable, with views of the gardens or vineyards. The bathrooms, equipped with marble bathtubs and walk-in showers, offer modern and luxurious comfort.

Culinary Offers

The gourmet restaurant at Hostellerie de Levernois, awarded one star in the Michelin guide, offers refined cuisine, highlighting local and seasonal products. The chef, recognized for his creativity and expertise, creates tasting menus that delight the taste buds and offer an exceptional culinary experience.

The hostelry also has a brasserie, offering traditional Burgundian cuisine in a relaxed and friendly setting. Guests can enjoy dishes such as gougère, beef bourguignon and escargots de Bourgogne, accompanied by carefully selected local wines.

Activities and Services

L'Hostellerie de Levernois offers a range of activities for its guests, from relaxation to sport. The hotel's spa offers a variety of wellness treatments, from massages to facials, performed with high-quality products. Guests can also enjoy the heated outdoor swimming pool, jacuzzi and fitness room.

The surrounding gardens and vineyards are perfect for leisurely walks, meditation sessions or outdoor yoga sessions. The hostelry also offers guided excursions to explore the vineyards of Beaune, the surrounding hiking trails and the tourist sites of the region.

Germigney Castle

History and Architecture

Château de Germigney, located in the village of Port-Lesney, is a magnificent 18th century residence surrounded by English gardens and green parks. The castle, with its elegant facades and sumptuous interiors, offers a romantic and refined setting. The owners have carefully restored the property to preserve its historic character while incorporating modern amenities for guest comfort.

The rooms and suites at Château de Germigney are decorated with antique furniture, works of art and refined textiles, offering an elegant and warm ambiance. The bathrooms, equipped with marble bathtubs and walk-in showers, offer modern and luxurious comfort.

Culinary Offers

The Château de Germigney's gourmet restaurant, led by a Michelin-starred chef, offers inventive and refined cuisine, highlighting local and seasonal products. The tasting menu offers an exceptional culinary experience, with creative and flavorful dishes, carefully presented to delight the eyes and taste buds.

The chateau also has an elegant bar, offering a selection of French and international wines, champagnes and cocktails. Customers can enjoy their favorite drinks in an intimate atmosphere, with comfortable seating and refined decoration.

Activities and Services

Château de Germigney offers a range of activities for its guests, from relaxation to sport. The hotel's spa offers a variety of wellness treatments, from massages to facials, performed with high-quality products. Guests can also enjoy the heated outdoor swimming pool, jacuzzi and fitness room.

The castle's gardens and grounds are perfect for leisurely walks, meditation sessions or outdoor yoga sessions. The castle also offers guided excursions to explore the village of Port-Lesney, the surrounding hiking trails and the region's attractions.

Bussière Abbey

History and Architecture

Bussière Abbey, located near Dijon, is a magnificent example of Cistercian architecture. Founded in the 12th century, this abbey has been carefully restored to preserve its historic character while offering first-rate modern comfort. Surrounded by formal gardens and green parks, the abbey offers an idyllic setting for a romantic getaway or peaceful retreat.

The interiors of the abbey are sumptuously decorated with antique furniture, artwork and fine textiles. The rooms and suites offer an elegant and warm atmosphere, with views of the gardens or the park. The bathrooms, equipped with marble bathtubs and walk-in showers, offer modern and luxurious comfort.

Culinary Offers

The gourmet restaurant at Abbaye de la Bussière, led by a Michelin-starred chef, offers inventive and refined cuisine, highlighting local and seasonal products. The tasting menu offers an exceptional culinary experience, with creative and flavorful dishes, carefully presented to delight the eyes and taste buds.

The abbey also has an elegant bar, offering a selection of French and international wines, champagnes and cocktails. Customers can enjoy their favorite drinks in an intimate atmosphere, with comfortable seating and refined decoration.

Activities and Services

Abbaye de la Bussière offers a range of activities for its guests, from relaxation to sport. The hotel's spa offers a variety of wellness treatments, from massages to facials, performed with high-quality products. Guests can also enjoy the heated outdoor swimming pool, jacuzzi and fitness room.

The abbey's gardens and grounds are perfect for leisurely walks, meditation sessions or outdoor yoga sessions. The abbey also offers guided excursions to explore the city of Dijon, the surrounding hiking trails and the region's tourist sites.

Castle of Vault-de-Lugny

History and Architecture

The Château de Vault-de-Lugny, located near Avallon, is a magnificent 13th century residence surrounded by a moat and French gardens. The castle, with its elegant facades and sumptuous interiors, offers a romantic and refined setting. The owners have carefully restored the property to preserve its historic character while incorporating modern amenities for guest comfort.

The rooms and suites at Château de Vault-de-Lugny are decorated with antique furniture, works of art and refined textiles, offering an elegant and warm ambiance. The bathrooms, equipped with marble bathtubs and walk-in showers, offer modern and luxurious comfort.

Culinary Offers

The gourmet restaurant at Château de Vault-de-Lugny, led by a Michelin-starred chef, offers inventive and refined cuisine, highlighting local and seasonal products. The tasting menu offers an exceptional culinary experience, with creative and flavorful dishes, carefully presented to delight the eyes and taste buds.

The château also has an elegant bar, offering a selection of French and international wines, champagnes and cocktails. Customers can enjoy their favorite drinks in an intimate atmosphere, with comfortable seating and refined decoration.

Activities and Services

Château de Vault-de-Lugny offers a range of activities for its guests, from relaxation to sport. The hotel's spa offers a variety of wellness treatments, from massages to facials, performed with high-quality products. Guests can also enjoy the heated indoor swimming pool, jacuzzi and fitness room.

The castle's gardens and grounds are perfect for leisurely walks, meditation sessions or outdoor yoga sessions. The castle also offers guided excursions to explore the town of Avallon, surrounding hiking trails and area sights.

Conclusion

The Relais & Châteaux in Burgundy-Franche-Comté offer unique and unforgettable experiences, combining luxury, comfort and historical heritage. Each establishment, with its enchanting setting, warm welcome, exceptional gastronomy and enriching activities, offers total immersion in the French art of living. Whether for a romantic getaway, a peaceful retreat or a cultural exploration, the Relais & Châteaux of the Burgundy-Franche-Comté region are must-see destinations.

By discovering these exceptional establishments, you will be transported to a world where every detail is designed to delight the senses and create lasting memories. This chapter has presented a detailed overview of some of the most prestigious Relais & Châteaux in the region, offering a glimpse of the unique experience that awaits you in each of these enchanting locations.

- Château de Gilly

The Château de Gilly, located in the heart of Burgundy, between Dijon and Beaune, is a true historical and architectural gem. Former residence of the abbots of Cîteaux, this 14th century castle has been carefully restored to offer a luxurious and refined setting to its visitors. In this chapter, we will explore in detail the history and architecture of Château de Gilly, its culinary offerings, the activities and services offered, and the unique experiences it offers.

History and Architecture

A Monastic History

Château de Gilly has a rich and fascinating history dating back to the Middle Ages. Originally built in the 14th century as a fortified residence for the abbots of Cîteaux Abbey, the castle played an important role in the region. The abbots of Cîteaux, founders of the Cistercian order, transformed this residence into a place of refuge and meditation, while welcoming dignitaries and pilgrims.

Over the centuries, the castle has undergone several architectural transformations, while retaining its medieval charm. After the French Revolution, the castle passed through the hands of different owners before finally being restored and transformed into a luxury hotel.

Elegant and Authentic Architecture

The architecture of Château de Gilly reflects its monastic and medieval history, with fortified elements, moats and French gardens. The stone facades, turrets and slate roofs add to the charm and elegance of the castle. The carefully maintained gardens provide a peaceful and picturesque setting for strolling and relaxing.

The interiors of the castle are sumptuously decorated with antique furniture, tapestries and works of art, creating a warm and refined ambiance. The rooms and suites, each unique, are tastefully furnished and offer magnificent views of the gardens or surrounding area. The bathrooms, equipped with marble bathtubs and walk-in showers, offer modern and luxurious comfort.

Culinary Offers

The Clos Prieur Restaurant

The Château de Gilly's gourmet restaurant, Le Clos Prieur, is run by a talented chef who offers refined and inventive cuisine, highlighting local and seasonal products. The restaurant is located in a vaulted room dating from the 14th century, offering an intimate and historic atmosphere.

The tasting menu is a true symphony of flavors, with dishes such as pan-fried duck foie gras, Charolais beef fillet, roast pigeon and seasonal fruit desserts. Each dish is carefully prepared and artistically presented, providing an exceptional dining experience.

The restaurant also has an impressive wine list, highlighting the great wines of Burgundy. Sommeliers are available to advise customers and help them choose the wines that will perfectly accompany their meal.

The Castle Bar

Le Bar du Château is a cozy and elegant venue where guests can relax and savor a selection of wines, champagnes, cocktails and spirits. The bar, located in a former guard room with exposed beams and a fireplace, offers a warm and welcoming atmosphere.

Guests can enjoy their favorite drinks in comfortable seats, while enjoying the view of the castle gardens. Wine tastings and mixology workshops are held regularly, allowing guests to discover new flavors and perfect their beverage knowledge.

Activities and Services

The Spa and Wellness Treatments

Château de Gilly offers a range of wellness treatments for its guests, from massages to facials, carried out with high quality products. The spa, located in a quiet wing of the castle, is a place of rest and relaxation, perfect for recharging your batteries after a day exploring the region.

Professional therapists use advanced techniques and luxury products to ensure optimal results and a luxurious experience. Guests can also enjoy the heated outdoor swimming pool, jacuzzi and fitness room to complete their relaxing experience.

Outdoor activities

The gardens and grounds of Château de Gilly are perfect for leisurely walks, meditation sessions or outdoor yoga sessions. Guests can also enjoy the heated outdoor swimming pool, tennis court and fitness room.

The hotel also offers guided excursions to explore the region's vineyards, surrounding hiking trails and Burgundy sights. Guests can discover picturesque villages, historic castles and local markets. Bicycles are also available to explore the region in an ecological and active way.

Cultural Activities and Experiences

Château de Gilly regularly organizes cultural events and unique experiences for its guests. Private concerts, literary readings and art exhibitions are often held in the castle's lounges or gardens. These events offer immersion in the local cultural scene and allow guests to meet artists, writers and musicians.

Guests can also participate in cooking workshops, baking classes and chocolate tastings, led by local chefs. These workshops offer an opportunity to learn Burgundian cooking techniques and taste delicious creations. The castle also offers yoga and meditation classes, led by qualified instructors, in the hotel's gardens or wellness areas.

Special Events and Unique Experiences

Weddings and Receptions

Château de Gilly is an ideal venue for intimate weddings and private receptions. The castle's gardens and lounges provide a romantic and elegant setting for ceremonies and receptions. Hotel staff work closely with couples to create tailor-made events, taking into account every detail, from decor to personalized menus.

The hotel's chefs create wedding menus that reflect the tastes and preferences of the bride and groom, using seasonal ingredients and local produce. The professional and attentive service teams ensure that every event goes off without a hitch. Couples can also enjoy luxurious suites for their wedding night, with special services such as massages, in-room breakfasts and welcome gifts.

Seminars and Business Meetings

The Château de Gilly offers an exceptional setting for seminars, conferences and business meetings. The castle's private lounges, equipped with the latest technology, offer flexible spaces for events of different sizes. Hotel teams work with event organizers to create tailor-made programs, including coffee breaks, business lunches and dinners.

Team-building activities and excursions can also be organized to strengthen team cohesion and provide moments of relaxation outside of work sessions. Guests can take advantage of the hotel's wellness facilities to unwind after a day of meetings, with spa treatments, yoga sessions and massages.

Unique Experiences

Château de Gilly offers unique experiences to make each stay memorable. These include private dinners in exclusive locations within the castle, such as the library or the gardens, offering an intimate and romantic atmosphere. Guests can also participate in wine tasting workshops, led by expert sommeliers, to discover the secrets of Burgundy wines.

Wellness getaways are also available, including personalized relaxation and relaxation programs, spa treatments, yoga and meditation sessions, as well as healthy and nutritious meals. These programs are designed to help clients recharge their batteries and regain physical and mental balance.

Seasonal and Thematic Offers

Château de Gilly regularly offers seasonal and thematic offers to enrich its customers' experience. At Christmas, the castle is decked out in festive decorations and offers special menus , cookie decorating workshops and Christmas market visits. In summer, gourmet picnics can be organized in the gardens or on the terraces.

Romantic getaways are also offered, including candlelit dinners, duo massages and horse-drawn carriage rides in the surrounding area. For culture lovers, special packages including tickets for exhibitions, shows and concerts are available, offering complete immersion in the cultural life of the region.

Conclusion

Château de Gilly is much more than just a luxury hotel; it is a destination in itself, offering a unique and unforgettable experience in the heart of the magnificent Burgundy region. With its rich history, impressive architecture, refined culinary offerings and a variety of activities and services, this establishment is the ideal place to relax, recharge and discover the French art of living.

Whether for a romantic getaway, a wellness retreat, an intimate wedding or a business meeting, Château de Gilly promises an exceptional experience, marked by luxury, comfort and elegance. Guests leave with unforgettable memories, enriched by the unique culture, gastronomy and hospitality of this iconic Burgundy château.

- Le Relais Bernard Loiseau

Located in the charming village of Saulieu, in the heart of Burgundy, Le Relais Bernard Loiseau is an emblematic place of French gastronomy. This prestigious establishment, a member of the Relais & Châteaux chain, combines tradition and innovation to offer an exceptional experience to its visitors. In this chapter, we will explore in detail the history and architecture of Relais Bernard Loiseau, its culinary offerings, the activities and services offered, and the unique experiences it offers.

History and Architecture

An Exceptional Culinary Heritage

Relais Bernard Loiseau owes its name to the illustrious chef Bernard Loiseau, who acquired the establishment in 1982. Thanks to his talent and passion for cooking, Bernard Loiseau quickly transformed the restaurant into a gastronomic reference, obtaining three stars in the Michelin guide in 1991. His unique approach to cooking, focused on simplicity, purity of flavors and the use of the best local products, marked the history of French gastronomy.

After the tragic death of Bernard Loiseau in 2003, his wife Dominique Loiseau continued to perpetuate his legacy with the help of chef Patrick Bertron , Bernard's loyal collaborator. Today, Relais Bernard Loiseau remains a gastronomic institution, honoring the memory of its founder while innovating and evolving.

Elegant and Friendly Architecture

Relais Bernard Loiseau is located in a magnificent Burgundian house, surrounded by lush gardens and picturesque landscapes. The architecture of the property reflects the traditional charm of the region, with stone facades, wooden shutters and tiled roofs. The interiors are tastefully decorated, combining classic and contemporary elements to create a warm and elegant ambiance.

The rooms and suites at Relais Bernard Loiseau are furnished with refined furniture, works of art and quality textiles. Each room is unique, offering views of the gardens or the village of Saulieu. The bathrooms, equipped with marble bathtubs and walk-in showers, offer modern and luxurious comfort.

Culinary Offers

The Gourmet Restaurant

The gourmet restaurant at Relais Bernard Loiseau, led by chef Patrick Bertron , offers refined and inventive cuisine, highlighting local and seasonal products. Patrick Bertron , who worked alongside Bernard Loiseau for many years, continues the spirit of his mentor while bringing his own creative touch to the kitchen.

The tasting menu is a true symphony of flavors, with dishes such as duck foie gras, roast pigeon, Charolais beef fillet and seasonal fruit desserts. Each dish is carefully prepared and artistically presented, providing an exceptional dining experience. The restaurant has retained its two Michelin stars, a testament to its continued excellence.

La Table de la Côte d'Or

La Table de la Côte d'Or is another dining option within Relais Bernard Loiseau, offering traditional Burgundian cuisine in a relaxed and friendly setting. The menu features iconic dishes from the region, such as beef bourguignon, Burgundy escargots and tarte Tatin. Guests can enjoy these delicious dishes accompanied by carefully selected local wines.

The Bar and Lounge

The Relais Bernard Loiseau bar is a cozy and elegant place where guests can relax and savor a selection of wines, champagnes, cocktails and spirits. The bar, decorated with wood paneling and comfortable armchairs, offers an intimate and welcoming atmosphere.

The lounge, on the other hand, is a friendly space where guests can gather for informal chats, read a book or simply enjoy the view of the gardens. Wine tastings and mixology workshops are held regularly, allowing guests to discover new flavors and perfect their beverage knowledge.

Activities and Services

The Spa and Wellness Treatments

Le Relais Bernard Loiseau offers a range of wellness treatments for its guests, ranging from massages to facial treatments, carried out with high quality products. The spa, located in a quiet wing of the establishment, is a place of rest and relaxation, perfect for recharging your batteries after a day exploring the region.

Professional therapists use advanced techniques and luxury products to ensure optimal results and a luxurious experience. Guests can also enjoy the heated indoor swimming pool, jacuzzi, sauna and steam room to complete their relaxation experience.

Outdoor activities

The gardens and grounds of Relais Bernard Loiseau are perfect for leisurely walks, meditation sessions or outdoor yoga sessions. Guests can also enjoy the heated outdoor swimming pool, tennis court and fitness room.

The hotel also offers guided excursions to explore the region's vineyards, surrounding hiking trails and Burgundy sights. Guests can discover picturesque villages, historic castles and local markets. Bicycles are also available to explore the region in an ecological and active way.

Cultural Activities and Experiences

Le Relais Bernard Loiseau regularly organizes cultural events and unique experiences for its guests. Private concerts, literary readings and art exhibitions are often organized in the establishment's lounges or gardens. These events offer immersion in the local cultural scene and allow guests to meet artists, writers and musicians.

Guests can also participate in cooking workshops, baking classes and chocolate tastings, led by local chefs. These workshops offer an opportunity to learn Burgundian cooking techniques and taste delicious creations. The Relais Bernard Loiseau also offers yoga and meditation classes, led by qualified instructors, in the hotel's gardens or wellness areas.

Special Events and Unique Experiences

Weddings and Receptions

The Relais Bernard Loiseau is an ideal venue for organizing intimate weddings and private receptions. The property's gardens and lounges provide a romantic and elegant setting for ceremonies and receptions. Hotel staff work closely with couples to create tailor-made events, taking into account every detail, from decor to personalized menus.

The hotel's chefs create wedding menus that reflect the tastes and preferences of the bride and groom, using seasonal ingredients and local produce. The professional and attentive service teams ensure that every event goes off without a hitch. Couples can also enjoy luxurious suites for their wedding night, with special services such as massages, in-room breakfasts and welcome gifts.

Seminars and Business Meetings

The Relais Bernard Loiseau offers an exceptional setting for seminars, conferences and business meetings. The property's private lounges, equipped with the latest technology, offer flexible spaces for events of different sizes. Hotel teams work with event organizers to create tailor-made programs, including coffee breaks, business lunches and dinners.

Team-building activities and excursions can also be organized to strengthen team cohesion and provide moments of relaxation outside of work sessions. Guests can take advantage of the hotel's wellness facilities to unwind after a day of meetings, with spa treatments, yoga sessions and massages.

Unique Experiences

The Relais Bernard Loiseau offers unique experiences to make each stay memorable. These include private dinners in exclusive locations within the establishment, such as the library or gardens, offering an intimate and romantic atmosphere. Guests can also participate in wine tasting workshops, led by expert sommeliers, to discover the secrets of Burgundy wines.

Wellness getaways are also available, including personalized relaxation and relaxation programs, spa treatments, yoga and meditation sessions, as well as healthy and nutritious meals. These programs are designed to help clients recharge their batteries and regain physical and mental balance.

Seasonal and Thematic Offers

The Relais Bernard Loiseau regularly offers seasonal and thematic offers to enrich its customers' experience. At Christmas, the establishment is decked out in festive decorations and offers special menus, cookie decorating workshops and Christmas market visits. In summer, gourmet picnics can be organized in the gardens or on the terraces.

Romantic getaways are also offered, including candlelit dinners, duo massages and horse-drawn carriage rides in the surrounding area. For culture lovers, special packages including tickets for exhibitions, shows and concerts are available, offering complete immersion in the cultural life of the region.

Conclusion

The Relais Bernard Loiseau is much more than just a luxury hotel; it is a destination in itself, offering a unique and unforgettable experience in the heart of the magnificent Burgundy region. With its rich history, impressive architecture, refined culinary offerings and a variety of activities and services, this establishment is the ideal place to relax, recharge and discover the French art of living.

Whether for a romantic getaway, a wellness retreat, an intimate wedding or a business meeting, the Relais Bernard Loiseau promises an exceptional experience, marked by luxury, comfort and elegance. Guests leave with unforgettable memories, enriched by the unique culture, gastronomy and hospitality of this iconic Burgundy establishment.

- Hostellerie de Levernois

The Hostellerie de Levernois is an elegant residence located a few kilometers from Beaune, in the heart of the Burgundian vineyards. This prestigious Relais & Châteaux offers an enchanting setting, refined cuisine and warm hospitality, making each stay a memorable experience. In this chapter, we will explore in detail the history and architecture of Hostellerie de Levernois, its culinary offerings, the activities and services offered, and the unique experiences it offers.

History and Architecture

A Story of Refinement and Elegance

Hostellerie de Levernois is nestled in an 18th-century residence, surrounded by lush gardens and vineyards. Over the centuries, this property has evolved from a private residence to a luxury hotel. The current owners have carefully restored the house to preserve its historic character while incorporating modern amenities for guest comfort.

The proximity of Beaune, capital of Burgundy wines, and the famous vineyards of the Côte de Beaune gives the Hostellerie de Levernois an ideal location for wine and gastronomy lovers.

Elegant and Authentic Architecture

The architecture of the Hostellerie de Levernois reflects the charm and elegance of the Burgundian countryside. The stone facades, wooden shutters and tiled roofs add to the authentic character of the establishment. The carefully maintained gardens provide a peaceful and picturesque setting for strolling and relaxing.

The interiors of the hostelry are tastefully decorated, combining classic and contemporary elements to create a warm and refined atmosphere. The rooms and suites, each unique, are furnished with antique furniture, works of art and quality textiles. The bathrooms, equipped with marble bathtubs and walk-in showers, offer modern and luxurious comfort.

Culinary Offers

The Gourmet Restaurant

The gourmet restaurant at Hostellerie de Levernois, awarded one star in the Michelin guide, is run by a talented chef who offers refined and inventive cuisine, highlighting local and seasonal products. The restaurant is located in an elegant room overlooking the gardens, offering an intimate and serene atmosphere.

The tasting menu is a true symphony of flavors, with dishes such as duck foie gras, Charolais beef fillet, roast pigeon and seasonal fruit desserts. Each dish is carefully prepared and artistically presented, providing an exceptional dining experience. Sommeliers are available to advise customers and help them choose the wines that will perfectly accompany their meal.

Brewery

The Hostellerie de Levernois brasserie offers traditional Burgundian cuisine in a relaxed and friendly setting. The menu offers emblematic dishes of the region, such as gougère, beef bourguignon and Burgundy escargots. Guests can enjoy these delicious dishes accompanied by carefully selected local wines.

The brasserie is the ideal place for a relaxed lunch or informal dinner, with a warm and welcoming ambiance.

The Bar and Lounge

The Hostellerie de Levernois bar is a cozy and elegant place where guests can relax and savor a selection of wines, champagnes, cocktails and spirits. The bar, decorated with wood paneling and comfortable armchairs, offers an intimate and welcoming atmosphere.

The lounge is a friendly space where guests can gather for informal chats, read a book or simply enjoy the view of the gardens. Wine tastings and mixology workshops are held regularly, allowing guests to discover new flavors and perfect their beverage knowledge.

Activities and Services

The Spa and Wellness Treatments

L'Hostellerie de Levernois offers a range of wellness treatments for its guests, ranging from massages to facial treatments, carried out with high quality products. The spa, located in a quiet wing of the establishment, is a place of rest and relaxation, perfect for recharging your batteries after a day exploring the region.

Professional therapists use advanced techniques and luxury products to ensure optimal results and a luxurious experience. Guests can also enjoy the heated outdoor swimming pool, jacuzzi, sauna and steam room to complete their relaxation experience.

Outdoor activities

The gardens and grounds of Hostellerie de Levernois are perfect for leisurely walks, meditation sessions or outdoor yoga sessions. Guests can also enjoy the heated outdoor swimming pool, tennis court and fitness room.

The hotel also offers guided excursions to explore the region's vineyards, surrounding hiking trails and Burgundy sights. Guests can discover picturesque villages, historic castles and local markets. Bicycles are also available to explore the region in an ecological and active way.

Cultural Activities and Experiences

L'Hostellerie de Levernois regularly organizes cultural events and unique experiences for its guests. Private concerts, literary readings and art exhibitions are often organized in the establishment's lounges or gardens. These events offer immersion in the local cultural scene and allow guests to meet artists, writers and musicians.

Guests can also participate in cooking workshops, baking classes and chocolate tastings, led by local chefs. These workshops offer an opportunity to learn Burgundian cooking techniques and taste delicious creations. L'Hostellerie de Levernois also offers yoga and meditation classes, led by qualified instructors, in the hotel's gardens or wellness areas.

Special Events and Unique Experiences

Weddings and Receptions

L'Hostellerie de Levernois is an ideal venue for organizing intimate weddings and private receptions. The property's gardens and lounges provide a romantic and elegant setting for ceremonies and receptions. Hotel staff work closely with couples to create tailor-made events, taking into account every detail, from decor to personalized menus.

The hotel's chefs create wedding menus that reflect the tastes and preferences of the bride and groom, using seasonal ingredients and local produce. The professional and attentive service teams ensure that every event goes off without a hitch. Couples can also enjoy luxurious suites for their wedding night, with special services such as massages, in-room breakfasts and welcome gifts.

Seminars and Business Meetings

The Hostellerie de Levernois offers an exceptional setting for seminars, conferences and business meetings. The property's private lounges, equipped with the latest technology, offer flexible spaces for events of different sizes. Hotel teams work with event organizers to create tailor-made programs, including coffee breaks, business lunches and dinners.

Team-building activities and excursions can also be organized to strengthen team cohesion and provide moments of relaxation outside of work sessions. Guests can take advantage of the hotel's wellness facilities to unwind after a day of meetings, with spa treatments, yoga sessions and massages.

Unique Experiences

L'Hostellerie de Levernois offers unique experiences to make each stay memorable. These include private dinners in exclusive locations within the establishment, such as the library or gardens, offering an intimate and romantic atmosphere. Guests can also participate in wine tasting workshops, led by expert sommeliers, to discover the secrets of Burgundy wines.

Wellness getaways are also available, including personalized relaxation and relaxation programs, spa treatments, yoga and meditation sessions, as well as healthy and nutritious meals. These programs are designed to help clients recharge their batteries and regain physical and mental balance.

Seasonal and Thematic Offers

L'Hostellerie de Levernois regularly offers seasonal and thematic offers to enrich its customers' experience. At Christmas, the establishment is decked out in festive decorations and offers special menus, cookie decorating workshops and Christmas market visits. In summer, gourmet picnics can be organized in the gardens or on the terraces.

Romantic getaways are also offered, including candlelit dinners, duo massages and horse-drawn carriage rides in the surrounding area. For culture lovers, special packages including tickets for exhibitions, shows and concerts are available, offering complete immersion in the cultural life of the region.

Conclusion

The Hostellerie de Levernois is much more than just a luxury hotel; it is a destination in itself, offering a unique and unforgettable experience in the heart of the magnificent Burgundy region. With its rich history, impressive architecture, refined culinary offerings and a variety of activities and services, this establishment is the ideal place to relax, recharge and discover the French art of living.

Whether for a romantic getaway, a wellness retreat, an intimate wedding or a business meeting, Hostellerie de Levernois promises an exceptional experience, marked by luxury, comfort and elegance. Guests leave with unforgettable memories, enriched by the unique culture, gastronomy and hospitality of this iconic Burgundy establishment.

Chapter 4: Relais & Châteaux in New Aquitaine

1. General Presentation of the Region

Nouvelle-Aquitaine, the largest administrative region in France, is a true paradise for lovers of culture, nature and gastronomy. Located in the southwest of the country, this region offers a diversity of landscapes, a rich heritage and an exceptional culinary scene. This chapter explores in detail the geographical, historical, cultural and economic characteristics of New Aquitaine, highlighting the treasures that make this region an essential destination.

Geography and Landscapes

A Diversity of Landscapes

New Aquitaine extends over more than 84,000 square kilometers, encompassing varied landscapes that range from Atlantic beaches to the Pyrenees mountains, including forests, plains and vineyards. This geographical diversity offers a multitude of outdoor activities and natural discoveries.

The Atlantic coast, with its sandy beaches, dunes and pine forests, is a popular destination for surfing, swimming and relaxation. Beach resorts such as Biarritz, Arcachon and Royan attract visitors from all over the world, while the islands of Ré and Oléron offer picturesque landscapes and a peaceful ambiance.

The Pyrenees mountains, which form the natural border with Spain, are ideal for hiking, skiing and climbing. The Pyrenees National Park protects exceptional biodiversity, with rare species of flora and fauna, as well as spectacular landscapes of snow-capped peaks, green valleys and glacial lakes.

Rivers and Lakes

New Aquitaine is crossed by several important rivers, including the Dordogne, the Garonne, the Charente and the Adour. These waterways add to the scenic beauty and provide opportunities for boating, fishing and water activities. River valleys, such as the Dordogne Valley and the Garonne Valley, are dotted with castles, picturesque villages and vineyards, creating breathtaking panoramas.

The region's lakes, such as Lac de Vassivière, Lac d'Hourtin-Carcans and Lac de Saint-Pardoux, are popular destinations for swimming, sailing, fishing and picnicking. The glacial lakes of the Pyrenees, in particular, offer crystal clear waters and picturesque beaches, ideal for relaxing in summer.

History and Heritage

The Origins of the Region

New Aquitaine has a rich and complex history, marked by the influence of numerous civilizations. The first traces of human occupation date back to prehistory, with sites such as the Lascaux Caves and the Rouffignac Cave, which are home to cave paintings and archaeological remains.

The Celts, then the Romans, occupied the region and left numerous vestiges, such as the arenas of Saintes, the Gallo-Roman theater of Bordeaux and the thermal baths of Chassenon. The city of Bordeaux, formerly called Burdigala , became an important commercial and cultural center during the Roman Empire.

The Middle Ages and the Hundred Years' War

The Middle Ages was a period of great prosperity for New Aquitaine, notably thanks to the Duchy of Aquitaine. The region became a strategic issue during the Hundred Years' War, opposing France and England. Eleanor of Aquitaine, one of the most famous figures of this period, married successively the King of France Louis VII and the King of England Henry II, making Aquitaine a territory under English influence.

Bastides, fortified towns typical of this era, were built to protect populations and promote trade. Monpazier, Domme and Beaumont-du-Périgord are among the best preserved bastides and offer a fascinating insight into medieval town planning.

The Renaissance and the Classical Age

The Renaissance brought an artistic and architectural renewal to New Aquitaine. The Loire castles, although located mainly in the Centre-Val de Loire region, influenced the architectural style of many buildings in New Aquitaine. The Château de La Rochefoucauld, the Château de Bonaguil and the Château de Puyguilhem are remarkable examples of Renaissance architecture in the region.

The Classical Age also saw the construction of numerous mansions and monuments, particularly in Bordeaux. The Place de la Bourse, with its famous Three Graces fountain and its reflecting pool, is a masterpiece of 18th century architecture. The city of La Rochelle, with its fortified port and its medieval towers, testifies to the maritime importance of the region.

Culture and Traditions

Cultural life

Nouvelle-Aquitaine is a hotbed of creativity and culture, with a vibrant arts scene and a rich tradition of festivals and events. Bordeaux, the regional capital, is known for its National Opera, its contemporary art museums and its film festival, Bordeaux Fête le Vin.

Music festivals, such as the Francofolies de La Rochelle, the Saint-Émilion International Jazz Festival and the Périgueux Guitar Festival, attract artists and spectators from all over the world. The Angoulême Comics Festival is another major event, celebrating comics and graphic novels.

The region is also famous for its tableware and crafts. Local markets, fairs and flea markets are opportunities to discover and purchase unique artisanal products, such as Limoges porcelain, Saintes pottery and Nontron knives.

Gastronomy and Local Products

The gastronomy of New Aquitaine is one of the most renowned in France, highlighting local products and culinary traditions. The region is particularly famous for its wines, seafood, truffles, ducks and cheeses.

Bordeaux wines are among the most prestigious in the world, with renowned appellations such as Saint-Émilion, Médoc, Pomerol and Sauternes. The wines of Bergerac, Cognac and Jurançon are also renowned for their quality and diversity.

Seafood, such as Marennes-Oléron oysters, Bouchot mussels and pink shrimp, are specialties of the Atlantic coast. Foie gras, confits and duck breasts are staples of Périgord cuisine, while Périgord noir truffles add a touch of luxury to many dishes.

The region's cheeses, such as Cabécou, Rocamadour , Chabichou du Poitou and Ossau-Iraty, are appreciated for their unique flavor and exceptional quality. Each cheese has its own history, manufacturing techniques and taste characteristics.

Local Festivals and Traditions

The Nouvelle-Aquitaine region is rich in festivals and traditions, which bear witness to its history and culture. Village festivals, agricultural fairs and folk festivals are opportunities to celebrate local customs and continue traditions.

The harvest festivals, in particular, are a highlight of regional life. Every fall, the vineyards are filled with grape pickers, who harvest the grapes by hand. The harvest is followed by parties and celebrations, with wine tastings, festive meals and musical entertainment.

Christmas markets, such as those in Bordeaux, Limoges and Pau, are also popular events, attracting visitors from across the region. The markets offer a variety of artisanal products, culinary specialties and gifts, creating a festive and warm atmosphere.

Economy and Innovation

Tourism

Tourism is one of the pillars of the economy of New Aquitaine, attracting millions of visitors from all over the world each year. The diversity of landscapes, cultural richness and historical heritage are all assets that make this region a popular destination.

The region's tourist infrastructure is of high quality, with a diverse range of accommodation, starred restaurants, wellness centers and leisure activities. The airports of Bordeaux, Biarritz and La Rochelle, as well as rail and road links, facilitate access to the region. Sustainable and responsible tourism is also encouraged, with initiatives aimed at preserving the environment and promoting local heritage.

Agriculture and Products

Terroir

Agriculture plays an essential role in the economy of the Nouvelle-Aquitaine region, with varied and quality production. Vineyards, cattle and duck breeding, cereal crops and cheese production are among the main agricultural activities.

Agricultural products, such as wine, foie gras, seafood, meat, cereals and fruits, are renowned for their excellence and diversity. Farmers' markets, agricultural cooperatives and short circuits promote the marketing of local products and support the rural economy.

Quality labels, such as the AOC (Appellation d'Origine Contrôlée) and the IGP (Protected Geographical Indication), guarantee the authenticity and quality of local products. Visitors can discover these products during tastings, farm tours and food festivals.

Industry and Innovation

The Nouvelle-Aquitaine region is also a hub of innovation and industrial development, with varied sectors such as aeronautics, agri-food, metallurgy, the pharmaceutical industry and renewable energies. Competitiveness clusters, such as Aerospace Valley (aeronautics and space) and Agri Sud-Ouest Innovation (agriculture and agri-food), promote innovation and collaboration between economic and scientific players.

Transportation infrastructure, such as highways, high-speed train lines and seaports, supports the region's economic development. The proximity of Spain and the presence of large metropolises such as Bordeaux facilitate commercial exchanges and international collaborations. The Nouvelle-Aquitaine region is a key player in the French economy, contributing to its dynamism and international influence.

Conclusion

The Nouvelle-Aquitaine region is an exceptional destination, rich in history, culture and varied landscapes. Whether to enjoy the beaches of the Atlantic, explore the mountains of the Pyrenees, discover the famous vineyards or savor the local gastronomy, there is something for everyone.

The Relais & Châteaux of the Nouvelle-Aquitaine region capture the essence of this diversity and offer their guests unforgettable experiences, combining luxury, comfort and authenticity. Each establishment, with its enchanting setting, warm welcome, exceptional gastronomy and enriching activities, offers total immersion in the French art of living.

By discovering the Relais & Châteaux de Nouvelle-Aquitaine, you will be transported into a world where every detail is designed to delight the senses and create lasting memories. This chapter presented a detailed overview of the region, integrating geographical, historical, cultural and economic aspects to provide a comprehensive understanding of this unique destination.

- History and Heritage

The Nouvelle-Aquitaine region, located in the southwest of France, is a land rich in history and heritage. Its towns, villages and castles tell fascinating stories dating back millennia. In this chapter, we will explore in detail key moments in the history of Nouvelle-Aquitaine, its iconic monuments and its cultural contributions.

The First Civilizations

Antiquity and the First Colonies

New Aquitaine has traces of human occupation dating back to prehistory. The Lascaux caves, located in the Dordogne, are among the most famous prehistoric sites in the world. Discovered in 1940, these caves are home to cave paintings dating back over 17,000 years, depicting animals such as bison, horses and deer. These works of art demonstrate the skill and creativity of the region's first inhabitants.

The Celts, then the Romans, also left their mark on the region. The Romans founded several important cities, including Bordeaux (Burdigala), Périgueux (Vesunna) and Saintes (Mediolanum Santonum). These cities were thriving commercial and cultural centers, with theaters, baths and temples. The arenas of Saintes and the Gallo-Roman theater of Bordeaux are remarkable vestiges of this period.

The Middle Ages: The Golden Age of Aquitaine

The Duchy of Aquitaine

The Middle Ages was a period of great prosperity for New Aquitaine, notably thanks to the Duchy of Aquitaine. Eleanor of Aquitaine, one of the most emblematic figures of this era, played a crucial role in the history of the region. Heir to the duchy, she became Queen of France through her marriage to Louis VII, then Queen of England after her union with Henry II Plantagenet. Under his influence, the Duchy of Aquitaine became a major cultural and political center in Europe.

During the Hundred Years' War, Aquitaine was a strategic issue between France and England. The region came under English and French control several times, and numerous castles and fortifications were built to protect the territories. The bastides, fortified towns typical of this era, such as Monpazier, Domme and Beaumont-du-Périgord, are remarkable examples of medieval town planning.

The Emblematic Monuments of the Middle Ages

The Saint-André Cathedral in Bordeaux, built in the 12th and 13th centuries, is a masterpiece of Gothic architecture. Listed as a UNESCO world heritage site, it is famous for its bell tower, the Pey-Berland tower, which offers a breathtaking view of the city.

Bonaguil Castle , located near Fumel, is another impressive example of medieval architecture. Built in the 13th century and remodeled in the 15th century, this fortified castle is remarkably well preserved and offers a fascinating insight into the defense techniques of the period.

The Renaissance and the Classical Age

The Renaissance in New Aquitaine

The Renaissance brought an artistic and architectural renewal to New Aquitaine. The Loire castles, although located mainly in the Centre-Val de Loire region, influenced the architectural style of many buildings in New Aquitaine. The Château de La Rochefoucauld, built in the 15th century and remodeled during the Renaissance, is a remarkable example of this period. With its imposing towers, spiral staircases and French gardens, it perfectly illustrates the marriage of medieval and Renaissance architecture.

Puyguilhem Castle , located in Dordogne, is another example of Renaissance architecture in New Aquitaine. Built in the early 16th century, this castle is famous for its sculpted facades, slate roofs and ornately decorated interiors.

The Classical Age and Baroque Monuments

The Classical Age also saw the construction of numerous mansions and monuments, particularly in Bordeaux. The city experienced economic growth thanks to the wine trade and maritime trading. Place de la Bourse, designed by architect Ange-Jacques Gabriel in the 18th century, is a masterpiece of classical French architecture. Its perfect symmetry, its elegance and its water mirror, which reflects the facades, make it one of the most photographed sites in Bordeaux.

The city of La Rochelle, with its fortified port and its medieval towers, testifies to the maritime importance of the region. The Chaîne, Lanterne and Saint-Nicolas towers are vestiges of the old medieval wall and offer a breathtaking view of the port and the ocean.

Modern and Contemporary Times

The French Revolution and the 19th Century

The French Revolution of 1789 brought significant changes to New Aquitaine. Feudal structures were abolished, the property of the Church and the nobility was confiscated and redistributed, and departments were created to replace the old provinces. Bordeaux became the prefecture of Gironde, and other cities such as Pau, Limoges and La Rochelle became important administrative centers.

The 19th century was a period of rapid transformation for New Aquitaine, with industrialization and urbanization. Technological progress and the rise of the railways stimulated the economic development of the region. Bordeaux became a major industrial and commercial center, with industries such as shipbuilding, wine production, and food manufacturing.

World Wars and Reconstruction

The 20th century was marked by two world wars which had a profound impact on New Aquitaine. During the First World War, the region was an important production and logistics center for the war effort. Soldiers from the region participated in fighting on the Western Front, and many memorials were erected in their honor.

The Second World War brought new challenges, with the German occupation and the Resistance. The region was the scene of numerous acts of resistance, and heroic figures such as Jean Moulin and Jacques Chaban-Delmas played a crucial role in the fight against the occupier. The cities of Bordeaux and La Rochelle were bombed, and many historic buildings were damaged or destroyed.

After the war, New Aquitaine undertook a period of reconstruction and modernization. Infrastructure was rebuilt, cities renovated and industries revitalized. Tourism became a key sector of the economy, attracting visitors from around the world to discover the historical and cultural treasures of the region.

Cultural and Architectural Heritage

UNESCO Sites

New Aquitaine has several UNESCO World Heritage sites, which bear witness to the richness of its cultural and architectural heritage. Among them, we find:

- Bordeaux, Port de la Lune: Listed in 2007, the historic center of Bordeaux is an exceptional example of classical and neoclassical town planning. The city is recognized for its quays, public squares, historic buildings and its role in the international wine trade.

- The routes to Saint-Jacques-de-Compostelle: Several sites in New Aquitaine are part of the pilgrimage routes leading to Saint-Jacques-de-Compostelle, listed as UNESCO world heritage sites. Among them, the Saint-Front cathedral in Périgueux, the Sainte-Marie church in Saint-Bertrand-de-Comminges and the Valentré bridge in Cahors.

- Lascaux Cave: Although the original cave is closed to the public to preserve it, the exact replica, Lascaux IV, allows visitors to discover the famous cave paintings of this prehistoric cave.

Historical Monuments and Museums

New Aquitaine is home to numerous historical monuments and museums that tell the history of the region and highlight its cultural heritage. Among them, we find:

- The Aquitaine Museum in Bordeaux: This museum traces the history of Bordeaux and the Aquitaine region, from prehistory to the present day. It houses collections of archaeology, ethnography and natural history, as well as works of art and everyday objects.

- The Château de Pau: Former residence of the kings of Navarre and birthplace of King Henri IV, the Château de Pau is a national museum which presents collections of art and history, as well as furniture and objects of era.

- The Bordeaux Museum of Fine Arts: This museum has a rich collection of paintings, sculptures and drawings, ranging from the Middle Ages to the contemporary era. It houses works by masters such as Rubens, Delacroix, Matisse and Picasso.

- The Prehistory Museum of Les Eyzies-de-Tayac: Located in the heart of the Vézère valley, this museum presents archaeological and paleontological collections, as well as reconstructions of prehistoric life.

Conclusion

New Aquitaine is a region rich in history and heritage, where every street corner, every village and every castle tells a unique story. From Roman remains to medieval fortifications, from Renaissance castles to 19th century industrial sites, the region offers an incredible diversity of monuments and historical sites.

The Relais & Châteaux of the Nouvelle-Aquitaine region capture the essence of this historical and cultural wealth, offering their guests unforgettable experiences. Each establishment, with its enchanting setting, warm welcome, exceptional gastronomy and enriching activities, offers total immersion in the history and heritage of the region.

By discovering the Relais & Châteaux de Nouvelle-Aquitaine, you will be transported into a world where every detail is designed to delight the senses and create lasting memories. This chapter explored the many facets of the region's history and heritage, revealing how each era helped shape this unique and fascinating destination.

- Gastronomy and Wine

The Nouvelle-Aquitaine region, located in the southwest of France, is a true paradise for food and wine lovers. Thanks to its exceptional local products, its ancestral culinary traditions and its prestigious vineyards, New Aquitaine offers an unrivaled culinary experience. In this chapter, we will explore the gastronomic aspects of the region in detail, highlighting the local produce, iconic dishes, renowned chefs, starred restaurants and wines that this region is famous for.

The Roots of Neo-Aquitaine Gastronomy

Local Products

New Aquitaine is a fertile and varied land which produces a great diversity of local products. Among the most emblematic products, we find:

- Marennes-Oléron Oysters: These oysters, raised in the Marennes-Oléron basin, are renowned for their delicate taste and firm texture. They are often eaten plain, with a squeeze of lemon or a shallot sauce.
- Foie Gras du Périgord: Foie gras is one of the most famous specialties of the region. It is often served in a terrine, pâté or pan-fried, accompanied by fruit preserves or gingerbread.
- Black Périgord Truffles: The black truffle, also called "black diamond", is a precious and aromatic mushroom that grows in the forests of Périgord. It is used to flavor dishes such as omelettes, pastas and risottos.

- Ducks and Geese of the South-West: Duck and goose confit, breasts and gizzards are essential specialties of the region. These products are often cooked slowly in their own fat to achieve a tender, flavorful texture.
- Seafood from the Arcachon Basin: The Arcachon Basin is a region rich in seafood, such as mussels, shrimp and scallops. These products are often enjoyed fresh or cooked in a simple manner to highlight their natural flavor.

Cheeses

Nouvelle-Aquitaine is also renowned for its cheeses, each having its own character and manufacturing techniques. Among the most famous, we find:

- Chabichou du Poitou: This goat's cheese, originally from Poitou, is made from raw milk and has a white, creamy paste , with a thin, pleated rind. It has a delicate and slightly tangy taste.
- Rocamadour : This small goat's cheese, produced in Quercy, is matured for around two weeks, which gives it a melting texture and a soft, creamy taste.
- Bleu des Causses: This blue cheese, made in the Lot, is similar to Roquefort but is matured in natural cellars. It has a blue paste and a powerful, spicy taste.
- L'Ossau-Iraty: This sheep's cheese, produced in the Pyrenees, has a firm and melting paste, with a natural rind. It has a sweet and fruity taste, with hints of hazelnut.
- Salers: This raw cow's milk cheese, made in the Massif Central, has an uncooked pressed paste and a natural rind. It has an intense and rustic taste, with aromas of hay and flowers.

Emblematic Dishes of Regional Cuisine

Duck Confit

Duck confit is one of the most emblematic dishes of South-West cuisine. It is prepared by slowly cooking duck legs in their own fat until they are meltingly tender. Duck confit is often served with potatoes fried in duck fat and a green salad.

Duck breast

Duck breast, or duck fillet, is another classic dish from the region. The duck breast is generally grilled or pan-fried and served rosé , accompanied by red fruit or citrus sauces. It is often accompanied by seasonal vegetables or potatoes.

Foie gras

Foie gras is a must in neo-Aquitaine gastronomy. It can be prepared in different ways: in a terrine, in a pâté, pan-fried or raw. Foie gras is often served as a starter, accompanied by fig jam, onion chutney or gingerbread.

Sarladaise Potato

Sarladaise potatoes are a specialty of the town of Sarlat, in Dordogne. The potatoes are cut into slices, then slowly cooked in duck fat with garlic and parsley. They are crispy on the outside and tender on the inside.

Porcini mushrooms à la Bordelaise

Porcini mushrooms, or porcini mushrooms , are a specialty of the Bordeaux region. They are usually sautéed with garlic, parsley and butter, then served as an accompaniment to meats or fish. Bordeaux-style porcini mushrooms are appreciated for their firm texture and intense taste.

Star Chefs and Restaurants

The Pioneers of Regional Haute Cuisine

Nouvelle-Aquitaine has always been a hotbed of culinary creativity, attracting talented chefs who have been able to highlight local products and culinary traditions. Pioneers of regional haute cuisine, such as Michel Guérard and Joël Robuchon, helped make the region a leading gastronomic destination.

Michel Guérard , chef of the restaurant Les Prés d'Eugénie in Eugénie-les-Bains, is considered one of the founders of French "nouvelle cuisine". His cuisine, light and inventive, has been rewarded with three stars in the Michelin guide. Joël Robuchon, for his part, opened his first restaurant in Bordeaux before becoming one of the most famous chefs in the world, with numerous starred establishments.

Contemporary Chefs

Today, the Nouvelle-Aquitaine region continues to attract renowned chefs, who perpetuate the tradition of haute cuisine while innovating and experimenting with new flavors. Among the most famous contemporary chefs, we find:

- Nicolas Masse: Chef of the La Grand'Vigne restaurant at Sources de Caudalie, near Bordeaux, Nicolas Masse offers refined and elegant cuisine, highlighting local and seasonal products. Its restaurant has been awarded two stars in the Michelin guide.
- Vivien Durand: Chef of the restaurant Le Prince Noir in Lormont, near Bordeaux, Vivien Durand offers inventive and daring cuisine, mixing regional and international influences. Its restaurant has been awarded a Michelin star.
- Thierry Marx: Chef of the restaurant Le Saint-James in Bouliac, near Bordeaux, Thierry Marx is known for his creative and experimental cuisine, using modern techniques and high quality ingredients. Its restaurant has been awarded a Michelin star.

Star Restaurants

The Nouvelle-Aquitaine region is home to numerous Michelin-starred restaurants, each offering a unique and unforgettable culinary experience. Among the most famous, we find:

- Les Prés d'Eugénie in Eugénie-les-Bains: Chef Michel Guérard offers light and inventive cuisine, highlighting local and seasonal products. The restaurant has been awarded three stars in the Michelin guide.
- La Grand'Vigne aux Sources de Caudalie: Chef Nicolas Masse offers refined and elegant cuisine, highlighting local and seasonal products. The restaurant has been awarded two stars in the Michelin guide.
- Le Prince Noir in Lormont: Chef Vivien Durand offers inventive and daring cuisine, mixing regional and international influences. The restaurant has been awarded a Michelin star.
- Le Saint-James in Bouliac: Chef Thierry Marx offers creative and experimental cuisine, using modern techniques and high-quality ingredients. The restaurant has been awarded a Michelin star.

Wines of Nouvelle-Aquitaine

Bordeaux Wines

The Bordeaux region is world famous for its wines, which are among the most prestigious and sought-after in the world. The vineyards of Bordeaux extend over approximately 120,000 hectares and are divided into several sub-regions, each with their own characteristics and appellations. Among the main appellations, we find:

- Saint-Émilion: Located on the right bank of the Dordogne, the Saint-Émilion region is known for its red wines made mainly from the Merlot grape variety. Saint-Émilion wines are renowned for their richness, complexity and aging potential.
- Médoc: Located on the left bank of the Gironde, the Médoc region produces powerful and tannic red wines, made mainly from Cabernet Sauvignon and Merlot grape varieties. The most famous appellations of Médoc are Margaux, Pauillac, Saint-Julien and Saint-Estèphe.
- Pomerol: Located near Saint-Émilion, the Pomerol region is known for its rich and velvety red wines, made mainly from the Merlot grape variety. Pomerol wines are renowned for their finesse, elegance and aging potential.
- Sauternes: Located in the Graves region, the Sauternes region is famous for its sweet white wines, made mainly from the Sémillon, Sauvignon Blanc and Muscadelle grape varieties. Sauternes wines are renowned for their sweetness, complexity and aging potential.

Bergerac and Dordogne Wines

The Bergerac region, located east of Bordeaux, produces a wide diversity of wines, including red, white, rosé and sweet wines. The main appellations of Bergerac are:

- Bergerac: This appellation produces quality red, white and rosé wines, made from the same grape varieties as those of Bordeaux. Bergerac red wines are generally rich and fruity, while white wines are fresh and aromatic.

- Monbazillac: Located south of Bergerac, the Monbazillac appellation is famous for its sweet white wines, made mainly from the Sémillon, Sauvignon Blanc and Muscadelle grape varieties. Monbazillac wines are renowned for their sweetness, complexity and aging potential.
- Pécharmant : Located north of Bergerac, the Pécharmant appellation produces powerful and tannic red wines, made mainly from Cabernet Sauvignon, Cabernet Franc, Merlot and Malbec grape varieties. Pécharmant wines are renowned for their richness, complexity and aging potential.

Wines of the South West

The South West region, which encompasses part of Nouvelle-Aquitaine, also produces a wide diversity of wines, including red, white, rosé and sparkling wines. The main appellations of the South-West are:

- Cahors: Located in the Lot valley, the Cahors appellation is famous for its powerful and tannic red wines, made mainly from the Malbec grape variety. Cahors wines are renowned for their richness, complexity and aging potential.
- Madiran: Located in the foothills of the Pyrenees, the Madiran appellation produces robust and tannic red wines, made mainly from the Tannat grape variety . Madiran wines are renowned for their structure, complexity and aging potential.
- Jurançon: Located in the foothills of the Pyrenees, the Jurançon appellation produces dry and sweet white wines, made mainly from the Petit Manseng and Gros Manseng grape varieties . Jurançon wines are renowned for their freshness, complexity and aging potential.

Oenological Experiences

Wine Tastings

Relais & Châteaux in the Nouvelle-Aquitaine region often offer unique wine experiences for their guests. From private tastings to vineyard visits, these experiences allow you to discover the region's wines and learn the secrets of Bordeaux, Bergerac and South-West viticulture.

Customers can participate in tasting workshops, led by expert sommeliers, to learn how to identify the aromas and flavors of wines from Bordeaux, Bergerac and the South West. Guided tours of the wine estates allow you to discover the winemaking processes, meet the winemakers and taste wines directly from the source.

Food and Wine Pairings

The Relais & Châteaux also offer food and wine pairings, allowing you to savor Nouvelle-Aquitaine wines in harmony with local cuisine. These pairings highlight the flavors of the dishes and wines, providing a complete and unforgettable gastronomic experience.

Chefs from Michelin-starred restaurants collaborate with sommeliers to create tasting menus that highlight the region's wines. Each dish is carefully paired with a wine, allowing guests to discover new combinations of flavors and textures.

Conclusion

The Nouvelle-Aquitaine region is a true land of gastronomy and wine, offering unparalleled richness and diversity. Neo-Aquitaine cuisine, with its authentic flavors and quality local products, is a pillar of the region's art of living. Wines from Bordeaux, Bergerac and the South West, renowned for their complexity and elegance, perfectly complement this culinary experience.

The Relais & Châteaux of the Nouvelle-Aquitaine region capture the essence of this gastronomic richness, offering their guests unique and unforgettable culinary and wine experiences. Each establishment, with its enchanting setting, warm welcome, exceptional gastronomy and enriching activities, offers total immersion in the French art of living.

By discovering the Relais & Châteaux de Nouvelle-Aquitaine, you will be transported into a world where every detail is designed to delight the senses and create lasting memories. This chapter explored the multiple facets of the region's gastronomy and wines, revealing how each element contributes to making this destination a true oasis of flavors and culinary pleasures.

2. Addresses and Descriptions

New Aquitaine is rich in Relais & Châteaux, each offering a unique experience combining luxury, comfort and regional charm. These establishments are spread throughout the region, from the vineyards of Bordeaux to the beaches of the Atlantic coast, including the mountains of the Pyrenees. In this chapter, we will explore some of the most prestigious addresses and describe in detail what makes them special.

Château Cordeillan-Bages

History and Architecture

Château Cordeillan-Bages , located in the heart of Médoc, is an elegant 17th century Chartreuse surrounded by prestigious vineyards. This historic estate belongs to the Cazes family, also owner of the famous Château Lynch- Bages . The castle has been transformed into a luxury hotel, while preserving its charm and historic character. The interiors of the castle are tastefully decorated, mixing classic and contemporary elements to create a warm and refined atmosphere.

Culinary Offers

The Château Cordeillan-Bages restaurant , led by a Michelin-starred chef, offers inventive and refined cuisine, highlighting local and seasonal products. The tasting menu offers an exceptional culinary experience, with creative and flavorful dishes, carefully presented to delight the eyes and taste buds. The carefully selected wine list highlights the great wines of Médoc and other prestigious wine-growing regions.

Activities and Services

Château Cordeillan-Bages offers a range of activities for its guests, from relaxation to sport. Guests can enjoy the heated outdoor swimming pool, spa and fitness room. Guided tours of the surrounding vineyards and wine tastings are also organized. Guests can learn about the winemaking process, meet winemakers and taste wines straight from the source.

The Springs of Caudalie

History and Architecture

Les Sources de Caudalie, located in Martillac, near Bordeaux, is a luxury hotel complex surrounded by vineyards and forests. Inspired by the traditional architecture of the region's wine cellars, the hotel is made up of several stone and wooden buildings, creating an authentic and elegant atmosphere. Interiors are decorated with antique furniture, artwork and fine textiles, providing a warm and welcoming ambiance.

Culinary Offers

Les Sources de Caudalie is home to several restaurants, including La Grand'Vigne , awarded two stars in the Michelin guide. The chef, Nicolas Masse, offers inventive and elegant cuisine, highlighting local and seasonal products. The tasting menu offers an exceptional culinary experience, with creative and flavorful dishes, carefully presented to delight the eyes and taste buds. The hotel also has a brasserie, La Table du Lavoir, offering traditional cuisine in a relaxed and friendly setting.

Activities and Services

Les Sources de Caudalie offer a range of activities for their guests, from relaxation to sport. The hotel's spa, specializing in vinotherapy, offers a variety of wellness treatments, from massages to facials, performed with high quality products. Guests can also enjoy the heated outdoor swimming pool, jacuzzi and fitness room. Guided tours of the surrounding vineyards and wine tastings are also organized, allowing guests to experience the winemaking process and taste wines directly from the source.

Post Office Relay

History and Architecture

Le Relais de la Poste, located in Magescq, Landes, is a charming 19th-century Landes house surrounded by lush gardens and forests. The hotel has been carefully restored to preserve its historic character while providing first-rate modern comfort. The interiors are tastefully decorated, mixing classic and contemporary elements to create a warm and refined atmosphere.

Culinary Offers

The Relais de la Poste's gourmet restaurant, led by a Michelin-starred chef, offers inventive and refined cuisine, highlighting local and seasonal products. The tasting menu offers an exceptional culinary experience, with creative and flavorful dishes, carefully presented to delight the eyes and taste buds. The restaurant also has an impressive wine list, highlighting the great wines of Bordeaux and other prestigious wine regions.

Activities and Services

Le Relais de la Poste offers a range of activities for its guests, from relaxation to sport. The hotel's spa offers a variety of wellness treatments, from massages to facials, performed with high-quality products. Guests can also enjoy the heated outdoor swimming pool, jacuzzi and fitness room. Guided excursions to explore the Landes forests, Atlantic beaches and surrounding villages are also organized.

Palace Hotel

History and Architecture

The Hôtel du Palais, located in Biarritz, is a sumptuous palace built in the 19th century for Empress Eugénie, wife of Napoleon III. This iconic hotel, with its majestic facade and lush gardens, offers breathtaking views of the Atlantic Ocean. The hotel's interiors are sumptuously decorated with antique furniture, artwork and fine textiles, providing an elegant and luxurious ambiance.

Culinary Offers

The gourmet restaurant at the Hôtel du Palais, led by a Michelin-starred chef, offers inventive and refined cuisine, highlighting local and seasonal products. The tasting menu offers an exceptional culinary experience, with creative and flavorful dishes, carefully presented to delight the eyes and taste buds. The restaurant also has an impressive wine list, highlighting the great wines of Bordeaux and other prestigious wine regions.

Activities and Services

The Hôtel du Palais offers a range of activities for its guests, from relaxation to sport. The hotel's spa, specializing in thalassotherapy, offers a variety of wellness treatments, from massages to facials, performed with high quality products. Guests can also enjoy the heated outdoor swimming pool, jacuzzi and fitness room. Guided excursions to explore the beaches of Biarritz, the Pyrenees and the surrounding Basque villages are also organized.

Domaine de la Tortinière

History and Architecture

Domaine de la Tortinière , located in Veigné, near Tours, is an elegant 19th-century château surrounded by formal gardens and forests. The hotel has been carefully restored to preserve its historic character while providing first-rate modern comfort. The interiors are tastefully decorated, mixing classic and contemporary elements to create a warm and refined atmosphere.

Culinary Offers

The gourmet restaurant at Domaine de la Tortinière , led by a talented chef, offers inventive and refined cuisine, highlighting local and seasonal products. The tasting menu offers an exceptional culinary experience, with creative and flavorful dishes, carefully presented to delight the eyes and taste buds. The restaurant also has an impressive wine list, highlighting the great wines of the Loire and other prestigious wine regions.

Activities and Services

Domaine de la Tortinière offers a range of activities for its guests, from relaxation to sport. The hotel's spa offers a variety of wellness treatments, from massages to facials, performed with high-quality products. Guests can also enjoy the heated outdoor swimming pool, jacuzzi and fitness room. Guided excursions to explore the Loire châteaux, gardens and surrounding vineyards are also organized.

Conclusion

The Relais & Châteaux in Nouvelle-Aquitaine offer unique and unforgettable experiences, combining luxury, comfort and historical heritage. Each establishment, with its enchanting setting, warm welcome, exceptional gastronomy and enriching activities, offers total immersion in the French art of living. Whether for a romantic getaway, a peaceful retreat or a cultural exploration, the Relais & Châteaux of the Nouvelle-Aquitaine region are must-see destinations.

By discovering these exceptional establishments, you will be transported to a world where every detail is designed to delight the senses and create lasting memories. This chapter has presented a detailed overview of some of the most prestigious Relais & Châteaux in the region, offering a glimpse of the unique experience that awaits you in each of these enchanting locations.

- Les Prés d'Eugénie - Maison Guérard

Les Prés d'Eugénie - Maison Guérard is a jewel of French gastronomy and hospitality, located in Eugénie-les-Bains, in the Landes. This iconic establishment, founded by the famous chef Michel Guérard , is a haven of peace and refinement, where discreet luxury and culinary excellence combine to offer an unforgettable experience. In this chapter, we will explore the history and architecture of Les Prés d'Eugénie, its culinary offerings, the activities and services offered, and the unique experiences it offers.

History and Architecture

A Story of Passion and Excellence

Les Prés d'Eugénie - Maison Guérard was founded by Michel Guérard and his wife Christine in 1974. Michel Guérard , pioneer of "nouvelle cuisine", quickly made his restaurant a place of pilgrimage for lovers of gastronomy. The restaurant was awarded three Michelin stars in 1977, an honor it has retained ever since.

The estate is located in Eugénie-les-Bains, a small spa town renowned for its waters with curative properties. The Guérard couple transformed an old mansion into a charming hotel, surrounded by lush gardens and shaded parks. Today, Les Prés d'Eugénie is an internationally renowned establishment, combining tradition and innovation.

Elegant and Authentic Architecture

Les Prés d'Eugénie is a collection of carefully restored historic buildings, combining elegance and authenticity. The estate includes the 18th century mansion, renovated outbuildings and cottages nestled in the gardens. The interiors are tastefully decorated, mixing classic and contemporary elements to create a warm and refined atmosphere.

Rooms and suites are furnished with antique furniture, artwork and quality textiles, offering modern and luxurious comfort. Each room is unique, with views of the gardens, parks or shaded terraces. The bathrooms, equipped with marble bathtubs and walk-in showers, offer optimal comfort for relaxing and recharging your batteries.

Culinary Offers

The Gourmet Restaurant

The gourmet restaurant of Les Prés d'Eugénie, managed by Michel Guérard , offers inventive and refined cuisine, highlighting local and seasonal products. Michel Guérard is known for his creativity and expertise, which is reflected in each dish. The tasting menu offers an exceptional culinary experience, with dishes such as "Filet of Sole with Vermouth" and "Free Range Pigeon with Lemongrass".

The carefully selected wine list highlights the great wines of Bordeaux, Burgundy and other prestigious wine regions. Sommeliers are available to advise customers and help them choose the wines that will perfectly accompany their meal.

Slimming and Gourmet Cuisine

Michel Guérard is also a pioneer of "slimming and gourmet cuisine", a culinary approach that combines pleasure and health. Dishes are designed to be both delicious and light, using innovative cooking techniques and fresh, quality ingredients. This kitchen is ideal for those who want to enjoy refined dishes while taking care of their well-being.

The slimming menu offers dishes such as "Roasted Sea Bass Fillet with Sweet Spices" and "Val Sauté with Aromatic Herbs". Each dish is carefully prepared to preserve the natural flavors of the ingredients while minimizing fat and calories.

The Restaurant "La Ferme aux Grives"

For a more relaxed dining experience, Les Prés d'Eugénie also offers the restaurant "La Ferme aux Grives". Located in an old restored farm, this restaurant offers traditional South-West cuisine, highlighting local products and family recipes. Customers can enjoy dishes such as "Duck Confit", "Cassoulet" and "Tarte Tatin" in a warm and friendly atmosphere.

Activities and Services

The Spa and Wellness Treatments

Les Prés d'Eugénie offers a range of well-being treatments for its customers, ranging from massages to facial treatments, carried out with high quality products. The spa, located in a peaceful and luxurious setting, is a place of rest and relaxation, perfect for recharging your batteries after a day exploring the region.

Professional therapists use advanced techniques and luxury products to ensure optimal results and a luxurious experience. Guests can also enjoy the heated outdoor swimming pool, jacuzzi, sauna and steam room to complete their relaxation experience.

Outdoor activities

The gardens and park of Les Prés d'Eugénie are perfect for leisurely walks, meditation sessions or outdoor yoga sessions. Guests can also enjoy the heated outdoor swimming pool, tennis court and fitness room.

The hotel also offers guided excursions to explore the surroundings of Eugénie-les-Bains, the hiking trails and the tourist sites of Landes and Béarn. Guests can discover picturesque villages, local markets and stunning natural landscapes.

Cultural Activities and Experiences

Les Prés d'Eugénie regularly organizes cultural events and unique experiences for its guests. Private concerts, literary readings and art exhibitions are often organized in the establishment's lounges or gardens. These events offer immersion in the local cultural scene and allow guests to meet artists, writers and musicians.

Guests can also participate in cooking workshops, baking classes and chocolate tastings, led by local chefs. These workshops offer an opportunity to learn Southwestern cooking techniques and taste delicious creations. Les Prés d'Eugénie also offers yoga and meditation classes, led by qualified instructors, in the hotel's gardens or wellness areas.

Special Events and Unique Experiences

Weddings and Receptions

Les Prés d'Eugénie is an ideal venue for organizing intimate weddings and private receptions. The property's gardens and lounges provide a romantic and elegant setting for ceremonies and receptions. Hotel staff work closely with couples to create tailor-made events, taking into account every detail, from decor to personalized menus.

The hotel's chefs create wedding menus that reflect the tastes and preferences of the bride and groom, using seasonal ingredients and local produce. The professional and attentive service teams ensure that every event goes off without a hitch. Couples can also enjoy luxurious suites for their wedding night, with special services such as massages, in-room breakfasts and welcome gifts.

Seminars and Business Meetings

Les Prés d'Eugénie offers an exceptional setting for seminars, conferences and business meetings. The property's private lounges, equipped with the latest technology, offer flexible spaces for events of different sizes. Hotel teams work with event organizers to create tailor-made programs, including coffee breaks, business lunches and dinners.

Team-building activities and excursions can also be organized to strengthen team cohesion and provide moments of relaxation outside of work sessions. Guests can take advantage of the hotel's wellness facilities to unwind after a day of meetings, with spa treatments, yoga sessions and massages.

Unique Experiences

Les Prés d'Eugénie offers unique experiences to make each stay memorable. These include private dinners in exclusive locations within the establishment, such as the library or gardens, offering an intimate and romantic atmosphere. Customers can also participate in wine tasting workshops, led by expert sommeliers, to discover the secrets of Bordeaux and Landes wines.

Wellness getaways are also available, including personalized relaxation and relaxation programs, spa treatments, yoga and meditation sessions, as well as healthy and nutritious meals. These programs are designed to help clients recharge their batteries and regain physical and mental balance.

Seasonal and Thematic Offers

Les Prés d'Eugénie regularly offers seasonal and thematic offers to enrich its customers' experience. At Christmas, the establishment is decked out in festive decorations and offers special menus, cookie decorating workshops and Christmas market visits. In summer, gourmet picnics can be organized in the gardens or on the terraces.

Romantic getaways are also offered, including candlelit dinners, duo massages and horse-drawn carriage rides in the surrounding area. For culture lovers, special packages including tickets for exhibitions, shows and concerts are available, offering complete immersion in the cultural life of the region.

Conclusion

Les Prés d'Eugénie - Maison Guérard is much more than just a luxury hotel; it is a destination in itself, offering a unique and unforgettable experience in the heart of the magnificent Landes region. With its rich history, impressive architecture, refined culinary offerings and a variety of activities and services, this establishment is the ideal place to relax, recharge and discover the French art of living.

Whether for a romantic getaway, a wellness retreat, an intimate wedding or a business meeting, Les Prés d'Eugénie promises an exceptional experience, marked by luxury, comfort and elegance. Guests leave with unforgettable memories, enriched by the unique culture, gastronomy and hospitality of this emblematic establishment of New Aquitaine.

- Château Cordeillan-Bages

Château Cordeillan-Bages , located in the heart of Médoc, is an emblematic place in the Nouvelle-Aquitaine region, combining wine-growing tradition and luxury hospitality. This Relais & Châteaux is recognized not only for its enchanting setting, but also for its starred cuisine and its exceptional wine offering. In this chapter, we will explore the history and architecture of Château Cordeillan-Bages , its culinary offerings, the activities and services offered, and the unique experiences it offers.

History and Architecture

A Wine Heritage

Château Cordeillan-Bages is an elegant 17th century Chartreuse, located in Pauillac, in the heart of the famous Médoc vineyards. This historic estate belongs to the Cazes family, also owner of the famous Château Lynch- Bages , a Grand Cru Classé of Pauillac. The castle has been transformed into a luxury hotel, while preserving its charm and historic character.

The architecture of the castle reflects the classic style of wine-growing residences in the region, with its stone facades, wooden shutters and tiled roofs. Surrounded by carefully maintained gardens and prestigious vineyards, Château Cordeillan-Bages offers an idyllic setting for a relaxing getaway and oenological discovery.

A Careful Restoration

The interiors of Château Cordeillan-Bages are tastefully decorated, mixing classic and contemporary elements to create a warm and refined atmosphere. Rooms and suites are furnished with antique furniture, artwork and quality textiles, offering modern and luxurious comfort. Each room is unique, with views of the gardens, vineyards or interior courtyards. The bathrooms, equipped with marble bathtubs and walk-in showers, offer optimal comfort for relaxing and recharging your batteries.

Culinary Offers

The Gourmet Restaurant

The Château Cordeillan-Bages restaurant, led by a Michelin-starred chef, offers inventive and refined cuisine, highlighting local and seasonal products. The talented and creative chef creates dishes that are both visually stunning and deliciously flavorful. The tasting menu offers an exceptional culinary experience, with dishes such as "Filet de Bœuf de Bazas" and "Lobster Bleu à la Bordelaise".

The carefully selected wine list highlights the great wines of the Médoc, as well as wines from other prestigious wine-growing regions. Sommeliers are available to advise customers and help them choose the wines that will perfectly accompany their meal.

Baggage Table

For a more casual dining experience, Château Cordeillan-Bages also offers La Table de Bages, located in the village of Bages, close to the château. This chic bistro offers traditional South-West cuisine, highlighting local products and family recipes. Customers can enjoy dishes such as "Duck Confit", "Cassoulet" and "Tarte Tatin" in a warm and friendly atmosphere.

Activities and Services

The Spa and Wellness Treatments

Château Cordeillan-Bages offers a range of wellness treatments for its guests, ranging from massages to facial treatments, carried out with high quality products. The spa, located in a peaceful and luxurious setting, is a place of rest and relaxation, perfect for recharging your batteries after a day exploring the vineyards.

Professional therapists use advanced techniques and luxury products to ensure optimal results and a luxurious experience. Guests can also enjoy the heated outdoor swimming pool, jacuzzi, sauna and steam room to complete their relaxation experience.

Outdoor activities

The gardens and grounds of Château Cordeillan-Bages are perfect for leisurely walks, meditation sessions or outdoor yoga sessions. Guests can also enjoy the heated outdoor swimming pool, tennis court and fitness room.

The hotel also offers guided excursions to explore the surrounding vineyards and tourist sites of the Médoc. Guests can discover prestigious wine châteaux, participate in wine tastings and learn the secrets of Bordeaux viticulture. Bicycles are also available to explore the region in an ecological and active way.

Cultural Activities and Experiences

Château Cordeillan-Bages regularly organizes cultural events and unique experiences for its guests. Private concerts, literary readings and art exhibitions are often organized in the establishment's lounges or gardens. These events offer immersion in the local cultural scene and allow guests to meet artists, writers and musicians.

Guests can also participate in cooking workshops, baking classes and chocolate tastings, led by local chefs. These workshops offer an opportunity to learn Southwestern cooking techniques and taste delicious creations. Château Cordeillan-Bages also offers yoga and meditation classes, led by qualified instructors, in the hotel's gardens or wellness areas.

Special Events and Unique Experiences

Weddings and Receptions

Château Cordeillan-Bages is an ideal venue for organizing intimate weddings and private receptions. The property's gardens and lounges provide a romantic and elegant setting for ceremonies and receptions. Hotel staff work closely with couples to create tailor-made events, taking into account every detail, from decor to personalized menus.

The hotel's chefs create wedding menus that reflect the tastes and preferences of the bride and groom, using seasonal ingredients and local produce. The professional and attentive service teams ensure that every event goes off without a hitch. Couples can also enjoy luxurious suites for their wedding night, with special services such as massages, in-room breakfasts and welcome gifts.

Seminars and Business Meetings

Château Cordeillan-Bages offers an exceptional setting for seminars, conferences and business meetings. The property's private lounges, equipped with the latest technology, offer flexible spaces for events of different sizes. Hotel teams work with event organizers to create tailor-made programs, including coffee breaks, business lunches and dinners.

Team-building activities and excursions can also be organized to strengthen team cohesion and provide moments of relaxation outside of work sessions. Guests can take advantage of the hotel's wellness facilities to unwind after a day of meetings, with spa treatments, yoga sessions and massages.

Unique Experiences

Château Cordeillan-Bages offers unique experiences to make each stay memorable. These include private dinners in exclusive locations within the establishment, such as the library or gardens, offering an intimate and romantic atmosphere. Guests can also participate in wine tasting workshops, led by expert sommeliers, to discover the secrets of Bordeaux and Médoc wines.

Wellness getaways are also available, including personalized relaxation and relaxation programs, spa treatments, yoga and meditation sessions, as well as healthy and nutritious meals. These programs are designed to help clients recharge their batteries and regain physical and mental balance.

Seasonal and Thematic Offers

Château Cordeillan-Bages regularly offers seasonal and thematic offers to enrich its customers' experience. At Christmas, the establishment is decked out in festive decorations and offers special menus, cookie decorating workshops and Christmas market visits. In summer, gourmet picnics can be organized in the gardens or on the terraces.

Romantic getaways are also offered, including candlelit dinners, duo massages and horse-drawn carriage rides in the surrounding area. For culture lovers, special packages including tickets for exhibitions, shows and concerts are available, offering complete immersion in the cultural life of the region.

Conclusion

Château Cordeillan-Bages is much more than just a luxury hotel; it is a destination in itself, offering a unique and unforgettable experience in the heart of the magnificent Médoc region. With its rich history, impressive architecture, refined culinary offerings and a variety of activities and services, this establishment is the ideal place to relax, recharge and discover the French art of living.

Whether for a romantic getaway, a wellness retreat, an intimate wedding or a business meeting, Château Cordeillan-Bages promises an exceptional experience, marked by luxury, comfort and elegance. Guests leave with unforgettable memories, enriched by the unique culture, gastronomy and hospitality of this emblematic establishment of New Aquitaine.

- Pavia Hotel

Located in the heart of Saint-Émilion, the Hôtel de Pavie is a prestigious establishment that embodies the essence of luxury and the region's wine-growing tradition. Nestled in a medieval village listed as a UNESCO World Heritage Site, this hotel is renowned for its warm hospitality, its enchanting setting, and its starred cuisine. In this chapter, we will explore the history and architecture of Hôtel de Pavie, its culinary offerings, the activities and services offered, and the unique experiences it offers.

History and Architecture

A Rich and Medieval History

The Hôtel de Pavie is located in a historic building that has stood the test of time, located in the picturesque village of Saint-Émilion. This old residence, dating from the 13th century, has been transformed into a luxury hotel while preserving its medieval charm. Saint-Émilion, with its cobbled streets and historic buildings, offers an ideal setting for this exceptional establishment.

Authentic Architecture

The architecture of the Hôtel de Pavie reflects the rich heritage of Saint-Émilion. The stone facade, vaults and exposed beams recall the medieval history of the region. The hotel's interiors are elegantly decorated, combining classic and contemporary elements to create a warm and refined ambiance. The rooms and suites, each unique, offer breathtaking views of the village, the vineyards and the Dordogne valley. The bathrooms, equipped with marble bathtubs and walk-in showers, offer modern and luxurious comfort.

Culinary Offers

The Gourmet Restaurant

The gourmet restaurant at the Hôtel de Pavie, led by chef Yannick Alléno , offers inventive and refined cuisine, highlighting local and seasonal products. Yannick Alléno , three-Michelin-starred, is known for his creative approach and culinary expertise. The tasting menu offers an exceptional culinary experience, with dishes such as "Lobster Bleu de Bretagne" and "Farm Pigeon with Black Truffle".

The carefully selected wine list highlights the great wines of Saint-Émilion and other prestigious wine regions. Sommeliers are available to advise customers and help them choose the wines that will perfectly accompany their meal.

The Brasserie Le Bistrot de l'Hôtel de Pavie

For a more relaxed dining experience, the Hôtel de Pavie also offers Le Bistrot de l'Hôtel de Pavie, located in an old restored building. This bistro offers traditional French cuisine, highlighting local products and family recipes. Customers can enjoy dishes such as "Duck Confit", "Boeuf Bourguignon" and "Crème Brûlée" in a warm and friendly atmosphere.

Activities and Services

The Spa and Wellness Treatments

Hôtel de Pavie offers a range of wellness treatments for its guests, from massages to facials, performed with high quality products. The spa, located in a peaceful and luxurious setting, is a place of rest and relaxation, perfect for recharging your batteries after a day exploring the vineyards.

Professional therapists use advanced techniques and luxury products to ensure optimal results and a luxurious experience. Guests can also enjoy the heated outdoor swimming pool, jacuzzi, sauna and steam room to complete their relaxation experience.

Outdoor activities

The gardens and grounds of Hôtel de Pavie are perfect for leisurely walks, meditation sessions or outdoor yoga sessions. Guests can also enjoy the heated outdoor swimming pool and fitness room.

The hotel also offers guided excursions to explore the surrounding vineyards and sights of Saint-Émilion. Guests can discover prestigious wine châteaux, participate in wine tastings and learn the secrets of Bordeaux viticulture. Bicycles are also available to explore the region in an ecological and active way.

Cultural Activities and Experiences

Hôtel de Pavie regularly organizes cultural events and unique experiences for its guests. Private concerts, literary readings and art exhibitions are often organized in the establishment's lounges or gardens. These events offer immersion in the local cultural scene and allow guests to meet artists, writers and musicians.

Guests can also participate in cooking workshops, baking classes and chocolate tastings, led by local chefs. These workshops offer an opportunity to learn Southwestern cooking techniques and taste delicious creations. Hôtel de Pavie also offers yoga and meditation classes, led by qualified instructors, in the hotel's gardens or wellness areas.

Special Events and Unique Experiences

Weddings and Receptions

The Hôtel de Pavie is an ideal venue for hosting intimate weddings and private receptions. The property's gardens and lounges provide a romantic and elegant setting for ceremonies and receptions. Hotel staff work closely with couples to create tailor-made events, taking into account every detail, from decor to personalized menus.

The hotel's chefs create wedding menus that reflect the tastes and preferences of the bride and groom, using seasonal ingredients and local produce. The professional and attentive service teams ensure that every event goes off without a hitch. Couples can also enjoy luxurious suites for their wedding night, with special services such as massages, in-room breakfasts and welcome gifts.

Seminars and Business Meetings

The Hôtel de Pavie offers an exceptional setting for seminars, conferences and business meetings. The property's private lounges, equipped with the latest technology, offer flexible spaces for events of different sizes. Hotel teams work with event organizers to create tailor-made programs, including coffee breaks, business lunches and dinners.

Team-building activities and excursions can also be organized to strengthen team cohesion and provide moments of relaxation outside of work sessions. Guests can take advantage of the hotel's wellness facilities to unwind after a day of meetings, with spa treatments, yoga sessions and massages.

Unique Experiences

The Hôtel de Pavie offers unique experiences to make each stay memorable. These include private dinners in exclusive locations within the establishment, such as the library or gardens, offering an intimate and romantic atmosphere. Guests can also participate in wine tasting workshops, led by expert sommeliers, to discover the secrets of the wines of Saint-Émilion and the Bordeaux region.

Wellness getaways are also available, including personalized relaxation and relaxation programs, spa treatments, yoga and meditation sessions, as well as healthy and nutritious meals. These programs are designed to help clients recharge their batteries and regain physical and mental balance.

Seasonal and Thematic Offers

The Hôtel de Pavie regularly offers seasonal and thematic offers to enrich its guests' experience. At Christmas, the establishment is decked out in festive decorations and offers special menus, cookie decorating workshops and Christmas market visits. In summer, gourmet picnics can be organized in the gardens or on the terraces.

Romantic getaways are also offered, including candlelit dinners, duo massages and horse-drawn carriage rides in the surrounding area. For culture lovers, special packages including tickets for exhibitions, shows and concerts are available, offering complete immersion in the cultural life of the region.

Conclusion

The Hôtel de Pavie is much more than just a luxury hotel; it is a destination in itself, offering a unique and unforgettable experience in the heart of the magnificent Saint-Émilion region. With its rich history, impressive architecture, refined culinary offerings and a variety of activities and services, this establishment is the ideal place to relax, recharge and discover the French art of living.

Whether for a romantic getaway, a wellness retreat, an intimate wedding or a business meeting, the Hôtel de Pavie promises an exceptional experience, marked by luxury, comfort and elegance. Guests leave with unforgettable memories, enriched by the unique culture, gastronomy and hospitality of this emblematic establishment of New Aquitaine.

Chapter 5: Relais & Châteaux in Auvergne-Rhône-Alpes

1. General Presentation of the Region

Auvergne-Rhône-Alpes is a region located in east-central France, famous for its geographical diversity, cultural richness and historical heritage. From the majesty of the Alps to the dormant volcanoes of Auvergne, the vineyards of Beaujolais and dynamic cities like Lyon and Grenoble, this region offers a multitude of unique landscapes and experiences. This chapter explores in detail the geographical, historical, cultural and economic characteristics of Auvergne-Rhône-Alpes, highlighting the treasures that make this region an essential destination.

Geography and Landscapes

A Diversity of Landscapes

Auvergne-Rhône-Alpes extends over a vast area of more than 69,000 square kilometers, encompassing varied landscapes that range from the snow-capped mountains of the Alps to the dormant volcanoes of Auvergne, via river valleys, plains agriculture and vineyards. This geographical diversity offers a multitude of outdoor activities and natural discoveries.

The Alps, with their iconic peaks such as Mont Blanc, offer exceptional opportunities for skiing, mountaineering, hiking and other mountain sports. World-famous ski resorts like Chamonix, Courchevel, and Les Deux Alpes attract visitors from around the world for their impeccable ski slopes and breathtaking scenery.

The Auvergne volcanoes, grouped in the Auvergne Volcanoes regional natural park, constitute one of the largest volcanic groups in Europe. Visitors can explore craters, volcanic lakes and lush forests, and enjoy spectacular panoramic views from peaks such as Puy de Dôme.

Rivers and Lakes

The region is crossed by several important rivers, including the Rhône, the Saône, the Isère and the Allier. These waterways add to the scenic beauty and provide opportunities for boating, fishing and water activities. River valleys, like the Rhône Valley and the Saône Valley, are dotted with picturesque villages, vineyards and historic sites, creating breathtaking panoramas.

The region's lakes, such as Lake Geneva, Lake Annecy and Lake Bourget, are popular destinations for swimming, sailing, fishing and picnicking. Lake Annecy, with its crystal clear waters and surrounding mountains, is often considered one of the most beautiful lakes in Europe.

History and Heritage

The Origins of the Region

Auvergne-Rhône-Alpes has a rich and complex history, marked by the influence of numerous civilizations. The first traces of human occupation date back to prehistory, with sites such as the Chauvet and Pech Merle caves, which house cave paintings and archaeological remains.

The Romans also left their mark on the region, founding important cities like Lyon (Lugdunum), Vienne and Saint-Romain-en-Gal. Lyon became a major administrative and commercial center of Roman Gaul, and its Roman remains, such as the ancient theater and baths, are still visible today.

The Middle Ages and the Renaissance

The Middle Ages were a period of great prosperity for the region, with the construction of numerous castles, churches and abbeys. Medieval towns, such as Le Puy-en-Velay, Thiers and Clermont-Ferrand, bear witness to the religious and economic importance of the region at that time.

The Renaissance brought an artistic and architectural renewal to Auvergne-Rhône-Alpes. Lyon became a cultural and intellectual center, attracting artists, writers and scholars. The city is still famous today for its traboules, covered passages typical of this era, and its private mansions.

Culture and Traditions

Cultural life

Auvergne-Rhône-Alpes is a hotbed of creativity and culture, with a vibrant arts scene and a rich tradition of festivals and events. Lyon, the regional capital, is known for its internationally renowned festivals, such as the Fête des Lumières, the Nuits de Fourvière and the Festival Lumière.

Music festivals, such as Jazz à Vienne, the Berlioz Festival in La Côte-Saint-André and the Chaise-Dieu Music Festival, attract artists and spectators from around the world. The region is also famous for its tableware and crafts. Local markets, fairs and flea markets are opportunities to discover and purchase unique artisanal products, such as cutlery from Thiers, pottery from Saint-Uze and textiles from Ardèche.

Gastronomy and Local Products

The gastronomy of Auvergne-Rhône-Alpes is one of the most renowned in France, highlighting local products and culinary traditions. The region is particularly famous for its cheeses, charcuterie, wines and local specialties.

The region's cheeses, such as Saint-Nectaire, Bleu d'Auvergne, Reblochon, Beaufort and Comté, are appreciated for their unique flavor and exceptional quality. Each cheese has its own history, manufacturing techniques and taste characteristics.

Cold meats, such as Morteau sausage, Auvergne ham and Lyon rosette, are essential in regional cuisine. The region is also renowned for its wines, with prestigious appellations such as Burgundy wines, Savoie wines, Côtes du Rhône and Beaujolais.

Iconic dishes of the region include Savoyard fondue, tartiflette, gratin dauphinois, Auvergne stew and quenelle Lyonnaise. Farmers' markets, Michelin-starred restaurants and traditional inns offer a variety of culinary delights to satisfy all tastes.

Local Festivals and Traditions

The Auvergne-Rhône-Alpes region is rich in festivals and traditions, which bear witness to its history and culture. Village festivals, agricultural fairs and folk festivals are opportunities to celebrate local customs and continue traditions.

The harvest festivals, in particular, are a highlight of regional life. Every fall, the vineyards are filled with grape pickers, who harvest the grapes by hand. The harvest is followed by parties and celebrations, with wine tastings, festive meals and musical entertainment.

Christmas markets, such as those in Lyon, Grenoble and Annecy, are also popular events, attracting visitors from across the region. The markets offer a variety of artisanal products, culinary specialties and gifts, creating a festive and warm atmosphere.

Economy and Innovation

Tourism

Tourism is one of the pillars of the economy of Auvergne-Rhône-Alpes, attracting millions of visitors from all over the world each year. The diversity of landscapes, cultural richness and historical heritage are all assets that make this region a popular destination.

The region's tourist infrastructure is of high quality, with a diverse range of accommodation, starred restaurants, wellness centers and leisure activities. The airports of Lyon, Grenoble and Clermont-Ferrand, as well as rail and road links, facilitate access to the region. Sustainable and responsible tourism is also encouraged, with initiatives aimed at preserving the environment and promoting local heritage.

Agriculture and Local Products

Agriculture plays an essential role in the economy of the Auvergne-Rhône-Alpes region, with varied and quality production. Vineyards, cattle and sheep breeding, cereal crops and cheese production are among the main agricultural activities.

Agricultural products, such as wine, cheese, meat, cereals and fruits, are renowned for their excellence and diversity. Farmers' markets, agricultural cooperatives and short circuits promote the marketing of local products and support the rural economy.

Quality labels, such as the AOC (Appellation d'Origine Contrôlée) and the IGP (Protected Geographical Indication), guarantee the authenticity and quality of local products. Visitors can discover these products during tastings, farm tours and food festivals.

Industry and Innovation

The Auvergne-Rhône-Alpes region is also a hub of innovation and industrial development, with varied sectors such as aeronautics, agri-food, metallurgy, the pharmaceutical industry and renewable energies. Competitiveness clusters, such as Lyonbiopôle (health) and Minalogic (micro-nanotechnologies and software), promote innovation and collaboration between economic and scientific players.

Transportation infrastructure, such as highways, high-speed train lines and seaports, supports the region's economic development. The proximity of Italy and Switzerland and the presence of large metropolises such as Lyon and Grenoble facilitate commercial exchanges and international collaborations. The Auvergne-Rhône-Alpes region is a key player in the French economy, contributing to its dynamism and international influence.

Conclusion

The Auvergne-Rhône-Alpes region is an exceptional destination, rich in history, culture and varied landscapes. Whether to enjoy the snow-capped peaks of the Alps, explore the volcanoes of Auvergne, discover the prestigious vineyards or savor the local gastronomy, there is something for everyone.

The Relais & Châteaux of the Auvergne-Rhône-Alpes region capture the essence of this diversity and offer their guests unforgettable experiences, combining luxury, comfort and authenticity. Each establishment, with its enchanting setting, warm welcome, exceptional gastronomy and enriching activities, offers total immersion in the French art of living.

By discovering the Relais & Châteaux of Auvergne-Rhône-Alpes, you will be transported into a world where every detail is designed to delight the senses and create lasting memories. This chapter presented a detailed overview of the region, integrating geographical, historical, cultural and economic aspects to provide a comprehensive understanding of this unique destination.

- History and Heritage

Auvergne-Rhône-Alpes is a region rich in history and heritage, where each town and village tells a unique story. From Roman remains to medieval castles, from Romanesque churches to modern buildings, the region offers an incredible diversity of monuments and historical sites. In this chapter, we will explore key moments in the history of Auvergne-Rhône-Alpes, its iconic monuments and its cultural contributions.

The First Civilizations

Antiquity and the Romans

The history of Auvergne-Rhône-Alpes dates back to prehistory, with sites such as the ornate caves of Chauvet and Pech Merle, home to cave paintings dating back over 30,000 years. These works of art demonstrate the skill and creativity of the region's first inhabitants.

The Romans left an indelible mark on the region. Lyon (Lugdunum), founded in 43 BC. BC, became the capital of Gaul and a major administrative, commercial and cultural center. The Roman remains of Lyon, such as the ancient theater, the thermal baths and the aqueduct, are still visible today and testify to the importance of the city at that time. Vienna, another important Roman city, also has remarkable monuments such as the Temple of Augustus and Livia and the ancient theater.

The Celtic and Gaulish Peoples

Before the arrival of the Romans, the region was inhabited by Celtic and Gallic peoples. The Arverni, one of the most powerful Gallic tribes, occupied the territory of present-day Auvergne. Vercingetorix, the famous Arverni leader, led the resistance against the Romans at the Battle of Alesia in 52 BC. The archaeological sites of Gergovie and Corent offer a fascinating insight into Gallic civilization and its heritage.

The Middle Ages: Castles and Churches

Medieval Castles

The Middle Ages were a period of great prosperity and development for Auvergne-Rhône-Alpes. Many castles were built to protect territories and assert the power of local lords. Among the region's most iconic castles are Château de Murol, perched on an extinct volcano in Auvergne, and Château de Montrottier, with its imposing towers and collections of weapons and armor.

The region's fortresses bear witness to the advanced defense techniques of medieval times. The Château de Tournoël , dominating the Limagne plain, and the Château de Polignac, located on a volcanic peak, are remarkable examples of medieval military architecture.

Romanesque Churches and Abbeys

Auvergne-Rhône-Alpes is also famous for its Romanesque churches and abbeys, which bear witness to the religious importance of the region in the Middle Ages. Cluny Abbey, founded in the 10th century, is one of the largest monasteries in the medieval West and a major spiritual and intellectual center. Although the abbey was largely destroyed during the French Revolution, its impressive remains still attract visitors from around the world.

The Notre-Dame-du-Port basilica in Clermont-Ferrand, listed as a UNESCO world heritage site, is a masterpiece of Auvergne Romanesque architecture. Its mosaics, sculptures and ornate capitals are exceptionally beautiful. The Saint-Nectaire church, another remarkable example of Auvergne Romanesque art, is known for its frescoes and its historic capitals.

The Renaissance and the Classical Age

The Influence of the Renaissance

The Renaissance brought an artistic and architectural renewal to Auvergne-Rhône-Alpes. Lyon, in particular, became a major cultural and intellectual center, attracting artists, writers and scholars.

The traboules of Lyon, covered passages connecting the interior courtyards of buildings, are a unique testimony to the Renaissance architecture and the urban history of the city.

Renaissance mansions, such as the Hôtel de Gadagne in Lyon and the Château de Chamerolles in the Loiret, illustrate the influence of the Renaissance on regional architecture. These buildings, with their elegant facades, interior courtyards and gardens, reflect the taste for refinement and humanism of this era.

Monuments of the Classical Age

The Classical Age also saw the construction of many notable monuments and buildings in the region. The Palais de l'Isle in Annecy, a medieval castle transformed into a palace, is an iconic example of classical architecture. Its stone facades, turrets and moats make it a picturesque and unmissable site.

The city of Grenoble, with its Bastille Fort, is another example of classical architecture. The fort, built in the 17th century to protect the town, offers a breathtaking view of the Alps and the Grésivaudan valley. The Grenoble cable car, inaugurated in 1934, allows visitors to easily access the fort and enjoy the spectacular panoramas.

Modern and Contemporary Times

The French Revolution and the 19th Century

The French Revolution of 1789 brought significant changes to Auvergne-Rhône-Alpes. Feudal structures were abolished, the property of the Church and the nobility was confiscated and redistributed, and departments were created to replace the old provinces. Lyon, Grenoble and Clermont-Ferrand became important administrative centers.

The 19th century was a period of rapid transformation for the region, with industrialization and urbanization. Technological advances and the rise of railroads stimulated economic development. Lyon became a major industrial and commercial center, with industries such as silk, chemicals and metallurgy. The network of Lyon silk workers, or canuts, played a crucial role in the economic growth of the city.

World Wars and Reconstruction

The 20th century was marked by two world wars which had a profound impact on Auvergne-Rhône-Alpes. During the First World War, the region was an important production and logistics center for the war effort. Soldiers from the region participated in fighting on the Western Front, and many memorials were erected in their honor.

The Second World War brought new challenges, with the German occupation and the Resistance. Lyon became an important center of the French Resistance, with heroic figures such as Jean Moulin, head of the National Council of the Resistance. Cities in the region, such as Annecy and Grenoble, were bombed, and many historic buildings were damaged or destroyed.

After the war, the region undertook a period of reconstruction and modernization. Infrastructure was rebuilt, cities renovated and industries revitalized. Tourism became a key sector of the economy, attracting visitors from around the world to discover the historical and cultural treasures of the region.

Cultural and Architectural Heritage

UNESCO Sites

Auvergne-Rhône-Alpes has several UNESCO World Heritage sites, which bear witness to the richness of its cultural and architectural heritage. Among them, we find:

- Lyon, historic site: Listed in 1998, the historic center of Lyon is an exceptional example of town planning and architecture, with its traboules, private mansions and public squares.
- The Routes of Saint-Jacques-de-Compostelle: Several sites in Auvergne-Rhône-Alpes are part of the pilgrimage routes leading to Saint-Jacques-de-Compostelle, such as the Notre-Dame-du-Port basilica in Clermont- Ferrand and the Saint-Nectaire church.
- The Chaîne des Puys tectonic hotspot - Limagne fault: Listed in 2018, this exceptional natural site in Auvergne illustrates the geological and tectonic processes which have shaped the volcanic landscape of the region.

Historical Monuments and Museums

Auvergne-Rhône-Alpes is home to numerous historical monuments and museums that tell the history of the region and highlight its cultural heritage. Among them, we find:

- The Musée des Confluences in Lyon: This museum of natural history, anthropology and civilizations, located at the confluence of the Rhône and the Saône, offers fascinating exhibitions on the evolution of humanity and the diversity of cultures .
- The Grenoble Museum: This art museum houses a rich collection of paintings, sculptures and drawings, ranging from the Middle Ages to the contemporary era. It is renowned for its works by masters such as Rubens, Delacroix, Gauguin and Picasso.
Quilliot Art Museum in Clermont-Ferrand: This museum presents art collections from the Middle Ages to the 20th century, with works by masters such as Philippe de Champaigne, Théodore Géricault and Jean-Auguste-Dominique Ingres.
- The Museum of the Resistance and Deportation of Isère in Grenoble: This museum traces the history of the Resistance in Isère during the Second World War, with exhibitions on resistance networks, the maquis and concentration camps .

Conclusion

Auvergne-Rhône-Alpes is a region rich in history and heritage, where every street corner, every village and every castle tells a unique story. From Roman remains to medieval fortifications, from Romanesque churches to modern buildings, the region offers an incredible diversity of monuments and historical sites.

The Relais & Châteaux of the Auvergne-Rhône-Alpes region capture the essence of this historical and cultural wealth, offering their guests unforgettable experiences. Each establishment, with its enchanting setting, warm welcome, exceptional gastronomy and enriching activities, offers total immersion in the history and heritage of the region.

By discovering the Relais & Châteaux of Auvergne-Rhône-Alpes, you will be transported into a world where every detail is designed to delight the senses and create lasting memories. This chapter explored the many facets of the region's history and heritage, revealing how each era helped shape this unique and fascinating destination.

- Gastronomy and Wine

The Auvergne-Rhône-Alpes region, located in east-central France, is a true land of gastronomy and wine. Thanks to its exceptional local products, its ancestral culinary traditions and its prestigious vineyards, this region offers an unrivaled culinary experience. In this chapter, we will explore the gastronomic aspects of the region in detail, highlighting the local produce, iconic dishes, renowned chefs, starred restaurants and wines that this region is famous for.

The Roots of Regional Gastronomy

Local Products

Auvergne-Rhône-Alpes is a region rich in local products, which constitute the basis of its renowned cuisine. Among the most emblematic products, we find:

- Cheeses: The region is famous for its numerous cheeses, each having its own character and manufacturing techniques. Among the most famous, we find Saint-Nectaire, Bleu d'Auvergne, Reblochon, Beaufort , Comté and Cantal. These cheeses are often used in traditional dishes or tasted alone to fully appreciate their flavors.
- Charcuteries: Morteau and Montbéliard sausages, Auvergne ham, Lyon rosette and Savoie diots are charcuterie specialties of the region. They are often accompanied by potatoes, lentils or sauerkraut.
- Truffles: The black Drôme truffle, also called "black diamond", is a precious and aromatic mushroom that grows in the region's forests. It is used to flavor dishes such as omelettes, pastas and risottos.
- Fruits and Vegetables: Potatoes from Île de Ré, green lentils from Puy, chestnuts from Ardèche and blueberries from the mountains are flagship products of the region. They are often used in traditional dishes or made into jams, soups and desserts.
- Meat and Poultry: The region is renowned for its quality meats, such as Charolais beef, Sisteron lamb and Bresse chicken. These meats are often grilled, roasted or simmered in traditional dishes.

Emblematic Dishes of Regional Cuisine

The Savoyard Fondue

Savoyard fondue is one of the most emblematic dishes of Alpine cuisine. It is prepared by melting several types of cheese (usually Beaufort , Emmental and Comté) in white wine and garlic, then dipping pieces of bread into it using long forks. Fondue is often accompanied by cold meats and pickles.

Raclette

Raclette is another traditional Alpine dish, made with the cheese of the same name. The cheese is melted and scraped over potatoes, pickles and onions, often accompanied by a variety of cold cuts. This convivial dish is especially popular during the winter months.

Tartiflette

Tartiflette is a gratin of potatoes, bacon, onions and reblochon, a pressed Savoyard cheese. This comforting and generous dish is ideal for cold winter days. It is often served with a green salad to balance the rich, creamy flavors.

The potato gratin

Gratin dauphinois is a traditional dish from the Dauphiné region, prepared with thinly sliced potatoes, crème fraîche, milk, garlic and butter. Everything is cooked slowly in the oven until the potatoes are tender and the top is golden. This dish often accompanies roast meats or fish.

The Auvergne Potée

Auvergne stew is a rustic stew made with pork (shank, blade or breast), cabbage, potatoes, carrots and turnips. This slow-cooked dish is rich and flavorful, ideal for cold winter days. It is often accompanied by country bread and mustard.

Star Chefs and Restaurants

The Pioneers of Regional Haute Cuisine

Auvergne-Rhône-Alpes has always been a hotbed of culinary creativity, attracting talented chefs who have been able to highlight local products and culinary traditions. Among the pioneers of regional haute cuisine is Paul Bocuse, considered one of the greatest French chefs of all time. His restaurant, L'Auberge du Pont de Collonges near Lyon, has maintained three Michelin stars for more than 50 years.

Contemporary Chefs

Today, the region continues to attract renowned chefs, who continue the tradition of haute cuisine while innovating and experimenting with new flavors. Among the most famous contemporary chefs, we find:

- Anne-Sophie Pic: Chef of the Maison Pic restaurant in Valence, Anne-Sophie Pic is the only woman in France to hold three Michelin stars. Its cuisine, refined and inventive, highlights local and seasonal products.
- Emmanuel Renaut: Chef of the Flocons de Sel restaurant in Megève, Emmanuel Renaut offers inventive and elegant cuisine, highlighting local and seasonal products. Its restaurant has been awarded three Michelin stars.
- Laurent Petit: Chef at Clos des Sens in Annecy, Laurent Petit offers creative cuisine that respects local products. Its restaurant has been awarded three Michelin stars.

Star Restaurants

Auvergne-Rhône-Alpes is home to numerous Michelin-starred restaurants, each offering a unique and unforgettable culinary experience. Among the most famous, we find:

- L'Auberge du Pont de Collonges in Collonges-au-Mont-d'Or: The restaurant of the legendary Paul Bocuse, famous for his traditional French cuisine and impeccable service. Although Paul Bocuse has passed away, his culinary legacy lives on through his establishment.
- Maison Pic in Valence: Anne-Sophie Pic's restaurant, offering inventive and refined cuisine. The tasting menu offers dishes such as blue lobster, royal langoustine and Racan pigeon.
- Flocons de Sel in Megève: Emmanuel Renaut's restaurant, offering inventive and elegant cuisine. The tasting menu offers dishes such as duck foie gras, beef fillet and lake fish.
- Le Clos des Sens in Annecy: Laurent Petit's restaurant, offering creative cuisine that respects local products. The tasting menu offers dishes such as lake pike, river trout and Bresse pigeon.

Wines of Auvergne-Rhône-Alpes

Beaujolais Wines

The Beaujolais region, located north of Lyon, is famous for its fruity and light red wines, made mainly from the Gamay grape variety. Beaujolais wines are divided into several appellations, the best known of which are:

- Beaujolais Nouveau: A young and fruity wine, marketed each year on the third Thursday of November. It is celebrated with festivities around the world.
- Beaujolais Villages: Wines of better quality than Beaujolais Nouveau, from specific villages in the region.
- Les Crus du Beaujolais: Ten superior quality wines, each with its own character and taste characteristics. Among the most famous, we find Morgon, Fleurie, Moulin-à-Vent and Brouilly.

Wines of the Rhône Valley

The Rhône Valley is one of the oldest wine regions in France, famous for its powerful red wines and aromatic white wines. The region is divided into two parts: the north and the south of the Rhône valley. The main appellations of the Rhône valley are:

- Côte-Rôtie: Located in the north of the Rhône valley, this appellation produces powerful and tannic red wines, made mainly from the Syrah grape variety.
- Hermitage: Also located in the north, this appellation is famous for its rich and complex red wines, as well as its elegant white wines, made from the Marsanne and Roussanne grape varieties.
- Châteauneuf-du-Pape: Located in the south of the Rhône valley, this appellation produces full-bodied and spicy red wines, made mainly from the Grenache, Syrah and Mourvèdre grape varieties.
- Gigondas: Also located in the south, this appellation produces robust and fruity red wines, made mainly from Grenache, Syrah and Mourvèdre grape varieties.

Savoie Wines

The Savoie region, located in the Alps, is known for its fresh and aromatic white wines, made primarily from the Jacquère, Altesse and Roussanne grape varieties. The main appellations of Savoie are:

- Savoie wine: An appellation which encompasses a wide variety of white, red and rosé wines, produced throughout the region.
- Roussette de Savoie: A specific appellation for white wines made from the Altesse grape variety, offering floral and fruity aromas.
- Crémant de Savoie: A sparkling wine made using the traditional method, offering fine bubbles and pleasant freshness.

Oenological Experiences

Wine Tastings

Relais & Châteaux in the Auvergne-Rhône-Alpes region often offer unique wine experiences for their guests. From private tastings to vineyard visits, these experiences allow you to discover the region's wines and learn the secrets of viticulture in Beaujolais, the Rhône valley and Savoie.

Guests can participate in tasting workshops, led by expert sommeliers, to learn how to identify the aromas and flavors of regional wines. Guided tours of the wine estates allow you to discover the winemaking processes, meet the winemakers and taste wines directly from the source.

Food and Wine Pairings

The Relais & Châteaux also offer food and wine pairings, allowing you to savor Auvergne-Rhône-Alpes wines in harmony with local cuisine. These pairings highlight the flavors of the dishes and wines, providing a complete and unforgettable gastronomic experience.

Chefs from Michelin-starred restaurants collaborate with sommeliers to create tasting menus that highlight the region's wines. Each dish is carefully paired with a wine, allowing guests to discover new combinations of flavors and textures.

Conclusion

The Auvergne-Rhône-Alpes region is a true land of gastronomy and wine, offering unparalleled richness and diversity. Regional cuisine, with its authentic flavors and quality local products, is a pillar of the region's art of living. Wines from Beaujolais, the Rhône Valley and Savoie, renowned for their complexity and elegance, perfectly complement this culinary experience.

The Relais & Châteaux of the Auvergne-Rhône-Alpes region capture the essence of this gastronomic richness, offering their guests unique and unforgettable culinary and wine experiences. Each establishment, with its enchanting setting, warm welcome, exceptional gastronomy and enriching activities, offers total immersion in the French art of living.

By discovering the Relais & Châteaux of Auvergne-Rhône-Alpes, you will be transported into a world where every detail is designed to delight the senses and create lasting memories. This chapter explored the multiple facets of the region's gastronomy and wines, revealing how each element contributes to making this destination a true oasis of flavors and culinary pleasures.

2. Addresses and Descriptions

The Auvergne-Rhône-Alpes region is home to numerous Relais & Châteaux, each offering a unique experience combining luxury, comfort and regional charm. These establishments are spread throughout the region, from the Alpine mountains to the volcanoes of Auvergne, via the vineyards of Beaujolais and the Rhône valleys. In this chapter, we will explore some of the most prestigious addresses and describe in detail what makes them special.

Domaine des Hauts de Loire

History and Architecture

Located in the charming village of Onzain, Domaine des Hauts de Loire is an elegant 19th-century residence nestled in the heart of the Loire Valley. This castle, surrounded by 70 hectares of forests and vineyards, offers an enchanting and peaceful setting. The architecture of the estate reflects the classic style of the region's residences, with its stone facades, wooden shutters and slate roofs.

Culinary Offers

The gourmet restaurant at Domaine des Hauts de Loire, led by a Michelin-starred chef, offers inventive and refined cuisine, highlighting local and seasonal products. The tasting menu offers an exceptional culinary experience, with dishes such as "Roasted Farm Pigeon" and "Filet of Zander with White Butter". The carefully selected wine list highlights the great wines of the Loire Valley and other prestigious wine regions.

Activities and Services

Domaine des Hauts de Loire offers a range of activities for its guests, from relaxation to sport. Guests can enjoy the heated outdoor swimming pool, tennis court and fitness room. Guided tours of the surrounding vineyards and wine tastings are also organized. Guests can learn about the winemaking process, meet winemakers and taste wines straight from the source.

Codignat Castle

History and Architecture

Château de Codignat , located in Bort-l'Étang, near Clermont-Ferrand, is a magnificent 15th century medieval castle. Surrounded by vast gardens and forests, this castle offers a romantic and historic setting. The interiors are decorated with antique furniture, tapestries and works of art, creating a warm and refined ambiance.

Culinary Offers

Codignat 's gourmet restaurant , led by a talented chef, offers inventive and refined cuisine, highlighting local and seasonal products. The tasting menu offers an exceptional culinary experience, with dishes such as "Charolais Beef Filet" and "Duck with Orange". The carefully selected wine list highlights the great wines of Auvergne and other prestigious wine regions.

Activities and Services

Château de Codignat offers a range of activities for its guests, from relaxation to sport. Guests can enjoy the heated outdoor swimming pool, tennis court and fitness room. Guided excursions to explore Auvergne's volcanoes, medieval castles and surrounding villages are also organized.

Marie's Farms

History and Architecture

Les Fermes de Marie, located in Megève, is a set of traditional Savoyard farms transformed into a luxury hotel. This unique resort, surrounded by mountains and forests, offers an authentic and warm setting. The interiors are decorated with natural materials, wooden furniture and quality textiles, creating a cozy and elegant ambiance.

Culinary Offers

The Fermes de Marie gourmet restaurant, led by a starred chef, offers inventive and refined cuisine, highlighting local and seasonal products. The tasting menu offers an exceptional culinary experience, with dishes such as "Filet of Mountain Trout" and "Ravioles de Royans". The carefully selected wine list highlights the great wines of Savoie and other prestigious wine regions.

Activities and Services

Les Fermes de Marie offer a range of activities for their guests, from relaxation to sport. The hotel's spa offers a variety of wellness treatments, from massages to facials, performed with high-quality products. Guests can also enjoy the heated outdoor swimming pool, jacuzzi and fitness room. Guided excursions to explore the Alps mountains, ski slopes and surrounding villages are also organized.

Bagnols Castle

History and Architecture

Château de Bagnols, located in Beaujolais, is a magnificent 13th century medieval castle surrounded by vineyards and French gardens. This historic castle has been carefully restored to preserve its authentic character while providing first-rate modern comfort. The interiors are decorated with antique furniture, tapestries and works of art, creating a warm and refined ambiance.

Culinary Offers

The Château de Bagnols gourmet restaurant, led by a talented chef, offers inventive and refined cuisine, highlighting local and seasonal products. The tasting menu offers an exceptional culinary experience, with dishes such as "Pigeon de Bresse" and "Foie Gras de Canard". The carefully selected wine list highlights the great wines of Beaujolais and other prestigious wine regions.

Activities and Services

Château de Bagnols offers a range of activities for its guests, from relaxation to sport. Guests can enjoy the heated outdoor swimming pool, tennis court and fitness room. Guided tours of the surrounding vineyards and wine tastings are also organized, allowing guests to experience the winemaking process and taste wines directly from the source.

Hotel Les Barmes de l'Ours

History and Architecture

Hôtel Les Barmes de l'Ours, located in Val d'Isère, is an elegant mountain hotel offering a luxurious and comfortable setting. Nestled at the foot of the ski slopes, this hotel is ideal for winter sports enthusiasts. The interiors are decorated with natural materials, wooden furniture and quality textiles, creating a warm and elegant ambiance.

Culinary Offers

The gourmet restaurant at the Hotel Les Barmes de l'Ours, led by a starred chef, offers inventive and refined cuisine, highlighting local and seasonal products. The tasting menu offers an exceptional culinary experience, with dishes such as "Veal Fillet" and "Fontaine Salmon". The carefully selected wine list highlights the great wines of Savoie and other prestigious wine regions.

Activities and Services

Hôtel Les Barmes de l'Ours offers a range of activities for its guests, from relaxation to sport. The hotel's spa offers a variety of wellness treatments, from massages to facials, performed with high-quality products. Guests can also enjoy the heated indoor swimming pool, jacuzzi and fitness room. Guided excursions to explore the ski slopes, hiking trails and surrounding villages are also organized.

Conclusion

The Relais & Châteaux in Auvergne-Rhône-Alpes offer unique and unforgettable experiences, combining luxury, comfort and historical heritage. Each establishment, with its enchanting setting, warm welcome, exceptional gastronomy and enriching activities, offers total immersion in the French art of living. Whether for a romantic getaway, a peaceful retreat or a cultural exploration, the Relais & Châteaux of the Auvergne-Rhône-Alpes region are must-see destinations.

By discovering these exceptional establishments, you will be transported to a world where every detail is designed to delight the senses and create lasting memories. This chapter has presented a detailed overview of some of the most prestigious Relais & Châteaux in the region, offering a glimpse of the unique experience that awaits you in each of these enchanting locations.

- The Château de Bagnols

The Château de Bagnols, located in the heart of Beaujolais, is a medieval jewel offering a unique experience combining history, luxury and gastronomy. Surrounded by vineyards and French gardens, this 13th century castle is a living testimony to the architecture and heritage of the Auvergne-Rhône-Alpes region. In this chapter, we will explore the history and architecture of Château de Bagnols, its culinary offerings, the activities and services offered, and the unique experiences it offers.

History and Architecture

A Medieval Heritage

The Château de Bagnols was built in 1217 by Guichard d'Oingt, a powerful feudal lord. Over the centuries, the castle has gone through many historical periods, each leaving its mark on the architecture and decoration. Transformed into a luxury residence, it has been carefully restored to preserve its authentic character while offering first-rate modern comfort.

The architecture of the castle is typical of medieval fortresses, with its moat, imposing towers and thick walls of golden Beaujolais stone. The interiors are decorated with antique furniture, tapestries and works of art, creating a warm and refined ambiance.

A Careful Restoration

The interiors of Château de Bagnols reflect its rich heritage, with decorative elements ranging from the Renaissance to the 18th century. Each room and suite is unique, offering breathtaking views of the gardens, vineyards or interior courtyard. The bathrooms, equipped with marble bathtubs and walk-in showers, offer optimal comfort for relaxing and recharging your batteries.

Culinary Offers

The Gourmet Restaurant

The Château de Bagnols gourmet restaurant, led by a talented chef, offers inventive and refined cuisine, highlighting local and seasonal products. The tasting menu offers an exceptional culinary experience, with dishes such as "Roasted Bresse Pigeon with Sweet Spices" and "Duck Foie Gras in Terrine". The carefully selected wine list highlights the great wines of Beaujolais and other prestigious wine regions.

The restaurant's setting matches its cuisine, with elegantly decorated dining rooms, stone fireplaces and views of the gardens and vineyards. Guests can also dine al fresco on the terrace, enjoying the tranquility and beauty of the natural surroundings.

Regional Cuisine

The cuisine at Château de Bagnols places particular emphasis on local products, with dishes inspired by the culinary traditions of Beaujolais and the Auvergne-Rhône-Alpes region. Menus change regularly to reflect the seasons and local harvests. Customers can taste specialties such as the "Tarte aux Pralines Roses" and the "Gratin Dauphinois", accompanied by carefully selected wines to enhance each dish.

Activities and Services

The Spa and Wellness Treatments

Château de Bagnols offers a range of wellness treatments for its guests, ranging from massages to facial treatments, carried out with high quality products. The spa, located in a peaceful and luxurious setting, is a place of rest and relaxation, perfect for recharging your batteries after a day exploring the vineyards.

Professional therapists use advanced techniques and luxury products to ensure optimal results and a luxurious experience. Guests can also enjoy the heated outdoor swimming pool, jacuzzi, sauna and steam room to complete their relaxation experience.

Outdoor activities

The gardens and grounds of Château de Bagnols are perfect for leisurely walks, meditation sessions or outdoor yoga sessions. Guests can also enjoy the heated outdoor swimming pool and fitness room.

The hotel also offers guided excursions to explore the surrounding vineyards and tourist sites of Beaujolais. Guests can discover prestigious wine châteaux, participate in wine tastings and learn the secrets of regional viticulture. Bicycles are also available to explore the region in an ecological and active way.

Cultural Activities and Experiences

Château de Bagnols regularly organizes cultural events and unique experiences for its guests. Private concerts, literary readings and art exhibitions are often organized in the establishment's lounges or gardens. These events offer immersion in the local cultural scene and allow guests to meet artists, writers and musicians.

Guests can also participate in cooking workshops, baking classes and chocolate tastings, led by local chefs. These workshops offer an opportunity to learn Beaujolais cooking techniques and taste delicious creations. Château de Bagnols also offers yoga and meditation classes, led by qualified instructors, in the hotel's gardens or wellness areas.

Special Events and Unique Experiences

Weddings and Receptions

Château de Bagnols is an ideal venue for organizing intimate weddings and private receptions. The property's gardens and lounges provide a romantic and elegant setting for ceremonies and receptions. Hotel staff work closely with couples to create tailor-made events, taking into account every detail, from decor to personalized menus.

The hotel's chefs create wedding menus that reflect the tastes and preferences of the bride and groom, using seasonal ingredients and local produce. The professional and attentive service teams ensure that every event goes off without a hitch. Couples can also enjoy luxurious suites for their wedding night, with special services such as massages, in-room breakfasts and welcome gifts.

Seminars and Business Meetings

The Château de Bagnols offers an exceptional setting for seminars, conferences and business meetings. The property's private lounges, equipped with the latest technology, offer flexible spaces for events of different sizes. Hotel teams work with event organizers to create tailor-made programs, including coffee breaks, business lunches and dinners.

Team-building activities and excursions can also be organized to strengthen team cohesion and provide moments of relaxation outside of work sessions. Guests can take advantage of the hotel's wellness facilities to unwind after a day of meetings, with spa treatments, yoga sessions and massages.

Unique Experiences

Château de Bagnols offers unique experiences to make each stay memorable. These include private dinners in exclusive locations within the establishment, such as the library or gardens, offering an intimate and romantic atmosphere. Guests can also participate in wine tasting workshops, led by expert sommeliers, to discover the secrets of Beaujolais and Bordeaux region wines.

Wellness getaways are also available, including personalized relaxation and relaxation programs, spa treatments, yoga and meditation sessions, as well as healthy and nutritious meals. These programs are designed to help clients recharge their batteries and regain physical and mental balance.

Seasonal and Thematic Offers

Château de Bagnols regularly offers seasonal and thematic offers to enrich its customers' experience. At Christmas, the establishment is decked out in festive decorations and offers special menus, cookie decorating workshops and Christmas market visits. In summer, gourmet picnics can be organized in the gardens or on the terraces.

Romantic getaways are also offered, including candlelit dinners, duo massages and horse-drawn carriage rides in the surrounding area. For culture lovers, special packages including tickets for exhibitions, shows and concerts are available, offering complete immersion in the cultural life of the region.

Conclusion

The Château de Bagnols is much more than just a luxury hotel; it is a destination in itself, offering a unique and unforgettable experience in the heart of the magnificent Beaujolais region. With its rich history, impressive architecture, refined culinary offerings and a variety of activities and services, this establishment is the ideal place to relax, recharge and discover the French art of living.

Whether for a romantic getaway, a wellness retreat, an intimate wedding or a business meeting, Château de Bagnols promises an exceptional experience, marked by luxury, comfort and elegance. Guests leave with unforgettable memories, enriched by the unique culture, gastronomy and hospitality of this emblematic establishment of the Auvergne-Rhône-Alpes region.

- Le Clos des Sens

Le Clos des Sens, located in Annecy-le-Vieux, is an exceptional Relais & Châteaux that embodies the essence of luxury, gastronomy and refinement. Nestled in the heart of the Alps mountains and overlooking Lake Annecy, this establishment offers a unique experience where every detail is designed to delight the senses. In this chapter, we will explore the history and architecture of Clos des Sens, its culinary offerings, the activities and services offered, and the unique experiences it offers.

History and Architecture

A Story of Passion

Le Clos des Sens was founded by Laurent Petit, a passionate chef who transformed a bourgeois house into a sanctuary of haute cuisine. Since its opening, Clos des Sens has gained international recognition for its inventive cuisine and warm hospitality. Laurent Petit has created a place where the art of living and cuisine meet, offering his customers an unforgettable experience.

Contemporary and Elegant Architecture

The architecture of Clos des Sens combines the charm of the old and the modernity of contemporary design. The house, originally built in the early 20th century, has been tastefully renovated to provide a luxurious and elegant setting. Interiors are decorated with natural materials, custom furniture and artwork, creating a warm and sophisticated ambiance.

The rooms and suites are carefully furnished, offering breathtaking views of Lake Annecy or the hotel gardens. Each room is unique, with distinctive design elements and modern amenities to ensure optimal comfort. The bathrooms, fitted with marble bathtubs and walk-in showers, provide a luxurious setting in which to relax and rejuvenate.

Culinary Offers

The Gourmet Restaurant

The Clos des Sens restaurant, led by chef Laurent Petit, offers inventive and refined cuisine, highlighting local and seasonal products. Laurent Petit, three-starred in the Michelin guide, is recognized for his creative approach and technical mastery. The tasting menu offers an exceptional culinary experience, with dishes such as "Filet de Féra du Lac d'Annecy" and "Agneau de Sisteron en Coûte de Sel".

The restaurant's setting matches its cuisine, with an elegantly decorated dining room, tables spaced for maximum privacy, and panoramic views of the lake and mountains. Guests can also dine al fresco on the terrace, enjoying the beauty of the natural surroundings.

Locavore Cuisine

The cuisine at Clos des Sens places particular emphasis on local products, with a locavore philosophy that favors fresh, seasonal ingredients from local producers. Menus change regularly to reflect the seasons and local harvests. Guests can taste specialties such as "Roasted Savoie Cepe" and "Chocolat Grand Cru Valrhona", accompanied by carefully selected wines to enhance each dish.

The wine list

The Clos des Sens wine list is carefully selected to offer an exceptional wine experience. Sommeliers are available to advise customers and help them choose the wines that will perfectly accompany their meal. The selection highlights the great wines of the Auvergne-Rhône-Alpes region, as well as wines from other prestigious wine-growing regions in France and around the world.

Activities and Services

The Spa and Wellness Treatments

Le Clos des Sens offers a range of wellness treatments for its customers, ranging from massages to facial treatments, carried out with high quality products. The spa, located in a peaceful and luxurious setting, is a place of rest and relaxation, perfect for recharging your batteries after a day exploring the region.

Professional therapists use advanced techniques and luxury products to ensure optimal results and a luxurious experience. Guests can also enjoy the heated outdoor swimming pool, jacuzzi, sauna and steam room to complete their relaxation experience.

Outdoor activities

The gardens and grounds of Clos des Sens are perfect for leisurely walks, meditation sessions or outdoor yoga sessions. Guests can also enjoy the heated outdoor swimming pool and fitness room.

The hotel also offers guided excursions to explore the surroundings of Lake Annecy and the Alps mountains. Guests can discover scenic hiking trails, renowned ski slopes and charming alpine villages. Bicycles are also available to explore the region in an ecological and active way.

Cultural Activities and Experiences

Le Clos des Sens regularly organizes cultural events and unique experiences for its guests. Private concerts, literary readings and art exhibitions are often organized in the establishment's lounges or gardens. These events offer immersion in the local cultural scene and allow guests to meet artists, writers and musicians.

Guests can also participate in cooking workshops, baking classes and chocolate tastings, led by local chefs. These workshops offer an opportunity to learn regional cooking techniques and taste delicious creations. Le Clos des Sens also offers yoga and meditation classes, led by qualified instructors, in the hotel's gardens or wellness areas.

Special Events and Unique Experiences

Weddings and Receptions

Le Clos des Sens is an ideal venue for organizing intimate weddings and private receptions. The property's gardens and lounges provide a romantic and elegant setting for ceremonies and receptions. Hotel staff work closely with couples to create tailor-made events, taking into account every detail, from decor to personalized menus.

The hotel's chefs create wedding menus that reflect the tastes and preferences of the bride and groom, using seasonal ingredients and local produce. The professional and attentive service teams ensure that every event goes off without a hitch. Couples can also enjoy luxurious suites for their wedding night, with special services such as massages, in-room breakfasts and welcome gifts.

Seminars and Business Meetings

Le Clos des Sens offers an exceptional setting for seminars, conferences and business meetings. The property's private lounges, equipped with the latest technology, offer flexible spaces for events of different sizes. Hotel teams work with event organizers to create tailor-made programs, including coffee breaks, business lunches and dinners.

Team-building activities and excursions can also be organized to strengthen team cohesion and provide moments of relaxation outside of work sessions. Guests can take advantage of the hotel's wellness facilities to unwind after a day of meetings, with spa treatments, yoga sessions and massages.

Unique Experiences

Le Clos des Sens offers unique experiences to make each stay memorable. These include private dinners in exclusive locations within the establishment, such as the library or gardens, offering an intimate and romantic atmosphere. Guests can also participate in wine tasting workshops, led by expert sommeliers, to discover the secrets of wines from the region and France.

Wellness getaways are also available, including personalized relaxation and relaxation programs, spa treatments, yoga and meditation sessions, as well as healthy and nutritious meals. These programs are designed to help clients recharge their batteries and regain physical and mental balance.

Seasonal and Thematic Offers

Le Clos des Sens regularly offers seasonal and thematic offers to enrich its customers' experience. At Christmas, the establishment is decked out in festive decorations and offers special menus, cookie decorating workshops and Christmas market visits. In summer, gourmet picnics can be organized in the gardens or on the terraces.

Romantic getaways are also offered, including candlelit dinners, duo massages and horse-drawn carriage rides in the surrounding area. For culture lovers, special packages including tickets for exhibitions, shows and concerts are available, offering complete immersion in the cultural life of the region.

Conclusion

Le Clos des Sens is much more than just a luxury hotel; it is a destination in itself, offering a unique and unforgettable experience in the heart of the magnificent Annecy region. With its rich history, impressive architecture, refined culinary offerings and a variety of activities and services, this establishment is the ideal place to relax, recharge and discover the French art of living.

Whether for a romantic getaway, a wellness retreat, an intimate wedding or a business meeting, Clos des Sens promises an exceptional experience, marked by luxury, comfort and elegance. Guests leave with unforgettable memories, enriched by the unique culture, gastronomy and hospitality of this emblematic establishment of the Auvergne-Rhône-Alpes region.

- Hotel & Spa Le Doge

Located in the heart of the city of Casablanca in Morocco, Hotel & Spa Le Doge is an iconic establishment that embodies the elegance and charm of Art Deco. This luxury hotel, a member of the Relais & Châteaux chain, offers a unique experience where refinement and comfort are guaranteed. In this chapter, we will explore the history and architecture of Hotel & Spa Le Doge, its culinary offerings, the activities and services offered, and the unique experiences it offers.

History and Architecture

An Art Deco Heritage

Hotel & Spa Le Doge is a magnificent villa built in the 1930s by an Italian entrepreneur for his wife. The hotel's Art Deco architecture is a testament to Casablanca's golden age, a time when the city was a cultural and economic crossroads. The villa has been carefully restored to preserve its old-world charm while providing top-notch modern comfort.

The architecture of Hotel & Spa Le Doge reflects the distinctive style of Art Deco, with its geometric facades, wrought iron balconies and richly decorated interiors. Every detail, from the crystal chandeliers to the wall murals, has been designed to create an elegant and sophisticated ambiance.

A Careful Restoration

The interiors of Hôtel & Spa Le Doge are decorated with antique furniture, works of art and quality textiles, creating a warm and refined atmosphere. Each room and suite is unique, with distinctive design elements and modern amenities to ensure optimal comfort. The bathrooms, fitted with marble bathtubs and walk-in showers, provide a luxurious setting in which to relax and rejuvenate.

Culinary Offers

The Gourmet Restaurant

The gourmet restaurant at the Hotel & Spa Le Doge, led by a talented chef, offers inventive and refined cuisine, highlighting local and seasonal products. The tasting menu offers an exceptional culinary experience, with dishes such as "Chicken Tagine with Preserved Lemons" and "Beef Fillet with Moroccan Spices". The carefully selected wine list highlights the great Moroccan wines and other prestigious wine regions.

The restaurant's setting matches its cuisine, with an elegantly decorated dining room, tables spaced for maximum privacy, and views of the gardens. Guests can also dine al fresco on the terrace, enjoying the tranquility and beauty of the natural surroundings.

Fusion Cuisine

The cuisine at Hôtel & Spa Le Doge places particular emphasis on local products, with a fusion of Moroccan and Mediterranean flavors. Menus change regularly to reflect the seasons and local harvests. Guests can enjoy specialties such as "Couscous Royal" and "Pastilla au Pigeon", accompanied by carefully selected wines to enhance each dish.

Activities and Services

The Spa and Wellness Treatments

Hotel & Spa Le Doge offers a range of wellness treatments for its guests, from massages to facials, performed with high quality products. The spa, located in a peaceful and luxurious setting, is a place of rest and relaxation, perfect for recharging your batteries after a day exploring Casablanca.

Professional therapists use advanced techniques and luxury products to ensure optimal results and a luxurious experience. Guests can also enjoy the traditional hammam, jacuzzi and fitness room to complete their relaxation experience.

Outdoor activities

The gardens and terraces of Hôtel & Spa Le Doge are perfect for leisurely walks, meditation sessions or outdoor yoga sessions. Guests can also enjoy the heated outdoor swimming pool and fitness room.

The hotel also offers guided excursions to explore the surrounding areas of Casablanca. Guests can discover historic sites, local markets and beautiful beaches. Bicycles are also available to explore the city in an ecological and active way.

Cultural Activities and Experiences

Hôtel & Spa Le Doge regularly organizes cultural events and unique experiences for its guests. Private concerts, literary readings and art exhibitions are often organized in the establishment's lounges or gardens. These events offer immersion in the local cultural scene and allow guests to meet artists, writers and musicians.

Guests can also participate in cooking workshops, baking classes and tea tastings, led by local chefs. These workshops provide an opportunity to learn Moroccan cooking techniques and taste delicious creations. Hotel & Spa Le Doge also offers yoga and meditation classes, led by qualified instructors, in the hotel's gardens or wellness areas.

Special Events and Unique Experiences

Weddings and Receptions

Hotel & Spa Le Doge is an ideal venue for intimate weddings and private receptions. The property's gardens and lounges provide a romantic and elegant setting for ceremonies and receptions. Hotel staff work closely with couples to create tailor-made events, taking into account every detail, from decor to personalized menus.

The hotel's chefs create wedding menus that reflect the tastes and preferences of the bride and groom, using seasonal ingredients and local produce. The professional and attentive service teams ensure that every event goes off without a hitch. Couples can also enjoy luxurious suites for their wedding night, with special services such as massages, in-room breakfasts and welcome gifts.

Seminars and Business Meetings

The Hotel & Spa Le Doge offers an exceptional setting for seminars, conferences and business meetings. The property's private lounges, equipped with the latest technology, offer flexible spaces for events of different sizes. Hotel teams work with event organizers to create tailor-made programs, including coffee breaks, business lunches and dinners.

Team-building activities and excursions can also be organized to strengthen team cohesion and provide moments of relaxation outside of work sessions. Guests can take advantage of the hotel's wellness facilities to unwind after a day of meetings, with spa treatments, yoga sessions and massages.

Unique Experiences

Hôtel & Spa Le Doge offers unique experiences to make every stay memorable. These include private dinners in exclusive locations within the establishment, such as the library or gardens, offering an intimate and romantic atmosphere. Guests can also participate in wine tasting workshops, led by expert sommeliers, to discover the secrets of Moroccan and regional wines.

Wellness getaways are also available, including personalized relaxation and relaxation programs, spa treatments, yoga and meditation sessions, as well as healthy and nutritious meals. These programs are designed to help clients recharge their batteries and regain physical and mental balance.

Seasonal and Thematic Offers

Hôtel & Spa Le Doge regularly offers seasonal and thematic offers to enrich its guests' experience. At Christmas, the establishment is decked out in festive decorations and offers special menus, cookie decorating workshops and Christmas market visits. In summer, gourmet picnics can be organized in the gardens or on the terraces.

Romantic getaways are also offered, including candlelit dinners, duo massages and horse-drawn carriage rides in the surrounding area. For culture lovers, special packages including tickets for exhibitions, shows and concerts are available, offering complete immersion in the cultural life of the region.

Conclusion

Hotel & Spa Le Doge is much more than just a luxury hotel; it is a destination in itself, offering a unique and unforgettable experience in the heart of the magnificent city of Casablanca. With its rich history, impressive architecture, fine culinary offerings and a variety of activities and services, this establishment is the ideal place to relax, recharge and discover the Moroccan art of living.

Whether for a romantic getaway, a wellness retreat, an intimate wedding or a business meeting, Hotel & Spa Le Doge promises an exceptional experience, marked by luxury, comfort and elegance. Guests leave with unforgettable memories, enriched by the unique culture, gastronomy and hospitality of this iconic establishment in the region.

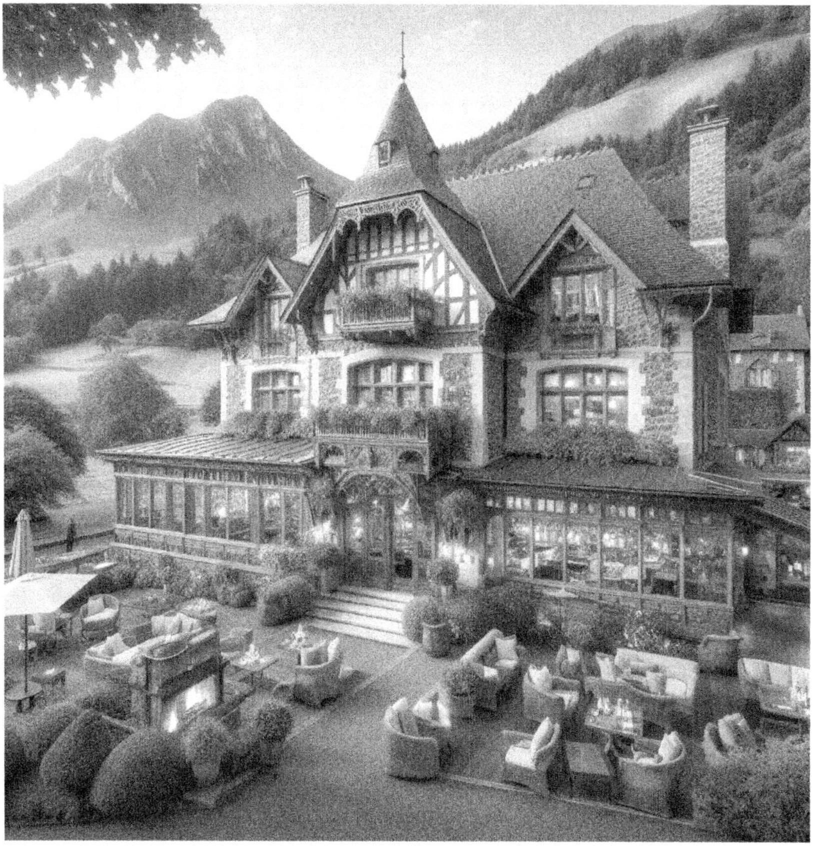

Chapter 6: Relais & Châteaux in Occitanie

1. General Presentation of the Region

Occitanie, located in the south of France, is a multifaceted region, offering exceptional geographic, historical and cultural wealth. With its vast landscapes, its historic towns, its living traditions and its renowned gastronomy, Occitanie is an essential destination for travelers in search of authenticity and diversity. This chapter explores in detail the geographical, historical, cultural and economic characteristics of Occitanie, highlighting the treasures that make this region a unique destination.

Geography and Landscapes

A Diversity of Landscapes

Occitanie extends over a vast area of more than 72,000 square kilometers, encompassing a great diversity of landscapes. The region extends from the Pyrenees mountains to the Mediterranean, passing through the plains of Languedoc, the plateaus of the Massif Central , and the fertile valleys of the Garonne and Tarn rivers. This geographical diversity offers a multitude of outdoor activities and natural discoveries.

The Pyrenees, with their snow-capped peaks, dense forests and deep valleys, offer exceptional opportunities for skiing, mountaineering, hiking and other mountain sports. World-famous ski resorts, such as Font- Romeu , Saint-Lary-Soulan and Ax-les-Thermes, attract visitors from all over the world for their impeccable ski slopes and breathtaking scenery.

The Mediterranean coastline, with its sandy beaches, rocky coves and protected lagoons, is a popular destination for swimming, sailing, scuba diving and other water activities. Coastal towns, such as Montpellier, Sète and Perpignan, offer a unique combination of culture, gastronomy and seaside leisure.

Rivers and Lakes

The region is crossed by several important rivers, including the Garonne, the Tarn, the Hérault and the Aude. These waterways add to the scenic beauty and provide opportunities for boating, fishing and water activities. River valleys, such as the Garonne Valley and the Lot Valley, are dotted with picturesque villages, vineyards and historic sites, creating breathtaking panoramas.

Lakes in the region, such as Lac de Saint-Ferréol, Lac de Pareloup and Lac de Salagou, are popular destinations for swimming, sailing, fishing and picnicking. Lake Saint-Ferréol, in particular, is a UNESCO World Heritage Site due to its key role in the Canal du Midi canal system.

History and Heritage

The Origins of the Region

Occitania has a rich and complex history, marked by the influence of numerous civilizations. The first traces of human occupation date back to prehistory, with sites such as the caves of Niaux and Pech Merle, which house cave paintings and archaeological remains.

The Romans also left their mark on the region, founding important cities like Nîmes (Nemausus), Narbonne (Narbo Martius) and Toulouse (Tolosa). The Roman remains of the region, such as the Pont du Gard, the Maison Carrée and the arenas of Nîmes, are still visible today and testify to the importance of the region at that time.

The Middle Ages and the Renaissance

The Middle Ages was a period of great prosperity for Occitania, with the construction of numerous castles, churches and abbeys. Medieval towns, such as Carcassonne, Albi and Cahors, bear witness to the religious and economic importance of the region at that time.

The Renaissance brought an artistic and architectural renewal to Occitania. Toulouse, in particular, became a cultural and intellectual center, attracting artists, writers and scholars. The city is still famous today for its mansions and pink brick buildings, which earned it the nickname "pink city".

Culture and Traditions

Cultural life

Occitanie is a hotbed of creativity and culture, with a vibrant arts scene and a rich tradition of festivals and events. Toulouse, the regional capital, is known for its internationally renowned festivals, such as the Roque- d'Anthéron Piano Festival , the Carcassonne Festival and the Marciac Jazz Festival.

Music, theater and dance festivals attract artists and spectators from around the world. The region is also famous for its tableware and crafts. Local markets, fairs and flea markets are opportunities to discover and purchase unique artisanal products, such as Anduze pottery, Mazamet textiles and Laguiole knives.

Gastronomy and Local Products

The gastronomy of Occitanie is one of the most renowned in France, highlighting local products and culinary traditions. The region is particularly famous for its wines, cheeses, charcuterie and local specialties.

Occitanie wines, such as Cahors wine, Gaillac wine, Fronton wine and Madiran wine, are appreciated for their unique flavor and exceptional quality. Each wine has its own history, manufacturing techniques and taste characteristics.

Cheeses, such as Roquefort , Pélardon and Laguiole, are essential in regional cuisine. Cold meats, such as Lacaune ham, Aveyron sausage and Toulouse sausage, are also very popular.

Iconic dishes of the region include cassoulet, cod brandade, garbure and apple croustade. Farmers' markets, Michelin-starred restaurants and traditional inns offer a variety of culinary delights to satisfy all tastes.

Local Festivals and Traditions

Occitanie is rich in festivals and traditions, which bear witness to its history and culture. Village festivals, agricultural fairs and folk festivals are opportunities to celebrate local customs and continue traditions.

The harvest festivals, in particular, are a highlight of regional life. Every fall, the vineyards are filled with grape pickers, who harvest the grapes by hand. The harvest is followed by parties and celebrations, with wine tastings, festive meals and musical entertainment.

Christmas markets, such as those in Toulouse, Montpellier and Perpignan, are also popular events, attracting visitors from across the region. The markets offer a variety of artisanal products, culinary specialties and gifts, creating a festive and warm atmosphere.

Economy and Innovation

Tourism

Tourism is one of the pillars of Occitania's economy, attracting millions of visitors from all over the world each year. The diversity of landscapes, cultural richness and historical heritage are all assets that make this region a popular destination.

The region's tourist infrastructure is of high quality, with a diverse range of accommodation, starred restaurants, wellness centers and leisure activities. The airports of Toulouse, Montpellier and Perpignan, as well as rail and road links, facilitate access to the region. Sustainable and responsible tourism is also encouraged, with initiatives aimed at preserving the environment and promoting local heritage.

Agriculture and Local Products

Agriculture plays an essential role in the economy of Occitania, with varied and quality production. Vineyards, cattle and sheep breeding, cereal crops and cheese production are among the main agricultural activities.

Agricultural products, such as wine, cheese, meat, cereals and fruits, are renowned for their excellence and diversity. Farmers' markets, agricultural cooperatives and short circuits promote the marketing of local products and support the rural economy.

Quality labels, such as the AOC (Appellation d'Origine Contrôlée) and the IGP (Protected Geographical Indication), guarantee the authenticity and quality of local products. Visitors can discover these products during tastings, farm tours and food festivals.

Industry and Innovation

The Occitanie region is also a hub of innovation and industrial development, with varied sectors such as aeronautics, agri-food, metallurgy, the pharmaceutical industry and renewable energies. Competitiveness clusters, such as Aerospace Valley (aeronautics) and Agri Sud-Ouest Innovation (agriculture and agri-food), promote innovation and collaboration between economic and scientific players.

Transportation infrastructure, such as highways, high-speed train lines and seaports, supports the region's economic development. The proximity of Spain and the Mediterranean, as well as the presence of large metropolises such as Toulouse and Montpellier, facilitate commercial exchanges and international collaborations. The Occitanie region is a key player in the French economy, contributing to its dynamism and international influence.

Conclusion

Occitanie is an exceptional region, rich in history, culture and varied landscapes. Whether to enjoy the snow-capped peaks of the Pyrenees, explore the beaches of the Mediterranean, discover the prestigious vineyards or savor the local gastronomy, there is something for everyone.

The Relais & Châteaux of the Occitanie region capture the essence of this diversity and offer their guests unforgettable experiences, combining luxury, comfort and authenticity. Each establishment, with its enchanting setting, warm welcome, exceptional gastronomy and enriching activities, offers total immersion in the French art of living.

By discovering the Relais & Châteaux d'Occitanie, you will be transported into a world where every detail is designed to delight the senses and create lasting memories. This chapter presented a detailed overview of the region, integrating geographical, historical, cultural and economic aspects to provide a comprehensive understanding of this unique destination.

- History and Heritage

Occitanie is a region rich in history and heritage, where each town, each village and each monument tells a unique story. From Roman remains to medieval fortifications, from Romanesque abbeys to Renaissance castles, Occitania offers an incredible diversity of historical sites and architectural monuments. In this chapter, we will explore key moments in Occitania's history, its iconic monuments and its cultural contributions.

The First Civilizations

Antiquity and the Romans

The history of Occitania dates back to prehistoric times, with sites such as the ornate caves of Niaux and Pech Merle, home to cave paintings dating back thousands of years. These works of prehistoric art demonstrate the skill and creativity of the region's first inhabitants.

The Romans left an indelible mark on Occitania. The region was an important commercial and strategic crossroads in the Roman Empire. Cities like Nîmes (Nemausus), Narbonne (Narbo Martius) and Toulouse (Tolosa) became major administrative and commercial centers. Roman remains, such as the Pont du Gard, the Maison Carrée, the arenas of Nîmes and the ramparts of Toulouse, are still visible today and bear witness to the grandeur of Roman architecture.

The Celtic and Gaulish Peoples

Before the arrival of the Romans, the region was inhabited by Celtic and Gallic peoples. The Arecomic Volques and the Tectosages were among the most influential Gallic tribes in Occitania. They left traces of their culture and their way of life through archaeological sites such as the oppidum of Ensérune and the site of Montlaurès .

The Middle Ages: Castles and Churches

Medieval Castles

The Middle Ages was a period of great prosperity for Occitania, with the construction of numerous castles to protect the territories and assert the power of local lords. Among the most emblematic castles in the region is the city of Carcassonne, a perfectly preserved medieval fortress, listed as a UNESCO World Heritage Site. Its ramparts, its towers and its count's castle offer a breathtaking view of the Aude valley.

Cathar castles, such as Montségur, Peyrepertuse and Quéribus, are also striking testimonies of this era. These fortresses perched on steep cliffs are symbols of the resistance of the Cathars, a dissident Christian sect, against the Crusades and the Inquisition.

Romanesque Churches and Abbeys

Occitania is also famous for its Romanesque churches and abbeys, which bear witness to the region's religious importance in the Middle Ages. The abbey of Saint-Guilhem-le-Désert, founded in the 9th century, is a masterpiece of Romanesque architecture. Located in an exceptional natural setting, it attracts pilgrims and visitors from all over the world.

The Saint-Sernin Basilica in Toulouse, one of the largest Romanesque churches in Europe, is another remarkable example of Occitan Romanesque art. Built between the 11th and 13th centuries, it is famous for its imposing dimensions, its sculpted capitals and its saints' relics.

The Renaissance and the Classical Age

The Influence of the Renaissance

The Renaissance brought an artistic and architectural renewal to Occitania. Toulouse, in particular, became a major cultural and intellectual center, attracting artists, writers and scholars. The city is still famous today for its mansions and pink brick buildings, which earned it the nickname "pink city".

Renaissance mansions, such as the Hôtel d' Assézat and the Hôtel de Bernuy , illustrate the influence of the Renaissance on regional architecture. These buildings, with their elegant facades, interior courtyards and gardens, reflect the taste for refinement and humanism of this era.

Monuments of the Classical Age

The Classical Age also saw the construction of many notable monuments and buildings in the region. The Pont Neuf in Toulouse, completed in the 17th century, is an iconic example of classical architecture. This stone bridge, with its majestic arches, crosses the Garonne and connects the two banks of the city.

The city of Montpellier, with its mansions and elegant squares, is another example of classical architecture in Occitania. Place de la Comédie, with its opera house and fountains, is the vibrant heart of the city.

Modern and Contemporary Times

The French Revolution and the 19th Century

The French Revolution of 1789 brought significant changes to Occitania. Feudal structures were abolished, the property of the Church and the nobility was confiscated and redistributed, and departments were created to replace the old provinces. Toulouse, Montpellier and Nîmes became important administrative centers.

The 19th century was a period of rapid transformation for the region, with industrialization and urbanization. Technological advances and the rise of railroads stimulated economic development. Toulouse became a major industrial and commercial center, with industries such as chemicals, textiles and aeronautics.

World Wars and Reconstruction

The 20th century was marked by two world wars which had a profound impact on Occitania. During the First World War, the region was an important production and logistics center for the war effort. Soldiers from the region participated in fighting on the Western Front, and many memorials were erected in their honor.

The Second World War brought new challenges, with the German occupation and the Resistance. Toulouse became an important center of the French Resistance, with heroic figures such as Jean Moulin, head of the National Council of the Resistance. Cities in the region, such as Nîmes and Perpignan, were bombed, and many historic buildings were damaged or destroyed.

After the war, the region undertook a period of reconstruction and modernization. Infrastructure was rebuilt, cities renovated and industries revitalized. Tourism became a key sector of the economy, attracting visitors from around the world to discover the historical and cultural treasures of the region.

Cultural and Architectural Heritage

UNESCO Sites

Occitanie has several UNESCO World Heritage sites, which testify to the richness of its cultural and architectural heritage. Among them, we find:

- The city of Carcassonne: Listed in 1997, this perfectly preserved medieval fortress is an exceptional example of military architecture. Its ramparts, its towers and its count's castle offer a breathtaking view of the Aude valley.
- The Pont du Gard: Listed in 1985, this Roman aqueduct bridge is a masterpiece of ancient engineering. Built in the 1st century AD, it is still intact and attracts visitors from all over the world.
- The Canal du Midi: Registered in 1996, this 240 kilometer canal connects the Garonne to the Mediterranean. Built in the 17th century, it is considered one of the greatest engineering works of its time.

Historical Monuments and Museums

Occitanie is home to numerous historical monuments and museums that tell the history of the region and highlight its cultural heritage. Among them, we find:

- The Musée des Augustins in Toulouse: This art museum houses a rich collection of paintings, sculptures and art objects, ranging from the Middle Ages to the contemporary era. It is located in a former Augustinian convent, a masterpiece of southern Gothic architecture.
- The Fabre Museum in Montpellier: This museum presents art collections ranging from the Renaissance to the 19th century, with works by masters such as Rubens, Delacroix, Courbet and Ingres.
- The Soulages museum in Rodez: This museum is dedicated to the work of Pierre Soulages, one of the greatest contemporary French artists. It presents an exceptional collection of his paintings, engravings and stained glass windows.

Conclusion

Occitanie is a region rich in history and heritage, where every street corner, every village and every monument tells a unique story. From Roman remains to medieval fortifications, from Romanesque churches to modern buildings, the region offers an incredible diversity of monuments and historical sites.

The Relais & Châteaux of the Occitanie region capture the essence of this historical and cultural wealth, offering their guests unforgettable experiences. Each establishment, with its enchanting setting, warm welcome, exceptional gastronomy and enriching activities, offers total immersion in the history and heritage of the region.

By discovering the Relais & Châteaux d'Occitanie, you will be transported into a world where every detail is designed to delight the senses and create lasting memories. This chapter explored the many facets of the region's history and heritage, revealing how each era helped shape this unique and fascinating destination.

- Gastronomy and Wine

Occitanie, located in the south of France, is a region renowned for its gastronomic richness and its prestigious vineyards. The diversity of its terroirs, the quality of its local products and its culinary traditions make it an essential destination for lovers of good food and fine wines. In this chapter, we will explore the gastronomic aspects of the region in detail, highlighting the local produce, iconic dishes, renowned chefs, starred restaurants and wines that this region is famous for.

The Roots of Regional Gastronomy

Local Products

Occitanie is a region rich in local products, which constitute the basis of its renowned cuisine. Among the most emblematic products, we find:

- Wines: The region is famous for its numerous vineyards and its prestigious appellations. Among the best known, we find Cahors , Gaillac, Madiran, Fronton, Minervois, Corbières and Saint-Chinian. Each wine has its own characteristics, reflecting the diversity of the region's terroirs.
- Cheeses: Occitanie produces a wide variety of cheeses, each having its own character and manufacturing techniques. Among the most famous, we find Roquefort , Pélardon, Laguiole and Bleu des Causses. These cheeses are often used in traditional dishes or tasted alone to fully appreciate their flavors.
- Charcuteries: The region is also renowned for its charcuteries, such as Lacaune ham, Aveyron sausage, Toulouse sausage and duck confit. They are often accompanied by local vegetables or country bread.
- Truffles: The Quercy black truffle, also called "black diamond", is a precious and aromatic mushroom that grows in the region's forests. It is used to flavor dishes such as omelettes, pastas and risottos.
- Fruits and Vegetables: Lectoure melons, Cévennes sweet onions, Lauragais asparagus and Marmande tomatoes are flagship products of the region. They are often used in traditional dishes or made into jams, soups and desserts.

Emblematic Dishes of Regional Cuisine

Cassoulet

Cassoulet is one of the most emblematic dishes of Occitan cuisine. This stew of white beans, pork, Toulouse sausage and duck confit is cooked slowly in a cassole, a terracotta terrine. Cassoulet is particularly appreciated in winter for its comforting and nourishing qualities.

Cod Brandade

Cod brandade is a specialty of Nîmes, prepared with desalinated cod, olive oil, garlic and milk. The cod is mashed and mixed with the other ingredients to obtain a smooth puree, often served with toast or potatoes.

La Garbure

Garbure is a thick soup made from vegetables, white beans, potatoes and duck or ham confit. Originally from Béarn, this rustic soup is particularly appreciated in winter for its comforting and nourishing qualities. It is often accompanied by country bread and red wine.

Apple Crisp

Apple crisp, also called Gascon pastis, is a traditional dessert from Occitania. This pastry is made with thinly sliced apples, sugar, butter and armagnac, all wrapped in a thin, crispy pastry. The croustade is often served warm, accompanied by crème fraîche or vanilla ice cream.

Occitan Wines

Cahors Wines

Cahors wines, produced in the Lot valley, are famous for their dark color and powerful aromas. Made mainly from the Malbec grape variety, these red wines are distinguished by their richness and complexity. Cahors wines go perfectly with meat dishes, stews and cheeses with character.

Gaillac Wines

Gaillac wines, produced in Tarn, offer a wide diversity of styles, from red wines to white wines including sparkling wines. Native grape varieties such as Duras, Braucol and Mauzac give Gaillac wines unique aromas and distinctive flavors. Gaillac wines are often associated with local dishes and regional specialties.

Fronton Wines

Fronton wines, produced north of Toulouse, are made mainly from the Négrette grape variety, which gives them fruity and spicy aromas. These red wines are renowned for their freshness and character, and pair well with charcuterie, grilled meats and spicy dishes.

The wines of Minervois and Corbières

The wines of Minervois and Corbières, produced in Languedoc, are robust and generous red wines, made mainly from the Grenache, Syrah and Carignan grape varieties. These wines are appreciated for their aromas of red fruits, spices and scrubland. They go perfectly with meat dishes, stews and cheeses.

The Wines of Saint-Chinian

Saint-Chinian wines, produced in Hérault, offer a wide diversity of styles, from red wines to rosé wines and white wines. The Grenache, Syrah and Mourvèdre grape varieties give Saint-Chinian wines fruity and spicy aromas. These wines are often associated with local dishes and regional specialties.

Star Chefs and Restaurants

The Pioneers of Regional Haute Cuisine

Occitanie has always been a hotbed of culinary creativity, attracting talented chefs who have been able to highlight local products and culinary traditions. Among the pioneers of regional haute cuisine is André Daguin, considered one of the greatest French chefs of all time . His restaurant, L'Hôtel de France in Auch, maintained two Michelin stars for several decades.

Contemporary Chefs

Today, the region continues to attract renowned chefs, who continue the tradition of haute cuisine while innovating and experimenting with new flavors. Among the most famous contemporary chefs, we find:

- Michel Sarran: Chef of the Michel Sarran restaurant in Toulouse, Michel Sarran is renowned for his inventive and refined cuisine, highlighting local and seasonal products. Its restaurant has been awarded two Michelin stars.
- Gilles Goujon: Chef at L'Auberge du Vieux Puits in Fontjoncouse, Gilles Goujon offers creative and elegant cuisine, highlighting local and seasonal products. Its restaurant has been awarded three Michelin stars.
- Franck Putelat : Chef of the Restaurant Le Parc in Carcassonne, Franck Putelat offers inventive and elegant cuisine, highlighting local and seasonal products. Its restaurant has been awarded two Michelin stars.

Star Restaurants

Occitanie is home to numerous Michelin-starred restaurants, each offering a unique and unforgettable culinary experience. Among the most famous, we find:

- Le Jardin des Sens in Montpellier: The restaurant of the Pourcel brothers , famous for its creative and refined cuisine, highlighting local and seasonal products. The tasting menu offers dishes such as "Lobster Bleu de Bretagne" and "Agneau de Lait des Pyrénées".
- Le Puits Saint-Jacques in Pujaudran: Bernard Bach's restaurant, renowned for its inventive and elegant cuisine. The tasting menu offers dishes such as "Duck Foie Gras" and "Filet de Bœuf de l'Aveyron".
- La Table de Michel Dussau in Agen: Michel Dussau 's restaurant , offering creative cuisine that respects local products. The tasting menu offers dishes such as "Duck Breast" and "Crispy Black Truffle".

Oenological Experiences

Wine Tastings

Relais & Châteaux in the Occitanie region often offer unique wine experiences for their guests. From private tastings to vineyard tours, these experiences allow you to discover the region's wines and learn the secrets of local viticulture.

Guests can participate in tasting workshops, led by expert sommeliers, to learn how to identify the aromas and flavors of regional wines. Guided tours of the wine estates allow you to discover the winemaking processes, meet the winemakers and taste wines directly from the source.

Food and Wine Pairings

The Relais & Châteaux also offer food and wine pairings, allowing you to savor Occitanie wines in harmony with local cuisine. These pairings highlight the flavors of the dishes and wines, providing a complete and unforgettable gastronomic experience.

Chefs from Michelin-starred restaurants collaborate with sommeliers to create tasting menus that highlight the region's wines. Each dish is carefully paired with a wine, allowing guests to discover new combinations of flavors and textures.

Conclusion

Occitanie is a true land of gastronomy and wine, offering unparalleled richness and diversity. Regional cuisine, with its authentic flavors and quality local products, is a pillar of the region's art of living. The wines of Cahors, Gaillac, Fronton, Minervois, Corbières and Saint-Chinian, renowned for their complexity and elegance, perfectly complement this culinary experience.

The Relais & Châteaux of the Occitanie region capture the essence of this gastronomic richness, offering their guests unique and unforgettable culinary and wine experiences. Each establishment, with its enchanting setting, warm welcome, exceptional gastronomy and enriching activities, offers total immersion in the French art of living.

By discovering the Relais & Châteaux d'Occitanie, you will be transported into a world where every detail is designed to delight the senses and create lasting memories. This chapter explored the multiple facets of the region's gastronomy and wines, revealing how each element contributes to making this destination a true oasis of flavors and culinary pleasures.

2. Addresses and Descriptions

Occitanie is home to numerous Relais & Châteaux, each offering a unique experience combining luxury, comfort and regional charm. These establishments are spread throughout the region, from the mountains of the Pyrenees to the plains of Languedoc, via the vineyards of Quercy and the historic towns of Tarn. In this chapter, we will explore some of the most prestigious addresses and describe in detail what makes them special.

Château de la Treyne

History and Architecture

Château de la Treyne , located on the banks of the Dordogne, is a magnificent 14th-century castle surrounded by formal gardens and forests. This historic residence has been carefully restored to preserve its authentic character while offering first-rate modern comfort. The architecture of the castle, with its imposing towers, moat and stone walls, evokes the elegance and charm of medieval times.

Culinary Offers

The Château de la Treyne gourmet restaurant , led by chef Stéphane Andrieux, offers inventive and refined cuisine, highlighting local and seasonal products. The tasting menu offers an exceptional culinary experience, with dishes such as "Roasted Pigeon with Sweet Spices" and "Filet of Zander with White Butter". The carefully selected wine list highlights the great wines of Quercy and other prestigious wine regions.

Activities and Services

Château de la Treyne offers a range of activities for its guests, from relaxation to sport. Guests can enjoy the heated outdoor swimming pool, tennis court and gardens for leisurely walks. Guided excursions are also organized to explore the surrounding area, including the Lacave caves, the picturesque villages of Rocamadour and Sarlat, and the vineyards of Cahors.

The Old Castillon

History and Architecture

Le Vieux Castillon, located in Castillon-du-Gard, is a charming hotel nestled in a picturesque medieval village. This 15th century residence has been transformed into a luxury hotel, offering a romantic and elegant setting. The interiors are decorated with natural materials, wooden furniture and quality textiles, creating a warm and sophisticated ambiance.

Culinary Offers

The gourmet restaurant at Vieux Castillon offers inventive and refined cuisine, highlighting local and seasonal products. The tasting menu offers an exceptional culinary experience, with dishes such as "Filet de Veau de l'Aveyron" and "Salmon de Fontaine". The carefully selected wine list highlights the great wines of the Languedoc region and other prestigious wine regions.

Activities and Services

Le Vieux Castillon offers a range of activities for its guests, from relaxation to sport. Guests can enjoy the heated outdoor swimming pool, sun terraces and gardens for moments of relaxation. Guided excursions are also organized to explore the surrounding area, including the Pont du Gard, the vineyards of Châteauneuf-du-Pape and local markets.

The Auriac Estate

History and Architecture

Le Domaine d'Auriac, located in Carcassonne, is a luxury hotel nestled in the heart of the Languedoc countryside. This elegant 18th century residence, surrounded by lush gardens and a golf course, offers a peaceful and refined setting. The interiors are decorated with antique furniture, artwork and quality textiles, creating a warm and sophisticated ambiance.

Culinary Offers

The Domaine d'Auriac's gourmet restaurant, led by chef Philippe Deschamps, offers inventive and refined cuisine, highlighting local and seasonal products. The tasting menu offers an exceptional culinary experience, with dishes such as "Duck Foie Gras" and "Pyrenees Suckling Lamb". The carefully selected wine list highlights the great wines of Languedoc and other prestigious wine regions.

Activities and Services

Domaine d'Auriac offers a range of activities for its guests, from relaxation to sport. Guests can enjoy the 18-hole golf course, heated outdoor swimming pool and gardens for moments of relaxation. Guided excursions are also organized to explore the surrounding area, including the medieval city of Carcassonne, the Cathar castles and the region's vineyards.

Mercuès Castle

History and Architecture

Château de Mercuès, located near Cahors, is a majestic 13th century castle perched on a hill overlooking the Lot valley. This historic residence has been transformed into a luxury hotel, offering an elegant and refined setting. The architecture of the castle, with its imposing towers, moat and stone walls, evokes the elegance and charm of medieval times.

Culinary Offers

The Château de Mercuès gourmet restaurant, led by chef Julien Poisot , offers inventive and refined cuisine, highlighting local and seasonal products. The tasting menu offers an exceptional culinary experience, with dishes such as "Roasted Racan Pigeon" and "Filet of Zander with Beurre Blanc". The carefully selected wine list highlights the great wines of Cahors and other prestigious wine regions.

Activities and Services

Château de Mercuès offers a range of activities for its guests, from relaxation to sport. Guests can enjoy the heated outdoor swimming pool, gardens and terraces for moments of relaxation. Guided excursions are also organized to explore the surrounding area, including the vineyards of Cahors, the caves of Pech Merle and the picturesque villages of Saint-Cirq-Lapopie and Puy-l'Évêque.

The Rimbaud Reserve

History and Architecture

La Réserve Rimbaud, located in Montpellier, is a gourmet restaurant nestled in an exceptional natural setting, on the banks of the Lez. The restaurant, housed in an old bourgeois house, offers a breathtaking view of the river and the surrounding gardens. The interiors are decorated with natural materials, wooden furniture and artwork, creating a warm and elegant ambiance.

Culinary Offers

The gourmet restaurant at La Réserve Rimbaud, led by chef Charles Fontès, offers inventive and refined cuisine, highlighting local and seasonal products. The tasting menu offers an exceptional culinary experience, with dishes such as "Homard Bleu de Bretagne" and "Agneau de Slait des Pyrénées". The carefully selected wine list highlights the great wines of Languedoc and other prestigious wine regions.

Activities and Services

La Réserve Rimbaud offers a range of activities for its guests, from relaxation to sport. Guests can enjoy the gardens and terraces for moments of relaxation. Guided excursions are also organized to explore the surrounding area, including the historic city of Montpellier, the Mediterranean beaches and the region's vineyards.

Conclusion

The Relais & Châteaux in Occitanie offer unique and unforgettable experiences, combining luxury, comfort and historical heritage. Each establishment, with its enchanting setting, warm welcome, exceptional gastronomy and enriching activities, offers total immersion in the French art of living. Whether for a romantic getaway, a peaceful retreat or a cultural exploration, the Relais & Châteaux of the Occitanie region are must-see destinations.

By discovering these exceptional establishments, you will be transported to a world where every detail is designed to delight the senses and create lasting memories. This chapter has presented a detailed overview of some of the most prestigious Relais & Châteaux in the region, offering a glimpse of the unique experience that awaits you in each of these enchanting locations.

- Mercuès Castle

Château de Mercuès, located near Cahors, is a majestic 13th century castle, offering a unique blend of history, luxury and refinement. Perched on a hill overlooking the Lot valley, this iconic château is not only an exceptional accommodation, but also a wine estate producing renowned wines. In this chapter, we will explore the history and architecture of Château de Mercuès, its culinary offerings, the activities and services offered, and the unique experiences it offers.

History and Architecture

A Medieval Heritage

The Château de Mercuès was built in the 13th century by the bishops of Cahors, who made it their summer residence. Over the centuries, the castle was enlarged and embellished, becoming a true impregnable fortress. Its strategic position overlooking the Lot valley gave it military and symbolic importance. In 1983, Georges Vigouroux, a passionate winemaker, acquired the château and began its restoration, preserving its historic character while transforming it into a luxury hotel and renowned wine estate.

Eclectic Architecture

The architecture of the Château de Mercuès reflects the different eras of its history. Medieval features, such as imposing towers, moats and ramparts, coexist harmoniously with additions from later centuries, including elegant lounges and sumptuously decorated bedrooms. The interiors of the castle are a true homage to the French art of living, with antique furniture, works of art and refined textiles.

The rooms and suites of the castle offer breathtaking views of the Lot valley, the French gardens and the surrounding vineyards. Each room is unique, with distinctive design elements and modern amenities to ensure optimal comfort. The bathrooms, fitted with marble bathtubs and walk-in showers, provide a luxurious setting in which to relax and rejuvenate.

Culinary Offers

The Gourmet Restaurant

The Château de Mercuès gourmet restaurant, led by chef Julien Poisot , offers inventive and refined cuisine, highlighting local and seasonal products. The tasting menu offers an exceptional culinary experience, with dishes such as "Roasted Racan Pigeon" and "Filet of Zander with Beurre Blanc". Chef Poisot , with his mastery of culinary techniques and his love for local produce, creates dishes that are both innovative and deeply rooted in the region's culinary tradition.

The restaurant's setting matches its cuisine, with elegantly decorated dining rooms, tables spaced for maximum privacy, and panoramic views of the gardens and vineyards. Guests can also dine al fresco on the terrace, enjoying the tranquility and beauty of the natural surroundings.

Regional Cuisine

The cuisine at Château de Mercuès places particular emphasis on local products, with a locavore philosophy that favors fresh, seasonal ingredients from local producers. Menus change regularly to reflect the seasons and local harvests. Guests can taste specialties such as "Roasted Savoie Cepe" and "Chocolat Grand Cru Valrhona", accompanied by carefully selected wines to enhance each dish.

The wine list

Château de Mercuès is also a renowned wine estate, producing exceptional Cahors wines. The restaurant's wine list highlights the estate's wines, made mainly from the Malbec grape variety, as well as wines from other prestigious wine regions in France and around the world. The château's sommeliers are available to advise guests and help them choose the wines that will perfectly accompany their meal.

Activities and Services

The Spa and Wellness Treatments

Château de Mercuès offers a range of wellness treatments for its guests, ranging from massages to facial treatments, carried out with high quality products. The spa, located in a peaceful and luxurious setting, is a place of rest and relaxation, perfect for recharging your batteries after a day exploring the vineyards.

Professional therapists use advanced techniques and luxury products to ensure optimal results and a luxurious experience. Guests can also enjoy the heated outdoor swimming pool, jacuzzi, sauna and steam room to complete their relaxation experience.

Outdoor activities

The gardens and grounds of Château de Mercuès are perfect for leisurely walks, meditation sessions or outdoor yoga sessions. Guests can also enjoy the heated outdoor swimming pool and fitness room.

The castle also offers guided excursions to explore the surrounding area, including the vineyards of Cahors, the caves of Pech Merle, and the picturesque villages of Saint-Cirq-Lapopie and Puy-l'Évêque. Guests can discover prestigious wine châteaux, participate in wine tastings and learn the secrets of the region's viticulture.

Cultural Activities and Experiences

Château de Mercuès regularly organizes cultural events and unique experiences for its guests. Private concerts, literary readings and art exhibitions are often organized in the establishment's lounges or gardens. These events offer immersion in the local cultural scene and allow guests to meet artists, writers and musicians.

Guests can also participate in cooking workshops, baking classes and chocolate tastings, led by local chefs. These workshops offer an opportunity to learn Southwestern cooking techniques and taste delicious creations. Château de Mercuès also offers yoga and meditation classes, led by qualified instructors, in the hotel's gardens or wellness areas.

Special Events and Unique Experiences

Weddings and Receptions

Château de Mercuès is an ideal venue for organizing intimate weddings and private receptions. The property's gardens and lounges provide a romantic and elegant setting for ceremonies and receptions. Hotel staff work closely with couples to create tailor-made events, taking into account every detail, from decor to personalized menus.

The hotel's chefs create wedding menus that reflect the tastes and preferences of the bride and groom, using seasonal ingredients and local produce. The professional and attentive service teams ensure that every event goes off without a hitch. Couples can also enjoy luxurious suites for their wedding night, with special services such as massages, in-room breakfasts and welcome gifts.

Seminars and Business Meetings

The Château de Mercuès offers an exceptional setting for seminars, conferences and business meetings. The property's private lounges, equipped with the latest technology, offer flexible spaces for events of different sizes. Hotel teams work with event organizers to create tailor-made programs, including coffee breaks, business lunches and dinners.

Team-building activities and excursions can also be organized to strengthen team cohesion and provide moments of relaxation outside of work sessions. Guests can take advantage of the hotel's wellness facilities to unwind after a day of meetings, with spa treatments, yoga sessions and massages.

Unique Experiences

Château de Mercuès offers unique experiences to make each stay memorable. These include private dinners in exclusive locations within the establishment, such as the library or gardens, offering an intimate and romantic atmosphere. Customers can also participate in wine tasting workshops, led by expert sommeliers, to discover the secrets of the wines of Cahors and the region.

Wellness getaways are also available, including personalized relaxation and relaxation programs, spa treatments, yoga and meditation sessions, as well as healthy and nutritious meals. These programs are designed to help clients recharge their batteries and regain physical and mental balance.

Seasonal and Thematic Offers

Château de Mercuès regularly offers seasonal and thematic offers to enrich its customers' experience. At Christmas, the establishment is decked out in festive decorations and offers special menus, cookie decorating workshops and Christmas market visits. In summer, gourmet picnics can be organized in the gardens or on the terraces.

Romantic getaways are also offered, including candlelit dinners, duo massages and horse-drawn carriage rides in the surrounding area. For culture lovers, special packages including tickets for exhibitions, shows and concerts are available, offering complete immersion in the cultural life of the region.

Conclusion

The Château de Mercuès is much more than just a luxury hotel; it is a destination in itself, offering a unique and unforgettable experience in the heart of the magnificent Quercy region. With its rich history, impressive architecture, refined culinary offerings and a variety of activities and services, this establishment is the ideal place to relax, recharge and discover the French art of living.

Whether for a romantic getaway, a wellness retreat, an intimate wedding or a business meeting, Château de Mercuès promises an exceptional experience, marked by luxury, comfort and elegance. Guests leave with unforgettable memories, enriched by the unique culture, gastronomy and hospitality of this emblematic establishment of the Occitanie region.

- Auriac Estate

Le Domaine d'Auriac, located in Carcassonne, is a luxury hotel nestled in the heart of the Languedoc countryside, offering an idyllic and peaceful setting close to the famous medieval city of Carcassonne. This historic estate, surrounded by lush gardens and a golf course, embodies the charm and elegance of Occitania. In this chapter, we will explore the history and architecture of Domaine d'Auriac, its culinary offerings, the activities and services offered, and the unique experiences it offers.

History and Architecture

A Historical Heritage

The Domaine d'Auriac was built in the 19th century on the ruins of an old Benedictine abbey. The property has been carefully restored to preserve its historic character while providing top-notch modern comfort. The estate is surrounded by formal gardens, woods and meadows, creating a serene and enchanting setting for visitors.

Elegant Architecture

The architecture of Domaine d'Auriac reflects the classic style of French country houses, with its stone facades, wooden shutters and slate roofs. The interiors are decorated with antique furniture, artwork and quality textiles, creating a warm and sophisticated ambiance.

The estate's rooms and suites offer stunning views of the gardens, golf course and surrounding countryside. Each room is unique, with distinctive design elements and modern amenities to ensure optimal comfort. The bathrooms, fitted with marble bathtubs and walk-in showers, provide a luxurious setting in which to relax and rejuvenate.

Culinary Offers

The Gourmet Restaurant

The Domaine d'Auriac's gourmet restaurant, led by chef Philippe Deschamps, offers inventive and refined cuisine, highlighting local and seasonal products. Michelin-starred chef Deschamps is renowned for his mastery of culinary techniques and his love for local products. The tasting menu offers an exceptional culinary experience, with dishes such as "Duck Foie Gras" and "Pyrenees Suckling Lamb".

The restaurant's setting matches its cuisine, with an elegantly decorated dining room, tables spaced for maximum privacy, and panoramic views of the gardens and golf course. Guests can also dine al fresco on the terrace, enjoying the tranquility and beauty of the natural surroundings.

Regional Cuisine

The cuisine at Domaine d'Auriac places particular emphasis on local products, with a locavore philosophy that favors fresh, seasonal ingredients from local producers. Menus change regularly to reflect the seasons and local harvests. Customers can enjoy specialties such as "Magret de Canard" and "Croustillant de Truffle Noire", accompanied by carefully selected wines to enhance each dish.

The wine list

The restaurant's wine list highlights the great wines of Languedoc, as well as wines from other prestigious wine-growing regions in France and around the world. The estate's sommeliers are available to advise customers and help them choose the wines that will perfectly accompany their meal.

Activities and Services

The Spa and Wellness Treatments

Domaine d'Auriac offers a range of wellness treatments for its clients, ranging from massages to facial treatments, carried out with high quality products. The spa, located in a peaceful and luxurious setting, is a place of rest and relaxation, perfect for recharging your batteries after a day exploring the region.

Professional therapists use advanced techniques and luxury products to ensure optimal results and a luxurious experience. Guests can also enjoy the heated outdoor swimming pool, jacuzzi, sauna and steam room to complete their relaxation experience.

Outdoor activities

Domaine d'Auriac is surrounded by beautiful gardens, meadows and woods, perfect for leisurely walks, meditation sessions or outdoor yoga sessions. Guests can also enjoy the estate's 18-hole golf course, considered one of the best in the region.

The estate also offers guided excursions to explore the surrounding area, including the medieval city of Carcassonne, the Cathar castles and the vineyards of Languedoc. Guests can discover prestigious wine châteaux, participate in wine tastings and learn the secrets of the region's viticulture.

Cultural Activities and Experiences

Domaine d'Auriac regularly organizes cultural events and unique experiences for its guests. Private concerts, literary readings and art exhibitions are often organized in the establishment's lounges or gardens. These events offer immersion in the local cultural scene and allow guests to meet artists, writers and musicians.

Guests can also participate in cooking workshops, baking classes and chocolate tastings, led by local chefs. These workshops offer an opportunity to learn Languedoc cooking techniques and taste delicious creations. Domaine d'Auriac also offers yoga and meditation classes, led by qualified instructors, in the hotel's gardens or wellness areas.

Special Events and Unique Experiences

Weddings and Receptions

Domaine d'Auriac is an ideal venue for organizing intimate weddings and private receptions. The property's gardens and lounges provide a romantic and elegant setting for ceremonies and receptions. Hotel staff work closely with couples to create tailor-made events, taking into account every detail, from decor to personalized menus.

The hotel's chefs create wedding menus that reflect the tastes and preferences of the bride and groom, using seasonal ingredients and local produce. The professional and attentive service teams ensure that every event goes off without a hitch. Couples can also enjoy luxurious suites for their wedding night, with special services such as massages, in-room breakfasts and welcome gifts.

Seminars and Business Meetings

The Domaine d'Auriac offers an exceptional setting for seminars, conferences and business meetings. The property's private lounges, equipped with the latest technology, offer flexible spaces for events of different sizes. Hotel teams work with event organizers to create tailor-made programs, including coffee breaks, business lunches and dinners.

Team-building activities and excursions can also be organized to strengthen team cohesion and provide moments of relaxation outside of work sessions. Guests can take advantage of the hotel's wellness facilities to unwind after a day of meetings, with spa treatments, yoga sessions and massages.

Unique Experiences

Domaine d'Auriac offers unique experiences to make each stay memorable. These include private dinners in exclusive locations within the establishment, such as the library or gardens, offering an intimate and romantic atmosphere. Guests can also participate in wine tasting workshops, led by expert sommeliers, to discover the secrets of Languedoc and regional wines.

Wellness getaways are also available, including personalized relaxation and relaxation programs, spa treatments, yoga and meditation sessions, as well as healthy and nutritious meals. These programs are designed to help clients recharge their batteries and regain physical and mental balance.

Seasonal and Thematic Offers

Domaine d'Auriac regularly offers seasonal and thematic offers to enrich its customers' experience. At Christmas, the establishment is decked out in festive decorations and offers special menus, cookie decorating workshops and Christmas market visits. In summer, gourmet picnics can be organized in the gardens or on the terraces.

Romantic getaways are also offered, including candlelit dinners, duo massages and horse-drawn carriage rides in the surrounding area. For culture lovers, special packages including tickets for exhibitions, shows and concerts are available, offering complete immersion in the cultural life of the region.

Conclusion

The Domaine d'Auriac is much more than just a luxury hotel; it is a destination in itself, offering a unique and unforgettable experience in the heart of the magnificent Languedoc region. With its rich history, impressive architecture, refined culinary offerings and a variety of activities and services, this establishment is the ideal place to relax, recharge and discover the French art of living.

Whether for a romantic getaway, a wellness retreat, an intimate wedding or a business meeting, Domaine d'Auriac promises an exceptional experience, marked by luxury, comfort and elegance. Guests leave with unforgettable memories, enriched by the unique culture, gastronomy and hospitality of this emblematic establishment of the Occitanie region.

- Old Castillon

Le Vieux Castillon, located in the charming medieval village of Castillon-du-Gard, is a luxury hotel that embodies the essence of refinement and elegance of Occitania. Nestled between vineyards and olive groves, this establishment offers an idyllic and peaceful setting, close to emblematic historical sites such as the Pont du Gard. In this chapter, we will explore the history and architecture of Vieux Castillon, its culinary offerings, the activities and services offered, and the unique experiences it offers.

History and Architecture

A Medieval Heritage

Le Vieux Castillon is a magnificent 15th century residence, located in the heart of the village of Castillon-du-Gard. This village, with its cobbled streets and stone houses, has retained all its medieval charm. The hotel, a former coaching inn, has been carefully restored to preserve its authentic character while offering modern and luxurious comfort.

Elegant Architecture

The architecture of Vieux Castillon reflects the typical style of Provençal residences, with its golden stone facades, wooden shutters and tiled roofs. The interiors are decorated with natural materials, wooden furniture and quality textiles, creating a warm and sophisticated ambiance.

The hotel's rooms and suites offer breathtaking views of the gardens, the surrounding countryside and the medieval village. Each room is unique, with distinctive design elements and modern amenities to ensure optimal comfort. The bathrooms, fitted with marble bathtubs and walk-in showers, provide a luxurious setting in which to relax and rejuvenate.

Culinary Offers

The Gourmet Restaurant

The gourmet restaurant at Vieux Castillon offers inventive and refined cuisine, highlighting local and seasonal products. The chef, passionate about the region's gastronomy, creates dishes that combine tradition and modernity, offering an exceptional culinary experience. The tasting menu offers dishes such as "Filet de Veau de l'Aveyron" and "Salmon de Fontaine".

The restaurant's setting matches its cuisine, with an elegantly decorated dining room, tables spaced for maximum privacy, and panoramic views of the gardens and surrounding countryside. Guests can also dine al fresco on the terrace, enjoying the tranquility and beauty of the natural surroundings.

Regional Cuisine

The cuisine of Vieux Castillon places particular emphasis on local products, with a locavore philosophy that favors fresh, seasonal ingredients from local producers. Menus change regularly to reflect the seasons and local harvests. Guests can enjoy specialties such as "Tian de Légumes Provençaux" and "Tarte aux Figues", accompanied by carefully selected wines to enhance each dish.

The wine list

The restaurant's wine list highlights the great wines of Languedoc and neighboring wine regions such as the Rhône Valley. The hotel's sommeliers are available to advise guests and help them choose the wines that will perfectly accompany their meal.

Activities and Services

The Spa and Wellness Treatments

Le Vieux Castillon offers a range of wellness treatments for its guests, from massages to facials, carried out with high quality products. The spa, located in a peaceful and luxurious setting, is a place of rest and relaxation, perfect for recharging your batteries after a day exploring the region.

Professional therapists use advanced techniques and luxury products to ensure optimal results and a luxurious experience. Guests can also enjoy the heated outdoor swimming pool, jacuzzi, sauna and steam room to complete their relaxation experience.

Outdoor activities

The gardens and terraces of Vieux Castillon are perfect for leisurely walks, meditation sessions or outdoor yoga sessions. Guests can also enjoy the heated outdoor swimming pool, tennis courts and fitness room.

The hotel also offers guided excursions to explore the surrounding area, including the Pont du Gard, the vineyards of Châteauneuf-du-Pape, and local markets. Guests can discover prestigious wine châteaux, participate in wine tastings and learn the secrets of the region's viticulture.

Cultural Activities and Experiences

Le Vieux Castillon regularly organizes cultural events and unique experiences for its guests. Private concerts, literary readings and art exhibitions are often organized in the establishment's lounges or gardens. These events offer immersion in the local cultural scene and allow guests to meet artists, writers and musicians.

Guests can also participate in cooking workshops, baking classes and chocolate tastings, led by local chefs. These workshops offer an opportunity to learn Languedoc cooking techniques and taste delicious creations. Le Vieux Castillon also offers yoga and meditation classes, led by qualified instructors, in the hotel's gardens or wellness areas.

Special Events and Unique Experiences

Weddings and Receptions

Le Vieux Castillon is an ideal venue for intimate weddings and private receptions. The property's gardens and lounges provide a romantic and elegant setting for ceremonies and receptions. Hotel staff work closely with couples to create tailor-made events, taking into account every detail, from decor to personalized menus.

The hotel's chefs create wedding menus that reflect the tastes and preferences of the bride and groom, using seasonal ingredients and local produce. The professional and attentive service teams ensure that every event goes off without a hitch. Couples can also enjoy luxurious suites for their wedding night, with special services such as massages, in-room breakfasts and welcome gifts.

Seminars and Business Meetings

Le Vieux Castillon offers an exceptional setting for seminars, conferences and business meetings. The property's private lounges, equipped with the latest technology, offer flexible spaces for events of different sizes. Hotel teams work with event organizers to create tailor-made programs, including coffee breaks, business lunches and dinners.

Team-building activities and excursions can also be organized to strengthen team cohesion and provide moments of relaxation outside of work sessions. Guests can take advantage of the hotel's wellness facilities to unwind after a day of meetings, with spa treatments, yoga sessions and massages.

Unique Experiences

Le Vieux Castillon offers unique experiences to make each stay memorable. These include private dinners in exclusive locations within the establishment, such as the library or gardens, offering an intimate and romantic atmosphere. Guests can also participate in wine tasting workshops, led by expert sommeliers, to discover the secrets of Languedoc and regional wines.

Wellness getaways are also available, including personalized relaxation and relaxation programs, spa treatments, yoga and meditation sessions, as well as healthy and nutritious meals. These programs are designed to help clients recharge their batteries and regain physical and mental balance.

Seasonal and Thematic Offers

Le Vieux Castillon regularly offers seasonal and thematic offers to enrich its customers' experience. At Christmas, the establishment is decked out in festive decorations and offers special menus, cookie decorating workshops and Christmas market visits. In summer, gourmet picnics can be organized in the gardens or on the terraces.

Romantic getaways are also offered, including candlelit dinners, duo massages and horse-drawn carriage rides in the surrounding area. For culture lovers, special packages including tickets for exhibitions, shows and concerts are available, offering complete immersion in the cultural life of the region.

Conclusion

Le Vieux Castillon is much more than just a luxury hotel; it is a destination in itself, offering a unique and unforgettable experience in the heart of the magnificent Gard region. With its rich history, impressive architecture, refined culinary offerings and a variety of activities and services, this establishment is the ideal place to relax, recharge and discover the French art of living.

Whether for a romantic getaway, a wellness retreat, an intimate wedding or a business meeting, Vieux Castillon promises an exceptional experience, marked by luxury, comfort and elegance. Guests leave with unforgettable memories, enriched by the unique culture, gastronomy and hospitality of this emblematic establishment of the Occitanie region.

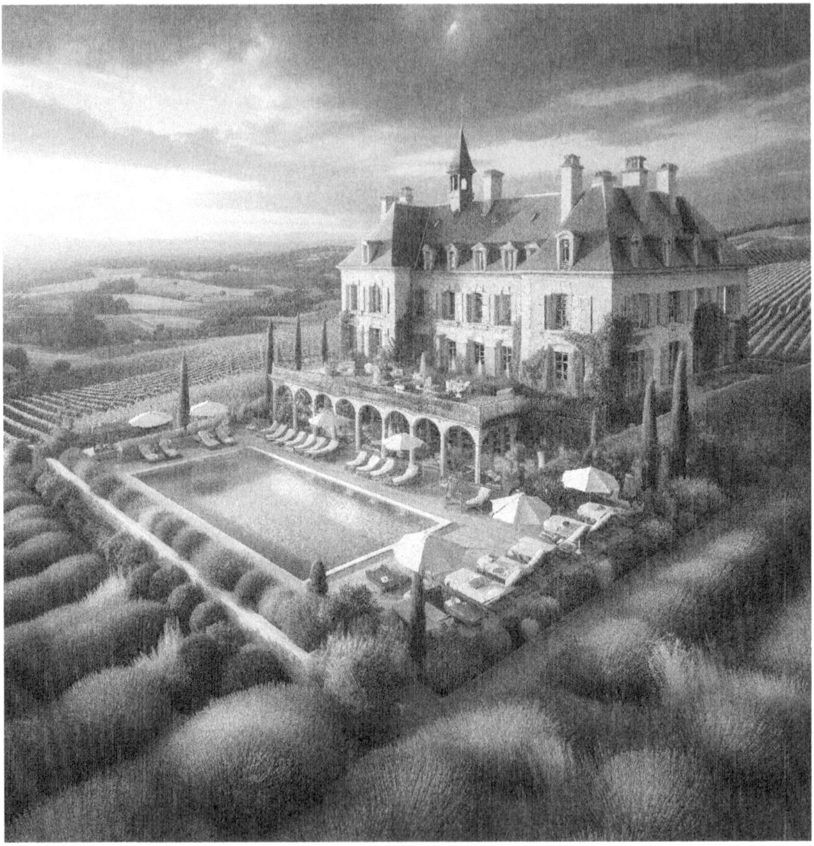

Chapter 7: Relais & Châteaux in Normandy

1. General Presentation of the Region

Normandy, located in the northwest of France, is a region rich in history, culture and varied landscapes. Known for its historic D-Day beaches, impressive chalk cliffs, charming villages and vast agricultural plains, Normandy offers a diversity of sites and experiences for visitors. This chapter explores in detail the geographical, historical, cultural and economic characteristics of Normandy, highlighting the treasures that make this region a unique destination.

Geography and Landscapes

A Spectacular Coast

Normandy is bordered by the English Channel, offering a spectacular coastline that stretches for around 600 kilometers. This coast is famous for its white chalk cliffs, notably those of Étretat, which offer breathtaking panoramas. The beaches of Deauville, Trouville and Cabourg are renowned for their charm and elegance, attracting visitors looking for relaxation and seaside leisure activities.

The landing beaches

The region is also famous for its World War II D-Day beaches, where Allied forces landed on June 6, 1944 to liberate Europe from Nazi occupation. Omaha, Utah, Gold, Juno and Sword beaches are important historical sites, with museums, military cemeteries and memorials that attract visitors from around the world.

A Green Countryside

The interior of Normandy is characterized by a green countryside, made up of meadows, groves, orchards and wheat fields. This agricultural region produces a wide variety of products, including milk, cheese, cider and apples. The Pays d'Auge, with its rolling hills and picturesque villages, is particularly renowned for its bucolic beauty.

Rivers and Natural Parks

Normandy is crossed by several major rivers, including the Seine, Orne and Eure, which add to the beauty of the landscape and provide opportunities for boating, fishing and water activities. Regional natural parks, such as the Parc Naturel Régional des Boucles de la Seine Normande and the Parc Naturel Régional du Perche, are popular destinations for hikes, excursions and wildlife observation.

History and Heritage

The Origins of the Region

Normandy has a rich and complex history, dating back to prehistoric times. The first traces of human occupation in the region include megalithic sites such as the Carnac alignments and the La Hague dolmens. The region has been marked by the influence of the Celts, Romans and Vikings, each leaving their mark on Norman culture and heritage.

The Viking Age and the Foundation of Normandy

In the 9th century, the Vikings, called Normans, invaded the region and settled there. In 911, King Charles III of France granted the territory to the Viking leader Rollo, who became the first Duke of Normandy. The region prospered under Norman rule, with the construction of castles, fortifications and abbeys.

The Conquest of England

Normandy is also famous for William the Conqueror's conquest of England in 1066. The Battle of Hastings and the Norman victory marked the beginning of a new era for England, with the introduction of Norman architecture , customs and laws. Mont-Saint-Michel, a fortified abbey located on a rocky island, is an iconic symbol of this period and attracts millions of visitors each year.

The Second World War

The Second World War left an indelible mark on Normandy, with the Landings of June 6, 1944, known as D-Day. This massive military operation was a turning point in the war, allowing the liberation of France and the 'Western Europe. The region's museums, military cemeteries and memorials bear witness to the historical significance of these events.

Culture and Traditions

Cultural life

Normandy is a hotbed of creativity and culture, with a vibrant arts scene and a rich tradition of festivals and events. Rouen, the regional capital, is known for its music, theater and visual arts festivals. The Normandy Impressionist festival celebrates the Impressionist movement, which found its inspiration in Normandy landscapes.

Gastronomy and Local Products

The gastronomy of Normandy is one of the most renowned in France, highlighting local products and culinary traditions. The region is particularly famous for its cheeses, notably Camembert , Livarot, Pont-l'Évêque and Neufchâtel. Cider, calvados and pommeau are emblematic drinks of Normandy, made from apples grown in local orchards.

Iconic dishes of Norman cuisine include Normandy sole, chicken valley d'Auge, duck Rouennaise and tripe à la mode de Caen. Local markets, Michelin-starred restaurants and traditional inns offer a variety of culinary delights to satisfy all tastes.

Local Festivals and Traditions

Normandy is rich in festivals and traditions, which bear witness to its history and culture. Village festivals, agricultural fairs and folk festivals are opportunities to celebrate local customs and continue traditions.

The apple and cider festivals, in particular, are major events in the region. Every fall, the orchards fill with apple pickers, and the presses begin to produce cider. The festivities include tastings, festive meals and musical entertainment.

Economy and Innovation

Tourism

Tourism is one of the pillars of Normandy's economy, attracting millions of visitors from all over the world each year. The diversity of landscapes, cultural richness and historical heritage are all assets that make this region a popular destination.

The region's tourist infrastructure is of high quality, with a diverse range of accommodation, starred restaurants, wellness centers and leisure activities. The airports of Deauville and Caen, as well as rail and road links, facilitate access to the region. Sustainable and responsible tourism is also encouraged, with initiatives aimed at preserving the environment and promoting local heritage.

Agriculture and Local Products

Agriculture plays an essential role in the economy of Normandy, with varied and quality production. Apple orchards, cattle and sheep breeding, cereal crops and cheese production are among the main agricultural activities.

Agricultural products, such as milk, cheese, cider, calvados and apples, are renowned for their excellence and diversity. Farmers' markets, agricultural cooperatives and short circuits promote the marketing of local products and support the rural economy.

Quality labels, such as the AOP (Protected Designation of Origin) and the IGP (Protected Geographical Indication), guarantee the authenticity and quality of local products. Visitors can discover these products during tastings, farm tours and food festivals.

Industry and Innovation

Normandy is also a center of innovation and industrial development, with varied sectors such as the agri-food industry, the pharmaceutical industry, aeronautics and renewable energies. Competitiveness clusters, such as Nov@log (logistics) and Cosmetic Valley (cosmetics), promote innovation and collaboration between economic and scientific players.

Transportation infrastructure, such as highways, high-speed train lines and seaports, supports the region's economic development. The proximity of Paris, as well as the presence of large metropolises such as Rouen and Caen, facilitate commercial exchanges and international collaborations. The Normandy region is a key player in the French economy, contributing to its dynamism and international influence.

Conclusion

Normandy is an exceptional region, rich in history, culture and varied landscapes. Whether enjoying the historic D-Day beaches, exploring the spectacular cliffs of Étretat, discovering the picturesque villages of the Pays d'Auge or savoring the local gastronomy, there is something for everyone.

The Relais & Châteaux of the Normandy region capture the essence of this diversity and offer their guests unforgettable experiences, combining luxury, comfort and authenticity. Each establishment, with its enchanting setting, warm welcome, exceptional gastronomy and enriching activities, offers total immersion in the French art of living.

By discovering the Relais & Châteaux of Normandy, you will be transported into a world where every detail is designed to delight the senses and create lasting memories. This chapter presented a detailed overview of the region, integrating geographical, historical, cultural and economic aspects to provide a comprehensive understanding of this unique destination.

- History and Heritage

Normandy is a region rich in history and heritage, where each town, each village and each monument tells a unique story. From prehistoric remains to medieval castles, from Romanesque abbeys to the D-Day beaches, Normandy offers an incredible diversity of historical sites and architectural monuments. In this chapter, we will explore key moments in Normandy's history, its iconic monuments and its cultural contributions.

The First Civilizations

Prehistoric Sites

Normandy is home to numerous prehistoric sites which bear witness to human occupation of the region for millennia. Among the most famous, we find the menhirs of La Hague and the dolmens of the Fécamp region. These megaliths, dating back several thousand years, are silent witnesses to the first civilizations that inhabited the region.

The Celts and the Gauls

Before the arrival of the Romans, the region was inhabited by Celtic and Gallic tribes. The Gauls, notably the Calètes, the Lexoviens and the Viducasses, left traces of their culture and their way of life through archaeological sites and the remains of fortified villages. The oppida, like that of Jumièges, bear witness to the social and military organization of these peoples.

The Roman Era

The Roman Conquest

Normandy was conquered by the Romans in the 1st century BC. The Romans established important cities such as Rotomagus (Rouen), Juliobona (Lillebonne) and Noviomagus (Lisieux). These towns become administrative, commercial and cultural centers of the region. Roman remains, such as the Lillebonne thermal baths, aqueducts and theaters, bear witness to the importance of Roman influence.

Roads and Infrastructure

The Romans built a network of roads and infrastructure that facilitated trade and commerce in the region. The Roman road linking Lillebonne to Rouen is an example. These roads also help strengthen military control of the region and facilitate troop movements.

The Viking Age and the Foundation of Normandy

The Viking Invasion

In the 9th century, the Vikings, called Normans, invaded the region and settled there. In 911, King Charles III of France granted the territory to Rollo, a Viking leader, who became the first Duke of Normandy. Rollo and his successors established a dynasty that governed the region and developed its infrastructure and economy.

The Normandy Foundation

The concession of Normandy to Rollon marks the beginning of a period of prosperity for the region. The dukes of Normandy built castles, fortifications and abbeys to strengthen their power and protect their territories. The city of Rouen becomes the capital of the duchy and an important center of commerce and culture.

The Conquest of England

William the Conqueror

Normandy is famous for William the Conqueror's conquest of England in 1066. William, Duke of Normandy, led a military expedition that resulted in victory at the Battle of Hastings. He was crowned king of England and introduced Norman architecture, customs and laws to his new kingdom.

The Norman Heritage in England

William the Conqueror's conquest of England had a profound impact on the history and culture of both regions. The Normans built castles, cathedrals and monasteries in England, influencing architecture and art. The Abbaye aux Hommes and the Abbaye aux Dames in Caen, founded by Guillaume and his wife Mathilde, are emblematic examples of this influence.

The Middle Ages and the Renaissance

Castles and Fortifications

The Middle Ages saw the construction of numerous castles and fortifications in Normandy. These structures, such as the Château de Caen, Château de Falaise and Château de Gisors, are symbols of the power of the Dukes of Normandy and local lords. They play a key role in the defense of territory and the consolidation of power.

Abbeys and Monasteries

Normandy is also known for its abbeys and monasteries, which become centers of culture, learning and spirituality. Jumièges Abbey, founded in the 7th century, is one of the oldest and most important in the region. Mont-Saint-Michel Abbey, perched on a rocky island, is a masterpiece of medieval architecture and a major place of pilgrimage.

The Renaissance and Cultural Development

The Renaissance brought an artistic and intellectual renewal to Normandy. The cities of Rouen, Caen and Alençon became dynamic cultural centers, attracting artists, writers and scholars. Renaissance architecture, with its mansions, mansions and richly decorated churches, bears witness to this period of prosperity and creativity.

Modern and Contemporary Times

The Wars of Religion and the French Revolution

The religious wars of the 16th century and the French Revolution of the 18th century mark periods of profound upheaval and change in Normandy. Churches and monasteries are often damaged or destroyed, and Church property is confiscated and sold. The region is undergoing significant political, social and economic transformations.

The Second World War and the Landings

The Second World War had a major impact on Normandy, with the Landings of June 6, 1944, known as D-Day. This massive military operation led to the liberation of France and Western Europe. D-Day beaches, such as Omaha Beach and Utah Beach, are becoming important historical sites, with museums, military cemeteries and memorials.

Reconstruction and Development

After the war, Normandy undertook a period of reconstruction and modernization. Infrastructure is rebuilt, cities renovated and industries revitalized. Tourism is becoming a key sector of the economy, attracting visitors from around the world to discover the historical and cultural treasures of the region.

Cultural and Architectural Heritage

UNESCO Sites

Normandy has several UNESCO World Heritage sites, which bear witness to the richness of its cultural and architectural heritage. Among them, we find:

- Mont-Saint-Michel and its bay: Listed in 1979, this site is a masterpiece of medieval architecture, with its abbey perched on a rocky island surrounded by spectacular tides.
- The cliffs of Étretat: Although not individually listed, these cliffs are among the most emblematic natural landscapes of the region, immortalized by numerous artists, including Claude Monet.

Historical Monuments and Museums

Normandy is home to numerous historical monuments and museums that tell the history of the region and highlight its cultural heritage. Among them, we find:

- Notre-Dame de Rouen Cathedral: A masterpiece of Gothic architecture, famous for its imposing spiers and magnificent stained glass windows.
- The Rouen Museum of Fine Arts: This museum houses a rich collection of paintings, sculptures and art objects, ranging from the Middle Ages to the contemporary era.
- The Caen Memorial: A museum dedicated to the history of the Second World War, with exhibitions on the Landings, the Battle of Normandy and the French Resistance.

Conclusion

Normandy is a region rich in history and heritage, where every street corner, every village and every monument tells a unique story. From prehistoric remains to medieval fortifications, from Romanesque abbeys to the Landing beaches, the region offers an incredible diversity of monuments and historical sites.

The Relais & Châteaux of the Normandy region capture the essence of this historical and cultural wealth, offering their guests unforgettable experiences. Each establishment, with its enchanting setting, warm welcome, exceptional gastronomy and enriching activities, offers total immersion in the history and heritage of the region.

By discovering the Relais & Châteaux of Normandy, you will be transported into a world where every detail is designed to delight the senses and create lasting memories. This chapter explored the many facets of the region's history and heritage, revealing how each era helped shape this unique and fascinating destination.

- Gastronomy and Wine

Normandy is a region renowned for its gastronomic richness and its exceptional quality local products. Its cuisine is anchored in ancient culinary traditions, highlighting local products such as cheeses, seafood, apples and cider. In this chapter, we will explore the gastronomic aspects of the region, highlighting the local products, iconic dishes, renowned chefs, starred restaurants and wines that this region is famous for.

The Roots of Regional Gastronomy

Local Products

Normandy is a prosperous agricultural region, producing a wide variety of local products which form the basis of its renowned cuisine. Among the most emblematic products, we find:

- Cheeses: Normandy is famous for its world-famous cheeses. Among the best known, we find Camembert , Livarot, Pont-l'Évêque and Neufchâtel. These cheeses, made from cow's milk, are often enjoyed alone or used in traditional dishes.
- Apples: Normandy is also renowned for its apple orchards, producing a wide variety of apples used to make cider, calvados and pommeau. Apples are also used in many local dishes and desserts.
- Seafood: The Normandy coast, with its fishing ports such as Honfleur, Dieppe and Granville, provides an abundance of fresh seafood, including oysters, mussels, scallops and shrimp. These seafoods are often prepared simply to showcase their freshness.
- Meats: Normandy also produces high quality meats, notably Norman beef, pork and free-range chicken. Cold meats, such as andouille de Vire and black pudding, are also very popular.

Emblematic Dishes of Regional Cuisine

Norman Sole

Normandy sole is an emblematic dish of the region, showcasing local seafood. This dish is prepared with sole fillets cooked in a court-bouillon, then topped with a sauce made from white wine, crème fraîche and mushrooms, and garnished with shrimp, mussels and scallops. Normandy sole is often served with steamed potatoes or rice.

Poulet Vallée d'Auge

Chicken valley d'Auge is a traditional dish of Norman cuisine, prepared with chicken cooked in a sauce made from crème fraîche, cider and calvados, and garnished with apples and mushrooms. This rich and flavorful dish is often accompanied by fried potatoes or seasonal vegetables.

Duck a la Rouennaise

Duck à la Rouennaise, also known as duck au sang, is a sophisticated and refined dish, typical of the Rouen region. The duck is roasted and served with a rich sauce made from its own blood, liver and red wine. This complex dish is often prepared and served in fine dining restaurants in the area.

Tripe à la Mode in Caen

Tripe à la mode de Caen is a traditional dish of Norman cuisine, prepared with beef tripe slowly cooked in a cider and calvados broth, with vegetables and spices. This rustic and tasty dish is often served with country bread and cider.

Tatin pie

Tarte Tatin is an emblematic dessert of Normandy, prepared with caramelized apples cooked under puff pastry. This upside-down tart is often served warm, accompanied by crème fraîche or vanilla ice cream. The Tatin tart is a perfect example of the use of apples in Normandy pastries.

Normandy Wines and Ciders

The Cider

Cider is the emblematic drink of Normandy, made from apples grown in the region's orchards. There are several varieties of cider, ranging from sweet to hard cider, each with its own taste and fermentation characteristics. Cider is often served with local dishes, cheeses and desserts.

Calvados

Calvados is an apple brandy produced in Normandy, obtained by distillation of cider. This alcoholic drink, aged in oak barrels, is renowned for its complexity and rich aromas. Calvados is often enjoyed as a digestif, but it is also used in cooking to flavor sauces and desserts.

The Pommel

Pommeau is an aperitif drink made from apple must and calvados. This sweet and fruity drink is often served as an aperitif or as an accompaniment to desserts. Pommeau is a specialty of Normandy and is appreciated for its balance between sweetness and acidity.

Star Chefs and Restaurants

The Pioneers of Regional Haute Cuisine

Normandy has always been a hotbed of culinary creativity, attracting talented chefs who have been able to highlight local products and culinary traditions. Among the pioneers of regional haute cuisine, we find Michel Bruneau, considered one of the greatest chefs in the region. His restaurant, L'Hostellerie de la Renaissance in Argentan, maintained a Michelin star for several decades.

Contemporary Chefs

Today, the region continues to attract renowned chefs, who continue the tradition of haute cuisine while innovating and experimenting with new flavors. Among the most famous contemporary chefs, we find:

- Gilles Tournadre : Chef of the Gill restaurant in Rouen, Gilles Tournadre is renowned for his inventive and refined cuisine, highlighting local and seasonal products. Its restaurant has been awarded two Michelin stars.
- Alexandre Bourdas: Chef of the SaQuaNa restaurant in Honfleur, Alexandre Bourdas offers creative and elegant cuisine, highlighting seafood and seasonal vegetables. Its restaurant has been awarded two Michelin stars.
- David Gallienne : Chef at the Jardin des Plumes in Giverny, David Gallienne offers inventive and elegant cuisine, highlighting local and seasonal products. Its restaurant has been awarded a Michelin star.

Star Restaurants

Normandy is home to many Michelin-starred restaurants, each offering a unique and unforgettable culinary experience. Among the most famous, we find:

- Le Manoir du Lys in Bagnoles-de-l'Orne: Franck Quinton's restaurant, famous for its creative and refined cuisine, highlighting local and seasonal products. The tasting menu offers dishes such as "Filet de Veau de Normandie" and "Salmon de Fontaine".
- L'Espérance in Hérouville-Saint-Clair: Jean-Luc Tartarin's restaurant, renowned for its inventive and elegant cuisine. The tasting menu offers dishes such as "Duck Foie Gras" and "Suckling Lamb of the Pyrenees".
- La Ferme Saint-Siméon in Honfleur: Pascal Malherbe's restaurant, offering creative cuisine that respects local products. The tasting menu offers dishes such as "Duck Breast" and "Crispy Black Truffle".

Oenological Experiences

Cider and Calvados Tastings

Relais & Châteaux in the Normandy region often offer unique wine experiences for their guests. From private tastings to distillery visits, these experiences allow you to discover the region's ciders and calvados and learn the secrets of their making.

Customers can participate in tasting workshops, led by experts, to learn how to identify the aromas and flavors of the region's ciders and calvados. Guided tours of the orchards and distilleries allow you to discover the production processes, meet the producers and taste products directly from the source.

Food-Cider and Food-Calvados Pairings

The Relais & Châteaux also offer food-cider and food-calvados pairings, allowing you to enjoy Normandy drinks in harmony with local cuisine. These pairings highlight the flavors of dishes and drinks, providing a complete and unforgettable gastronomic experience.

Chefs from Michelin-starred restaurants collaborate with sommeliers to create tasting menus that highlight the region's ciders and calvados. Each dish is carefully paired with a drink, allowing guests to discover new combinations of flavors and textures.

Conclusion

Normandy is a true land of gastronomy and drinks, offering unrivaled richness and diversity. Regional cuisine, with its authentic flavors and quality local products, is a pillar of the region's art of living. The ciders, calvados and pommeaux, renowned for their complexity and elegance, perfectly complement this culinary experience.

The Relais & Châteaux of the Normandy region capture the essence of this gastronomic richness, offering their guests unique and unforgettable culinary and wine experiences. Each establishment, with its enchanting setting, warm welcome, exceptional gastronomy and enriching activities, offers total immersion in the French art of living.

By discovering the Relais & Châteaux of Normandy, you will be transported into a world where every detail is designed to delight the senses and create lasting memories. This chapter explored the many facets of the region's food and drink, revealing how each element contributes to making this destination a true oasis of flavors and culinary pleasures.

2. Addresses and Descriptions

Normandy is home to numerous Relais & Châteaux, each offering a unique experience combining luxury, comfort and regional charm. These establishments are spread throughout the region, from the beaches of the English Channel to the hills of the Pays d'Auge, via the green valleys of the Orne and the historic towns of Calvados. In this chapter, we will explore some of the most prestigious addresses and describe in detail what makes them special.

The Ablon Estate

History and Architecture

Domaine d'Ablon, located near Honfleur, is a magnificent 17th-century manor house surrounded by formal gardens and apple orchards. This historic residence has been carefully restored to preserve its authentic character while offering first-rate modern comfort. The architecture of the manor, with its stone facades, half-timbering and slate roofs, evokes the elegance and charm of the period.

Culinary Offers

Domaine d'Ablon offers an exceptional culinary experience, with dishes highlighting local and seasonal products. The establishment's chef creates gourmet menus inspired by Norman cuisine, using fresh, high-quality ingredients. Guests can taste specialties such as "Duck Breast in Cider" and "Roasted Camembert", accompanied by carefully selected wines.

Activities and Services

Domaine d'Ablon offers a range of activities for its guests, from relaxation to sport. Guests can enjoy the gardens for leisurely walks, meditation sessions or outdoor yoga sessions. Guided excursions are also organized to explore the surrounding area, including the town of Honfleur, the beaches of Deauville and the apple orchards. Cider and calvados tastings are also offered, allowing customers to discover the region's emblematic drinks.

The Impressionist Manor

History and Architecture

Le Manoir des Impressionnistes, located in Honfleur, is a charming 18th-century manor house overlooking the sea. This historic residence, surrounded by lush gardens, offers a peaceful and refined setting. The interiors are decorated with antique furniture, artwork and quality textiles, creating a warm and sophisticated ambiance.

Culinary Offers

The gourmet restaurant at Manoir des Impressionnistes offers inventive and refined cuisine, highlighting local and seasonal products. The chef, passionate about the region's gastronomy, creates dishes that combine tradition and modernity. The tasting menu offers dishes such as "Filet de Bass de Ligne" and "Soufflé au Calvados". The wine list highlights the region's great wines and other prestigious wine regions.

Activities and Services

Le Manoir des Impressionnistes offers a range of activities for its guests, from relaxation to sport. Guests can enjoy the outdoor swimming pool, gardens and terraces for moments of relaxation. Guided excursions are also organized to explore the surrounding area, including the town of Honfleur, the beaches of Trouville and local museums. The hotel's spa offers a range of wellness treatments, including massages, facials and yoga sessions.

Château La Chenevière

History and Architecture

Château La Chenevière , located near Bayeux, is an elegant 18th-century castle surrounded by English gardens and woods. This historic residence has been transformed into a luxury hotel, offering a romantic and elegant setting. The architecture of the castle, with its stone facades, turrets and mullioned windows, evokes the elegance and refinement of the period.

Culinary Offers

The Château La Chenevière gourmet restaurant , led by a talented chef, offers inventive and refined cuisine, highlighting local and seasonal products. The tasting menu offers an exceptional culinary experience, with dishes such as "Duck Foie Gras" and "Pyrenees Suckling Lamb". The carefully selected wine list highlights the region's great wines and other prestigious wine regions.

Activities and Services

Château La Chenevière offers a range of activities for its guests, from relaxation to sport. Guests can enjoy the heated outdoor swimming pool, gardens and terraces for moments of relaxation. Guided excursions are also organized to explore the surrounding area, including the town of Bayeux, the D-Day beaches and local museums. The castle also offers cooking classes, wine tastings and outdoor activities such as tennis and cycling.

The Château de Sassetot

History and Architecture

Château de Sassetot , located in Sassetot-le-Mauconduit, is a majestic 18th century castle surrounded by extensive gardens and woods. This historic residence, once the residence of Empress Elisabeth of Austria, has been transformed into a luxury hotel, offering an elegant and refined setting. The architecture of the castle, with its stone facades, towers and mullioned windows, evokes the elegance and charm of the era.

Culinary Offers

Sassetot 's gourmet restaurant offers inventive and refined cuisine, highlighting local and seasonal products. The chef, passionate about the region's gastronomy, creates dishes that combine tradition and modernity. The tasting menu offers dishes such as "Lobster Bleu de Bretagne" and "Tarte Tatin aux Pommes". The wine list highlights the region's great wines and other prestigious wine regions.

Activities and Services

Château de Sassetot offers a range of activities for its guests, from relaxation to sport. Guests can enjoy the gardens for leisurely walks, meditation sessions or outdoor yoga sessions. Guided excursions are also organized to explore the surrounding area, including the cliffs of Étretat, the beaches of Fécamp and local museums. The hotel's spa offers a range of wellness treatments, including massages, facials and yoga sessions.

Saint-Siméon Farm

History and Architecture

La Ferme Saint-Siméon , located in Honfleur, is a former 17th century coaching inn transformed into a luxury hotel. This historic residence, surrounded by lush gardens, offers a peaceful and refined setting. The interiors are decorated with antique furniture, artwork and quality textiles, creating a warm and sophisticated ambiance.

Culinary Offers

The gourmet restaurant at Ferme Saint-Siméon offers inventive and refined cuisine, highlighting local and seasonal products. The chef, passionate about the region's gastronomy, creates dishes that combine tradition and modernity. The tasting menu offers dishes such as "Filet de Veau de Normandie" and "Calvados Soufflé". The wine list highlights the region's great wines and other prestigious wine regions.

Activities and Services

La Ferme Saint-Siméon offers a range of activities for its guests, from relaxation to sport. Guests can enjoy the heated outdoor swimming pool, gardens and terraces for moments of relaxation. Guided excursions are also organized to explore the surrounding area, including the town of Honfleur, the beaches of Deauville and local museums. The hotel's spa offers a range of wellness treatments, including massages, facials and yoga sessions.

Conclusion

Relais & Châteaux in Normandy offer unique and unforgettable experiences, combining luxury, comfort and historical heritage. Each establishment, with its enchanting setting, warm welcome, exceptional gastronomy and enriching activities, offers total immersion in the French art of living. Whether for a romantic getaway, a peaceful retreat or a cultural exploration, the Relais & Châteaux of the Normandy region are must-see destinations.

By discovering these exceptional establishments, you will be transported to a world where every detail is designed to delight the senses and create lasting memories. This chapter has presented a detailed overview of some of the most prestigious Relais & Châteaux in the region, offering a glimpse of the unique experience that awaits you in each of these enchanting locations.

Chantore Castle

Château de Chantore , located in Bacilly near Mont-Saint-Michel, is a magnificent 18th-century castle surrounded by English gardens and woods. This architectural gem offers an idyllic and peaceful setting, perfect for a romantic getaway or a relaxing stay in Normandy. In this chapter, we will explore the history and architecture of Château de Chantore , its culinary offerings, the activities and services offered, and the unique experiences it offers.

History and Architecture

A Heritage of the 18th Century

Château de Chantore was built in the 18th century in an elegant classical style. The castle is nestled in a 19 hectare park, decorated with English gardens, meadows and woods. The property offers breathtaking views of Mont-Saint-Michel, adding a spectacular dimension to its enchanting setting.

Elegant Architecture

The architecture of Château de Chantore reflects the classic style of French country houses of the period, with its symmetrical facades, sash windows and slate roofs. Interiors are decorated with period furniture, artwork and fine textiles, creating a warm and sophisticated atmosphere.

The rooms and suites of the castle offer breathtaking views of the gardens, the park and, on a clear day, Mont-Saint-Michel. Each room is unique, with distinctive design elements and modern amenities to ensure optimal comfort. The bathrooms, fitted with marble bathtubs and walk-in showers, provide a luxurious setting in which to relax and rejuvenate.

Culinary Offers

The Gourmet Breakfast

Château de Chantore offers a gourmet breakfast served in the elegantly decorated dining room or on the terrace, with magnificent views of the gardens. Breakfast is composed of fresh, local products, including pastries, fruit, homemade jams, Norman cheeses, fresh eggs and pressed fruit juices. Guests can also enjoy hot drinks, such as coffee, tea and hot chocolate.

Meals on Demand

For lunches and dinners, the castle offers meals on request, prepared with local and seasonal ingredients. Menus can be customized based on guest preferences, providing a tailor-made dining experience. Meals are served in the privacy of the dining room, in the gardens or on the terrace, depending on the guests' wishes.

Regional Cuisine

The cuisine at Château de Chantore places particular emphasis on local products, with a locavore philosophy that favors fresh, seasonal ingredients from local producers. Guests can taste Norman specialties such as "Poulet Vallée d'Auge", "Roasted Camembert" and "Tarte Tatin", accompanied by carefully selected wines to enhance each dish.

Activities and Services

The Park and Gardens

The grounds and gardens of Château de Chantore are perfect for leisurely walks, meditation sessions or outdoor yoga sessions. Guests can explore the park's winding trails, discover the different species of trees and plants, and enjoy the serenity of the place. The park is also an ideal place to observe local wildlife, including birds and small mammals.

Outdoor activities

The castle offers a range of outdoor activities for its guests, including hiking, cycling and horseback riding. Guests can also organize picnics in the gardens or on the banks of the park's ponds. Guided excursions are also available to explore the surrounding area, including Mont-Saint-Michel, the beaches of Mont-Saint-Michel Bay and the region's picturesque villages.

Cultural Visits and Experiences

Château de Chantore regularly organizes cultural events and unique experiences for its guests. Private concerts, literary readings and art exhibitions are often organized in the establishment's lounges or gardens. These events offer immersion in the local cultural scene and allow guests to meet artists, writers and musicians.

Guests can also participate in cooking workshops, baking classes and chocolate tastings, led by local chefs. These workshops offer an opportunity to learn Norman cooking techniques and taste delicious creations. The castle also offers yoga and meditation classes, led by qualified instructors, in the hotel's gardens or wellness areas.

Special Events and Unique Experiences

Weddings and Receptions

Château de Chantore is an ideal venue for intimate weddings and private receptions. The property's gardens and lounges provide a romantic and elegant setting for ceremonies and receptions. Hotel staff work closely with couples to create tailor-made events, taking into account every detail, from decor to personalized menus.

The hotel's chefs create wedding menus that reflect the tastes and preferences of the bride and groom, using seasonal ingredients and local produce. The professional and attentive service teams ensure that every event goes off without a hitch. Couples can also enjoy luxurious suites for their wedding night, with special services such as massages, in-room breakfasts and welcome gifts.

Seminars and Business Meetings

The Château de Chantore offers an exceptional setting for seminars, conferences and business meetings. The property's private lounges, equipped with the latest technology, offer flexible spaces for events of different sizes. Hotel teams work with event organizers to create tailor-made programs, including coffee breaks, business lunches and dinners.

Team-building activities and excursions can also be organized to strengthen team cohesion and provide moments of relaxation outside of work sessions. Guests can take advantage of the hotel's

wellness facilities to unwind after a day of meetings, with spa treatments, yoga sessions and massages.

Unique Experiences

Château de Chantore offers unique experiences to make each stay memorable. These include private dinners in exclusive locations within the establishment, such as the library or gardens, offering an intimate and romantic atmosphere. Guests can also participate in wine tasting workshops, led by expert sommeliers, to discover the secrets of Normandy and regional wines.

Wellness getaways are also available, including personalized relaxation and relaxation programs, spa treatments, yoga and meditation sessions, as well as healthy and nutritious meals. These programs are designed to help clients recharge their batteries and regain physical and mental balance.

Seasonal and Thematic Offers

Château de Chantore regularly offers seasonal and thematic offers to enrich its customers' experience. At Christmas, the establishment is decked out in festive decorations and offers special menus, cookie decorating workshops and Christmas market visits. In summer, gourmet picnics can be organized in the gardens or on the terraces.

Romantic getaways are also offered, including candlelit dinners, duo massages and horse-drawn carriage rides in the surrounding area. For culture lovers, special packages including tickets for exhibitions, shows and concerts are available, offering complete immersion in the cultural life of the region.

Conclusion

Château de Chantore is much more than just a luxury hotel; it is a destination in itself, offering a unique and unforgettable experience in the heart of the magnificent Mont-Saint-Michel region. With its rich history, impressive architecture, refined culinary offerings and a variety of activities and services, this establishment is the ideal place to relax, recharge and discover the French art of living.

Whether for a romantic getaway, a wellness retreat, an intimate wedding or a business meeting, Château de Chantore promises an exceptional experience, marked by luxury, comfort and elegance. Guests leave with unforgettable memories, enriched by the unique culture, gastronomy and hospitality of this emblematic establishment of the Normandy region.

- La Ferme Saint-Siméon

La Ferme Saint-Siméon , located in Honfleur, is a former 17th century coaching inn transformed into a luxury hotel. Nestled in the heart of lush gardens and overlooking the sea, this historic residence offers an idyllic and peaceful setting. La Ferme Saint-Siméon is a place full of charm and elegance, perfect for a romantic getaway or a relaxing stay in Normandy. In this chapter, we will explore the history and architecture of La Ferme Saint-Siméon , its culinary offerings, the activities and services offered, and the unique experiences it offers.

History and Architecture

A Heritage of the 17th Century

La Ferme Saint-Siméon was built in the 17th century as a post house, welcoming travelers and artists. In the 19th century, the inn became a meeting place for impressionist painters such as Claude Monet, Eugène Boudin and Johan Jongkind, who found inspiration and refuge there. The residence is thus nicknamed "La Mère Toutain", after the name of its famous innkeeper.

Authentic Architecture

The architecture of La Ferme Saint-Siméon reflects the rustic charm of Norman farms, with its half-timbered facades, tiled roofs and brick chimneys. The interiors are decorated with antique furniture, artwork and quality textiles, creating a warm and sophisticated ambiance.

The hotel's rooms and suites offer breathtaking views of the gardens, the sea and the port of Honfleur. Each room is unique, with distinctive design elements and modern amenities to ensure optimal comfort. The bathrooms, fitted with marble bathtubs and walk-in showers, provide a luxurious setting in which to relax and rejuvenate.

Culinary Offers

The Gourmet Restaurant

The gourmet restaurant at La Ferme Saint-Siméon offers inventive and refined cuisine, highlighting local and seasonal products. The chef, passionate about the region's gastronomy, creates dishes that combine tradition and modernity, offering an exceptional culinary experience. The tasting menu offers dishes such as "Filet de Veau de Normandie" and "Calvados Soufflé". The wine list highlights the region's great wines and other prestigious wine regions.

Regional Cuisine

The cuisine at La Ferme Saint-Siméon places particular emphasis on local products, with a locavore philosophy that favors fresh, seasonal ingredients from local producers. Guests can enjoy Normandy specialties such as "Poulet Vallée d'Auge", "Roasted Camembert" and "Tarte Tatin", accompanied by carefully selected ciders and calvados.

The Gourmet Breakfast

Saint-Siméon 's gourmet breakfast is served in the elegantly decorated dining room or on the terrace, with magnificent views of the gardens and the sea. Breakfast is composed of fresh, local products, including pastries, fruit, homemade jams, Norman cheeses, fresh eggs and pressed fruit juices. Guests can also enjoy hot drinks, such as coffee, tea and hot chocolate.

Activities and Services

The Spa and Wellness Treatments

La Ferme Saint-Siméon offers a range of well-being treatments for its clients, ranging from massages to facial treatments, carried out with high quality products. The spa, located in a peaceful and luxurious setting, is a place of rest and relaxation, perfect for recharging your batteries after a day exploring the region.

Professional therapists use advanced techniques and luxury products to ensure optimal results and a luxurious experience. Guests can also enjoy the heated indoor swimming pool, jacuzzi, sauna and steam room to complete their relaxation experience.

Outdoor activities

The gardens and terraces of La Ferme Saint-Siméon are perfect for leisurely walks, meditation sessions or outdoor yoga sessions. Guests can also enjoy the proximity to the sea for water activities such as sailing, kayaking and fishing. Guided excursions are also organized to explore the surrounding area, including the town of Honfleur, the beaches of Deauville and the cliffs of Étretat.

Cultural Activities and Experiences

La Ferme Saint-Siméon regularly organizes cultural events and unique experiences for its clients. Private concerts, literary readings and art exhibitions are often organized in the establishment's lounges or gardens. These events offer immersion in the local cultural scene and allow guests to meet artists, writers and musicians.

Guests can also participate in cooking workshops, baking classes and chocolate tastings, led by local chefs. These workshops offer an opportunity to learn Norman cooking techniques and taste delicious creations. La Ferme Saint-Siméon also offers yoga and meditation classes, led by qualified instructors, in the hotel's gardens or wellness areas.

Special Events and Unique Experiences

Weddings and Receptions

La Ferme Saint-Siméon is an ideal venue for organizing intimate weddings and private receptions. The property's gardens and lounges provide a romantic and elegant setting for ceremonies and receptions. Hotel staff work closely with couples to create tailor-made events, taking into account every detail, from decor to personalized menus.

The hotel's chefs create wedding menus that reflect the tastes and preferences of the bride and groom, using seasonal ingredients and local produce. The professional and attentive service teams ensure that every event goes off without a hitch. Couples can also enjoy luxurious suites for their wedding night, with special services such as massages, in-room breakfasts and welcome gifts.

Seminars and Business Meetings

La Ferme Saint-Siméon offers an exceptional setting for seminars, conferences and business meetings. The property's private lounges, equipped with the latest technology, offer flexible spaces for events of different sizes. Hotel teams work with event organizers to create tailor-made programs, including coffee breaks, business lunches and dinners.

Team-building activities and excursions can also be organized to strengthen team cohesion and provide moments of relaxation outside of work sessions. Guests can take advantage of the hotel's wellness facilities to unwind after a day of meetings, with spa treatments, yoga sessions and massages.

Unique Experiences

La Ferme Saint-Siméon offers unique experiences to make each stay memorable. These include private dinners in exclusive locations within the establishment, such as the library or gardens, offering an intimate and romantic atmosphere. Guests can also participate in wine tasting workshops, led by expert sommeliers, to discover the secrets of Normandy and regional wines.

Wellness getaways are also available, including personalized relaxation and relaxation programs, spa treatments, yoga and meditation sessions, as well as healthy and nutritious meals. These programs are designed to help clients recharge their batteries and regain physical and mental balance.

Seasonal and Thematic Offers

La Ferme Saint-Siméon regularly offers seasonal and thematic offers to enrich its customers' experience. At Christmas, the establishment is decked out in festive decorations and offers special menus, cookie decorating workshops and Christmas market visits. In summer, gourmet picnics can be organized in the gardens or on the terraces.

Romantic getaways are also offered, including candlelit dinners, duo massages and horse-drawn carriage rides in the surrounding area. For culture lovers, special packages including tickets for exhibitions, shows and concerts are available, offering complete immersion in the cultural life of the region.

Conclusion

La Ferme Saint-Siméon is much more than just a luxury hotel; it is a destination in itself, offering a unique and unforgettable experience in the heart of the magnificent city of Honfleur. With its rich history, impressive architecture, refined culinary offerings and a variety of activities and services, this establishment is the ideal place to relax, recharge and discover the French art of living.

Whether for a romantic getaway, a wellness retreat, an intimate wedding or a business meeting, La Ferme Saint-Siméon promises an exceptional experience, marked by luxury, comfort and elegance. Guests leave with unforgettable memories, enriched by the unique culture, gastronomy and hospitality of this emblematic establishment of the Normandy region.

- The Manor of the Impressionists

Le Manoir des Impressionnistes, located in Honfleur, is a charming 18th-century manor house which offers an idyllic and peaceful setting overlooking the Seine estuary. This historic residence is a true haven of peace, imbued with the charm and elegance of the period. Le Manoir des Impressionnistes is the ideal location for a romantic getaway, relaxing retreat or cultural exploration in Normandy. In this chapter, we will explore the history and architecture of the Manoir des Impressionnistes, its culinary offerings, the activities and services offered, and the unique experiences it offers.

History and Architecture

A Heritage of the 18th Century

The Manoir des Impressionnistes was built in the 18th century and has retained its old-world charm while being modernized to offer contemporary comfort. The residence is surrounded by lush gardens and green meadows, offering breathtaking views of the Seine estuary. This historic mansion has attracted many artists over the years, including impressionist painters who found inspiration in its picturesque landscapes.

Elegant Architecture

The architecture of the Manoir des Impressionnistes reflects the classic style of French country houses of the period, with its stone facades, wooden shutters and slate roofs. Interiors are decorated with antique furniture, artwork and fine textiles, creating a warm and sophisticated atmosphere.

The hotel's rooms and suites offer breathtaking views of the gardens, the Seine estuary and the surrounding countryside. Each room is unique, with distinctive design elements and modern amenities to ensure optimal comfort. The bathrooms, fitted with marble bathtubs and walk-in showers, provide a luxurious setting in which to relax and rejuvenate.

Culinary Offers

The Gourmet Restaurant

The gourmet restaurant at Manoir des Impressionnistes offers inventive and refined cuisine, highlighting local and seasonal products. The chef, passionate about the region's gastronomy, creates dishes that combine tradition and modernity, offering an exceptional culinary experience. The tasting menu offers dishes such as "Filet de Bass de Ligne" and "Soufflé au Calvados". The wine list highlights the region's great wines and other prestigious wine regions.

Regional Cuisine

The cuisine at Manoir des Impressionnistes places particular emphasis on local products, with a locavore philosophy that favors fresh, seasonal ingredients from local producers. Guests can taste Norman specialties such as "Poulet Vallée d'Auge", "Roasted Camembert" and "Tarte Tatin", accompanied by carefully selected wines to enhance each dish.

The Gourmet Breakfast

The Manoir des Impressionnistes' gourmet breakfast is served in the elegantly decorated dining room or on the terrace, with magnificent views of the gardens and the Seine estuary. Breakfast is composed of fresh, local products, including pastries, fruit, homemade jams, Norman cheeses, fresh eggs and pressed fruit juices. Guests can also enjoy hot drinks, such as coffee, tea and hot chocolate.

Activities and Services

The Spa and Wellness Treatments

Le Manoir des Impressionnistes offers a range of well-being treatments for its clients, ranging from massages to facial treatments, carried out with high quality products. The spa, located in a peaceful and luxurious setting, is a place of rest and relaxation, perfect for recharging your batteries after a day exploring the region.

Professional therapists use advanced techniques and luxury products to ensure optimal results and a luxurious experience. Guests can also enjoy the heated outdoor swimming pool, jacuzzi, sauna and steam room to complete their relaxation experience.

Outdoor activities

The gardens and terraces of Manoir des Impressionnistes are perfect for leisurely walks, meditation sessions or outdoor yoga sessions. Guests can also enjoy the proximity to the sea for water activities such as sailing, kayaking and fishing. Guided excursions are also organized to explore the surrounding area, including the town of Honfleur, the beaches of Deauville and the cliffs of Étretat.

Cultural Activities and Experiences

Le Manoir des Impressionnistes regularly organizes cultural events and unique experiences for its guests. Private concerts, literary readings and art exhibitions are often organized in the establishment's lounges or gardens. These events offer immersion in the local cultural scene and allow guests to meet artists, writers and musicians.

Guests can also participate in cooking workshops, baking classes and chocolate tastings, led by local chefs. These workshops offer an opportunity to learn Norman cooking techniques and taste delicious creations. Le Manoir des Impressionnistes also offers yoga and meditation classes, led by qualified instructors, in the hotel's gardens or wellness areas.

Special Events and Unique Experiences

Weddings and Receptions

Le Manoir des Impressionnistes is an ideal venue for organizing intimate weddings and private receptions. The property's gardens and lounges provide a romantic and elegant setting for ceremonies and receptions. Hotel staff work closely with couples to create tailor-made events, taking into account every detail, from decor to personalized menus.

The hotel's chefs create wedding menus that reflect the tastes and preferences of the bride and groom, using seasonal ingredients and local produce. The professional and attentive service teams ensure that every event goes off without a hitch. Couples can also enjoy luxurious suites for their wedding night, with special services such as massages, in-room breakfasts and welcome gifts.

Seminars and Business Meetings

The Manoir des Impressionnistes offers an exceptional setting for seminars, conferences and business meetings. The property's private lounges, equipped with the latest technology, offer flexible spaces for events of different sizes. Hotel teams work with event organizers to create tailor-made programs, including coffee breaks, business lunches and dinners.

Team-building activities and excursions can also be organized to strengthen team cohesion and provide moments of relaxation outside of work sessions. Guests can take advantage of the hotel's wellness facilities to unwind after a day of meetings, with spa treatments, yoga sessions and massages.

Unique Experiences

Le Manoir des Impressionnistes offers unique experiences to make each stay memorable. These include private dinners in exclusive locations within the establishment, such as the library or gardens, offering an intimate and romantic atmosphere. Guests can also participate in wine tasting workshops, led by expert sommeliers, to discover the secrets of Normandy and regional wines.

Wellness getaways are also available, including personalized relaxation and relaxation programs, spa treatments, yoga and meditation sessions, as well as healthy and nutritious meals. These programs are designed to help clients recharge their batteries and regain physical and mental balance.

Seasonal and Thematic Offers

Le Manoir des Impressionnistes regularly offers seasonal and thematic offers to enrich its customers' experience. At Christmas, the establishment is decked out in festive decorations and offers special menus, cookie decorating workshops and Christmas market visits. In summer, gourmet picnics can be organized in the gardens or on the terraces.

Romantic getaways are also offered, including candlelit dinners, duo massages and horse-drawn carriage rides in the surrounding area. For culture lovers, special packages including tickets for exhibitions, shows and concerts are available, offering complete immersion in the cultural life of the region.

Conclusion

Le Manoir des Impressionnistes is much more than just a luxury hotel; it is a destination in itself, offering a unique and unforgettable experience in the heart of the magnificent city of Honfleur. With its rich history, impressive architecture, refined culinary offerings and a variety of activities and services, this establishment is the ideal place to relax, recharge and discover the French art of living.

Whether for a romantic getaway, a wellness retreat, an intimate wedding or a business meeting, Le Manoir des Impressionnistes promises an exceptional experience, marked by luxury, comfort and elegance. Guests leave with unforgettable memories, enriched by the unique culture, gastronomy and hospitality of this emblematic establishment of the Normandy region.

Chapter 8: Relais & Châteaux in Brittany

1. General Presentation of the Region

Brittany, located in the northwest of France, is a region rich in history, culture and spectacular landscapes. Known for its wild coasts, Celtic legends, medieval towns and gastronomic specialties, Brittany offers a diversity of sites and experiences for visitors. This chapter explores in detail the geographical, historical, cultural and economic characteristics of Brittany, highlighting the treasures that make this region a unique destination.

Geography and Landscapes

A Wild and Magnificent Coast

Brittany is surrounded by sea on three sides, with over 2,700 kilometers of spectacular coastline. The Breton coast is famous for its rugged cliffs, sandy beaches, secret coves and picturesque islands. The Emerald and Pink Granite coasts and the Crozon peninsula are among the most remarkable, offering breathtaking panoramas and opportunities for hiking, water sports and relaxation.

The Breton Islands

Brittany has many islands, each with its own character and attractions. Belle-Île-en-Mer, Groix, Ouessant, Molène and les Glénan are popular destinations for day trips or extended stays. These islands offer wild landscapes, idyllic beaches, charming villages and rich biodiversity.

A Green and Fertile Countryside

Inland Brittany is characterized by lush green countryside, made up of meadows, forests, valleys and hills. The Monts d'Arrée and the Montagnes Noires are the main hill ranges, offering panoramic views and hiking trails. The region's rivers and lakes add to the scenic beauty and provide opportunities for fishing, boating and water activities.

Regional Natural Parks

Brittany is home to several regional natural parks, such as the Armorique Regional Natural Park and the Brière Regional Natural Park. These parks protect local wildlife, while providing hiking trails, biking trails, and picnic areas for visitors. They are ideal places to discover the natural wealth of the region.

History and Heritage

Celtic Origins

Brittany has a rich and complex history, dating back to prehistoric times. The region is deeply marked by its Celtic heritage, with megalithic sites such as the alignments of Carnac, the menhirs of

Locmariaquer and the dolmens of Plouharnel. These monuments bear witness to the human occupation of the region for millennia.

Roman Influence

The Romans also left their mark in Brittany, with the construction of towns, roads and fortifications. Roman remains, such as the thermal baths of Carhaix and the aqueducts of Rennes, bear witness to the importance of the region in the Roman Empire.

The Breton Duchies and the Wars of Succession

Brittany was an independent duchy for several centuries, with its own dukes and institutions. The Breton wars of succession in the 14th century marked the region's history, ultimately leading to the union of Brittany with France in 1532. Castles and fortresses, such as Château de Fougères and Château de Josselin, bear witness to this tumultuous period.

Maritime Heritage

Brittany has a long maritime tradition, with historic ports such as Saint-Malo, Brest and Lorient. These ports were centers of trade, fishing and exploration, playing a key role in France's maritime history. The corsairs of Saint-Malo, explorers like Jacques Cartier and the large fishing companies contributed to the wealth and fame of the region.

Culture and Traditions

Breton Language and Culture

Brittany is proud of its distinct language and culture. Breton, a Celtic language, is still spoken in parts of the region and taught in schools. Breton culture is rich in musical traditions, with instruments such as the bombarde and the biniou, and traditional dances such as the an dro and the gavotte.

Fest-Noz and Festivals

Fest-noz, night parties with music and traditional dance, are popular events in Brittany, attracting thousands of participants. Festivals, such as the Festival Interceltique de Lorient, the Fête de la Musique in Rennes and the Festival des Vieilles Charrues, celebrate Breton culture and attract artists and visitors from around the world.

Gastronomy and Local Products

Brittany is renowned for its gastronomy, highlighting local products and culinary traditions. Crepes and pancakes, seafood, salted butter, cider and kouign-amann are among the most emblematic specialties. Local markets, Michelin-starred restaurants and traditional inns offer a variety of culinary delights to satisfy all tastes.

Local Festivals and Traditions

Brittany is rich in festivals and traditions, which bear witness to its history and culture. Village festivals, agricultural fairs and folk festivals are opportunities to celebrate local customs and continue traditions. Pardons, religious pilgrimages, are also important events in the life of Breton communities.

Economy and Innovation

Tourism

Tourism is a key sector of the Breton economy, attracting millions of visitors from all over the world each year. The diversity of landscapes, cultural richness and historical heritage are all assets that make this region a popular destination. The region's tourist infrastructure is of high quality, with a diverse range of accommodation, starred restaurants, wellness centers and leisure activities.

Agriculture and Seafood

Agriculture and fishing play an essential role in Brittany's economy. The region produces a wide variety of agricultural products, including vegetables, fruits, dairy products and quality meats. Seafood products, such as oysters, mussels, scallops and fish, are also very popular. Quality labels, such as the AOP (Protected Designation of Origin) and the IGP (Protected Geographical Indication), guarantee the authenticity and quality of local products.

Industry and Innovation

Brittany is also a center of innovation and industrial development, with various sectors such as agri-food, the naval industry, telecommunications and renewable energies. Competitiveness clusters, such as Valorial (agri-food) and Images & Réseaux (information and communication technologies), promote innovation and collaboration between economic and scientific players.

Transportation infrastructure, such as highways, high-speed train lines and seaports, supports the region's economic development. The proximity of Paris, as well as the presence of large metropolises such as Rennes and Brest, facilitate commercial exchanges and international collaborations. The Brittany region is a key player in the French economy, contributing to its dynamism and international influence.

Conclusion

Brittany is an exceptional region, rich in history, culture and varied landscapes. Whether enjoying the wild and beautiful coastlines, exploring the picturesque islands, discovering the medieval towns or savoring the local gastronomy, there is something for everyone.

The Relais & Châteaux of the Brittany region capture the essence of this diversity and offer their guests unforgettable experiences, combining luxury, comfort and authenticity. Each establishment, with its enchanting setting, warm welcome, exceptional gastronomy and enriching activities, offers total immersion in the French art of living.

By discovering the Relais & Châteaux de Bretagne, you will be transported into a world where every detail is designed to delight the senses and create lasting memories. This chapter presented a detailed overview of the region, integrating geographical, historical, cultural and economic aspects to provide a comprehensive understanding of this unique destination.

- History and Heritage

Brittany is a region steeped in history and legends, with a rich and diverse heritage stretching from prehistoric times to the present day. Its monuments, historic sites and cultural traditions bear witness to its tumultuous past and its unique identity. In this chapter, we will explore key moments in Brittany's history, its iconic monuments and its cultural contributions.

Prehistoric Origins

Megalithic Sites

Brittany is famous for its impressive megalithic sites, which are among the oldest and most fascinating in Europe. The Carnac alignments, with their thousands of menhirs aligned over several kilometers, are among the best known. These structures, erected between 4500 and 3300 BC, demonstrate the presence of advanced prehistoric civilizations. Other notable sites include the dolmens of Plouharnel, the cairns of Barnenez and the menhirs of Locmariaquer.

Celtic Legends and Myths

Brittany is also rich in Celtic legends, which mingle with its prehistoric sites. The forest of Brocéliande, for example, is famous for its associations with Arthurian legends, notably the stories of Merlin the Enchanter, the Fairy Morgana and the Knight Lancelot. These legends add a mystical dimension to Breton landscapes and continue to attract many visitors.

Roman Influence

The Roman Conquest

In the 1st century BC, Brittany was conquered by the Romans, who established their domination over the region. They build cities, roads and infrastructure that promote economic and cultural development. Roman remains, such as the thermal baths of Carhaix, the aqueducts of Rennes and the villas of Corseul, bear witness to this period of Roman influence.

Gallo-Roman Cities

The Gallo-Roman towns of Brittany, such as Condate (Rennes), Darioritum (Vannes) and Vorgium (Carhaix), became important administrative, commercial and cultural centers. They play a key role in the diffusion of Roman culture and the Romanization of local populations.

The Breton Duchies and the Middle Ages

The Birth of the Duchy of Brittany

In the 5th century, Brittany saw the arrival of the island Bretons, fleeing the Anglo-Saxon invasions in Great Britain. They settled in Armorique, giving birth to a new Breton identity. In the 9th century, Nominoë, considered the founding father of Brittany, unified the different Breton kingdoms and founded the Duchy of Brittany.

The Wars of Succession

The 14th and 15th centuries were marked by the Breton wars of succession, a series of dynastic conflicts between the supporters of Jean de Montfort and those of Charles de Blois. These wars ended with the victory of Jean de Montfort, who became Duke of Brittany. The duchy maintained its independence until its union with France in 1532.

Castles and Fortresses

Medieval Brittany is dotted with castles and fortresses, which bear witness to its tumultuous history and strategic position. Among the most famous are the Château de Fougères, one of the largest castles in Europe, the Château de Josselin, with its magnificent towers and gardens, and the Château de Suscinio , residence of the Dukes of Brittany. These fortresses play a key role in the defense of the duchy and in the consolidation of the power of the dukes.

The Renaissance and the Union with France

Union with France

In 1532, the Duchy of Brittany was officially united with the Kingdom of France, under the reign of François I. This union puts an end to Breton independence, but the region retains a certain autonomy and its cultural particularities. Renaissance castles, such as the Château des Ducs de Bretagne in Nantes, bear witness to this period of transition.

Cultural Development

The Renaissance brought an artistic and intellectual renewal to Brittany. The cities of Rennes, Nantes and Vannes became dynamic cultural centers, attracting artists, writers and scholars. Renaissance architecture, with its mansions, mansions and richly decorated churches, bears witness to this period of prosperity and creativity.

Maritime Heritage

Ports and Navigation

Brittany has a long maritime tradition, with historic ports such as Saint-Malo, Brest and Lorient. These ports were centers of trade, fishing and exploration, playing a key role in France's maritime history. The corsairs of Saint-Malo, explorers like Jacques Cartier and the large fishing companies contributed to the wealth and fame of the region.

Lighthouses and Semaphores

The Breton coast is dotted with lighthouses and semaphores, which demonstrate the importance of navigation and maritime safety. Among the most famous, we find the Pointe Saint-Mathieu lighthouse, the Eckmühl lighthouse and the Virgin Island lighthouse. These structures, often built in isolated and spectacular locations, are iconic symbols of Brittany.

The Revolution and Modern Times

French Revolution

The French Revolution of 1789 marked a period of upheaval for Brittany, as for the rest of the country. Feudal institutions are abolished, and the region is reorganized into departments. The property of the Church and the nobility was confiscated and sold, leading to profound transformations in Breton society.

The Second World War

Brittany played a strategic role during the Second World War, with its ports and naval bases. The region was occupied by German forces, who fortified the coast by building the Atlantic Wall. The cities of Brest, Lorient and Saint-Malo suffered major Allied bombings. Breton resistance was also active, contributing to the liberation of the region in 1944.

Reconstruction and Development

After the war, Brittany undertook a period of reconstruction and modernization. Infrastructure is rebuilt, cities renovated and industries revitalized. Tourism is becoming a key sector of the economy, attracting visitors from around the world to discover the historical and cultural treasures of the region.

Cultural and Architectural Heritage

UNESCO Sites

Brittany has several UNESCO World Heritage sites, which testify to the richness of its cultural and architectural heritage. Among them, we find:

- Mont-Saint-Michel and its bay: Although located in Normandy, Mont-Saint-Michel is often associated with Brittany because of its proximity. This site is a masterpiece of medieval architecture, with its abbey perched on a rocky island surrounded by spectacular tides.
- The Carnac alignments: This exceptional megalithic site, with its rows of menhirs and dolmens, is one of the most important in Europe and attracts researchers and visitors from all over the world.

Historical Monuments and Museums

Brittany is home to numerous historical monuments and museums that tell the history of the region and highlight its cultural heritage. Among them, we find:

- Saint-Corentin Cathedral in Quimper: A masterpiece of Gothic architecture, famous for its imposing spires and magnificent stained glass windows.
- The Rennes Museum of Fine Arts: This museum houses a rich collection of paintings, sculptures and art objects, ranging from the Middle Ages to the contemporary era.
- The Compagnie des Indes museum in Lorient: This museum traces the history of the Compagnie des Indes, which played a key role in maritime trade and exploration in the 18th century.

Conclusion

Brittany is a region rich in history and heritage, where every street corner, every village and every monument tells a unique story. From prehistoric remains to medieval castles, from Romanesque abbeys to majestic lighthouses, the region offers an incredible diversity of monuments and historic sites.

The Relais & Châteaux of the Brittany region capture the essence of this historical and cultural richness, offering their guests unforgettable experiences. Each establishment, with its enchanting setting, warm welcome, exceptional gastronomy and enriching activities, offers total immersion in the history and heritage of the region.

By discovering the Relais & Châteaux de Bretagne, you will be transported into a world where every detail is designed to delight the senses and create lasting memories. This chapter explored the many facets of the region's history and heritage, revealing how each era helped shape this unique and fascinating destination.

- Gastronomy and Wine

Brittany is a region renowned for its gastronomic richness and exceptional local products. Its cuisine is anchored in ancient traditions, highlighting seafood, vegetables from its fertile lands, and unique local specialties. In this chapter, we will explore the gastronomic aspects of the region, highlighting the local products, iconic dishes, renowned chefs, starred restaurants and wines that this region is famous for.

The Roots of Regional Gastronomy

Seafood

Brittany, with its 2,700 kilometers of coastline, is a paradise for seafood lovers. Breton seafood is among the most popular in the world, and it constitutes an essential part of regional cuisine.

- Oysters: Brittany is famous for its oysters, particularly those from Cancale and Belon. They are appreciated for their iodized flavor and delicate texture.
- Scallops: Breton scallops, fished mainly in the bay of Saint-Brieuc, are renowned for their delicate taste and superior quality.
- Lobsters and Langoustines: The region produces high quality shellfish, notably blue lobsters and langoustines, often served grilled or in sauce.
- Fish: Breton fishing ports provide a wide variety of fresh fish, such as sea bass, sole, mackerel and monkfish, often prepared in a simple way to highlight their freshness.

Products of the Earth

Brittany is also a fertile agricultural land, producing a wide variety of vegetables, fruits and dairy products.

- Vegetables: Artichokes from Brittany, onions from Roscoff, potatoes from the island of Batz and carrots from Créances are some of the emblematic vegetables of the region.
- Fruits: Apples are omnipresent in Brittany, used to make cider, calvados and desserts. Plougastel strawberries are also very famous.
- Dairy Products: Breton salted butter is famous for its richness and unique taste, and it is used in many local recipes. Breton cheeses, such as goat's cheese from Pays de Redon and cow's cheese from Pays Nantais, are also very popular.

Local Specialties

Brittany has many unique culinary specialties, often linked to its traditions and cultural heritage.

- Crêpes and Galettes: Sweet crepes and buckwheat pancakes are essentials of Breton cuisine. They are often topped with butter, sugar, jam, cheese, ham or eggs.
- Kouign-Amann: This butter and sugar cake, from Douarnenez, is a true Breton treat, known for its caramelized and melting texture.
- Far Breton: This prune flan is a traditional, simple and delicious dessert, often prepared for celebrations and special occasions.
- La Cotriade: This traditional fish soup, similar to bouillabaisse, is prepared with fresh fish, potatoes and herbs, and served with bread and butter.

Wines and Ciders of Brittany

The Cider

Cider is the emblematic drink of Brittany, made from apples grown in the region's orchards. There are several varieties of cider, ranging from sweet to hard cider, each with its own taste and fermentation characteristics. Cider is often served with pancakes and pancakes, or as a refreshing drink at any time of the day.

The Chouchen

Chouchen is a traditional Breton alcoholic drink, made from fermented honey. It is often compared to mead, but with a distinct and unique flavor. Chouchen is generally consumed as an aperitif or digestive.

The Lambig

Lambig is a cider brandy, distilled from cider and aged in oak barrels . This strong drink is similar to Norman calvados, but with characteristics specific to Brittany. Lambig is often enjoyed as a digestive, but it is also used in cooking to flavor sauces and desserts.

Star Chefs and Restaurants

The Pioneers of Regional Haute Cuisine

Brittany has always been a hotbed of culinary creativity, attracting talented chefs who have been able to highlight local products and culinary traditions. Among the pioneers of regional haute cuisine is Olivier Roellinger , considered one of the region's greatest chefs. His restaurant, Les Maisons de Bricourt in Cancale, maintained three Michelin stars for several years.

Contemporary Chefs

Today, the region continues to attract renowned chefs, who continue the tradition of haute cuisine while innovating and experimenting with new flavors. Among the most famous contemporary chefs, we find:

- Dominique Crenn : Originally from Brittany, Dominique Crenn became the first female chef in the United States to receive three Michelin stars for her restaurant Atelier Crenn in San Francisco.
- Jean-Yves Bordier: Master butter refiner in Saint-Malo, Jean-Yves Bordier is famous for his artisanal butters and matured cheeses. His workshop is an essential destination for lovers of quality butter.
- Hugo Roellinger : Son of Olivier Roellinger , Hugo perpetuates the family tradition with his restaurant Le Coquillage in Cancale, offering inventive cuisine that respects local products.

Star Restaurants

Brittany is home to many Michelin-starred restaurants, each offering a unique and unforgettable culinary experience. Among the most famous, we find:

Roellinger 's restaurant , offering inventive cuisine that respects local products. The tasting menu offers dishes such as "Homard Bleu de Bretagne" and "Saint-Pierre aux Algues".
- Le Manoir de Lan- Kerellec in Trébeurden: Laurent Bacquer 's restaurant , renowned for its creative and refined cuisine, highlighting seafood. The tasting menu offers dishes such as "Turbot Sauvage" and "Kouign -Amann Revisited."
Carro 's restaurant , offering inventive and elegant cuisine, highlighting products from the land and sea. The tasting menu offers dishes such as the "Bar de Ligne" and the "Far Unstructured Breton".

Oenological Experiences

Cider and Chouchen Tastings

Relais & Châteaux in the Brittany region often offer unique wine experiences for their guests. From private tastings to cider house visits, these experiences allow you to discover the region's ciders and chouchens and learn the secrets of their production.

Customers can participate in tasting workshops, led by experts, to learn how to identify the aromas and flavors of the region's ciders and chouchens. Guided tours of the orchards and distilleries allow you to discover the production processes, meet the producers and taste products directly from the source.

Food-Cider and Food-Chouchen Pairings

The Relais & Châteaux also offer food-cider and food-chouchen pairings, allowing you to savor the drinks of Brittany in harmony with the local cuisine. These pairings highlight the flavors of dishes and drinks, providing a complete and unforgettable gastronomic experience.

Chefs from Michelin-starred restaurants collaborate with sommeliers to create tasting menus that highlight the region's ciders and chouchens. Each dish is carefully paired with a drink, allowing guests to discover new combinations of flavors and textures.

Conclusion

Brittany is a true land of gastronomy and drinks, offering unrivaled richness and diversity. Regional cuisine, with its authentic flavors and quality local products, is a pillar of the region's art of living. Ciders, chouchens and lambigs , renowned for their complexity and elegance, perfectly complement this culinary experience.

The Relais & Châteaux of the Brittany region capture the essence of this gastronomic richness, offering their guests unique and unforgettable culinary and wine experiences. Each establishment, with its enchanting setting, warm welcome, exceptional gastronomy and enriching activities, offers total immersion in the French art of living.

By discovering the Relais & Châteaux de Bretagne, you will be transported into a world where every detail is designed to delight the senses and create lasting memories. This chapter explored the many facets of the region's food and drink, revealing how each element contributes to making this destination a true oasis of flavors and culinary pleasures.

2. Addresses and Descriptions

Brittany is a region rich in history, culture and spectacular landscapes. Its Relais & Châteaux offer a unique experience combining luxury, comfort and regional charm. These establishments, located in emblematic places of the region, offer unforgettable stays in the heart of Breton nature, from its wild coasts to its picturesque villages. In this chapter, we will discover some of the most prestigious addresses and describe in detail what makes them special.

Domaine de Rochevilaine

History and Architecture

The Domaine de Rochevilaine is a superb hotel located in Billiers, on the Rhuys peninsula. This area is made up of several traditional Breton buildings, some of which date back to the 13th century. Nestled on the edge of the Atlantic Ocean, it offers stunning views of the sea and cliffs. The architecture of the estate reflects the charm of Breton residences, with its stone walls, slate roofs and landscaped gardens.

Culinary Offers

The Domaine de Rochevilaine gourmet restaurant , led by a talented chef, offers inventive and refined cuisine, highlighting local and seasonal products. The tasting menu offers dishes such as "Homard Bleu de Bretagne" and "Turbot Sauvage". The carefully selected wine list highlights the region's great wines and other prestigious wine regions.

Activities and Services

Domaine de Rochevilaine offers a range of activities for its guests, from relaxation to sport. Guests can enjoy the heated indoor swimming pool, spa, sauna and hammam for moments of relaxation. Guided excursions are also organized to explore the surrounding area, including the salt marshes of Guérande, the medieval town of Vannes and the beaches of the Rhuys peninsula. The estate also offers cooking classes, wine tastings and outdoor activities such as golfing and cycling.

Castel Clara Thalasso & Spa

History and Architecture

Castel Clara Thalasso & Spa is located in Belle-Île-en-Mer, a picturesque island off the southern coast of Brittany. This luxury hotel offers an exceptional setting with spectacular views of the Atlantic Ocean and the surrounding cliffs. The hotel's architecture combines traditional Breton elements with modern touches, creating an elegant and comfortable atmosphere.

Culinary Offers

Castel Clara's gourmet restaurant, led by a renowned chef, offers inventive and refined cuisine, highlighting local and seasonal products. The tasting menu offers dishes such as "Saint-Pierre aux Algues" and "Kouign-Amann Revisité". The wine list highlights the region's great wines and other prestigious wine regions.

Activities and Services

Castel Clara Thalasso & Spa offers a range of activities for its guests, from relaxation to sport. Guests can enjoy the heated outdoor swimming pool, thalassotherapy spa, sauna and hammam for moments of relaxation. Guided excursions are also organized to explore the surrounding area, including the coastal hiking trails, sandy beaches and picturesque villages of Belle-Île-en-Mer. The hotel also offers yoga classes, meditation sessions and water activities such as sailing and kayaking.

The Brittany & Spa

History and Architecture

Brittany & Spa, located in Roscoff, is a luxury hotel housed in a former 17th century privateer's residence. This establishment offers a romantic and historic setting, with breathtaking views of the Ile de Batz and the English Channel. The hotel's architecture reflects the charm of traditional Breton houses, with its stone walls, wooden shutters and slate roofs.

Culinary Offers

The Brittany & Spa's gourmet restaurant, led by a talented chef, offers inventive and refined cuisine, highlighting local and seasonal products. The tasting menu offers dishes such as "Homard Bleu de Bretagne" and "Bar de Ligne". The carefully selected wine list highlights the region's great wines and other prestigious wine regions.

Activities and Services

Brittany & Spa offers a range of activities for its guests, from relaxation to sport. Guests can enjoy the heated indoor swimming pool, spa, sauna and hammam for moments of relaxation. Guided excursions are also organized to explore the surrounding area, including the island of Batz, the exotic gardens of Roscoff and the region's sandy beaches. The hotel also offers cooking classes, wine tastings and outdoor activities such as golfing and cycling.

Locguénolé Castle

History and Architecture

Château de Locguénolé, located in Kervignac near Lorient, is a magnificent 19th century castle surrounded by extensive gardens and woods. This historic residence, formerly the residence of the Polignac family, has been transformed into a luxury hotel, offering a romantic and elegant setting. The architecture of the castle, with its stone facades, towers and mullioned windows, evokes the elegance and refinement of the period.

Culinary Offers

Locguénolé 's gourmet restaurant offers inventive and refined cuisine, highlighting local and seasonal products. The chef, passionate about the region's gastronomy, creates dishes that combine tradition and modernity. The tasting menu offers dishes such as "Duck Foie Gras" and "Suckling Lamb of the

Pyrenees". The carefully selected wine list highlights the region's great wines and other prestigious wine regions.

Activities and Services

Château de Locguénolé offers a range of activities for its guests, from relaxation to sport. Guests can enjoy the heated outdoor swimming pool, gardens and terraces for moments of relaxation. Guided excursions are also organized to explore the surrounding area, including the city of Lorient, the beaches of the Breton coast and the region's historic sites. The castle also offers cooking classes, wine tastings and outdoor activities such as tennis and cycling.

Ti Al Lannec Hotel Restaurant & Spa

History and Architecture

The Ti Al Lannec Hotel Restaurant & Spa, located in Trébeurden, is a luxury hotel nestled on a hill overlooking the sea. This historic residence offers a peaceful and refined setting, with spectacular views of the Pink Granite Coast and the surrounding islands. The hotel's architecture combines traditional Breton elements with modern touches, creating an elegant and comfortable atmosphere.

Culinary Offers

Lannec 's gourmet restaurant , led by a talented chef, offers inventive and refined cuisine, highlighting local and seasonal products. The tasting menu offers dishes such as the "Turbot Sauvage" and the "Kouign-Amann Revisited". The carefully selected wine list highlights the region's great wines and other prestigious wine regions.

Activities and Services

The Ti Al Lannec Hotel Restaurant & Spa offers a range of activities for its guests, from relaxation to sport. Guests can enjoy the heated indoor swimming pool, spa, sauna and hammam for moments of relaxation. Guided excursions are also organized to explore the surrounding area, including the coastal walking trails, sandy beaches and picturesque villages of the Pink Granite Coast. The hotel also offers yoga classes, meditation sessions and water activities such as sailing and kayaking.

Conclusion

The Relais & Châteaux in Brittany offer unique and unforgettable experiences, combining luxury, comfort and historical heritage. Each establishment, with its enchanting setting, warm welcome, exceptional gastronomy and enriching activities, offers total immersion in the French art of living. Whether for a romantic getaway, a peaceful retreat or a cultural exploration, the Relais & Châteaux of the Brittany region are must-see destinations.

By discovering these exceptional establishments, you will be transported to a world where every detail is designed to delight the senses and create lasting memories. This chapter has presented a detailed overview of some of the most prestigious Relais & Châteaux in the region, offering a glimpse of the unique experience that awaits you in each of these enchanting locations.

- Castel Clara Thalasso & Spa

The Castel Clara Thalasso & Spa, located in Belle-Île-en-Mer, is a luxury establishment offering a unique and unforgettable experience on this picturesque island of Brittany. With its spectacular views of the Atlantic Ocean and surrounding cliffs, this haven of peace combines traditional Breton charm with modern comfort. In this chapter, we will explore the history and architecture of Castel Clara Thalasso & Spa, its culinary offerings, the activities and services offered, and the unique experiences it offers.

History and Architecture

A Maritime Heritage

Belle-Île-en-Mer, the largest of the Breton islands, is a place rich in history and culture. The Castel Clara Thalasso & Spa, built in a traditional Breton style, fits perfectly into this unique maritime landscape. The property takes its name from Goulphar Bay , where it is located, offering panoramic views of the cliffs and ocean.

Elegant Architecture

The architecture of Castel Clara Thalasso & Spa reflects the charm of Breton residences, with its stone facades, slate roofs and landscaped gardens. Interiors are decorated with contemporary furniture, artwork and fine textiles, creating a warm and sophisticated atmosphere.

The hotel's rooms and suites offer breathtaking views of the ocean, gardens or cliffs. Each room is unique, with distinctive design elements and modern amenities to ensure optimal comfort. The bathrooms, fitted with marble bathtubs and walk-in showers, provide a luxurious setting in which to relax and rejuvenate.

Culinary Offers

The Gourmet Restaurant

Castel Clara's gourmet restaurant, led by a renowned chef, offers inventive and refined cuisine, highlighting local and seasonal products. The tasting menu offers dishes such as "Homard Bleu de Bretagne" and "Turbot Sauvage". The wine list highlights the region's great wines and other prestigious wine regions.

The restaurant's setting matches its cuisine, with an elegantly decorated dining room, tables spaced for maximum privacy, and panoramic ocean views. Guests can also dine al fresco on the terrace, enjoying the tranquility and beauty of the natural surroundings.

Regional Cuisine

The cuisine at Castel Clara Thalasso & Spa places particular emphasis on local products, with a locavore philosophy that favors fresh, seasonal ingredients from local producers. Guests can enjoy Breton specialties such as "Kouign-Amann", "Bar de Ligne" and "Crêpes Suzette", accompanied by carefully selected ciders and chouchens.

The Gourmet Breakfast

Castel Clara's gourmet breakfast is served in the elegantly decorated dining room or on the terrace, with magnificent views of the ocean. Breakfast is composed of fresh, local products, including pastries, fruit, homemade jams, Breton cheeses, fresh eggs and pressed fruit juices. Guests can also enjoy hot drinks, such as coffee, tea and hot chocolate.

Activities and Services

The Thalasso Spa and Well-Being Treatments

The Castel Clara Thalasso & Spa offers a range of wellness treatments for its guests, from massages to facial treatments, carried out with high quality products. The thalasso spa, located in a peaceful and luxurious setting, is a place of rest and relaxation, perfect for recharging your batteries after a day of exploring the island.

Professional therapists use advanced techniques and luxury products to ensure optimal results and a luxurious experience. Guests can also enjoy the heated indoor swimming pool, jacuzzi, sauna and steam room to complete their relaxation experience.

Outdoor activities

The gardens and terraces of Castel Clara are perfect for leisurely walks, meditation sessions or outdoor yoga sessions. Guests can also take advantage of the proximity to the ocean for water activities such as sailing, kayaking and fishing. Guided excursions are also organized to explore the surrounding area, including the coastal hiking trails, sandy beaches and picturesque villages of Belle-Île-en-Mer.

Cultural Activities and Experiences

Castel Clara regularly organizes cultural events and unique experiences for its guests. Private concerts, literary readings and art exhibitions are often organized in the establishment's lounges or gardens. These events offer immersion in the local cultural scene and allow guests to meet artists, writers and musicians.

Guests can also participate in cooking workshops, baking classes and chocolate tastings, led by local chefs. These workshops offer an opportunity to learn Breton cooking techniques and taste delicious creations. Castel Clara also offers yoga and meditation classes, led by qualified instructors, in the hotel's gardens or wellness areas.

Special Events and Unique Experiences

Weddings and Receptions

Castel Clara Thalasso & Spa is an ideal venue for organizing intimate weddings and private receptions. The property's gardens and lounges provide a romantic and elegant setting for ceremonies and receptions. Hotel staff work closely with couples to create tailor-made events, taking into account every detail, from decor to personalized menus.

The hotel's chefs create wedding menus that reflect the tastes and preferences of the bride and groom, using seasonal ingredients and local produce. The professional and attentive service teams ensure that every event goes off without a hitch. Couples can also enjoy luxurious suites for their wedding night, with special services such as massages, in-room breakfasts and welcome gifts.

Seminars and Business Meetings

Castel Clara Thalasso & Spa offers an exceptional setting for seminars, conferences and business meetings. The property's private lounges, equipped with the latest technology, offer flexible spaces for events of different sizes. Hotel teams work with event organizers to create tailor-made programs, including coffee breaks, business lunches and dinners.

Team-building activities and excursions can also be organized to strengthen team cohesion and provide moments of relaxation outside of work sessions. Guests can take advantage of the hotel's wellness facilities to unwind after a day of meetings, with spa treatments, yoga sessions and massages.

Unique Experiences

Castel Clara Thalasso & Spa offers unique experiences to make each stay memorable. These include private dinners in exclusive locations within the establishment, such as the library or gardens, offering an intimate and romantic atmosphere. Customers can also participate in wine tasting workshops, led by expert sommeliers, to discover the secrets of the wines of Brittany and the region.

Wellness getaways are also available, including personalized relaxation and relaxation programs, spa treatments, yoga and meditation sessions, as well as healthy and nutritious meals. These programs are designed to help clients recharge their batteries and regain physical and mental balance.

Seasonal and Thematic Offers

Castel Clara Thalasso & Spa regularly offers seasonal and thematic offers to enrich its customers' experience. At Christmas, the establishment is decked out in festive decorations and offers special menus, cookie decorating workshops and Christmas market visits. In summer, gourmet picnics can be organized in the gardens or on the terraces.

Romantic getaways are also offered, including candlelit dinners, duo massages and horse-drawn carriage rides in the surrounding area. For culture lovers, special packages including tickets for exhibitions, shows and concerts are available, offering complete immersion in the cultural life of the region.

Conclusion

Castel Clara Thalasso & Spa is much more than just a luxury hotel; it is a destination in itself, offering a unique and unforgettable experience in the heart of the magnificent island of Belle-Île-en-Mer. With its rich history, impressive architecture, refined culinary offerings and a variety of activities and services, this establishment is the ideal place to relax, recharge and discover the French art of living.

Whether for a romantic getaway, a wellness retreat, an intimate wedding or a business meeting, Castel Clara Thalasso & Spa promises an exceptional experience, marked by luxury, comfort and elegance. Guests leave with unforgettable memories, enriched by the unique culture, gastronomy and hospitality of this emblematic establishment of the Brittany region.

- Hotel Brittany & Spa

The Brittany Hotel & Spa, located in Roscoff, is a luxury establishment installed in a former 17th century privateer's residence. This hotel offers a romantic and historic setting, with breathtaking views of the Ile de Batz and the English Channel. Brittany & Spa combines the charm of the past with modern comfort, offering its guests a unique and unforgettable experience. In this chapter, we will explore the history and architecture of the Brittany Hotel & Spa, its culinary offerings, the activities and services offered, and the unique experiences it offers.

History and Architecture

A Corsair Legacy

Roscoff, a historic port on the north coast of Brittany, is known for its rich maritime past and its privateers. The Brittany Hotel & Spa is housed in a 17th century privateer's residence, offering an immersion in the history of this fascinating period. The residence has been carefully restored to preserve its authentic character while offering first-rate modern comfort.

Elegant Architecture

The architecture of Hôtel Brittany & Spa reflects the charm of traditional Breton houses, with its stone walls, wooden shutters and slate roofs. Interiors are decorated with antique furniture, artwork and fine textiles, creating a warm and sophisticated atmosphere.

The hotel's rooms and suites offer breathtaking views of the sea, the gardens or the Ile de Batz. Each room is unique, with distinctive design elements and modern amenities to ensure optimal comfort. The bathrooms, fitted with marble bathtubs and walk-in showers, provide a luxurious setting in which to relax and rejuvenate.

Culinary Offers

The Gourmet Restaurant

The gourmet restaurant at the Brittany & Spa Hotel, led by a talented chef, offers inventive and refined cuisine, highlighting local and seasonal products. The tasting menu offers dishes such as "Homard Bleu de Bretagne" and "Bar de Ligne". The carefully selected wine list highlights the region's great wines and other prestigious wine regions.

The restaurant's setting matches its cuisine, with an elegantly decorated dining room, tables spaced for maximum privacy, and panoramic ocean views. Guests can also dine al fresco on the terrace, enjoying the tranquility and beauty of the natural surroundings.

Regional Cuisine

The cuisine at Hôtel Brittany & Spa places particular emphasis on local products, with a locavore philosophy that favors fresh, seasonal ingredients from local producers. Guests can enjoy Breton specialties such as "Kouign-Amann", "Bar de Ligne" and "Crêpes Suzette", accompanied by carefully selected ciders and chouchens.

The Gourmet Breakfast

The gourmet breakfast at Hôtel Brittany & Spa is served in the elegantly decorated dining room or on the terrace, with a magnificent view of the ocean. Breakfast is composed of fresh, local products, including pastries, fruit, homemade jams, Breton cheeses, fresh eggs and pressed fruit juices. Guests can also enjoy hot drinks, such as coffee, tea and hot chocolate.

Activities and Services

The Spa and Wellness Treatments

Hôtel Brittany & Spa offers a range of wellness treatments for its guests, from massages to facials, performed with high quality products. The spa, located in a peaceful and luxurious setting, is a place of rest and relaxation, perfect for recharging your batteries after a day exploring the region.

Professional therapists use advanced techniques and luxury products to ensure optimal results and a luxurious experience. Guests can also enjoy the heated indoor swimming pool, jacuzzi, sauna and steam room to complete their relaxation experience.

Outdoor activities

The gardens and terraces of the Brittany Hotel & Spa are perfect for leisurely walks, meditation sessions or outdoor yoga sessions. Guests can also enjoy the proximity to the sea for water activities such as sailing, kayaking and fishing. Guided excursions are also organized to explore the surrounding area, including the island of Batz, the exotic gardens of Roscoff and the region's sandy beaches.

Cultural Activities and Experiences

Hôtel Brittany & Spa regularly organizes cultural events and unique experiences for its guests. Private concerts, literary readings and art exhibitions are often organized in the establishment's lounges or gardens. These events offer immersion in the local cultural scene and allow guests to meet artists, writers and musicians.

Guests can also participate in cooking workshops, baking classes and chocolate tastings, led by local chefs. These workshops offer an opportunity to learn Breton cooking techniques and taste delicious creations. Hôtel Brittany & Spa also offers yoga and meditation classes, led by qualified instructors, in the hotel's gardens or wellness areas.

Special Events and Unique Experiences

Weddings and Receptions

The Brittany Hotel & Spa is an ideal venue for intimate weddings and private receptions. The property's gardens and lounges provide a romantic and elegant setting for ceremonies and receptions. Hotel staff work closely with couples to create tailor-made events, taking into account every detail, from decor to personalized menus.

The hotel's chefs create wedding menus that reflect the tastes and preferences of the bride and groom, using seasonal ingredients and local produce. The professional and attentive service teams ensure that every event goes off without a hitch. Couples can also enjoy luxurious suites for their wedding night, with special services such as massages, in-room breakfasts and welcome gifts.

Seminars and Business Meetings

The Brittany Hotel & Spa offers an exceptional setting for seminars, conferences and business meetings. The property's private lounges, equipped with the latest technology, offer flexible spaces for events of different sizes. Hotel teams work with event organizers to create tailor-made programs, including coffee breaks, business lunches and dinners.

Team-building activities and excursions can also be organized to strengthen team cohesion and provide moments of relaxation outside of work sessions. Guests can take advantage of the hotel's wellness facilities to unwind after a day of meetings, with spa treatments, yoga sessions and massages.

Unique Experiences

Hôtel Brittany & Spa offers unique experiences to make every stay memorable. These include private dinners in exclusive locations within the establishment, such as the library or gardens, offering an intimate and romantic atmosphere. Customers can also participate in wine tasting workshops, led by expert sommeliers, to discover the secrets of the wines of Brittany and the region.

Wellness getaways are also available, including personalized relaxation and relaxation programs, spa treatments, yoga and meditation sessions, as well as healthy and nutritious meals. These programs are designed to help clients recharge their batteries and regain physical and mental balance.

Seasonal and Thematic Offers

The Brittany Hotel & Spa regularly offers seasonal and thematic offers to enrich its guests' experience. At Christmas, the establishment is decked out in festive decorations and offers special menus, cookie decorating workshops and Christmas market visits. In summer, gourmet picnics can be organized in the gardens or on the terraces.

Romantic getaways are also offered, including candlelit dinners, duo massages and horse-drawn carriage rides in the surrounding area. For culture lovers, special packages including tickets for exhibitions, shows and concerts are available, offering complete immersion in the cultural life of the region.

Conclusion

The Brittany Hotel & Spa is much more than just a luxury hotel; it is a destination in itself, offering a unique and unforgettable experience in the heart of the magnificent town of Roscoff. With its rich history, impressive architecture, refined culinary offerings and a variety of activities and services, this establishment is the ideal place to relax, recharge and discover the French art of living.

Whether for a romantic getaway, a wellness retreat, an intimate wedding or a business meeting, the Brittany Hotel & Spa promises an exceptional experience, marked by luxury, comfort and elegance. Guests leave with unforgettable memories, enriched by the unique culture, gastronomy and hospitality of this emblematic establishment of the Brittany region.

- The Castel Marie-Louise

Castel Marie-Louise, located in La Baule, is a luxury establishment offering a refined and elegant experience on the Atlantic coast of Brittany. Nestled in an enchanting setting with manicured gardens and stunning ocean views, this historic mansion combines the charm of traditional architecture with modern comfort. In this chapter, we will explore the history and architecture of Castel Marie-Louise, its culinary offerings, the activities and services offered, and the unique experiences it offers.

History and Architecture

An Aristocratic Heritage

The Castel Marie-Louise was built in the early 20th century by Louis Lajarrige, a visionary real estate developer, who wanted to create a luxury hotel to attract the aristocracy and high society to La Baule. This Anglo-Norman style manor reflects the elegance and refinement of the period, with its stone facades, turrets and ornate balconies.

Elegant Architecture

The architecture of Castel Marie-Louise is a perfect example of the Anglo-Norman style, with rich decorative elements and noble materials. Interiors are decorated with antique furniture, artwork and fine textiles, creating a warm and sophisticated atmosphere.

The hotel's rooms and suites offer breathtaking views of the gardens or the Atlantic Ocean. Each room is unique, with distinctive design elements and modern amenities to ensure optimal comfort. The bathrooms, fitted with marble bathtubs and walk-in showers, provide a luxurious setting in which to relax and rejuvenate.

Culinary Offers

The Gourmet Restaurant

The Castel Marie-Louise's gourmet restaurant, led by a talented chef, offers inventive and refined cuisine, highlighting local and seasonal products. The tasting menu offers dishes such as "Lobster Bleu de Bretagne" and "Filet de Bass de Ligne". The carefully selected wine list highlights the region's great wines and other prestigious wine regions.

The restaurant's setting matches its cuisine, with an elegantly decorated dining room, tables spaced for maximum privacy, and panoramic ocean views. Guests can also dine al fresco on the terrace, enjoying the tranquility and beauty of the natural surroundings.

Regional Cuisine

The cuisine at Castel Marie-Louise places particular emphasis on local products, with a locavore philosophy that favors fresh, seasonal ingredients from local producers. Guests can enjoy Breton specialties such as "Kouign-Amann", "Bar de Ligne" and "Crêpes Suzette", accompanied by carefully selected ciders and chouchens.

The Gourmet Breakfast

Castel Marie-Louise's gourmet breakfast is served in the elegantly decorated dining room or on the terrace, with magnificent views of the gardens and the ocean. Breakfast is composed of fresh, local products, including pastries, fruit, homemade jams, Breton cheeses, fresh eggs and pressed fruit juices. Guests can also enjoy hot drinks, such as coffee, tea and hot chocolate.

Activities and Services

The Spa and Wellness Treatments

The Castel Marie-Louise offers a range of wellness treatments for its guests, ranging from massages to facial treatments, carried out with high quality products. The spa, located in a peaceful and luxurious setting, is a place of rest and relaxation, perfect for recharging your batteries after a day exploring the region.

Professional therapists use advanced techniques and luxury products to ensure optimal results and a luxurious experience. Guests can also enjoy the heated indoor swimming pool, jacuzzi, sauna and steam room to complete their relaxation experience.

Outdoor activities

The gardens and terraces of Castel Marie-Louise are perfect for leisurely walks, meditation sessions or outdoor yoga sessions. Guests can also enjoy the proximity to the beach for water activities such as sailing, kayaking and fishing. Guided excursions are also organized to explore the surrounding area, including the salt marshes of Guérande, the picturesque villages of Batz-sur-Mer and the beaches of La Baule.

Cultural Activities and Experiences

Castel Marie-Louise regularly organizes cultural events and unique experiences for its guests. Private concerts, literary readings and art exhibitions are often organized in the establishment's lounges or gardens. These events offer immersion in the local cultural scene and allow guests to meet artists, writers and musicians.

Guests can also participate in cooking workshops, baking classes and chocolate tastings, led by local chefs. These workshops offer an opportunity to learn Breton cooking techniques and taste delicious creations. The Castel Marie-Louise also offers yoga and meditation classes, led by qualified instructors, in the hotel's gardens or wellness areas.

Special Events and Unique Experiences

Weddings and Receptions

The Castel Marie-Louise is an ideal venue for organizing intimate weddings and private receptions. The property's gardens and lounges provide a romantic and elegant setting for ceremonies and receptions. Hotel staff work closely with couples to create tailor-made events, taking into account every detail, from decor to personalized menus.

The hotel's chefs create wedding menus that reflect the tastes and preferences of the bride and groom, using seasonal ingredients and local produce. The professional and attentive service teams ensure that every event goes off without a hitch. Couples can also enjoy luxurious suites for their wedding night, with special services such as massages, in-room breakfasts and welcome gifts.

Seminars and Business Meetings

The Castel Marie-Louise offers an exceptional setting for seminars, conferences and business meetings. The property's private lounges, equipped with the latest technology, offer flexible spaces for events of different sizes. Hotel teams work with event organizers to create tailor-made programs, including coffee breaks, business lunches and dinners.

Team-building activities and excursions can also be organized to strengthen team cohesion and provide moments of relaxation outside of work sessions. Guests can take advantage of the hotel's wellness facilities to unwind after a day of meetings, with spa treatments, yoga sessions and massages.

Unique Experiences

Castel Marie-Louise offers unique experiences to make each stay memorable. These include private dinners in exclusive locations within the establishment, such as the library or gardens, offering an intimate and romantic atmosphere. Customers can also participate in wine tasting workshops, led by expert sommeliers, to discover the secrets of the wines of Brittany and the region.

Wellness getaways are also available, including personalized relaxation and relaxation programs, spa treatments, yoga and meditation sessions, as well as healthy and nutritious meals. These programs are designed to help clients recharge their batteries and regain physical and mental balance.

Seasonal and Thematic Offers

The Castel Marie-Louise regularly offers seasonal and thematic offers to enrich its customers' experience. At Christmas, the establishment is decked out in festive decorations and offers special menus, cookie decorating workshops and Christmas market visits. In summer, gourmet picnics can be organized in the gardens or on the terraces.

Romantic getaways are also offered, including candlelit dinners, duo massages and horse-drawn carriage rides in the surrounding area. For culture lovers, special packages including tickets for exhibitions, shows and concerts are available, offering complete immersion in the cultural life of the region.

Conclusion

The Castel Marie-Louise is much more than just a luxury hotel; it is a destination in itself, offering a unique and unforgettable experience in the heart of the magnificent seaside resort of La Baule. With its rich history, impressive architecture, refined culinary offerings and a variety of activities and services, this establishment is the ideal place to relax, recharge and discover the French art of living.

Whether for a romantic getaway, a wellness retreat, an intimate wedding or a business meeting, Castel Marie-Louise promises an exceptional experience, marked by luxury, comfort and elegance. Guests leave with unforgettable memories, enriched by the unique culture, gastronomy and hospitality of this emblematic establishment of the Brittany region.

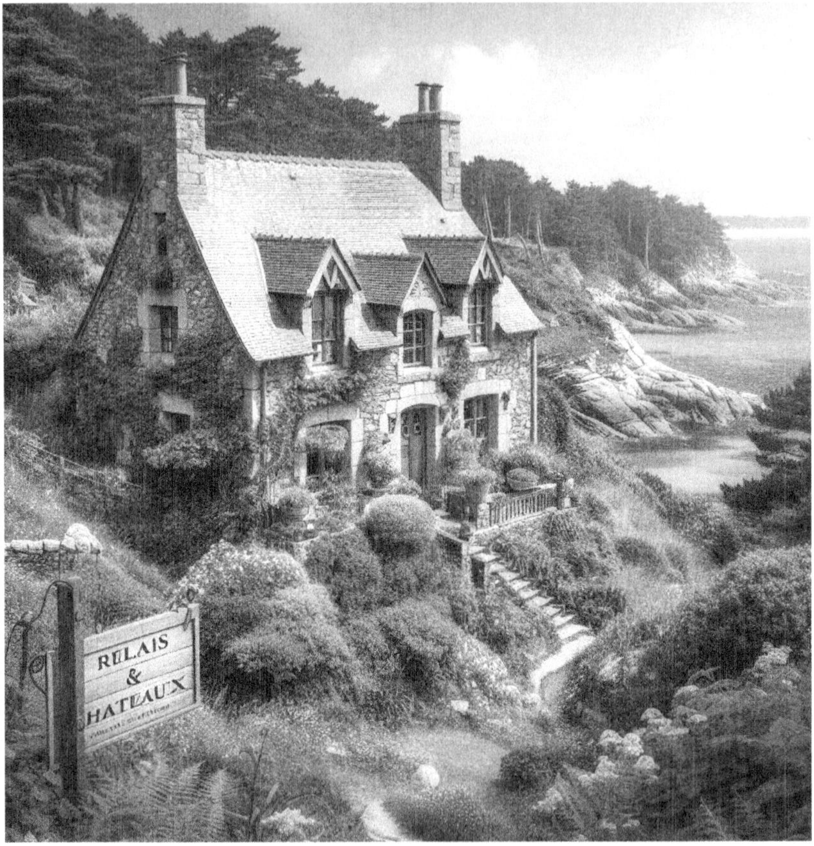
RELAIS
&
HATEAUX

Chapter 9: Relais & Châteaux in Pays de la Loire

1. General Presentation of the Region

The Pays de la Loire, located in the west of France, is a multifaceted region, offering exceptional cultural, historical and natural wealth. Known for its majestic castles, its renowned vineyards, its historic towns and its varied landscapes, the region attracts many visitors each year in search of discovery and relaxation. This chapter explores the geographical, historical, cultural and economic characteristics of the Pays de la Loire, highlighting the treasures that make this region an essential destination.

Geography and Landscapes

Exceptional Landscape Diversity

The Pays de la Loire is characterized by an impressive landscape diversity, ranging from river valleys to the Atlantic coasts, via fertile plains and green hills.

- The Loire Valley: Listed as a UNESCO world heritage site, the Loire Valley is famous for its picturesque landscapes, its sumptuous castles and its renowned vineyards. The Loire, France's longest river, flows through the region, offering panoramic views and opportunities for water recreation.
- The Atlantic Coasts: The fine sandy beaches, secret coves and seaside resorts of the Atlantic coast attract many visitors. The islands of Noirmoutier and Yeu, accessible by ferry, offer wild and preserved landscapes.
- The Marshes and Bocages: The salt marshes of Guérande, the Poitevin marshes and the bocages of Maine and Anjou are characteristic landscapes of the region, sheltering a rich biodiversity and offering opportunities for hikes and boat trips.

Regional Natural Parks

The Pays de la Loire is home to several regional natural parks, such as the Brière Regional Natural Park and the Loire-Anjou-Touraine Regional Natural Park. These parks protect local wildlife, while providing hiking trails, biking trails, and picnic areas for visitors. They are ideal places to discover the natural wealth of the region.

History and Heritage

Origins and Antiquity

The Pays de la Loire has a rich history dating back to Antiquity. The region was inhabited by the Celts, then conquered by the Romans, who left numerous remains, such as the thermal baths and aqueducts of Nantes and Angers.

The Middle Ages and the Renaissance

The Middle Ages and the Renaissance are significant periods in the history of Pays de la Loire, with the construction of numerous castles, abbeys and churches. Among the most famous, we find:

- The Château des Ducs de Bretagne in Nantes: Former residence of the Dukes of Brittany, this medieval castle now houses the Nantes history museum.
- The Château de Saumur: Overlooking the Loire, this fairytale castle is a remarkable example of medieval and Renaissance architecture.
- Fontevraud Abbey: One of the largest monastic cities in Europe, this abbey served as a necropolis for the Plantagenet dynasty.

Maritime and Industrial Heritage

The region also has a rich maritime and industrial past. The shipyards of Saint-Nazaire, the salt works of Guérande and the slate mines of Trélazé are all witnesses to this history. Nantes, former capital of the Dukes of Brittany, has become an important port and a dynamic industrial center over the centuries.

Culture and Traditions

Loire Language and Culture

Loire culture is marked by ancestral traditions and a regional language, Gallo, still spoken by some inhabitants. The region is rich in festivals, traditional markets and local festivals, which perpetuate customs and artisanal know-how.

Festivals and Events

Pays de la Loire is renowned for its festivals and cultural events, attracting artists and visitors from all over the world. Among the most famous, we find:

- The Anjou Festival: A theater festival taking place in the most beautiful heritage sites in the region.
- Les Folles Journees de Nantes: A classical music festival which offers concerts throughout the city of Nantes.
- The Saumur Wine Festival: An unmissable event for wine lovers, celebrating the region's wines with tastings and activities.

Gastronomy and Local Products

The Pays de la Loire is a leading gastronomic region, showcasing local products and culinary traditions. Regional specialties include:

- Loire Wines: The vineyards of the Loire Valley produce world-renowned wines, such as Muscadet, Saumur , Savennières and Chinon.
- Seafood: Vendée oysters, bouchot mussels and fresh Atlantic fish are essentials of local cuisine.
- Cheeses and Charcuteries: Nantes priest, Vendée mogette and Le Mans rillettes are specialties not to be missed.

Economy and Innovation

Tourism

Tourism is a key sector of the Pays de la Loire economy, attracting millions of visitors each year who come to discover the historical, cultural and natural treasures of the region. The region's tourist infrastructure is of high quality, with a diverse range of accommodation, starred restaurants, wellness centers and leisure activities.

Agriculture and Vineyards

Agriculture and viticulture play an essential role in the economy of Pays de la Loire. The region produces a wide variety of agricultural products, including vegetables, fruits, dairy products and quality meats. The vineyards of the Loire Valley are renowned for their exceptional wines, which attract wine lovers from around the world.

Industry and Innovation

Pays de la Loire is also a center of innovation and industrial development, with varied sectors such as aeronautics, automobiles, renewable energies and information technologies. Competitiveness clusters, such as EMC2 (Advanced Production Technologies) and ID4CAR (Intelligent Mobility), promote innovation and collaboration between economic and scientific players.

Transportation infrastructure, such as highways, high-speed train lines and seaports, supports the region's economic development. The proximity of Paris, as well as the presence of large metropolises such as Nantes and Angers, facilitate commercial exchanges and international collaborations. Pays de la Loire is a key player in the French economy, contributing to its dynamism and international influence.

Conclusion

The Pays de la Loire is an exceptional region, rich in history, culture and varied landscapes. Whether enjoying the majestic castles of the Loire Valley, exploring the beaches of the Atlantic coast, discovering historic towns or savoring the local gastronomy, there is something for everyone.

The region's Relais & Châteaux capture the essence of this diversity and offer their guests unforgettable experiences, combining luxury, comfort and authenticity. Each establishment, with its enchanting setting, warm welcome, exceptional gastronomy and enriching activities, offers total immersion in the French art of living.

By discovering the Relais & Châteaux des Pays de la Loire, you will be transported into a world where every detail is designed to delight the senses and create lasting memories. This chapter presented a detailed overview of the region, integrating geographical, historical, cultural and economic aspects to provide a comprehensive understanding of this unique destination.

- History and Heritage

The Pays de la Loire, with their diverse landscapes and historic towns, is a region rich in history and heritage. From prehistory to contemporary times, each period has left visible traces in monuments, castles, churches and archaeological sites. This chapter explores key moments in the history of Pays de la Loire, its emblematic monuments and its cultural contributions.

Prehistoric Origins and Antiquity

Prehistoric Sites

The Pays de la Loire is home to numerous prehistoric sites, witnesses to the first human occupations. Among the most notable, we find the megaliths of Carnac in neighboring Brittany, but also the dolmens and menhirs scattered throughout the region's departments. These megalithic monuments are the traces of the Neolithic cultures which populated the region more than 5000 years ago.

Roman Influence

With the Roman conquest in the 1st century BC, the Pays de la Loire region was integrated into the Roman Empire. The Romans built cities, roads and infrastructure there. Remains from this era include the Roman baths of Entrammes and the remains of the Gallo-Roman town of Jublains. The arenas of Doué-la-Fontaine also bear witness to this Roman influence.

The Middle Age

The Birth of Duchies and Counties

The Middle Ages is a period of formation and consolidation of local political entities. The counties of Anjou, Nantes and Maine emerge and play a crucial role in regional and national history. Local lords built castles to defend their lands and establish their authority.

Medieval Castles

The Pays de la Loire is famous for its numerous castles, built mainly from the 11th century. Among the most famous, we find:

- Angers Castle: Built in the 13th century, this impressive castle houses the famous Apocalypse Tapestry, a series of remarkable medieval tapestries.
- The Château de Saumur: Overlooking the Loire, this castle is a typical example of medieval architecture, transformed into a pleasure residence during the Renaissance.

- The Château de Nantes: Former residence of the Dukes of Brittany, this castle is a symbol of ducal power and the union of Brittany with France.

The Renaissance

The Loire Valley: The Garden of France

The Renaissance was a peak period for the Loire Valley, often nicknamed the "Garden of France". The kings of France and the nobility had sumptuous residences built there, influenced by Italian arts and architecture.

- The Château de Chambord: Although located in Centre-Val de Loire, it is close to the limits of the region and testifies to the splendor of Renaissance architecture.
- The Château de Brissac: The highest castle in France, with its seven floors, its 204 rooms and its magnificent landscaped park.
- The Château de Serrant: One of the most beautiful Renaissance castles, with its collections of furniture, books and art objects.

Churches and Abbeys

The churches and abbeys of Pays de la Loire also bear witness to the cultural richness of the region during the Renaissance. Fontevraud Abbey is one of the largest monastic cities in Europe, and Saint-Maurice Cathedral in Angers is a splendid example of Angevin Gothic architecture.

The Modern Era

Maritime and Industrial Heritage

The 17th and 18th centuries saw the rise of maritime trade and industry in the region. Nantes became a major port, notably thanks to the slave trade, a dark period in regional history. The salt works of Guérande, the shipyards of Saint-Nazaire and the forges of Pays de Retz are examples of this period of industrial development.

The Revolution and the Empire

The French Revolution and the Napoleonic Empire had a profound impact on the region. The Vendée Wars, a counter-revolutionary uprising, tore the region apart and left lasting traces. Monuments and memorials, such as the Lucs -sur-Boulogne memorial, recall these tragic events.

Contemporary Heritage

The industrial Revolution

The industrial revolution transformed the Pays de la Loire into a dynamic and innovative region. The mechanical, textile and agri-food industries are developing rapidly. Nantes and Saint-Nazaire became major industrial centers, with shipbuilding as a flagship activity.

The 20th Century and Today

The 20th century saw the modernization of infrastructure and the development of tourism. Cities in the region, such as Nantes, Angers and Le Mans, are modernizing while retaining their historical heritage. Today, the Pays de la Loire is a prosperous region, known for its quality of life, its cultural festivals and its economic dynamism.

UNESCO Sites and Historical Monuments

The Loire Valley, UNESCO world heritage

The Loire Valley is a UNESCO World Heritage Site for its exceptional cultural landscapes, castles and historic towns. This site includes a section of the river between Sully-sur-Loire and Chalonnes-sur-Loire, encompassing many remarkable monuments.

Historical Monuments and Museums

The region is home to numerous historical monuments and museums which tell the history of Pays de la Loire and highlight its cultural heritage. Among them, we find:

- Le Puy du Fou: A historical theme park offering grandiose shows and historical reenactments.
- The Museum of Fine Arts of Nantes: Housing a rich collection of art, ranging from the Middle Ages to the contemporary era.
- The Slate Museum in Trélazé: Illustrating the history of slate extraction in the region.

Conclusion

The Pays de la Loire is a region rich in history and heritage, where each town, each village and each monument tells a unique story. From prehistoric remains to Renaissance castles, from medieval abbeys to contemporary industries, the region offers an incredible diversity of historic sites and monuments.

Les Relais & Châteaux des Pays de la Loire capture the essence of this historical and cultural wealth, offering their guests unforgettable experiences. Each establishment, with its enchanting setting, warm welcome, exceptional gastronomy and enriching activities, offers total immersion in the history and heritage of the region.

By discovering the Relais & Châteaux des Pays de la Loire, you will be transported into a world where every detail is designed to delight the senses and create lasting memories. This chapter explored the many facets of the region's history and heritage, revealing how each era helped shape this unique and fascinating destination.

- Gastronomy and Wine

The Pays de la Loire is a region renowned for its gastronomic and wine richness. Local cuisine, influenced by the diversity of landscapes and local products, offers a palette of unique and authentic flavors. The world-famous wines of the Loire add an exceptional dimension to the region's culinary experience. In this chapter, we will explore the gastronomic aspects of Pays de la Loire, highlighting the local products, iconic dishes, renowned chefs, starred restaurants and wines that make this region famous.

Local Products

Seafood

The proximity to the Atlantic Ocean and rivers offers an abundance of fresh and tasty seafood.

- Oysters from Vendée: The Vendée coast is renowned for its fine and tasty oysters, particularly those from the bay of Bourgneuf and Noirmoutier.
- Bouchot Mussels: Raised on wooden stakes, bouchot mussels are a specialty of Aiguillon Bay.
- Fresh Fish: Sea bass, sole, mackerel and tuna are commonly caught and served in restaurants in the region.

Products of the Earth

The fertile lands of Pays de la Loire produce a wide variety of vegetables, fruits and dairy products.

- Vegetables: Nantes artichokes, Loire Valley leeks, and Mallemort asparagus are some of the region's emblematic vegetables.
- Fruits: Apples, pears and strawberries are widely grown, with specific varieties such as Reinette de Loire and Poire d'Anjou.
- Dairy Products: Nantes white butter, Loire Valley goat's cheese and Le Mans rillettes are very popular dairy products.

Regional Specialties

The Pays de la Loire has many unique culinary specialties, often linked to their traditions and history.

- Rillettes du Mans: A preparation of candied pork, often served on fresh bread.
- Le Gâteau Nantais: A soft cake made with almond powder and rum, typical of the city of Nantes.
- Préfou Vendéen: A bread topped with garlic butter, often served as an aperitif.

Loire Wines

A Diversity of Terroirs

The Loire Valley is one of the largest and most diverse wine regions in France. It is divided into several wine sub-regions, each producing distinct wines.

- Muscadet: Produced around Nantes, Muscadet is a dry and refreshing white wine, often associated with seafood.
- Saumur : This region produces white, red and sparkling wines, with grape varieties such as Chenin Blanc and Cabernet Franc.
- Sancerre and Pouilly-Fumé: Located further east, these vineyards are famous for their white wines made from Sauvignon Blanc, characterized by their freshness and minerality.
- Chinon and Bourgueil: These appellations produce robust red wines based on Cabernet Franc, often aged to develop complex aromas.

Wine Routes

The Loire wine routes offer picturesque routes through the vineyards, allowing visitors to discover the wine landscapes, visit the cellars and taste wines directly from the producers. Among the most popular are the Nantes wine route, the Anjou-Saumur wine route and the Touraine wine route.

Star Chefs and Restaurants

The Pioneers of Regional Haute Cuisine

Pays de la Loire has always been a hotbed of culinary creativity, attracting talented chefs who showcase local produce and culinary traditions. Among the pioneers of regional haute cuisine, we find Joël Robuchon, who began his career in Tours before becoming one of the most starred chefs in the world.

Contemporary Chefs

Today, the region continues to attract renowned chefs, who continue the tradition of haute cuisine while innovating and experimenting with new flavors. Among the most famous contemporary chefs, we find:

- Thierry Drapeau: Chef of the Thierry Drapeau restaurant in Saint-Sulpice-le-Verdon, renowned for his inventive cuisine that respects local products.
- Jean-Yves Guého : Chef at Atlantide 1874 in Nantes, Michelin-starred, offering refined and contemporary cuisine.

Star Restaurants

The Pays de la Loire is home to numerous Michelin-starred restaurants, each offering a unique and unforgettable culinary experience. Among the most famous, we find:

- L'Auberge de la Garenne in La Baule: This Michelin-starred restaurant offers refined cuisine highlighting seafood and land products.

- Le Favre d'Anne in Angers: Led by Pascal Favre d'Anne, this Michelin-starred restaurant offers inventive and elegant cuisine, inspired by local products.
- La Marine in Noirmoutier: Chef Alexandre Couillon offers daring and creative cuisine, rewarded with two Michelin stars.

Oenological Experiences

Wine Tastings

Relais & Châteaux des Pays de la Loire often offer unique wine experiences for their guests. From private tastings to vineyard visits, these experiences allow you to discover the wines of the Loire and learn the secrets of their making.

Customers can participate in tasting workshops, led by experts, to learn how to identify the aromas and flavors of regional wines. Guided tours of the vineyards and cellars allow you to discover the production processes, meet the winegrowers and taste wines directly from the source.

Food and Wine Pairings

Relais & Châteaux also offer food and wine pairings, allowing you to savor Loire wines in harmony with local cuisine. These pairings highlight the flavors of the dishes and wines, providing a complete and unforgettable gastronomic experience.

Chefs from Michelin-starred restaurants collaborate with sommeliers to create tasting menus that highlight the region's wines. Each dish is carefully paired with a wine, allowing guests to discover new combinations of flavors and textures.

Conclusion

The Pays de la Loire is a true land of gastronomy and wine, offering unparalleled richness and diversity. Regional cuisine, with its authentic flavors and quality local products, is a pillar of the region's art of living. Loire wines, renowned for their complexity and elegance, perfectly complement this culinary experience.

Les Relais & Châteaux des Pays de la Loire capture the essence of this gastronomic richness, offering their guests unique and unforgettable culinary and wine experiences. Each establishment, with its enchanting setting, warm welcome, exceptional gastronomy and enriching activities, offers total immersion in the French art of living.

By discovering the Relais & Châteaux des Pays de la Loire, you will be transported into a world where every detail is designed to delight the senses and create lasting memories. This chapter explored the multiple facets of the region's gastronomy and wines, revealing how each element contributes to making this destination a true oasis of flavors and culinary pleasures.

2. Addresses and Descriptions

Pays de la Loire is home to several Relais & Châteaux establishments, each offering a unique experience combining luxury, comfort and regional charm. These prestigious hotels and restaurants are located in iconic locations across the region, from historic towns to picturesque countryside. In this chapter, we will discover some of the most prestigious addresses and describe in detail what makes them special.

Domaine de la Bretesche

History and Architecture

Domaine de la Bretesche , located in Missillac, is a sumptuous estate which houses a luxury hotel and a golf course. The estate's castle, dating from the 15th century, is surrounded by a moat and landscaped gardens. The architecture of the castle, with its turrets and stone facades, evokes the elegance and refinement of the Renaissance.

Culinary Offers

The gourmet restaurant at Domaine de la Bretesche , led by a talented chef, offers inventive and refined cuisine, highlighting local and seasonal products. The tasting menu offers dishes such as "Lobster Bleu de Bretagne" and "Filet de Bœuf Charolais". The carefully selected wine list highlights the region's great wines and other prestigious wine regions.

Activities and Services

Domaine de la Bretesche offers a range of activities for its guests, from relaxation to sport. Guests can enjoy the heated outdoor swimming pool, spa, sauna and hammam for moments of relaxation. The 18-hole golf course, located in a picturesque setting, is one of the major assets of the estate. Guided excursions are also organized to explore the surrounding area, including the town of Guérande and its salt marshes.

Noirieux Castle

History and Architecture

Château de Noirieux , located in Briollay near Angers, is an elegant 17th century residence surrounded by extensive gardens and woods. This historic castle, once the residence of the Noirieux family , has been transformed into a luxury hotel offering a romantic and peaceful setting. The architecture of the castle, with its stone facades, turrets and mullioned windows, reflects the elegance of the period.

Culinary Offers

Noirieux's gourmet restaurant offers inventive and refined cuisine, highlighting local and seasonal products. The chef, passionate about the region's gastronomy, creates dishes that combine tradition and modernity. The tasting menu offers dishes such as "Duck Foie Gras" and "Racan Pigeon". The carefully selected wine list highlights the region's great wines and other prestigious wine regions.

Activities and Services

Château de Noirieux offers a range of activities for its guests, from relaxation to sport. Guests can enjoy the heated outdoor swimming pool, gardens and terraces for moments of relaxation. Guided excursions are also organized to explore the surrounding area, including the city of Angers, Angers Castle and the Anjou vineyard. The castle also offers cooking classes, wine tastings and outdoor activities such as cycling and hiking.

Maubreuil Castle

History and Architecture

Château de Maubreuil , located in Carquefou near Nantes, is an elegant 19th-century castle surrounded by landscaped gardens and woods. This historic residence, formerly the residence of the Maubreuil family , has been transformed into a luxury hotel offering a refined and peaceful setting. The architecture of the castle, with its stone facades, turrets and ornate balconies, reflects the elegance of the period.

Culinary Offers

The Château de Maubreuil gourmet restaurant offers inventive and refined cuisine, highlighting local and seasonal products. The chef, passionate about the region's gastronomy, creates dishes that combine tradition and modernity. The tasting menu offers dishes such as "Filet de Bœuf Charolais" and "Saint-Pierre aux Algues". The carefully selected wine list highlights the region's great wines and other prestigious wine regions.

Activities and Services

Château de Maubreuil offers a range of activities for its guests, from relaxation to sport. Guests can enjoy the heated outdoor swimming pool, spa, sauna and hammam for moments of relaxation. Guided excursions are also organized to explore the surrounding area, including the city of Nantes, the Château des Ducs de Bretagne and the Muscadet vineyard. The castle also offers cooking classes, wine tastings and outdoor activities such as golfing and cycling.

The Hauts de Loire

History and Architecture

Les Hauts de Loire, located in Onzain, is a magnificent 19th century hunting estate transformed into a luxury hotel. The manor, surrounded by vast gardens and woods, offers a peaceful and refined setting.

The architecture of the manor, with its stone facades, turrets and mullioned windows, reflects the elegance of the period.

Culinary Offers

The Hauts de Loire gourmet restaurant, led by a talented chef, offers inventive and refined cuisine, highlighting local and seasonal products. The tasting menu offers dishes such as "Lobster Bleu de Bretagne" and "Filet de Bass de Ligne". The carefully selected wine list highlights the region's great wines and other prestigious wine regions.

Activities and Services

Les Hauts de Loire offers a range of activities for its guests, from relaxation to sport. Guests can enjoy the heated outdoor swimming pool, spa, sauna and hammam for moments of relaxation. Guided excursions are also organized to explore the surrounding area, including the Loire Valley castles and Loire Valley vineyards. The estate also offers cooking classes, wine tastings and outdoor activities such as cycling and hiking.

Domaine des Hauts de Loire

History and Architecture

The Domaine des Hauts de Loire, located in Onzain, is a charming 19th century hunting estate transformed into a luxury hotel. This elegant mansion is surrounded by extensive gardens and forests, providing a peaceful and refined setting. The architecture of the manor, with its stone facades, turrets and mullioned windows, reflects the elegance of the period.

Culinary Offers

The Domaine des Hauts de Loire gourmet restaurant, led by a starred chef, offers inventive and refined cuisine, highlighting local and seasonal products. The tasting menu offers dishes such as "Homard Bleu de Bretagne" and "Turbot Sauvage". The carefully selected wine list highlights the region's great wines and other prestigious wine regions.

Activities and Services

Domaine des Hauts de Loire offers a range of activities for its guests, from relaxation to sport. Guests can enjoy the heated outdoor swimming pool, spa, sauna and hammam for moments of relaxation. Guided excursions are also organized to explore the surrounding area, including the Loire castles and the region's vineyards. The estate also offers cooking classes, wine tastings and outdoor activities such as cycling and hiking.

Conclusion

The Relais & Châteaux des Pays de la Loire offer unique and unforgettable experiences, combining luxury, comfort and historical heritage. Each establishment, with its enchanting setting, warm welcome, exceptional gastronomy and enriching activities, offers total immersion in the French art of living. Whether for a romantic getaway, a peaceful retreat or a cultural exploration, the Relais & Châteaux of the Pays de la Loire region are must-see destinations.

By discovering these exceptional establishments, you will be transported to a world where every detail is designed to delight the senses and create lasting memories. This chapter has presented a detailed overview of some of the most prestigious Relais & Châteaux in the region, offering a glimpse of the unique experience that awaits you in each of these enchanting locations.

- Domaine de La Bretesche

The Domaine de La Bretesche , located in Missillac, is an emblematic establishment of the Pays de la Loire, offering a luxurious and refined experience in the heart of an exceptional historical and natural setting. With its majestic castle, landscaped gardens and world-renowned golf course, Domaine de La Bretesche combines the charm of medieval architecture with modern comfort. In this chapter, we will explore the history and architecture of Domaine de La Bretesche , its culinary offerings, the activities and services offered, and the unique experiences it offers.

History and Architecture

A Medieval Heritage

The Domaine de La Bretesche has its origins in the 15th century, when the Château de La Bretesche was built by the de Montfort family, a line of Breton nobles. This castle, surrounded by moats and forests, served as a fortified residence and refuge in times of war. Over the centuries, the estate has been enlarged and embellished by its different owners, each bringing their personal touch to the architecture and gardens.

Elegant Architecture

The architecture of Domaine de La Bretesche reflects the elegance and refinement of the Renaissance, with its stone facades, turrets and mullioned windows. Interiors are decorated with antique furniture, artwork and fine textiles, creating a warm and sophisticated atmosphere.

The hotel's rooms and suites offer breathtaking views of the park, the golf course or the moat. Each room is unique, with distinctive design elements and modern amenities to ensure optimal comfort. The bathrooms, fitted with marble bathtubs and walk-in showers, provide a luxurious setting in which to relax and rejuvenate.

Culinary Offers

The Montague

Le Montaigu, the gourmet restaurant of Domaine de La Bretesche, is run by a talented chef who offers inventive and refined cuisine, highlighting local and seasonal products. The tasting menu offers dishes such as "Lobster Bleu de Bretagne" and "Filet de Bœuf Charolais". The carefully selected wine list highlights the region's great wines and other prestigious wine regions.

The restaurant's setting matches its cuisine, with an elegantly decorated dining room, tables spaced for maximum privacy, and panoramic views of the park. Guests can also dine al fresco on the terrace, enjoying the tranquility and beauty of the natural surroundings.

The club

The Club, located in the castle's former orangery, offers a more relaxed atmosphere with bistronomic cuisine. The dishes offered highlight quality local products, in a friendly and warm atmosphere. Guests can enjoy dishes such as "Langoustine Salad" or "Heart of Rumsteak", accompanied by regional wines.

The Gourmet Breakfast

Bretesche 's gourmet breakfast is served in the elegantly decorated dining room or on the terrace, with magnificent views of the gardens and park. Breakfast is composed of fresh, local products, including pastries, fruits, homemade jams, regional cheeses, fresh eggs and pressed fruit juices. Guests can also enjoy hot drinks, such as coffee, tea and hot chocolate.

Activities and Services

The Spa and Wellness Treatments

The Spa at Domaine de La Bretesche offers a range of wellness treatments for its guests, from massages to facials, carried out with high quality products. The spa, located in a peaceful and luxurious setting, is a place of rest and relaxation, perfect for recharging your batteries after a day exploring the region.

Professional therapists use advanced techniques and luxury products to ensure optimal results and a luxurious experience. Guests can also enjoy the heated indoor swimming pool, jacuzzi, sauna and steam room to complete their relaxation experience.

The Golf Course

The 18-hole golf course at Domaine de La Bretesche is one of the most beautiful in France, offering a picturesque setting with stunning views of the castle and gardens. Designed by British golf architect Henry Cotton, this course is both technical and accessible, providing an enjoyable challenge for golfers of all abilities.

Guests can benefit from golf lessons taught by professionals, as well as development courses to improve their game. The club house, located in the old orangery, offers a friendly setting in which to relax after a round of golf, with a bar and restaurant offering light meals and refreshing drinks.

Outdoor activities

The gardens and woods of Domaine de La Bretesche are perfect for leisurely walks, meditation sessions or outdoor yoga sessions. Guests can also take advantage of the proximity to the Guérande salt marshes for activities such as hiking, cycling and fishing. Guided excursions are also organized to explore the surrounding area, including the medieval town of Guérande and its ramparts, as well as the beaches of the Atlantic coast.

Cultural Activities and Experiences

Domaine de La Bretesche regularly organizes cultural events and unique experiences for its guests. Private concerts, literary readings and art exhibitions are often organized in the establishment's lounges or gardens. These events offer immersion in the local cultural scene and allow guests to meet artists, writers and musicians.

Guests can also participate in cooking workshops, baking classes and wine tastings, led by local chefs. These workshops offer an opportunity to learn regional cooking techniques and taste delicious creations. Domaine de La Bretesche also offers yoga and meditation classes, led by qualified instructors, in the hotel's gardens or wellness areas.

Special Events and Unique Experiences

Weddings and Receptions

Domaine de La Bretesche is an ideal venue for organizing intimate weddings and private receptions. The property's gardens and lounges provide a romantic and elegant setting for ceremonies and receptions. Hotel staff work closely with couples to create tailor-made events, taking into account every detail, from decor to personalized menus.

The hotel's chefs create wedding menus that reflect the tastes and preferences of the bride and groom, using seasonal ingredients and local produce. The professional and attentive service teams ensure that every event goes off without a hitch. Couples can also enjoy luxurious suites for their wedding night, with special services such as massages, in-room breakfasts and welcome gifts.

Seminars and Business Meetings

The Domaine de La Bretesche offers an exceptional setting for seminars, conferences and business meetings. The property's private lounges, equipped with the latest technology, offer flexible spaces for events of different sizes. Hotel teams work with event organizers to create tailor-made programs, including coffee breaks, business lunches and dinners.

Team-building activities and excursions can also be organized to strengthen team cohesion and provide moments of relaxation outside of work sessions. Guests can take advantage of the hotel's wellness facilities to unwind after a day of meetings, with spa treatments, yoga sessions and massages.

Unique Experiences

Domaine de La Bretesche offers unique experiences to make each stay memorable. These include private dinners in exclusive locations within the establishment, such as the library or gardens, offering an intimate and romantic atmosphere. Guests can also participate in wine tasting workshops, led by expert sommeliers, to discover the secrets of the region's wines.

Wellness getaways are also available, including personalized relaxation and relaxation programs, spa treatments, yoga and meditation sessions, as well as healthy and nutritious meals. These programs are designed to help clients recharge their batteries and regain physical and mental balance.

Seasonal and Thematic Offers

Domaine de La Bretesche regularly offers seasonal and thematic offers to enrich its customers' experience. At Christmas, the establishment is decked out in festive decorations and offers special menus, cookie decorating workshops and Christmas market visits. In summer, gourmet picnics can be organized in the gardens or on the terraces.

Romantic getaways are also offered, including candlelit dinners, duo massages and horse-drawn carriage rides in the surrounding area. For culture lovers, special packages including tickets for exhibitions, shows and concerts are available, offering complete immersion in the cultural life of the region.

Conclusion

Domaine de La Bretesche is much more than just a luxury hotel; it is a destination in itself, offering a unique and unforgettable experience in the heart of the magnificent Pays de la Loire countryside. With its rich history, impressive architecture, refined culinary offerings and a variety of activities and services, this establishment is the ideal place to relax, recharge and discover the French art of living.

Whether for a romantic getaway, a wellness retreat, an intimate wedding or a business meeting, Domaine de La Bretesche promises an exceptional experience, marked by luxury, comfort and elegance. Guests leave with unforgettable memories, enriched by the unique culture, gastronomy and hospitality of this emblematic establishment of the Pays de la Loire region.

- Château de Noirieux

Château de Noirieux , located in Briollay near Angers, is a jewel of the Pays de la Loire offering a luxurious and refined experience in an exceptional historical and natural setting. This elegant 17th century residence, surrounded by extensive gardens and woods, combines the charm of classic architecture with modern comfort. In this chapter, we will explore the history and architecture of Château de Noirieux , its culinary offerings, the activities and services offered, and the unique experiences it offers.

History and Architecture

An Aristocratic Heritage

The Château de Noirieux was built in the 17th century by the Noirieux family , a noble Angevin lineage. This castle, located on the banks of the Sarthe, served as a family residence for several centuries. Over time, the castle was enlarged and embellished by its different owners, each bringing their personal touch to the architecture and gardens.

Elegant Architecture

The architecture of Château de Noirieux reflects the elegance and refinement of the classical era, with its stone facades, turrets and mullioned windows. Interiors are decorated with antique furniture, artwork and fine textiles, creating a warm and sophisticated atmosphere.

The hotel's rooms and suites offer breathtaking views of the park, river or gardens. Each room is unique, with distinctive design elements and modern amenities to ensure optimal comfort. The bathrooms, fitted with marble bathtubs and walk-in showers, provide a luxurious setting in which to relax and rejuvenate.

Culinary Offers

The Gourmet Restaurant

Noirieux 's gourmet restaurant , led by a talented chef, offers inventive and refined cuisine, highlighting local and seasonal products. The tasting menu offers dishes such as "Duck Foie Gras" and "Racan Pigeon". The carefully selected wine list highlights the region's great wines and other prestigious wine regions.

The restaurant's setting matches its cuisine, with an elegantly decorated dining room, tables spaced for maximum privacy, and panoramic views of the park and river. Guests can also dine al fresco on the terrace, enjoying the tranquility and beauty of the natural surroundings.

The Bistro

The Bistro du Château de Noirieux offers a more relaxed atmosphere with bistronomic cuisine. The dishes offered highlight quality local products, in a friendly and warm atmosphere. Guests can enjoy dishes such as "Mushroom Risotto" or "Bass Fillet", accompanied by regional wines.

The Gourmet Breakfast

Noirieux 's gourmet breakfast is served in the elegantly decorated dining room or on the terrace, with magnificent views of the gardens and park. Breakfast is composed of fresh, local products, including pastries, fruits, homemade jams, regional cheeses, fresh eggs and pressed fruit juices. Guests can also enjoy hot drinks, such as coffee, tea and hot chocolate.

Activities and Services

The Spa and Wellness Treatments

Château de Noirieux offers a range of wellness treatments for its guests, ranging from massages to facials, carried out with high quality products. The spa, located in a peaceful and luxurious setting, is a place of rest and relaxation, perfect for recharging your batteries after a day exploring the region.

Professional therapists use advanced techniques and luxury products to ensure optimal results and a luxurious experience. Guests can also enjoy the heated outdoor swimming pool, jacuzzi, sauna and steam room to complete their relaxation experience.

Outdoor activities

The gardens and woods of Château de Noirieux are perfect for leisurely walks, meditation sessions or outdoor yoga sessions. Guests can also take advantage of the proximity to the Sarthe River for water activities such as canoeing and fishing. Guided excursions are also organized to explore the surrounding area, including the city of Angers, Angers Castle and the Anjou vineyard.

Cultural Activities and Experiences

Château de Noirieux regularly organizes cultural events and unique experiences for its guests. Private concerts, literary readings and art exhibitions are often organized in the establishment's lounges or gardens. These events offer immersion in the local cultural scene and allow guests to meet artists, writers and musicians.

Guests can also participate in cooking workshops, baking classes and wine tastings, led by local chefs. These workshops offer an opportunity to learn regional cooking techniques and taste delicious creations. Château de Noirieux also offers yoga and meditation classes, led by qualified instructors, in the hotel's gardens or wellness areas.

Special Events and Unique Experiences

Weddings and Receptions

Château de Noirieux is an ideal venue for intimate weddings and private receptions. The property's gardens and lounges provide a romantic and elegant setting for ceremonies and receptions. Hotel staff work closely with couples to create tailor-made events, taking into account every detail, from decor to personalized menus.

The hotel's chefs create wedding menus that reflect the tastes and preferences of the bride and groom, using seasonal ingredients and local produce. The professional and attentive service teams ensure that every event goes off without a hitch. Couples can also enjoy luxurious suites for their wedding night, with special services such as massages, in-room breakfasts and welcome gifts.

Seminars and Business Meetings

The Château de Noirieux offers an exceptional setting for seminars, conferences and business meetings. The property's private lounges, equipped with the latest technology, offer flexible spaces for events of different sizes. Hotel teams work with event organizers to create tailor-made programs, including coffee breaks, business lunches and dinners.

Team-building activities and excursions can also be organized to strengthen team cohesion and provide moments of relaxation outside of work sessions. Guests can take advantage of the hotel's wellness facilities to unwind after a day of meetings, with spa treatments, yoga sessions and massages.

Unique Experiences

Château de Noirieux offers unique experiences to make each stay memorable. These include private dinners in exclusive locations within the establishment, such as the library or gardens, offering an intimate and romantic atmosphere. Guests can also participate in wine tasting workshops, led by expert sommeliers, to discover the secrets of the region's wines.

Wellness getaways are also available, including personalized relaxation and relaxation programs, spa treatments, yoga and meditation sessions, as well as healthy and nutritious meals. These programs are designed to help clients recharge their batteries and regain physical and mental balance.

Seasonal and Thematic Offers

Château de Noirieux regularly offers seasonal and thematic offers to enrich its customers' experience. At Christmas, the establishment is decked out in festive decorations and offers special menus, cookie decorating workshops and Christmas market visits. In summer, gourmet picnics can be organized in the gardens or on the terraces.

Romantic getaways are also offered, including candlelit dinners, duo massages and horse-drawn carriage rides in the surrounding area. For culture lovers, special packages including tickets for exhibitions, shows and concerts are available, offering complete immersion in the cultural life of the region.

Conclusion

The Château de Noirieux is much more than just a luxury hotel; it is a destination in itself, offering a unique and unforgettable experience in the heart of the magnificent Pays de la Loire countryside. With its rich history, impressive architecture, refined culinary offerings and a variety of activities and services, this establishment is the ideal place to relax, recharge and discover the French art of living.

Whether for a romantic getaway, a wellness retreat, an intimate wedding or a business meeting, Château de Noirieux promises an exceptional experience, marked by luxury, comfort and elegance. Guests leave with unforgettable memories, enriched by the unique culture, gastronomy and hospitality of this emblematic establishment of the Pays de la Loire region.

- Relais de Chambord

Le Relais de Chambord, located in close proximity to the famous Château de Chambord, is a unique establishment that offers a luxurious and authentic stay experience in the heart of one of the most iconic regions of France. In the heart of the Loire Valley, this hotel combines the charm of traditional architecture with modern comfort, offering total immersion in the history and culture of the region. In this chapter, we will explore the history and architecture of Relais de Chambord, its culinary offerings, the activities and services offered, and the unique experiences it offers.

History and Architecture

A Renaissance Heritage

The Relais de Chambord is a few steps from the Château de Chambord, one of the most majestic castles of the Loire, built in the 16th century by François I. The castle is a masterpiece of the French Renaissance, known for its elaborate architecture, towers and double-revolving staircases. The Relais de Chambord is inspired by this historical grandeur, offering its guests a refined setting imbued with the spirit of the Renaissance.

Eclectic Architecture

The architecture of the Relais de Chambord combines traditional and contemporary elements. The hotel's facades, made of stone and wood, harmonize perfectly with the surrounding landscape. Interiors are decorated with elegant furniture, artwork and quality textiles, creating a warm and sophisticated atmosphere.

The hotel's rooms and suites offer breathtaking views of the Château de Chambord, the gardens or the Cosson River. Each room is unique, with distinctive design elements and modern amenities to ensure optimal comfort. The bathrooms, fitted with marble bathtubs and walk-in showers, provide a luxurious setting in which to relax and rejuvenate.

Culinary Offers

The Gourmet Restaurant

The Relais de Chambord's gourmet restaurant, led by a talented chef, offers inventive and refined cuisine, highlighting local and seasonal products. The tasting menu offers dishes such as "Filet of Zander de Loire" and "Roasted Pigeon with Spices". The carefully selected wine list highlights the region's great wines and other prestigious wine regions.

The restaurant's setting matches its cuisine, with an elegantly decorated dining room, tables spaced for maximum privacy, and panoramic views of the Château de Chambord. Guests can also dine al fresco on the terrace, enjoying the tranquility and beauty of the natural surroundings.

The Bistro

The Bistro du Relais de Chambord offers a more relaxed atmosphere with bistronomic cuisine. The dishes offered highlight quality local products, in a friendly and warm atmosphere. Guests can enjoy dishes such as "Mushroom Risotto" or "Duck Breast", accompanied by regional wines.

The Gourmet Breakfast

The Relais de Chambord's gourmet breakfast is served in the elegantly decorated dining room or on the terrace, with magnificent views of the gardens and the castle. Breakfast is composed of fresh, local products, including pastries, fruits, homemade jams, regional cheeses, fresh eggs and pressed fruit juices. Guests can also enjoy hot drinks, such as coffee, tea and hot chocolate.

Activities and Services

The Spa and Wellness Treatments

The Spa du Relais de Chambord offers a range of wellness treatments for its guests, from massages to facials, performed with high quality products. The spa, located in a peaceful and luxurious setting, is a place of rest and relaxation, perfect for recharging your batteries after a day exploring the region.

Professional therapists use advanced techniques and luxury products to ensure optimal results and a luxurious experience. Guests can also enjoy the heated outdoor swimming pool, jacuzzi, sauna and steam room to complete their relaxation experience.

Outdoor activities

The gardens and woods of Relais de Chambord are perfect for leisurely walks, meditation sessions or outdoor yoga sessions. Guests can also take advantage of the proximity to the Chambord Forest for activities such as hiking, cycling and fishing. Guided excursions are also organized to explore the surrounding area, including the Château de Chambord, the other châteaux of the Loire and the region's vineyards.

Cultural Activities and Experiences

Le Relais de Chambord regularly organizes cultural events and unique experiences for its guests. Private concerts, literary readings and art exhibitions are often organized in the establishment's lounges or gardens. These events offer immersion in the local cultural scene and allow guests to meet artists, writers and musicians.

Guests can also participate in cooking workshops, baking classes and wine tastings, led by local chefs. These workshops offer an opportunity to learn regional cooking techniques and taste delicious creations. The Relais de Chambord also offers yoga and meditation classes, led by qualified instructors, in the hotel's gardens or wellness areas.

Special Events and Unique Experiences

Weddings and Receptions

Le Relais de Chambord is an ideal venue for intimate weddings and private receptions. The property's gardens and lounges provide a romantic and elegant setting for ceremonies and receptions. Hotel staff work closely with couples to create tailor-made events, taking into account every detail, from decor to personalized menus.

The hotel's chefs create wedding menus that reflect the tastes and preferences of the bride and groom, using seasonal ingredients and local produce. The professional and attentive service teams ensure that every event goes off without a hitch. Couples can also enjoy luxurious suites for their wedding night, with special services such as massages, in-room breakfasts and welcome gifts.

Seminars and Business Meetings

The Relais de Chambord offers an exceptional setting for seminars, conferences and business meetings. The property's private lounges, equipped with the latest technology, offer flexible spaces for events of different sizes. Hotel teams work with event organizers to create tailor-made programs, including coffee breaks, business lunches and dinners.

Team-building activities and excursions can also be organized to strengthen team cohesion and provide moments of relaxation outside of work sessions. Guests can take advantage of the hotel's wellness facilities to unwind after a day of meetings, with spa treatments, yoga sessions and massages.

Unique Experiences

Le Relais de Chambord offers unique experiences to make each stay memorable. These include private dinners in exclusive locations within the establishment, such as the library or gardens, offering an intimate and romantic atmosphere. Guests can also participate in wine tasting workshops, led by expert sommeliers, to discover the secrets of the region's wines.

Wellness getaways are also available, including personalized relaxation and relaxation programs, spa treatments, yoga and meditation sessions, as well as healthy and nutritious meals. These programs are designed to help clients recharge their batteries and regain physical and mental balance.

Seasonal and Thematic Offers

The Relais de Chambord regularly offers seasonal and thematic offers to enrich its customers' experience. At Christmas, the establishment is decked out in festive decorations and offers special menus, cookie decorating workshops and Christmas market visits. In summer, gourmet picnics can be organized in the gardens or on the terraces.

Romantic getaways are also offered, including candlelit dinners, duo massages and horse-drawn carriage rides in the surrounding area. For culture lovers, special packages including tickets for exhibitions, shows and concerts are available, offering complete immersion in the cultural life of the region.

Conclusion

The Relais de Chambord is much more than just a luxury hotel; it is a destination in itself, offering a unique and unforgettable experience in the heart of the magnificent Loire Valley. With its rich history, impressive architecture, refined culinary offerings and a variety of activities and services, this establishment is the ideal place to relax, recharge and discover the French art of living.

Whether for a romantic getaway, a wellness retreat, an intimate wedding or a business meeting, the Relais de Chambord promises an exceptional experience, marked by luxury, comfort and elegance. Guests leave with unforgettable memories, enriched by the unique culture, gastronomy and hospitality of this emblematic establishment of the Pays de la Loire region.

Chapter 10: Relais & Châteaux in the Grand Est

1. General Presentation of the Region

The Grand Est region, located in the north-east of France, is a mosaic of landscapes, cultures and histories. This region, created in 2016 by the merger of Alsace, Lorraine and Champagne-Ardenne, offers an impressive diversity of natural sites, historic towns and cultural treasures. This chapter explores the geographical, historical, cultural and economic characteristics of the Grand Est, highlighting the treasures that make this region an essential destination.

Geography and Landscapes

Exceptional Landscape Diversity

The Grand Est is distinguished by the variety of its landscapes, ranging from fertile plains to forested mountains, rolling vineyards and winding rivers.

- The Vosges: This mountain range offers spectacular landscapes with its dense forests, glacial lakes and rounded peaks. The Vosges are ideal for outdoor activities like hiking, skiing and cycling.
- The Plain of Alsace: This fertile region, crossed by the Rhine, is famous for its vineyards, its picturesque villages and its bucolic landscapes.
- The Massif Ardennais: Located in the north of the region, this massif offers landscapes of wooded hills and deep valleys, perfect for nature activities and adventure sports.
- The Champagne Vineyards: The Champagne hillsides, listed as a UNESCO world heritage site, are renowned for their vineyard landscapes and their prestigious Champagne houses.

Regional Natural Parks

The Grand Est is home to several regional natural parks, such as the Ballons des Vosges Regional Natural Park and the Forêt d'Orient Regional Natural Park. These parks protect local wildlife while providing hiking trails, biking trails, and picnic areas for visitors. They are ideal places to discover the natural wealth of the region.

History and Heritage

Origins and Antiquity

The Grand Est has a rich history dating back to Antiquity. The region was inhabited by the Celts, then conquered by the Romans, who left numerous remains, such as the thermal baths of Grand and the Roman roads.

The Middle Ages and the Renaissance

The Middle Ages and the Renaissance were periods of great prosperity for the region, with the construction of numerous castles, cathedrals and fortified towns. Among the most famous, we find:

- Strasbourg Cathedral: A masterpiece of Gothic architecture, famous for its slender spire and astronomical clock.
- The Château du Haut-Koenigsbourg: A restored medieval fortress, offering spectacular views over the Alsace plain.
- Place Stanislas in Nancy: A dazzling example of 18th century town planning, listed as a UNESCO world heritage site.

Industrial Heritage and the World Wars

The Grand Est has also been a major industrial center, particularly for mining and steelmaking. Traces of this era are visible in cities like Metz and Mulhouse. The region was also marked by the two world wars, with memorial sites such as the Verdun Battlefield and the Maginot Line Memorial.

Culture and Traditions

Regional Language and Culture

The Grand Est is rich in regional cultures, with Germanic influences in Alsace and Lorraine, and a strong wine tradition in Champagne. The region is also known for its dialects, such as Alsatian and Lorraine, as well as its traditional festivals and Christmas markets.

Festivals and Events

The Grand Est is renowned for its festivals and cultural events, attracting artists and visitors from around the world. Among the most famous, we find:

- The Strasbourg Carnival: A festive event with parades, costumes and street shows.
- The Mirabelle Festival in Metz: A celebration of the Mirabelle plum, with tastings, concerts and fireworks.
- The Montmartre Harvest Festival in Paris: Although located in Paris, this event celebrates the wines of the Grand Est region, particularly those of Champagne.

Gastronomy and Local Products

The Grand Est is a leading gastronomic region, showcasing local products and culinary traditions. Regional specialties include:
- Alsace Wine: Alsatian vineyards produce renowned white wines, such as Riesling, Gewurztraminer and Pinot Gris.
- Choucroute: A traditional Alsatian dish made from fermented cabbage and various meats.

- Champagne: The Champagne vineyards produce the famous sparkling wines, appreciated throughout the world.
- La Quiche Lorraine: A savory tart made with bacon, eggs and cream, from Lorraine.

Economy and Innovation

Tourism

Tourism is a key sector of the economy of the Grand Est, attracting millions of visitors each year who come to discover the historical, cultural and natural treasures of the region. The region's tourist infrastructure is of high quality, with a diverse range of accommodation, starred restaurants, wellness centers and leisure activities.

Agriculture and Vineyards

Agriculture and viticulture play an essential role in the economy of the Grand Est. The region produces a wide variety of agricultural products, including grains, fruits, vegetables and dairy products. The vineyards of Champagne, Alsace and Lorraine are renowned for their exceptional wines, which attract wine lovers from around the world.

Industry and Innovation

The Grand Est is also a hub of innovation and industrial development, with varied sectors such as automobiles, aeronautics, information technologies and renewable energies. Competitiveness clusters, such as Materalia (innovative materials) and Hydreos (water management), promote innovation and collaboration between economic and scientific players.

Transportation infrastructure, such as highways, high-speed train lines and river ports, supports the region's economic development. The proximity of Germany, Switzerland and Luxembourg, as well as the presence of large metropolises such as Strasbourg and Reims, facilitate commercial exchanges and international collaborations. The Grand Est is a key player in the French economy, contributing to its dynamism and international influence.

Conclusion

The Grand Est is an exceptional region, rich in history, culture and varied landscapes. Whether enjoying majestic castles, exploring renowned vineyards, discovering historic towns or savoring local gastronomy, there is something for everyone.

The region's Relais & Châteaux capture the essence of this diversity and offer their guests unforgettable experiences, combining luxury, comfort and authenticity. Each establishment, with its enchanting setting, warm welcome, exceptional gastronomy and enriching activities, offers total immersion in the French art of living.

By discovering the Relais & Châteaux du Grand Est, you will be transported into a world where every detail is designed to delight the senses and create lasting memories. This chapter presented a detailed overview of the region, integrating geographical, historical, cultural and economic aspects to provide a comprehensive understanding of this unique destination.

- History and Heritage

The Grand Est region, formed by the merger of Alsace, Lorraine and Champagne-Ardenne, is a true crossroads of European history. This heritage-rich region offers an impressive diversity of monuments, historical sites and cultural treasures. In this chapter, we will explore key moments in the history of the Grand Est, its iconic monuments and its cultural contributions.

Prehistoric Origins and Antiquity

Prehistoric Sites

The Grand Est has a history that dates back to prehistory, with numerous archaeological sites testifying to human occupation since the Paleolithic. Notable sites include the caves of Saint-Anne-sur-Brivet in Champagne-Ardenne and the numerous dolmens and menhirs scattered throughout the region.

Roman Influence

The region was deeply marked by the Roman presence. The Romans left behind many remains, including Roman roads, aqueducts and thermal baths. The city of Reims, formerly Durocortorum , was an important city in Roman Gaul and still retains traces of this era today, such as the Porte de Mars.

The Middle Age

The Birth of Duchies and Counties

The Middle Ages is a period of formation and consolidation of local political entities. The duchies and counties of Alsace, Lorraine and Champagne play a crucial role in regional and national history. Local lords built castles to defend their lands and establish their authority.

Medieval Castles

The Grand Est is famous for its numerous medieval castles, built mainly from the 11th century. Among the most famous, we find:

- The Château du Haut-Koenigsbourg: Located in Alsace, this fortified castle offers a spectacular view of the Alsace plain and has been magnificently restored.

- The Château de Sedan: In Champagne-Ardenne, this castle is one of the largest medieval fortresses in Europe.

- The Château de Malbrouck: In Lorraine, this 15th century fortified castle is an impressive example of medieval military architecture.

Cathedrals and Churches

The Middle Ages also saw the construction of numerous cathedrals and churches, symbols of the religious power of the time. Among the most notable are:

- Strasbourg Cathedral: A masterpiece of Gothic architecture, famous for its slender spire and astronomical clock.
- Reims Cathedral: Another Gothic gem, where the kings of France were traditionally crowned.
- Metz Cathedral: Known for its exceptional stained glass windows, including those by Marc Chagall.

The Renaissance

The Renaissance and Art

The Renaissance brought a new wave of construction and decoration to the Grand Est, influenced by Italian arts and architecture. The castles and stately residences were adorned with new ornamentations and French-style gardens.

- The Palais des Rohan in Strasbourg: An example of classical and baroque architecture, this palace is today a museum.
- The Château de Lunéville: Nicknamed the "Versailles of Lorraine", this castle is a magnificent example of 18th century architecture.

The Modern Era

Wars and Conflicts

The Great East has been the scene of numerous conflicts over the centuries, notably during the wars of religion, the Thirty Years' War and the two world wars. These events have left indelible traces in the landscape and collective memory.

- The Maginot Line: A line of fortifications built to defend France against Germany, several sections of which are today open to visitors.
- The Verdun Battlefield: One of the most important sites of the First World War, with its trenches, forts and commemorative monuments.

The industrial Revolution

The industrial revolution transformed the Grand Est into a major economic center, with the development of the textile industry in Alsace, the steel industry in Lorraine and viticulture in

Champagne. Cities like Mulhouse, Nancy and Reims are experiencing rapid growth and modernization of their infrastructure.

Contemporary Heritage

World War II and Reconstruction

The Grand Est was heavily affected by the Second World War, with many villages and towns destroyed. Post-war reconstruction brought life back to the area, and memorials were erected to honor the memory of the victims.

- The Schirmeck Memorial: Dedicated to the memory of the deportees and victims of the war in Alsace.
- The Struthof: One of the rare Nazi concentration camps on French soil, today a site of memory.

Europe and Innovation

Today, the Grand Est is a dynamic and innovative region, integrated into the heart of Europe. Strasbourg, seat of the European Parliament, symbolizes the region's commitment to European unity and cooperation. Competitiveness clusters and research centers, such as the Fibers- Energivie cluster in Metz, place the region at the forefront of technological and environmental innovation.

UNESCO Sites and Historical Monuments

UNESCO World Heritage Sites

The Grand Est has several UNESCO World Heritage sites, testifying to its historical and cultural richness.

- The Fortifications of Vauban: Several sites fortified by Vauban, including Neuf-Brisach in Alsace.
- The Hillsides, Houses and Cellars of Champagne: A tribute to the art of viticulture in Champagne, inscribed for their exceptional universal value.

Historical Monuments and Museums

The region is home to numerous historical monuments and museums which tell the history of the Grand Est and highlight its cultural heritage. Among them, we find:

- The Unterlinden Museum in Colmar: Housing the famous Isenheim Altarpiece.
- The Center Pompidou-Metz: A modern and contemporary art museum, subsidiary of the Center Pompidou in Paris.
- The Musée de la Cour d'Or in Metz: An archeology and history museum, located in a former medieval convent.

Conclusion

The Grand Est is a region rich in history and heritage, where each town, each village and each monument tells a unique story. From Roman remains to Renaissance castles, from Gothic cathedrals to war memorial sites, the region offers an incredible diversity of historical sites and monuments.

Les Relais & Châteaux du Grand Est capture the essence of this historical and cultural wealth, offering their guests unforgettable experiences. Each establishment, with its enchanting setting, warm welcome, exceptional gastronomy and enriching activities, offers total immersion in the history and heritage of the region.

By discovering the Relais & Châteaux du Grand Est, you will be transported into a world where every detail is designed to delight the senses and create lasting memories. This chapter explored the many facets of the region's history and heritage, revealing how each era helped shape this unique and fascinating destination.

- Gastronomy and Wine

The Grand Est region, with its rich history and cultural diversity, is also a mecca for gastronomy and viticulture in France. Alsace, Lorraine and Champagne-Ardenne, which make up this region, each offer unique culinary specialties and world-renowned wines. This chapter explores the gastronomic delights of the Grand Est, highlighting the local produce, iconic dishes, renowned chefs, starred restaurants and wines that this region is famous for.

Local Products

Products of the Earth

The Grand Est is a fertile region that produces a wide variety of high-quality fruits, vegetables, meats and dairy products.

- Alsace Asparagus: Renowned for its delicate flavor, it is often served with a Dutch sauce or in a salad.
- Mirabelles of Lorraine: These small golden plums are used in many recipes, from tarts to jams, as well as for the production of liqueurs.
- Choucroute Cabbage: Grown mainly in Alsace, it is fermented to create the famous garnished sauerkraut.

Sea and River Products

Although the region is not coastal, its rivers and lakes provide an abundance of fish and seafood.

- Moselle Trout: This fish is often prepared blue or filleted, accompanied by local sauces.
- Crayfish: Used in dishes such as dumplings or in stews.

Cheeses and charcuterie

The Grand Est region is also known for its cheeses and charcuterie, which are essential elements of the local cuisine.

- Munster: A soft cheese with a washed rind, typical of Alsace, often served with cumin.
- Brie de Meaux: Although more associated with the Paris region, this cheese is also produced in Champagne.
- Rillettes de Lorraine: A specialty of pulled meat, often served on fresh bread.

Traditional dishes

Alsatian Specialties

Alsace is renowned for its generous and tasty cuisine, influenced by its German neighbors.

- Choucroute Garnie: A dish of fermented cabbage accompanied by various meats, such as sausages, pork and sometimes duck.
- Baeckeoffe : A stew of marinated meats and vegetables slowly cooked in a terracotta terrine.
- Tarte Flambée (Flammekueche): A thin bread dough covered with cream, bacon and onions, cooked in a wood oven.

Lorraine Specialties

Lorraine offers robust and comforting dishes, often based on meat and potatoes.

- Quiche Lorraine: A savory tart garnished with bacon, eggs and cream, sometimes with cheese.
- Pâté Lorrain: A puff pastry filled with meat marinated in white wine and spices.
- Les Macarons de Nancy: Small biscuits made with almonds, sugar and egg whites, a specialty of the city of Nancy.

Champagne Specialties

Champagne-Ardenne is known for its simple but delicious dishes, often accompanied by its famous sparkling wine.

- Jambon de Reims: A cooked, seasoned and pressed ham, often served with pickles.
- Andouillette de Troyes: A sausage made from pig pork and stomachs, seasoned with mustard or white wine.
- The Rose de Reims Biscuit: A dry biscuit, often dipped in champagne.

Wines of the Great East

Alsace Wines

Alsace wines are renowned for their quality and diversity. The region produces mainly white wines, although some reds and rosés are also produced.

- Riesling: A dry white wine, often considered one of the best wines of Alsace.
- Gewurztraminer: An aromatic white wine, often sweet and spicy, perfect to accompany spicy dishes or desserts.
- Pinot Gris: A rich, full-bodied white wine, with notes of ripe fruit and honey.

Wines of Lorraine

Lorraine is less known for its wines, but it nevertheless produces interesting wines, particularly in the Côtes de Toul.

- Le Gris de Toul: A light and fresh rosé wine, perfect for aperitifs and light meals.
- Pinot Noir: An elegant red wine, with aromas of red fruits and a beautiful tannic structure.

Champagne Wines

Champagne is world famous for its sparkling wines, produced using the traditional method.

- Champagne Brut: The most common style, with aromas of apple, pear, brioche and almond.
- Rosé Champagne: Made by adding red wine to the champagne vintage, offering notes of red fruits and a beautiful pink color.
- Vintage Champagne: Produced only in the best years, with complex aromas and great finesse.

Star Chefs and Restaurants

The Pioneers of Regional Haute Cuisine

The Grand Est has always been a hotbed of culinary creativity, attracting talented chefs who highlight local products and culinary traditions. Among the pioneers of regional haute cuisine, we find Emile Jung, who made the Auberge de l'Ill a temple of Alsatian gastronomy.

Contemporary Chefs

Today, the region continues to attract renowned chefs, who continue the tradition of haute cuisine while innovating and experimenting with new flavors. Among the most famous contemporary chefs, we find:

- Jean-Georges Klein: Chef of the Michelin-starred Villa René Lalique restaurant in Alsace, offering inventive and refined cuisine.
- Patrice Teisseire: Chef of the restaurant Le Jardin des Remparts in Beaune, renowned for its contemporary and elegant cuisine.

Star Restaurants

The Grand Est is home to numerous Michelin-starred restaurants, each offering a unique and unforgettable culinary experience. Among the most famous, we find:

- L'Auberge de l'Ill in Illhaeusern: This three-star Michelin restaurant, run by the Haeberlin family , offers sophisticated Alsatian cuisine.
- Le Crocodile in Strasbourg: Michelin-starred, this restaurant offers classic French cuisine with a contemporary touch.
- La Grenouillère in La Madeleine-sous-Montreuil: A Michelin-starred restaurant where chef Alexandre Gauthier offers inventive and daring cuisine.

Oenological Experiences

Wine Tastings

Relais & Châteaux du Grand Est often offer unique wine experiences for their guests. From private tastings to vineyard tours, these experiences allow you to discover the region's wines and learn the secrets of their making.

Customers can participate in tasting workshops, led by experts, to learn how to identify the aromas and flavors of regional wines. Guided tours of the vineyards and cellars allow you to discover the production processes, meet the winegrowers and taste wines directly from the source.

Food and Wine Pairings

The Relais & Châteaux also offer food and wine pairings, allowing you to savor Grand Est wines in harmony with local cuisine. These pairings highlight the flavors of the dishes and wines, providing a complete and unforgettable gastronomic experience.

Chefs from Michelin-starred restaurants collaborate with sommeliers to create tasting menus that highlight the region's wines. Each dish is carefully paired with a wine, allowing guests to discover new combinations of flavors and textures.

Conclusion

The Grand Est is a true land of gastronomy and wine, offering unparalleled richness and diversity. Regional cuisine, with its authentic flavors and quality local products, is a pillar of the region's art of living. Wines from Alsace, Lorraine and Champagne, renowned for their complexity and elegance, perfectly complement this culinary experience.

Les Relais & Châteaux du Grand Est capture the essence of this gastronomic richness, offering their guests unique and unforgettable culinary and wine experiences. Each establishment, with its enchanting setting, warm welcome, exceptional gastronomy and enriching activities, offers total immersion in the French art of living.

By discovering the Relais & Châteaux du Grand Est, you will be transported into a world where every detail is designed to delight the senses and create lasting memories. This chapter explored the multiple facets of the region's gastronomy and wines, revealing how each element contributes to making this destination a true oasis of flavors and culinary pleasures.

2. Addresses and Descriptions

The Grand Est region is home to several Relais & Châteaux establishments, each offering a unique experience combining luxury, comfort and regional charm. These prestigious hotels and restaurants are located in iconic locations across the region, from historic towns to picturesque countryside. In this chapter, we will discover some of the most prestigious addresses and describe in detail what makes them special.

Hotel Les Bas Rupts

History and Architecture

The Hôtel Les Bas Rupts , located in the Vosges in Gérardmer, is a charming establishment offering a luxurious experience in the heart of nature. This family hotel, founded in 1950, combines the authenticity of Vosges chalets with modern comfort. The wooden facades, flowered balconies and warm interiors make it a place of relaxation and rejuvenation.

Culinary Offers

The gourmet restaurant at Hôtel Les Bas Rupts offers inventive and refined cuisine, highlighting local and seasonal products. The chef creates dishes such as "Filet de Trout de la Vologne" and "Gibier des Vosges". The carefully selected wine list highlights the great wines of Alsace and other prestigious wine regions.

Activities and Services

Hôtel Les Bas Rupts offers a range of activities for its guests, from relaxation to sport. Guests can enjoy the indoor swimming pool, spa, sauna and hammam for moments of relaxation. Guided excursions are also organized to explore the surrounding area, including the Gérardmer and Longemer lakes, as well as the Vosges hiking trails.

Adomenil Castle

History and Architecture

Château d' Adoménil , located near Lunéville in Lorraine, is an elegant 18th-century residence surrounded by extensive gardens and woods. This historic castle, carefully restored, offers a romantic and peaceful setting. The architecture of the castle, with its stone facades and slate roofs, reflects the elegance of the period.

Culinary Offers

The Château d' Adoménil gourmet restaurant , led by a starred chef, offers inventive and refined cuisine, highlighting local and seasonal products. The tasting menu offers dishes such as "Duck Foie Gras" and "Racan Pigeon". The carefully selected wine list highlights the region's great wines and other prestigious wine regions.

Activities and Services

Château d' Adoménil offers a range of activities for its guests, from relaxation to sport. Guests can enjoy the heated outdoor swimming pool, gardens and terraces for moments of relaxation. Guided excursions are also organized to explore the surrounding area, including the town of Lunéville and its famous castle, as well as the Lorraine vineyard.

Hostellerie La Cheneaudière & Spa

History and Architecture

Hostellerie La Cheneaudière & Spa, located in Colroy-la-Roche in Alsace, is a charming establishment nestled in the heart of the Bruche valley. This family hotel, founded in 1974, combines the charm of Alsatian architecture with modern comfort. The wooden facades, flowered balconies and warm interiors make it a place of relaxation and rejuvenation.

Culinary Offers

The gourmet restaurant at Hostellerie La Cheneaudière offers inventive and refined cuisine, highlighting local and seasonal products. The chef creates dishes such as "Filet de Perch de la Bruche" and "Gibier de la Forêt Noire". The carefully selected wine list highlights the great wines of Alsace and other prestigious wine regions.

Activities and Services

Hostellerie La Cheneaudière offers a range of activities for its guests, from relaxation to sport. Guests can enjoy the 2,500 m^2 spa, with its indoor and outdoor swimming pools, saunas, hammams and treatment rooms for moments of relaxation. Guided excursions are also organized to explore the surrounding area, including the hiking trails of the Vosges and the picturesque villages of Alsace.

Domaine Les Crayères

History and Architecture

Domaine Les Crayères, located in Reims in Champagne, is an elegant castle surrounded by a seven-hectare park. This estate, built at the beginning of the 20th century, is a symbol of the elegance and refinement of the Belle Époque. The stone facades, slate roofs and landscaped gardens make it an exceptional place.

Culinary Offers

The gourmet restaurant at Domaine Les Crayères, led by a starred chef, offers inventive and refined cuisine, highlighting local and seasonal products. The tasting menu offers dishes such as "Lobster Bleu de Bretagne" and "Filet de Bœuf Charolais". The carefully selected wine list highlights the great wines of Champagne and other prestigious wine regions.

Activities and Services

Domaine Les Crayères offers a range of activities for its guests, from relaxation to sport. Guests can take advantage of the proximity to Champagne houses for tours and tastings. Guided excursions are also organized to explore the surrounding area, including the city of Reims, Notre-Dame de Reims Cathedral and the Champagne vineyards.

Auberge de l'Ill

History and Architecture
Auberge de l'Ill, located in Illhaeusern in Alsace, is a world-renowned establishment offering an exceptional gastronomic experience. Founded in 1882, this family inn combines the charm of Alsatian architecture with modern comfort. The wooden facades, flowered balconies and warm interiors make it a place of relaxation and culinary pleasure.

Culinary Offers

The gourmet restaurant at the Auberge de l'Ill, run by the Haeberlin family , offers inventive and refined cuisine, highlighting local and seasonal products. The tasting menu offers dishes such as "Duck Foie Gras" and "Lobster à la Presse". The carefully selected wine list highlights the great wines of Alsace and other prestigious wine regions.

Activities and Services

Auberge de l'Ill offers a range of activities for its guests, from relaxation to sport. Guests can enjoy walks along the Ill, tours of Alsace vineyards and guided excursions to explore the surrounding area, including the picturesque villages of the Alsace wine route and the hiking trails of the Vosges.

Conclusion

The Relais & Châteaux du Grand Est offer unique and unforgettable experiences, combining luxury, comfort and historical heritage. Each establishment, with its enchanting setting, warm welcome, exceptional gastronomy and enriching activities, offers total immersion in the French art of living. Whether for a romantic getaway, a peaceful retreat or a cultural exploration, the Relais & Châteaux of the Grand Est region are must-see destinations.

By discovering these exceptional establishments, you will be transported to a world where every detail is designed to delight the senses and create lasting memories. This chapter has presented a detailed overview of some of the most prestigious Relais & Châteaux in the region, offering a glimpse of the unique experience that awaits you in each of these enchanting locations.

Adoménil Castle

The Château d' Adoménil , located near Lunéville in Lorraine, is a jewel of the Grand Est region. This elegant 18th-century castle, surrounded by extensive gardens and woodland, offers a luxurious and refined experience in a romantic and peaceful setting. In this chapter, we will explore the history and architecture of Château d' Adoménil , its culinary offerings, the activities and services offered, and the unique experiences it offers.

History and Architecture

An Aristocratic Heritage

The Château d' Adoménil was built in the 18th century, at a time when Lorraine was an independent duchy under the supervision of France. This elegant residence served as a residence for the Lorraine nobility and has been carefully restored to preserve its old-world charm. The current owners have managed to preserve the authenticity of the place while modernizing it to offer all the necessary comfort to its guests.

Elegant Architecture

The architecture of Château d' Adoménil reflects the elegance and refinement of the classical era, with its stone facades, slate roofs and large mullioned windows. Interiors are decorated with antique furniture, artwork and fine textiles, creating a warm and sophisticated atmosphere.

The hotel's rooms and suites offer breathtaking views of the park, gardens or interior courtyard. Each room is unique, with distinctive design elements and modern amenities to ensure optimal comfort. The bathrooms, fitted with marble bathtubs and walk-in showers, provide a luxurious setting in which to relax and rejuvenate.

Culinary Offers

The Gourmet Restaurant

The Château d' Adoménil gourmet restaurant , led by a Michelin-starred chef, offers inventive and refined cuisine, highlighting local and seasonal products. The tasting menu offers dishes such as "Duck Foie Gras" and "Racan Pigeon". The carefully selected wine list highlights the region's great wines and other prestigious wine regions.

The restaurant's setting matches its cuisine, with an elegantly decorated dining room, tables spaced for maximum privacy, and panoramic views of the gardens. Guests can also dine al fresco on the terrace, enjoying the tranquility and beauty of the natural surroundings.

Regional Cuisine

The chef at Château d' Adoménil places particular emphasis on local products, with a locavore philosophy that favors fresh, seasonal ingredients from local producers. Guests can taste regional specialties such as "Filet de Zander de la Moselle" and "Tarte aux Mirabelles de Lorraine", accompanied by carefully selected local wines.

The Gourmet Breakfast

Adoménil 's gourmet breakfast is served in the elegantly decorated dining room or on the terrace, with magnificent views of the gardens and park. Breakfast is composed of fresh, local products, including pastries, fruits, homemade jams, regional cheeses, fresh eggs and pressed fruit juices. Guests can also enjoy hot drinks, such as coffee, tea and hot chocolate.

Activities and Services

The Spa and Wellness Treatments

Château d' Adoménil offers a range of wellness treatments for its guests, ranging from massages to facial treatments, carried out with high quality products. The spa, located in a peaceful and luxurious setting, is a place of rest and relaxation, perfect for recharging your batteries after a day exploring the region.

Professional therapists use advanced techniques and luxury products to ensure optimal results and a luxurious experience. Guests can also enjoy the heated outdoor swimming pool, jacuzzi, sauna and steam room to complete their relaxation experience.

Outdoor activities

The gardens and woods of Château d' Adoménil are perfect for leisurely walks, meditation sessions or outdoor yoga sessions. Guests can also take advantage of the proximity to the Meurthe River for water activities such as canoeing and fishing. Guided excursions are also organized to explore the surrounding area, including the town of Lunéville, its castle and its famous French gardens.

Cultural Activities and Experiences

Château d' Adoménil regularly organizes cultural events and unique experiences for its guests. Private concerts, literary readings and art exhibitions are often organized in the establishment's lounges or gardens. These events offer immersion in the local cultural scene and allow guests to meet artists, writers and musicians.

Guests can also participate in cooking workshops, baking classes and wine tastings, led by local chefs. These workshops offer an opportunity to learn regional cooking techniques and taste delicious creations. Château d' Adoménil also offers yoga and meditation classes, led by qualified instructors, in the hotel's gardens or wellness areas.

Special Events and Unique Experiences

Weddings and Receptions

Château d' Adoménil is an ideal venue for organizing intimate weddings and private receptions. The property's gardens and lounges provide a romantic and elegant setting for ceremonies and receptions. Hotel staff work closely with couples to create tailor-made events, taking into account every detail, from decor to personalized menus.

The hotel's chefs create wedding menus that reflect the tastes and preferences of the bride and groom, using seasonal ingredients and local produce. The professional and attentive service teams ensure that every event goes off without a hitch. Couples can also enjoy luxurious suites for their wedding night, with special services such as massages, in-room breakfasts and welcome gifts.

Seminars and Business Meetings

The Château d' Adoménil offers an exceptional setting for seminars, conferences and business meetings. The property's private lounges, equipped with the latest technology, offer flexible spaces for events of different sizes. Hotel teams work with event organizers to create tailor-made programs, including coffee breaks, business lunches and dinners.

Team-building activities and excursions can also be organized to strengthen team cohesion and provide moments of relaxation outside of work sessions. Guests can take advantage of the hotel's wellness facilities to unwind after a day of meetings, with spa treatments, yoga sessions and massages.

Unique Experiences

Château d' Adoménil offers unique experiences to make each stay memorable. These include private dinners in exclusive locations within the establishment, such as the library or gardens, offering an intimate and romantic atmosphere. Guests can also participate in wine tasting workshops, led by expert sommeliers, to discover the secrets of the region's wines.

Wellness getaways are also available, including personalized relaxation and relaxation programs, spa treatments, yoga and meditation sessions, as well as healthy and nutritious meals. These programs are designed to help clients recharge their batteries and regain physical and mental balance.

Seasonal and Thematic Offers

Château d' Adoménil regularly offers seasonal and thematic offers to enrich its customers' experience. At Christmas, the establishment is decked out in festive decorations and offers special menus, cookie decorating workshops and Christmas market visits. In summer, gourmet picnics can be organized in the gardens or on the terraces.

Romantic getaways are also offered, including candlelit dinners, duo massages and horse-drawn carriage rides in the surrounding area. For culture lovers, special packages including tickets for exhibitions, shows and concerts are available, offering complete immersion in the cultural life of the region.

Conclusion

The Château d' Adoménil is much more than just a luxury hotel; it is a destination in itself, offering a unique and unforgettable experience in the heart of the magnificent Lorraine region. With its rich history, impressive architecture, refined culinary offerings and a variety of activities and services, this establishment is the ideal place to relax, recharge and discover the French art of living.

Whether for a romantic getaway, a wellness retreat, an intimate wedding or a business meeting, Château d' Adoménil promises an exceptional experience, marked by luxury, comfort and elegance. Guests leave with unforgettable memories, enriched by the unique culture, gastronomy and hospitality of this emblematic establishment of the Grand Est region.

- Le Chambard

Le Chambard, located in Kaysersberg in Alsace, is a charming establishment offering a luxurious and authentic experience in the heart of one of the most beautiful regions of France. This Relais & Châteaux hotel combines the refinement of Alsatian hospitality with starred cuisine and modern wellness facilities. In this chapter, we will explore the history and architecture of Chambard, its culinary offerings, the activities and services offered, and the unique experiences it offers.

History and Architecture

An Alsatian Heritage

Le Chambard is located in Kaysersberg, a picturesque village in the heart of the Alsace wine route. Kaysersberg is famous for its medieval charm, half-timbered houses and surrounding vineyards. The establishment, founded by Olivier Nasti , embodies the elegance and authenticity of Alsace, combining tradition and modernity.

Elegant Architecture

The architecture of Chambard reflects the typically Alsatian style with its colorful facades, half-timbering and flowered balconies. Inside, the spaces are tastefully decorated, combining traditional and contemporary elements to create a warm and sophisticated atmosphere.

The hotel's rooms and suites offer breathtaking views of the village or the vineyards. Each room is unique, with distinctive design elements and modern amenities to ensure optimal comfort. The bathrooms, fitted with marble bathtubs and walk-in showers, provide a luxurious setting in which to relax and rejuvenate.

Culinary Offers

The Gourmet Restaurant

The Chambard gourmet restaurant, led by starred chef Olivier Nasti , offers inventive and refined cuisine, highlighting local and seasonal products. The tasting menu offers dishes such as "Duck Foie Gras" and "Turbot de Ligne". The carefully selected wine list highlights the great wines of Alsace and other prestigious wine regions.

The restaurant's setting matches its cuisine, with an elegantly decorated dining room, tables spaced for maximum privacy, and panoramic views of Kaysersberg village. Guests can also dine al fresco on the terrace, enjoying the tranquility and beauty of the natural surroundings.

The Winstub

The Winstub du Chambard offers a more relaxed atmosphere with traditional Alsatian bistronomic cuisine. The dishes offered highlight quality local products, in a friendly and warm atmosphere. Guests can enjoy dishes such as "Choucroute Garnie" or " Baeckeoffe ", accompanied by regional wines.

The Gourmet Breakfast

Chambard's gourmet breakfast is served in the elegantly decorated dining room or on the terrace, with magnificent views of the vineyards and the village. Breakfast is composed of fresh, local products, including pastries, fruits, homemade jams, regional cheeses, fresh eggs and pressed fruit juices. Guests can also enjoy hot drinks, such as coffee, tea and hot chocolate.

Activities and Services

The Spa and Wellness Treatments

The Spa du Chambard offers a range of wellness treatments for its clients, from massages to facials, performed with high quality products. The spa, located in a peaceful and luxurious setting, is a place of rest and relaxation, perfect for recharging your batteries after a day exploring the region.

Professional therapists use advanced techniques and luxury products to ensure optimal results and a luxurious experience. Guests can also enjoy the heated indoor swimming pool, jacuzzi, sauna and steam room to complete their relaxation experience.

Outdoor activities

The vineyards and surrounding hills of Chambard are perfect for leisurely walks, meditation sessions or outdoor yoga sessions. Guests can also enjoy the proximity to Vosges hiking trails for activities such as walking, cycling and fishing. Guided excursions are also organized to explore the surrounding area, including the picturesque villages of the Alsace wine route and the region's historic sites.

Cultural Activities and Experiences

Le Chambard regularly organizes cultural events and unique experiences for its guests. Private concerts, literary readings and art exhibitions are often organized in the establishment's lounges or gardens. These events offer immersion in the local cultural scene and allow guests to meet artists, writers and musicians.

Guests can also participate in cooking workshops, baking classes and wine tastings, led by local chefs. These workshops offer an opportunity to learn regional cooking techniques and taste delicious creations. Le Chambard also offers yoga and meditation classes, led by qualified instructors, in the hotel's gardens or wellness areas.

Special Events and Unique Experiences

Weddings and Receptions

Le Chambard is an ideal venue for intimate weddings and private receptions. The property's gardens and lounges provide a romantic and elegant setting for ceremonies and receptions. Hotel staff work closely with couples to create tailor-made events, taking into account every detail, from decor to personalized menus.

The hotel's chefs create wedding menus that reflect the tastes and preferences of the bride and groom, using seasonal ingredients and local produce. The professional and attentive service teams ensure that every event goes off without a hitch. Couples can also enjoy luxurious suites for their wedding night, with special services such as massages, in-room breakfasts and welcome gifts.

Seminars and Business Meetings

Le Chambard offers an exceptional setting for seminars, conferences and business meetings. The property's private lounges, equipped with the latest technology, offer flexible spaces for events of different sizes. Hotel teams work with event organizers to create tailor-made programs, including coffee breaks, business lunches and dinners.

Team-building activities and excursions can also be organized to strengthen team cohesion and provide moments of relaxation outside of work sessions. Guests can take advantage of the hotel's wellness facilities to unwind after a day of meetings, with spa treatments, yoga sessions and massages.

Unique Experiences

Le Chambard offers unique experiences to make each stay memorable. These include private dinners in exclusive locations within the establishment, such as the library or gardens, offering an intimate and romantic atmosphere. Guests can also participate in wine tasting workshops, led by expert sommeliers, to discover the secrets of the region's wines.

Wellness getaways are also available, including personalized relaxation and relaxation programs, spa treatments, yoga and meditation sessions, as well as healthy and nutritious meals. These programs are designed to help clients recharge their batteries and regain physical and mental balance.

Seasonal and Thematic Offers

Le Chambard regularly offers seasonal and thematic offers to enrich its customers' experience. At Christmas, the establishment is decked out in festive decorations and offers special menus, cookie decorating workshops and Christmas market visits. In summer, gourmet picnics can be organized in the gardens or on the terraces.

Romantic getaways are also offered, including candlelit dinners, duo massages and horse-drawn carriage rides in the surrounding area. For culture lovers, special packages including tickets for exhibitions, shows and concerts are available, offering complete immersion in the cultural life of the region.

Conclusion

Le Chambard is much more than just a luxury hotel; it is a destination in itself, offering a unique and unforgettable experience in the heart of the magnificent Alsace region. With its rich history, impressive architecture, refined culinary offerings and a variety of activities and services, this establishment is the ideal place to relax, recharge and discover the French art of living.

Whether for a romantic getaway, a wellness retreat, an intimate wedding or a business meeting, Le Chambard promises an exceptional experience, marked by luxury, comfort and elegance. Guests leave with unforgettable memories, enriched by the unique culture, gastronomy and hospitality of this emblematic establishment of the Grand Est region.

- Hostellerie La Cheneaudière

Hostellerie La Cheneaudière & Spa, located in Colroy-la-Roche in Alsace, is a charming establishment nestled in the heart of the Bruche valley. This Relais & Châteaux hotel combines the refinement of Alsatian hospitality with modern wellness facilities and starred cuisine. In this chapter, we will explore the history and architecture of La Cheneaudière , its culinary offerings, the activities and services offered, and the unique experiences it offers.

History and Architecture

A Family Heirloom

Founded in 1974 by the François family, La Cheneaudière is a family business that embodies the hospitality and charm of Alsace. The name " Cheneaudière " refers to the majestic oak trees that surround the property, creating a peaceful and natural setting.

Eclectic Architecture

The architecture of La Cheneaudière combines traditional Alsatian style and modern elements to offer a setting that is both warm and sophisticated. The wooden facades, flowered balconies and interiors elegantly decorated with natural materials such as stone and wood, create a welcoming and authentic atmosphere.

The hotel's rooms and suites offer breathtaking views of the Bruche valley or the gardens. Each room is unique, with distinctive design elements and modern amenities to ensure optimal comfort. The bathrooms, fitted with marble bathtubs and walk-in showers, provide a luxurious setting in which to relax and rejuvenate.

Culinary Offers

The Gourmet Restaurant

The gourmet restaurant of La Cheneaudière , led by a talented chef, offers inventive and refined cuisine, highlighting local and seasonal products. The tasting menu offers dishes such as "Filet de Perch de la Bruche" and "Gibier de la Forêt Noire". The carefully selected wine list highlights the great wines of Alsace and other prestigious wine regions.

The restaurant's setting matches its cuisine, with an elegantly decorated dining room, tables spaced for maximum privacy, and panoramic views of the valley and gardens. Guests can also dine al fresco on the terrace, enjoying the tranquility and beauty of the natural surroundings.

The Gourmet Breakfast

Cheneaudière 's gourmet breakfast is served in the dining room or on the terrace, offering magnificent views of the gardens and the valley. Breakfast is composed of fresh, local products, including pastries, fruits, homemade jams, regional cheeses, fresh eggs and pressed fruit juices. Guests can also enjoy hot drinks, such as coffee, tea and hot chocolate.

Activities and Services

The Spa and Wellness Treatments

The Spa de La Cheneaudière , spanning 2,500 m^2, offers a range of well-being treatments for its clients, ranging from massages to facial treatments, carried out with high quality products. The spa, located in a peaceful and luxurious setting, is a perfect place to relax and unwind after a day exploring the region.

Spa facilities include heated indoor and outdoor swimming pools, saunas, steam rooms, hot tubs and treatment rooms. Professional therapists use advanced techniques and luxury products to ensure optimal results and a luxurious experience.

Outdoor activities

The gardens and surrounding hills of La Cheneaudière are perfect for leisurely walks, meditation sessions or outdoor yoga sessions. Guests can also enjoy the proximity to Vosges hiking trails for activities such as walking, cycling and fishing. Guided excursions are also organized to explore the surrounding area, including the picturesque villages of the Alsace wine route and the region's historic sites.

Cultural Activities and Experiences

La Cheneaudière regularly organizes cultural events and unique experiences for its guests. Private concerts, literary readings and art exhibitions are often organized in the establishment's lounges or gardens. These events offer immersion in the local cultural scene and allow guests to meet artists, writers and musicians.

Guests can also participate in cooking workshops, baking classes and wine tastings, led by local chefs. These workshops offer an opportunity to learn regional cooking techniques and taste delicious creations. La Cheneaudière also offers yoga and meditation classes, led by qualified instructors, in the hotel's gardens or wellness areas.

Special Events and Unique Experiences

Weddings and Receptions

La Cheneaudière is an ideal venue for organizing intimate weddings and private receptions. The property's gardens and lounges provide a romantic and elegant setting for ceremonies and receptions. Hotel staff work closely with couples to create tailor-made events, taking into account every detail, from decor to personalized menus.

The hotel's chefs create wedding menus that reflect the tastes and preferences of the bride and groom, using seasonal ingredients and local produce. The professional and attentive service teams ensure that every event goes off without a hitch. Couples can also enjoy luxurious suites for their wedding night, with special services such as massages, in-room breakfasts and welcome gifts.

Seminars and Business Meetings

La Cheneaudière offers an exceptional setting for seminars, conferences and business meetings. The property's private lounges, equipped with the latest technology, offer flexible spaces for events of different sizes. Hotel teams work with event organizers to create tailor-made programs, including coffee breaks, business lunches and dinners.

Team-building activities and excursions can also be organized to strengthen team cohesion and provide moments of relaxation outside of work sessions. Guests can take advantage of the hotel's

wellness facilities to unwind after a day of meetings, with spa treatments, yoga sessions and massages.

Unique Experiences

La Cheneaudière offers unique experiences to make each stay memorable. These include private dinners in exclusive locations within the establishment, such as the library or gardens, offering an intimate and romantic atmosphere. Guests can also participate in wine tasting workshops, led by expert sommeliers, to discover the secrets of the region's wines.

Wellness getaways are also available, including personalized relaxation and relaxation programs, spa treatments, yoga and meditation sessions, as well as healthy and nutritious meals. These programs are designed to help clients recharge their batteries and regain physical and mental balance.

Seasonal and Thematic Offers

La Cheneaudière regularly offers seasonal and thematic offers to enrich its customers' experience. At Christmas, the establishment is decked out in festive decorations and offers special menus, cookie decorating workshops and Christmas market visits. In summer, gourmet picnics can be organized in the gardens or on the terraces.

Romantic getaways are also offered, including candlelit dinners, duo massages and horse-drawn carriage rides in the surrounding area. For culture lovers, special packages including tickets for exhibitions, shows and concerts are available, offering complete immersion in the cultural life of the region.

Conclusion

Hostellerie La Cheneaudière & Spa is much more than just a luxury hotel; it is a destination in itself, offering a unique and unforgettable experience in the heart of the magnificent Alsace region. With its rich history, impressive architecture, refined culinary offerings and a variety of activities and services, this establishment is the ideal place to relax, recharge and discover the French art of living.

Whether for a romantic getaway, a wellness retreat, an intimate wedding or a business meeting, La Cheneaudière promises an exceptional experience, marked by luxury, comfort and elegance. Guests leave with unforgettable memories, enriched by the unique culture, gastronomy and hospitality of this emblematic establishment of the Grand Est region.

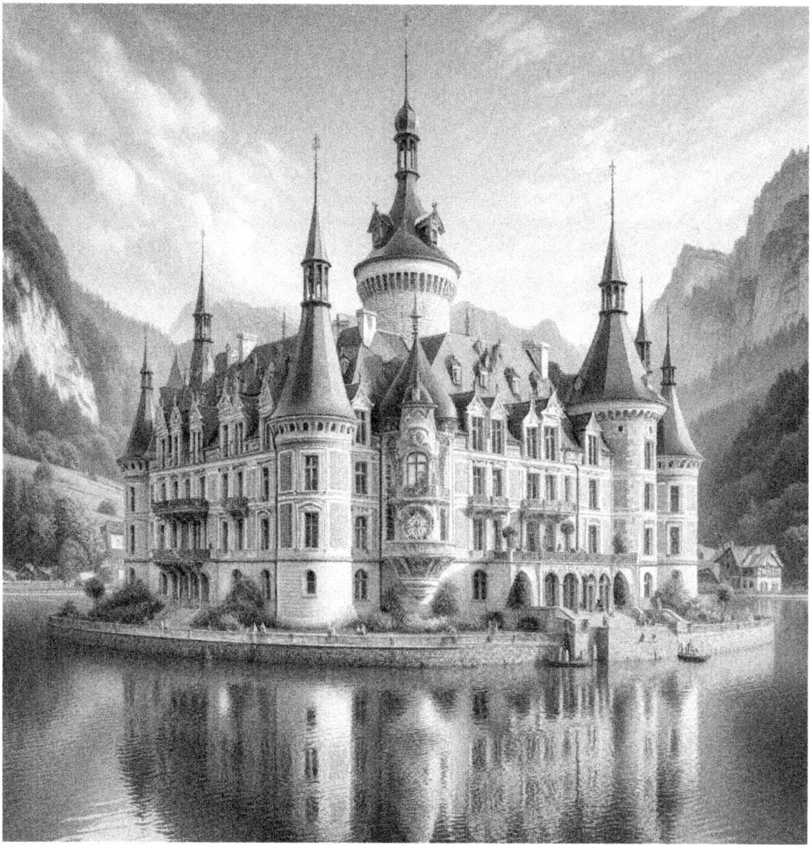

Chapter 11: Relais & Châteaux in Hauts-de-France

1. General Presentation of the Region

The Hauts-de-France region, located in the north of France, is a land of contrasts and riches, combining a rich historical heritage, varied landscapes and a living culture. This region, made up of the former Nord-Pas-de-Calais and Picardie regions, offers an impressive diversity of natural sites, historic towns and cultural treasures. This chapter explores the geographical, historical, cultural and economic characteristics of Hauts-de-France, highlighting the attractions that make this region an essential destination.

Geography and Landscapes

Exceptional Landscape Diversity

Hauts-de-France is distinguished by the variety of its landscapes, ranging from the beaches of the Opal Coast to the fertile plains of Artois, via the green forests of Picardy and the rolling hills of the Pays de Bray.

- The Opal Coast: Stretching 120 kilometers along the North Sea, this coast offers fine sandy beaches, spectacular cliffs and protected dunes. Beach resorts like Le Touquet-Paris-Plage and Wimereux are popular destinations for tourists.
- The Plains of Artois and Flanders: These agricultural regions are characterized by open fields, picturesque villages and windmills.
- The Forests of Compiègne and Chantilly: These vast forests offer wooded landscapes and picturesque hiking trails, ideal for outdoor activities.

Regional Natural Parks

Hauts-de-France is home to several regional natural parks, such as the Caps et Marais d'Opale Regional Natural Park and the Avesnois Regional Natural Park. These parks protect local wildlife while providing hiking trails, biking trails, and picnic areas for visitors. They are ideal places to discover the natural wealth of the region.

History and Heritage

Origins and Antiquity

Hauts-de-France has a history that dates back to Antiquity. The region was inhabited by the Celts before being conquered by the Romans. Remains from this era, such as Roman roads and baths, can still be seen today.

The Middle Ages and the Renaissance

The Middle Ages and the Renaissance were periods of great prosperity for the region, with the construction of numerous castles, cathedrals and fortified towns. Among the most famous, we find:

- Amiens Cathedral: A masterpiece of Gothic architecture, listed as a UNESCO world heritage site.
- The Château de Pierrefonds: A medieval castle magnificently restored by Viollet-le-Duc, offering a dive into the history of chivalry.
- The Remparts of Montreuil-sur-Mer: Well-preserved fortifications which bear witness to the strategic importance of the city in the Middle Ages.

The Modern Era and the World Wars

Hauts-de-France has been the scene of numerous conflicts over the centuries, notably during the world wars. The region retains many memorial sites and memorials.

- The Somme Battlefields: An emblematic site of the First World War, with museums, military cemeteries and preserved trenches.
- The Vimy Memorial: An impressive monument dedicated to the Canadian soldiers who fell during the Battle of Vimy Ridge in 1917.
- The Citadel of Lille: A masterpiece of military architecture designed by Vauban, used during various conflicts.

Culture and Traditions

Regional Language and Culture

Hauts-de-France is rich in regional cultures, with Flemish, Picardy and Artesian influences. The region is also known for its dialects, such as Ch'ti and Picard, as well as its traditional festivals and carnivals.

Festivals and Events

Hauts-de-France is renowned for its festivals and cultural events, attracting artists and visitors from around the world. Among the most famous, we find:

- The Dunkirk Carnival: A festive event with colorful parades, extravagant costumes and musical bands.
- La Braderie de Lille: The largest flea market in Europe, attracting millions of visitors each year.
- The Johannine Festivals of Compiègne: A historical reconstruction celebrating Joan of Arc with parades, shows and medieval markets.

Gastronomy and Local Products

Hauts-de-France is a leading gastronomic region, showcasing local products and culinary traditions. Regional specialties include:

- Moules-Frites: An emblematic dish, especially popular during the Lille clearance sale.
- Carbonnade Flemish: A beef stew simmered in beer, typical of Flemish cuisine.
- Maroilles : A soft cow's milk cheese with a washed rind, very popular in the region.
- Les Ficelles Picardes: Crepes topped with ham, mushrooms and cream, gratinated in the oven.

Economy and Innovation

Tourism

Tourism is a key sector of the Hauts-de-France economy, attracting millions of visitors each year who come to discover the historical, cultural and natural treasures of the region. The region's tourist infrastructure is of high quality, with a diverse range of accommodation, starred restaurants, wellness centers and leisure activities.

Agriculture and Local Products

Agriculture plays an essential role in the economy of Hauts-de-France. The region produces a wide variety of agricultural products, including grains, vegetables, fruits and dairy products. Local markets, like Wazemmes in Lille, are popular places to buy fresh, local produce.

Industry and Innovation

Hauts-de-France is also a hub of innovation and industrial development, with varied sectors such as automobiles, aeronautics, information technologies and renewable energies. Competitiveness clusters, such as the i-Trans cluster (transport and mobility) and the Matikem cluster (materials and chemistry), promote innovation and collaboration between economic and scientific players.

Transport infrastructure, such as motorways, high-speed train lines and the ports of Calais and Dunkirk, support the region's economic development. The proximity to Belgium, the Netherlands and the United Kingdom facilitates trade and international collaborations.

Conclusion

Hauts-de-France is an exceptional region, rich in history, culture and varied landscapes. Whether enjoying the beaches of the Opal Coast, exploring historic towns, discovering the battlefields or savoring the local gastronomy, there is something for everyone.

The region's Relais & Châteaux capture the essence of this diversity and offer their guests unforgettable experiences, combining luxury, comfort and authenticity. Each establishment, with its enchanting setting, warm welcome, exceptional gastronomy and enriching activities, offers total immersion in the French art of living.

By discovering the Relais & Châteaux des Hauts-de-France, you will be transported into a world where every detail is designed to delight the senses and create lasting memories. This chapter presented a detailed overview of the region, integrating geographical, historical, cultural and economic aspects to provide a comprehensive understanding of this unique destination.

- History and Heritage

Hauts-de-France, made up of the former Nord-Pas-de-Calais and Picardy regions, is rich in history and heritage. This region has played a crucial role in many of France's historic events and is home to a multitude of iconic sites, from medieval castles to battlefields of the World Wars. In this chapter, we will explore key moments in the history of Hauts-de-France, its emblematic monuments and its cultural contributions.

Prehistoric Origins and Antiquity

Prehistoric Sites

Hauts-de-France has a history that dates back to prehistory, with numerous archaeological sites testifying to human occupation since the Paleolithic. The discoveries of fossils and flint tools in sites such as the Biache-Saint-Vaast site show the antiquity of human presence in the region.

Roman Influence

The region was deeply marked by the Roman presence. The Romans left behind many remains, including Roman roads, baths and villas. The town of Bavay, formerly Bagacum, was an important administrative center of Roman Gaul. Today, you can visit the ancient Forum, one of the largest in the Roman Empire.

The Middle Age

The Birth of Duchies and Counties

The Middle Ages saw the formation and consolidation of many local political entities, such as the County of Flanders and the Duchy of Burgundy. The region became a major commercial and cultural crossroads, attracting merchants and artisans from across Europe.

Medieval Castles

Hauts-de-France is dotted with medieval castles, built mainly from the 11th century to defend the territories and establish the authority of local lords.

- The Château de Pierrefonds: Restored by Viollet-le-Duc in the 19th century, this medieval castle offers an insight into the military architecture of the Middle Ages.
- The Château de Coucy: Although in ruins, this castle remains impressive in terms of its size and its tumultuous history.
- The Dungeon of Bours : A rare example of a Romanesque dungeon still standing in the region.

Cathedrals and Churches

The Middle Ages also saw the construction of numerous cathedrals and churches, symbols of the religious power of the time.

- Amiens Cathedral: The largest cathedral in France, a masterpiece of Gothic architecture, listed as a UNESCO world heritage site.
- The Basilica of Saint-Quentin: Another example of Gothic architecture, known for its magnificent stained glass windows and detailed carvings.
- Saint-Riquier Abbey: Founded in the 7th century, this Benedictine abbey played a crucial role in the Christianization of the region.

The Renaissance and the Modern Era

The Renaissance and Art

The Renaissance brought a new wave of construction and decoration to Hauts-de-France, influenced by Italian arts and architecture. The castles and stately residences were adorned with new ornamentations and French-style gardens.

- The Palais Rihour in Lille: An example of flamboyant Gothic architecture, transformed during the Renaissance.
- The Château de Chantilly: Built and embellished during the Renaissance, it now houses one of the most beautiful art museums in France.

Wars and Conflicts

The Hauts-de-France region has been the scene of numerous conflicts over the centuries, notably during the wars of religion and the Franco-English wars. The fortifications of Vauban, like the citadel of Lille, testify to the strategic importance of the region.

World Wars

WWI

Hauts-de-France was deeply marked by the First World War. The region was the scene of decisive battles, and numerous monuments and military cemeteries bear witness to this past.

- The Somme Battlefields: One of the most emblematic sites of the war, with preserved trenches and commemorative museums.
- The Vimy Memorial: An impressive monument dedicated to the Canadian soldiers who fought at Vimy Ridge.
- The Notre-Dame-de-Lorette Cemetery: The largest French military cemetery, where more than 40,000 soldiers rest.

The Second World War

The Second World War also left indelible traces in the region, with memorial sites and vestiges of the Maginot Line.

- La Coupole d'Helfaut: A V2 missile launch base, today transformed into a museum on the Second World War.
- The Éperlecques Blockhaus: Another V2 launch base, which bears witness to the German occupation and Allied bombings.

Industrial Heritage

The industrial Revolution

The industrial revolution transformed Hauts-de-France into a major economic center, with the development of the textile, mining and steel industries. Cities like Lille, Roubaix and Tourcoing are experiencing rapid growth and modernization of their infrastructure.

- Les Mines de Lewarde: The largest mining museum in France, which traces the history of mining in the region.
- La Piscine de Roubaix: A former public bath transformed into a museum of art and industry, a unique example of industrial reconversion.

Contemporary Heritage

UNESCO Sites and Historical Monuments

Hauts-de-France has several UNESCO World Heritage sites, testifying to its historical and cultural richness.
- The Belfries of Belgium and France: Several belfries in the region are listed as world heritage sites for their historical and architectural value.
- The Roads to Santiago: Monuments such as the basilica of Saint-Quentin are part of the pilgrimage routes to Santiago de Compostela.

Museums and Cultural Centers

The region is home to numerous museums and cultural centers which tell the history of Hauts-de-France and highlight its cultural heritage.

- The Louvre-Lens: A branch of the Louvre Museum in Paris, which presents temporary exhibitions of prestigious collections.
- The Palais des Beaux-Arts in Lille: One of the largest museums in France, with a vast collection of paintings, sculptures and art objects.

Conclusion

Hauts-de-France is a region rich in history and heritage, where each town, each village and each monument tells a unique story. From Roman remains to medieval castles, from Gothic cathedrals to world war memorial sites, the region offers an incredible diversity of historic sites and monuments.

Les Relais & Châteaux des Hauts-de-France capture the essence of this historical and cultural wealth, offering their guests unforgettable experiences. Each establishment, with its enchanting setting, warm welcome, exceptional gastronomy and enriching activities, offers total immersion in the history and heritage of the region.

By discovering the Relais & Châteaux des Hauts-de-France, you will be transported into a world where every detail is designed to delight the senses and create lasting memories. This chapter explored the many facets of the region's history and heritage, revealing how each era helped shape this unique and fascinating destination.

- Gastronomy and Wine

The Hauts-de-France region is renowned for its rich culinary tradition and its exceptional local products. Combining Flemish, Picardy and Artesian influences, the gastronomy of Hauts-de-France is at once generous, authentic and refined. Regional culinary specialties, local products and wines from the region are all testimonies to the art of living in this part of northern France. In this chapter, we'll explore the gastronomic delights of Hauts-de-France, highlighting the local produce, iconic dishes, renowned chefs, Michelin-starred restaurants and wines that this region is famous for.

Local Products

Products of the Earth

Hauts-de-France is a fertile agricultural region, producing a wide variety of high-quality fruits, vegetables, meats and dairy products.

- Potatoes: Grown in abundance in the region, they are used in many traditional dishes, such as fries, mash and Parmentier hash.
- Endives: Called "chicons" in the North, they are eaten raw in salads or cooked, particularly in endives with ham.
- Beets: Used in salads, soups and stews.

Sea and River Products

The proximity to the North Sea and numerous rivers offers an abundance of fish and seafood.

- Mussels: Main ingredient of the famous mussels and fries, an essential dish of the region.
- Herring: Eaten marinated or smoked, they are often served with potatoes and onions.
- Scallops: Used in many refined dishes, they are particularly appreciated for their delicate flavor.

Cheeses and charcuterie

Hauts-de-France is also known for its cheeses and charcuterie, which are essential elements of the local cuisine.

- Maroilles : A soft cow's milk cheese with a washed rind, with a powerful and distinctive flavor.
- Vieux-Lille: A soft cheese with a washed rind, softer than Maroilles but with a pronounced flavor.
- Rillettes d'Ardenne: A specialty of pulled meat, often served on fresh bread.

Traditional dishes

Flemish Specialties

Flemish cuisine is rich and generous, with dishes that warm the heart and soul.

- Flemish Carbonnade: A beef stew simmered in beer, typical of Flemish cuisine, often served with fries or mash.
- Potjevleesch : A jellied meat dish, composed of chicken, rabbit, pork and veal, traditionally served cold with fries.
- Waterzooï: A creamy chicken or fish stew, garnished with vegetables and potatoes.

Picardy Specialties

Picardy cuisine is simple but tasty, showcasing local produce in a rustic and comforting way.

- Les Ficelles Picardes: Crepes topped with ham, mushrooms and cream, gratinated in the oven.
- Le Flamiche aux Poireaux: A savory tart garnished with leeks and cream, sometimes garnished with bacon or cheese.
- Amiens Duck Pâté: A pâté en croute, garnished with duck and pork meat, often served as a starter or aperitif.

Artesian Specialties

Artois, with its British and Flemish influences, offers robust and comforting dishes.

- The Welsh: A slice of bread covered with ham, melted cheddar and beer, then baked in the oven.
- Le Hochepot : A meat stew (often beef, pork and mutton) simmered with vegetables and spices.
- Les Cœurs d'Arras: Almond paste candies, a sweet specialty of the town of Arras.

Wines and Beers of Hauts-de-France

Beers of the Region

Hauts-de-France is a leading brewing region, with many craft breweries producing high quality beers.

- La Bière de Garde: A top-fermented beer, often amber, with a complex and malty flavor.
- La Ch'ti: A blond or amber beer, produced by the Castelain brewery, symbol of the region.
- Pelforth : A dark, blond or amber beer, known for its rich aromas and velvety texture.

Wines of the Region

Although Hauts-de-France is not a major wine region, some interesting wines are produced there, particularly fruit wines.

- Rhubarb Wine: Produced mainly in Picardy, this fruit wine offers a unique and refreshing flavor.
- Redcurrant Wine: Another fruit wine, sweet and slightly tart, perfect for desserts and aperitifs.

Star Chefs and Restaurants

The Pioneers of Regional Haute Cuisine

Hauts-de-France has always been a hotbed of culinary creativity, attracting talented chefs who highlight local products and culinary traditions. Among the pioneers of regional haute cuisine, we find Alexandre Gauthier, chef of the restaurant La Grenouillère in La Madelaine-sous-Montreuil, who has redefined regional cuisine with a modern and innovative approach.

Contemporary Chefs

Today, the region continues to attract renowned chefs, who continue the tradition of haute cuisine while innovating and experimenting with new flavors. Among the most famous contemporary chefs, we find:

- Marc Meurin : Chef at the Château de Beaulieu in Busnes, Michelin-starred, offering inventive and refined cuisine.
- Florent Ladeyn : Chef of the Le Vert Mont restaurant in Boeschepe, known for its locavore and environmentally friendly cuisine.

Star Restaurants

Hauts-de-France is home to numerous Michelin-starred restaurants, each offering a unique and unforgettable culinary experience. Among the most famous, we find:

- La Grenouillère in La Madelaine-sous-Montreuil: A Michelin-starred restaurant, managed by Alexandre Gauthier, offering modern and creative cuisine in a rustic and elegant setting.
- Le Château de Beaulieu in Busnes: Michelin-starred, this restaurant offers refined and inventive cuisine, highlighting local products from the region.

- Le Meurin in Busnes: Another Michelin-starred restaurant by Marc Meurin, offering high-quality gourmet cuisine.

Oenological and Culinary Experiences

Beer Tastings

Relais & Châteaux des Hauts-de-France often offer unique wine and culinary experiences for their guests. From private tastings to brewery tours, these experiences allow you to discover the region's beers and learn the secrets of their making.

Customers can participate in tasting workshops, led by experts, to learn how to identify the aromas and flavors of the region's beers. Guided brewery tours allow you to discover the production processes, meet the brewers and taste beers directly from the source.

Food and Beer Pairings

The Relais & Châteaux also offer food and beer pairings, allowing you to enjoy Hauts-de-France beers in harmony with local cuisine. These pairings highlight the flavors of the dishes and beers, offering a complete and unforgettable gastronomic experience.

Chefs from Michelin-starred restaurants collaborate with sommeliers and brewers to create tasting menus that highlight the region's beers. Each dish is carefully paired with a beer, allowing guests to discover new combinations of flavors and textures.

Conclusion

Hauts-de-France is a true land of gastronomy and beers, offering unparalleled richness and diversity. Regional cuisine, with its authentic flavors and quality local products, is a pillar of the region's art of living. Craft beers and fruit wines, renowned for their complexity and elegance, perfectly complement this culinary experience.

Les Relais & Châteaux des Hauts-de-France capture the essence of this gastronomic richness, offering their guests unique and unforgettable culinary and wine experiences. Each establishment, with its enchanting setting, warm welcome, exceptional gastronomy and enriching activities, offers total immersion in the French art of living.

By discovering the Relais & Châteaux des Hauts-de-France, you will be transported into a world where every detail is designed to delight the senses and create lasting memories. This chapter explored the multiple facets of the region's gastronomy and wines, revealing how each element contributes to making this destination a true oasis of flavors and culinary pleasures.

2. Addresses and Descriptions

Hauts-de-France is home to several Relais & Châteaux establishments, each offering a unique experience combining luxury, comfort and regional charm. These prestigious hotels and restaurants are located in iconic locations across the region, from historic towns to picturesque countryside. In this chapter, we will discover some of the most prestigious addresses and describe in detail what makes them special.

Montreuil Castle

History and Architecture

Château de Montreuil, located in Montreuil-sur-Mer, is a charming hotel offering a luxurious experience in the heart of one of the most beautiful medieval towns in France. This castle, dating from the 16th century, has been magnificently restored to preserve its old-world charm while providing modern comfort. The architecture of the castle, with its stone facades, turrets and landscaped gardens, reflects the elegance of the era.

Culinary Offers

The Château de Montreuil's gourmet restaurant, led by a starred chef, offers inventive and refined cuisine, highlighting local and seasonal products. The tasting menu offers dishes such as "Lobster Bleu de Bretagne" and "Filet de Bœuf Charolais". The carefully selected wine list highlights the region's great wines and other prestigious wine regions.

Activities and Services

Château de Montreuil offers a range of activities for its guests, from relaxation to sport. Guests can enjoy the heated outdoor swimming pool, gardens and terraces for moments of relaxation. Guided excursions are also organized to explore the surrounding area, including the ramparts of Montreuil-sur-Mer and the beaches of the Opal Coast.

The Chartreuse du Val Saint Esprit

History and Architecture

La Chartreuse du Val Saint Esprit, located in Gosnay, is a charming hotel located in a former Carthusian monastery from the 18th century. The establishment has retained its historic character while offering modern and luxurious facilities. The formal gardens, vaulted rooms and elegantly decorated rooms create a unique and serene atmosphere.

Culinary Offers

The gourmet restaurant at La Chartreuse du Val Saint Esprit offers inventive and refined cuisine, highlighting local and seasonal products. The chef prepares dishes such as "Duck Foie Gras" and

"Racan Pigeon". The carefully selected wine list highlights the region's great wines and other prestigious wine regions.

Activities and Services

La Chartreuse du Val Saint Esprit offers a range of activities for its guests, from relaxation to sport. Guests can enjoy gardens, tennis courts and equipped meeting rooms. Guided excursions are also organized to explore the surrounding area, including the city of Arras, its historic squares and monuments.

Beaulieu Castle

History and Architecture

Château de Beaulieu, located in Busnes, is an elegant 18th-century castle surrounded by extensive gardens and woods. This property has been carefully restored to provide a luxurious and authentic experience. The stone facades, slate roofs and tastefully decorated interiors reflect the elegance of the era.

Culinary Offers

The Château de Beaulieu's gourmet restaurant, led by starred chef Marc Meurin , offers inventive and refined cuisine, highlighting local and seasonal products. The tasting menu offers dishes such as "Lobster Bleu de Bretagne" and "Filet de Bœuf Charolais". The carefully selected wine list highlights the region's great wines and other prestigious wine regions.

Activities and Services

Château de Beaulieu offers a range of activities for its guests, from relaxation to sport. Guests can enjoy the heated outdoor swimming pool, gardens and terraces for moments of relaxation. Guided excursions are also organized to explore the surrounding area, including the town of Béthune and its surrounding areas.

La Grenouillère

History and Architecture

La Grenouillère, located in La Madelaine-sous-Montreuil, is a world-renowned establishment offering an exceptional gastronomic experience. Founded in the 19th century, this family-run inn combines the charm of rustic architecture with modern comfort. The wooden facades, flowered balconies and warm interiors make it a place of relaxation and culinary pleasure.

Culinary Offers

The gourmet restaurant of La Grenouillère, led by starred chef Alexandre Gauthier, offers inventive and refined cuisine, highlighting local and seasonal products. The tasting menu offers dishes such as "Duck Foie Gras" and "Lobster à la Presse". The carefully selected wine list highlights the region's great wines and other prestigious wine regions.

Activities and Services

La Grenouillère offers a range of activities for its guests, from relaxation to sport. Guests can enjoy walks along the Canche River, visits to the region's picturesque villages and guided excursions to explore the surrounding area, including the beaches of the Opal Coast and the surrounding hiking trails.

The Drôme Manor

History and Architecture

Le Manoir de la Drôme, located in Béthune, is an elegant 19th-century manor house surrounded by picturesque gardens. This historic manor house, carefully restored, offers a romantic and peaceful setting. The architecture of the manor, with its stone facades and slate roofs, reflects the elegance of the period.

Culinary Offers

The gourmet restaurant at Manoir de la Drôme, led by a starred chef, offers inventive and refined cuisine, highlighting local and seasonal products. The tasting menu offers dishes such as "Duck Foie Gras" and "Racan Pigeon". The carefully selected wine list highlights the region's great wines and other prestigious wine regions.

Activities and Services

Le Manoir de la Drôme offers a range of activities for its guests, from relaxation to sport. Guests can take advantage of the gardens, equipped meeting rooms and guided excursions to explore the surrounding area, including the town of Béthune and its historic monuments.

Conclusion

The Relais & Châteaux des Hauts-de-France offer unique and unforgettable experiences, combining luxury, comfort and historical heritage. Each establishment, with its enchanting setting, warm welcome, exceptional gastronomy and enriching activities, offers total immersion in the French art of living. Whether for a romantic getaway, a peaceful retreat or a cultural exploration, the Relais & Châteaux of the Hauts-de-France region are must-see destinations.

By discovering these exceptional establishments, you will be transported to a world where every detail is designed to delight the senses and create lasting memories. This chapter has presented a detailed overview of some of the most prestigious Relais & Châteaux in the region, offering a glimpse of the unique experience that awaits you in each of these enchanting locations.

- Montreuil Castle

The Château de Montreuil, located in the charming town of Montreuil-sur-Mer, is a true jewel of the Hauts-de-France region. This elegant 16th-century castle, with its historic atmosphere and lush gardens, offers a luxurious and authentic experience to its visitors. In this chapter, we will explore the history and architecture of Château de Montreuil, its culinary offerings, the activities and services offered, and the unique experiences it offers.

History and Architecture

A Historical Heritage

Montreuil Castle was built in the 16th century and has since witnessed many historic events. It served as a residence for noble families and played an important role in local history. The town of Montreuil-sur-Mer itself is rich in history, known for its medieval fortifications and its strategic role during past conflicts.

Elegant Architecture

The architecture of the Château de Montreuil reflects the elegance of the period, with its stone facades, turrets and landscaped gardens. Interiors are decorated with antique furniture, artwork and fine textiles, creating a warm and sophisticated atmosphere. The hotel's rooms and suites offer stunning views of the gardens or city walls. Each room is unique, with distinctive design elements and modern amenities to ensure optimal comfort.

Culinary Offers

The Gourmet Restaurant

The Château de Montreuil's gourmet restaurant, led by a starred chef, offers inventive and refined cuisine, highlighting local and seasonal products. The tasting menu offers dishes such as "Lobster Bleu de Bretagne" and "Filet de Bœuf Charolais". The carefully selected wine list highlights the region's great wines and other prestigious wine regions.

The restaurant's setting matches its cuisine, with an elegantly decorated dining room, tables spaced for maximum privacy, and panoramic views of the gardens. Guests can also dine al fresco on the terrace, enjoying the tranquility and beauty of the natural surroundings.

Regional Cuisine

The chef at Château de Montreuil places particular emphasis on local products, with a locavore philosophy that favors fresh, seasonal ingredients from local producers. Guests can taste regional specialties such as "Filet de Zander de la Canche" and "Tarte aux Pommes de Montreuil", accompanied by carefully selected local wines.

The Gourmet Breakfast

The Château de Montreuil's gourmet breakfast is served in the elegantly decorated dining room or on the terrace, with a magnificent view of the gardens and ramparts. Breakfast is composed of fresh, local products, including pastries, fruits, homemade jams, regional cheeses, fresh eggs and pressed fruit juices. Guests can also enjoy hot drinks, such as coffee, tea and hot chocolate.

Activities and Services

The Spa and Wellness Treatments

Château de Montreuil offers a range of wellness treatments for its guests, ranging from massages to facial treatments, carried out with high quality products. The spa, located in a peaceful and luxurious setting, is a perfect place to relax and unwind after a day exploring the region.

Professional therapists use advanced techniques and luxury products to ensure optimal results and a luxurious experience. Guests can also enjoy the heated outdoor swimming pool, jacuzzi, sauna and steam room to complete their relaxation experience.

Outdoor activities

The gardens and woods of Château de Montreuil are perfect for leisurely walks, meditation sessions or outdoor yoga sessions. Guests can also take advantage of the proximity to the Opal Coast beaches for water activities such as sailing and paddle boarding. Guided excursions are also organized to explore the surrounding area, including the ramparts of Montreuil-sur-Mer and the region's hiking trails.

Cultural Activities and Experiences

Château de Montreuil regularly organizes cultural events and unique experiences for its guests. Private concerts, literary readings and art exhibitions are often organized in the establishment's lounges or gardens. These events offer immersion in the local cultural scene and allow guests to meet artists, writers and musicians.

Guests can also participate in cooking workshops, baking classes and wine tastings, led by local chefs. These workshops offer an opportunity to learn regional cooking techniques and taste delicious creations. Château de Montreuil also offers yoga and meditation classes, led by qualified instructors, in the hotel's gardens or wellness areas.

Special Events and Unique Experiences

Weddings and Receptions

The Château de Montreuil is an ideal venue for organizing intimate weddings and private receptions. The property's gardens and lounges provide a romantic and elegant setting for ceremonies and receptions. Hotel staff work closely with couples to create tailor-made events, taking into account every detail, from decor to personalized menus.

The hotel's chefs create wedding menus that reflect the tastes and preferences of the bride and groom, using seasonal ingredients and local produce. The professional and attentive service teams ensure that every event goes off without a hitch. Couples can also enjoy luxurious suites for their wedding night, with special services such as massages, in-room breakfasts and welcome gifts.

Seminars and Business Meetings

The Château de Montreuil offers an exceptional setting for seminars, conferences and business meetings. The property's private lounges, equipped with the latest technology, offer flexible spaces for events of different sizes. Hotel teams work with event organizers to create tailor-made programs, including coffee breaks, business lunches and dinners.

Team-building activities and excursions can also be organized to strengthen team cohesion and provide moments of relaxation outside of work sessions. Guests can take advantage of the hotel's wellness facilities to unwind after a day of meetings, with spa treatments, yoga sessions and massages.

Unique Experiences

Château de Montreuil offers unique experiences to make each stay memorable. These include private dinners in exclusive locations within the establishment, such as the library or gardens, offering an intimate and romantic atmosphere. Guests can also participate in wine tasting workshops, led by expert sommeliers, to discover the secrets of the region's wines.

Wellness getaways are also available, including personalized relaxation and relaxation programs, spa treatments, yoga and meditation sessions, as well as healthy and nutritious meals. These programs are designed to help clients recharge their batteries and regain physical and mental balance.

Seasonal and Thematic Offers

Château de Montreuil regularly offers seasonal and thematic offers to enrich its customers' experience. At Christmas, the establishment is decked out in festive decorations and offers special menus, cookie decorating workshops and Christmas market visits. In summer, gourmet picnics can be organized in the gardens or on the terraces.

Romantic getaways are also offered, including candlelit dinners, duo massages and horse-drawn carriage rides in the surrounding area. For culture lovers, special packages including tickets for exhibitions, shows and concerts are available, offering complete immersion in the cultural life of the region.

Conclusion

The Château de Montreuil is much more than just a luxury hotel; it is a destination in itself, offering a unique and unforgettable experience in the heart of the magnificent Hauts-de-France region. With its rich history, impressive architecture, refined culinary offerings and a variety of activities and services, this establishment is the ideal place to relax, recharge and discover the French art of living.

Whether for a romantic getaway, a wellness retreat, an intimate wedding or a business meeting, Château de Montreuil promises an exceptional experience, marked by luxury, comfort and elegance. Guests leave with unforgettable memories, enriched by the unique culture, gastronomy and hospitality of this emblematic establishment of the Hauts-de-France region.

- The Chartreuse du Val Saint Esprit

La Chartreuse du Val Saint Esprit, located in Gosnay, is a prestigious establishment which combines history, luxury and gastronomy in an exceptional setting. This former Carthusian monastery from the 18th century, magnificently restored, offers its visitors a unique and unforgettable experience. In this chapter, we will explore the history and architecture of La Chartreuse du Val Saint Esprit, its culinary offerings, the activities and services offered, and the unique experiences it offers.

History and Architecture

A Monastic Heritage

The Chartreuse du Val Saint Esprit was founded in the 18th century as a Carthusian monastery. The Carthusian monks, known for their austere and contemplative lifestyle, built this place of prayer and contemplation. The monastery has survived centuries and historical upheavals, before being transformed into a luxury hotel which still retains the soul and authenticity of its past.

Elegant and Historic Architecture

The architecture of La Chartreuse du Val Saint Esprit reflects its monastic heritage, with its brick and stone facades, slate roofs and French-style gardens. Interiors are decorated with antique furniture, artwork and fine textiles, creating a warm and sophisticated atmosphere.

The hotel's rooms and suites offer breathtaking views of the gardens or the interior courtyard. Each room is unique, with distinctive design elements and modern amenities to ensure optimal comfort. The bathrooms, fitted with marble bathtubs and walk-in showers, provide a luxurious setting in which to relax and rejuvenate.

Culinary Offers

The Gourmet Restaurant

The gourmet restaurant at La Chartreuse du Val Saint Esprit, led by a talented chef, offers inventive and refined cuisine, highlighting local and seasonal products. The tasting menu offers dishes such as "Duck Foie Gras" and "Racan Pigeon". The carefully selected wine list highlights the region's great wines and other prestigious wine regions.

The restaurant's setting matches its cuisine, with an elegantly decorated dining room, tables spaced for maximum privacy, and panoramic views of the gardens. Guests can also dine al fresco on the terrace, enjoying the tranquility and beauty of the natural surroundings.

Regional Cuisine

The chef at La Chartreuse du Val Saint Esprit places particular emphasis on local products, with a locavore philosophy that favors fresh, seasonal ingredients from local producers. Guests can taste regional specialties such as "Filet de Zander de la Canche" and "Tarte aux Pommes de Gosnay", accompanied by carefully selected local wines.

The Gourmet Breakfast

La Chartreuse du Val Saint Esprit's gourmet breakfast is served in the elegantly decorated dining room or on the terrace, with magnificent views of the gardens. Breakfast is composed of fresh, local products, including pastries, fruits, homemade jams, regional cheeses, fresh eggs and pressed fruit juices. Guests can also enjoy hot drinks, such as coffee, tea and hot chocolate.

Activities and Services

The Spa and Wellness Treatments

La Chartreuse du Val Saint Esprit offers a range of well-being treatments for its customers, ranging from massages to facial treatments, carried out with high quality products. The spa, located in a peaceful and luxurious setting, is a perfect place to relax and unwind after a day exploring the region.

Professional therapists use advanced techniques and luxury products to ensure optimal results and a luxurious experience. Guests can also enjoy the heated indoor swimming pool, jacuzzi, sauna and steam room to complete their relaxation experience.

Outdoor activities

The gardens and woods of La Chartreuse du Val Saint Esprit are perfect for leisurely walks, meditation sessions or outdoor yoga sessions. Guests can also enjoy the proximity to hiking trails for activities such as walking and cycling. Guided excursions are also organized to explore the surrounding area, including the city of Arras, its historic squares and monuments.

Cultural Activities and Experiences

La Chartreuse du Val Saint Esprit regularly organizes cultural events and unique experiences for its guests. Private concerts, literary readings and art exhibitions are often organized in the establishment's lounges or gardens. These events offer immersion in the local cultural scene and allow guests to meet artists, writers and musicians.

Guests can also participate in cooking workshops, baking classes and wine tastings, led by local chefs. These workshops offer an opportunity to learn regional cooking techniques and taste delicious creations. La Chartreuse du Val Saint Esprit also offers yoga and meditation classes, led by qualified instructors, in the hotel's gardens or wellness areas.

Special Events and Unique Experiences

Weddings and Receptions

La Chartreuse du Val Saint Esprit is an ideal venue for organizing intimate weddings and private receptions. The property's gardens and lounges provide a romantic and elegant setting for ceremonies and receptions. Hotel staff work closely with couples to create tailor-made events, taking into account every detail, from decor to personalized menus.

The hotel's chefs create wedding menus that reflect the tastes and preferences of the bride and groom, using seasonal ingredients and local produce. The professional and attentive service teams ensure that every event goes off without a hitch. Couples can also enjoy luxurious suites for their wedding night, with special services such as massages, in-room breakfasts and welcome gifts.

Seminars and Business Meetings

La Chartreuse du Val Saint Esprit offers an exceptional setting for seminars, conferences and business meetings. The property's private lounges, equipped with the latest technology, offer flexible spaces for events of different sizes. Hotel teams work with event organizers to create tailor-made programs, including coffee breaks, business lunches and dinners.

Team-building activities and excursions can also be organized to strengthen team cohesion and provide moments of relaxation outside of work sessions. Guests can take advantage of the hotel's wellness facilities to unwind after a day of meetings, with spa treatments, yoga sessions and massages.

Unique Experiences

La Chartreuse du Val Saint Esprit offers unique experiences to make each stay memorable. These include private dinners in exclusive locations within the establishment, such as the library or gardens, offering an intimate and romantic atmosphere. Guests can also participate in wine tasting workshops, led by expert sommeliers, to discover the secrets of the region's wines.

Wellness getaways are also available, including personalized relaxation and relaxation programs, spa treatments, yoga and meditation sessions, as well as healthy and nutritious meals. These programs are designed to help clients recharge their batteries and regain physical and mental balance.

Seasonal and Thematic Offers

La Chartreuse du Val Saint Esprit regularly offers seasonal and thematic offers to enrich its customers' experience. At Christmas, the establishment is decked out in festive decorations and offers special menus, cookie decorating workshops and Christmas market visits. In summer, gourmet picnics can be organized in the gardens or on the terraces.

Romantic getaways are also offered, including candlelit dinners, duo massages and horse-drawn carriage rides in the surrounding area. For culture lovers, special packages including tickets for exhibitions, shows and concerts are available, offering complete immersion in the cultural life of the region.

Conclusion

La Chartreuse du Val Saint Esprit is much more than just a luxury hotel; it is a destination in itself, offering a unique and unforgettable experience in the heart of the magnificent Hauts-de-France region. With its rich history, impressive architecture, refined culinary offerings and a variety of activities and services, this establishment is the ideal place to relax, recharge and discover the French art of living.

Whether for a romantic getaway, a wellness retreat, an intimate wedding or a business meeting , La Chartreuse du Val Saint Esprit promises an exceptional experience, marked by luxury, comfort and elegance. Guests leave with unforgettable memories, enriched by the unique culture, gastronomy and hospitality of this emblematic establishment of the Hauts-de-France region.

- Beaulieu Castle

The Château de Beaulieu, located in Busnes in Hauts-de-France, is a prestigious establishment offering a unique experience combining history, luxury and gastronomy. This elegant 18th century castle, surrounded by vast gardens and woods, has been carefully restored to provide a romantic and refined setting for its visitors. In this chapter, we will explore the history and architecture of Château de Beaulieu, its culinary offerings, the activities and services offered, and the unique experiences it offers.

History and Architecture

An Aristocratic Heritage

Château de Beaulieu was built in the 18th century and served as a residence for noble families. It has witnessed many historical events and has retained its old-world charm through careful restoration. The history of the castle is closely linked to that of the region, marked by the elegance and refinement of the French aristocracy.

Elegant and Historic Architecture

The architecture of Château de Beaulieu reflects the elegance of the period, with its stone facades, slate roofs and French gardens. Interiors are decorated with antique furniture, artwork and fine textiles, creating a warm and sophisticated atmosphere. The hotel's rooms and suites offer breathtaking views of the gardens or park. Each room is unique, with distinctive design elements and modern amenities to ensure optimal comfort.

Culinary Offers

The Gourmet Restaurant

The Château de Beaulieu's gourmet restaurant, led by Michelin-starred chef Marc Meurin , offers inventive and refined cuisine, highlighting local and seasonal products. The tasting menu offers dishes such as "Lobster Bleu de Bretagne" and "Filet de Bœuf Charolais". The carefully selected wine list highlights the region's great wines and other prestigious wine regions.

The restaurant's setting matches its cuisine, with an elegantly decorated dining room, tables spaced for maximum privacy, and panoramic views of the gardens. Guests can also dine al fresco on the terrace, enjoying the tranquility and beauty of the natural surroundings.

Regional Cuisine

Chef Marc Meurin places particular emphasis on local products, with a locavore philosophy that favors fresh, seasonal ingredients from local producers. Guests can taste regional specialties such as "Filet de Zander de la Lys" and "Tarte au Maroilles", accompanied by carefully selected local wines.

The Gourmet Breakfast

Château de Beaulieu's gourmet breakfast is served in the elegantly decorated dining room or on the terrace, with magnificent views of the gardens. Breakfast is composed of fresh, local products, including pastries, fruits, homemade jams, regional cheeses, fresh eggs and pressed fruit juices. Guests can also enjoy hot drinks, such as coffee, tea and hot chocolate.

Activities and Services

The Spa and Wellness Treatments

Château de Beaulieu offers a range of wellness treatments for its guests, from massages to facials, carried out with high quality products. The spa, located in a peaceful and luxurious setting, is a perfect place to relax and unwind after a day exploring the region.

Professional therapists use advanced techniques and luxury products to ensure optimal results and a luxurious experience. Guests can also enjoy the heated outdoor swimming pool, jacuzzi, sauna and steam room to complete their relaxation experience.

Outdoor activities

The gardens and woods of Château de Beaulieu are perfect for leisurely walks, meditation sessions or outdoor yoga sessions. Guests can also enjoy the proximity to hiking trails for activities such as walking, cycling and fishing. Guided excursions are also organized to explore the surrounding area, including the town of Béthune, its historic squares and monuments.

Cultural Activities and Experiences

Château de Beaulieu regularly organizes cultural events and unique experiences for its guests. Private concerts, literary readings and art exhibitions are often organized in the establishment's lounges or gardens. These events offer immersion in the local cultural scene and allow guests to meet artists, writers and musicians.

Guests can also participate in cooking workshops, baking classes and wine tastings, led by local chefs. These workshops offer an opportunity to learn regional cooking techniques and taste delicious creations. Château de Beaulieu also offers yoga and meditation classes, led by qualified instructors, in the hotel's gardens or wellness areas.

Special Events and Unique Experiences

Weddings and Receptions

Château de Beaulieu is an ideal venue for intimate weddings and private receptions. The property's gardens and lounges provide a romantic and elegant setting for ceremonies and receptions. Hotel staff work closely with couples to create tailor-made events, taking into account every detail, from decor to personalized menus.

The hotel's chefs create wedding menus that reflect the tastes and preferences of the bride and groom, using seasonal ingredients and local produce. The professional and attentive service teams ensure that every event goes off without a hitch. Couples can also enjoy luxurious suites for their wedding night, with special services such as massages, in-room breakfasts and welcome gifts.

Seminars and Business Meetings

The Château de Beaulieu offers an exceptional setting for seminars, conferences and business meetings. The property's private lounges, equipped with the latest technology, offer flexible spaces for events of different sizes. Hotel teams work with event organizers to create tailor-made programs, including coffee breaks, business lunches and dinners.

Team-building activities and excursions can also be organized to strengthen team cohesion and provide moments of relaxation outside of work sessions. Guests can take advantage of the hotel's wellness facilities to unwind after a day of meetings, with spa treatments, yoga sessions and massages.

Unique Experiences

Château de Beaulieu offers unique experiences to make each stay memorable. These include private dinners in exclusive locations within the establishment, such as the library or gardens, offering an intimate and romantic atmosphere. Guests can also participate in wine tasting workshops, led by expert sommeliers, to discover the secrets of the region's wines.

Wellness getaways are also available, including personalized relaxation and relaxation programs, spa treatments, yoga and meditation sessions, as well as healthy and nutritious meals. These programs are designed to help clients recharge their batteries and regain physical and mental balance.

Seasonal and Thematic Offers

Château de Beaulieu regularly offers seasonal and thematic offers to enrich its customers' experience. At Christmas, the establishment is decked out in festive decorations and offers special menus, cookie decorating workshops and Christmas market visits. In summer, gourmet picnics can be organized in the gardens or on the terraces.

Romantic getaways are also offered, including candlelit dinners, duo massages and horse-drawn carriage rides in the surrounding area. For culture lovers, special packages including tickets for exhibitions, shows and concerts are available, offering complete immersion in the cultural life of the region.

Conclusion

The Château de Beaulieu is much more than just a luxury hotel; it is a destination in itself, offering a unique and unforgettable experience in the heart of the magnificent Hauts-de-France region. With its rich history, impressive architecture, refined culinary offerings and a variety of activities and services, this establishment is the ideal place to relax, recharge and discover the French art of living.

Whether for a romantic getaway, a wellness retreat, an intimate wedding or a business meeting, Château de Beaulieu promises an exceptional experience, marked by luxury, comfort and elegance. Guests leave with unforgettable memories, enriched by the unique culture, gastronomy and hospitality of this emblematic establishment of the Hauts-de-France region.

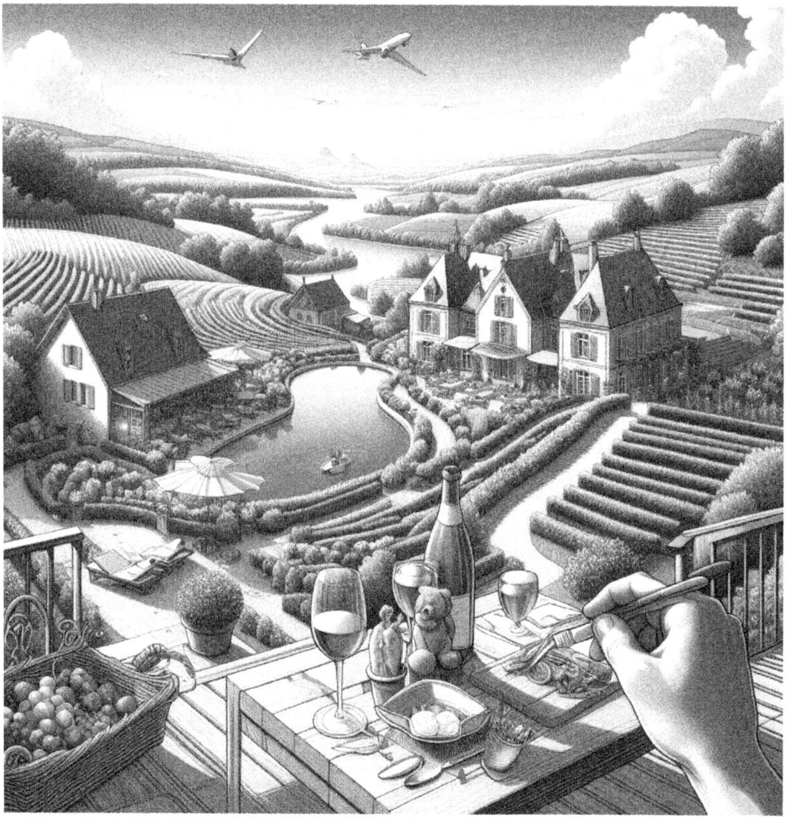

Chapter 12: Relais & Châteaux in Corsica

1. General Presentation of the Region

Corsica, nicknamed "Island of Beauty", is a unique French region, renowned for its breathtaking landscapes, its heavenly beaches, its imposing mountains, and its rich cultural and historical heritage. Located in the Mediterranean, approximately 200 kilometers southeast of the Côte d'Azur, Corsica offers an incomparable experience, where nature, tradition and modernity combine harmoniously. In this chapter, we will explore the geographical, historical, cultural and economic characteristics of Corsica, highlighting the attractions that make this island an essential destination.

Geography and Landscapes

Exceptional Landscape Diversity

Corsica stands out for the diversity of its landscapes, which range from fine sandy beaches to rugged mountains, dense forests and fertile valleys.

- The Beaches: Corsica is surrounded by magnificent beaches, such as those of Palombaggia , Santa Giulia, and Saleccia , with crystal clear waters and white sands.
- The Mountains: The island is crossed by a mountain range, the highest point of which is Monte Cinto at 2,706 meters. Hikes, including the famous GR20, offer spectacular views and challenges for outdoor enthusiasts.
- Forests and Valleys: The forests of Vizzavona and the valleys of Restonica and Asco are examples of the natural wealth of Corsica, offering hiking trails and picnic areas.

Natural Parks

Corsica is home to a regional natural park covering around 40% of the island, protecting a rich and varied fauna and flora. The Corsica Regional Natural Park includes nature reserves such as the Scandola Reserve , a UNESCO World Heritage Site, which is famous for its volcanic cliffs and marine biodiversity.

History and Heritage

Origins and Antiquity

Corsica has a millennia-old history, marked by numerous civilizations. Prehistoric remains, such as the menhirs of Filitosa, bear witness to human presence since the Neolithic period. The island was then colonized by the Phoenicians, the Greeks, then the Romans, who left traces of their passage, such as the ruins of the ancient city of Aléria.

The Middle Ages and the Renaissance

During the Middle Ages, Corsica was disputed by several powers, including the Pisans and the Genoese. The latter left a lasting legacy, notably through the citadels of Bonifacio and Calvi, as well as the Genoese towers which dot the coasts.

The Modern Era

Corsica played a strategic role in the conflicts between European powers. In 1768, it was ceded to France by the Republic of Genoa. The island is also the birthplace of Napoleon Bonaparte, born in Ajaccio in 1769, which adds an important historical dimension.

Culture and Traditions

Corsican Language and Culture

Corsica is rich in cultural traditions and has its own language, Corsican, which is still spoken by part of the population. Corsican culture is also manifested through polyphonic music, traditional songs and folk dances.

Festivals and Events

Corsica is renowned for its many festivals and cultural events, which celebrate music, gastronomy and local traditions. Among the most famous, we find:

- The Rencontres Polyphoniques de Calvi: A festival dedicated to Corsican and international polyphonic songs.
- A Fiera di U Casgiu : A cheese fair in Venaco, showcasing local products.
- The Lama Film Festival: An open-air film festival, which attracts filmmakers and film buffs from all over the world.

Gastronomy and Local Products

Corsica is a land of gastronomy, where local products play a central role in the cuisine. Regional specialties include:

- Charcuteries: Corsican charcuterie, such as lonzu , figatellu and prisuttu , is famous for its quality and unique taste.
- Cheeses: Brocciu, a fresh cheese made from sheep or goat's whey, is a key ingredient in Corsican cuisine.
- Wines: Corsica produces quality wines, with appellations like Patrimonio, Ajaccio and Calvi. Local grape varieties such as Niellucciu , Sciaccarellu and Vermentinu are particularly popular.
- Desserts: Canistrelli (dry biscuits), fiadoni (brocciu cakes) and nougats are typically Corsican sweet delights.

Economy and Innovation

Tourism

Tourism is a key sector of the Corsican economy, attracting millions of visitors each year who come to discover the natural and cultural treasures of the island. Corsica's tourist infrastructure is of high quality, with a diverse range of accommodation, starred restaurants, wellness centers and varied leisure activities.

Agriculture and Local Products

Agriculture plays an essential role in the Corsican economy, with the production of high quality fruits, vegetables, wines, cheeses and cold meats. Local markets, such as those in Ajaccio and Bastia, are popular places to buy fresh, local produce.

Crafts

Crafts are also an important sector in Corsica, with production of jewelry, knives, pottery and artisanal textiles. Local artisans perpetuate traditional know-how while innovating to create unique and authentic products.

Conclusion

Corsica is an exceptional region, rich in history, culture and varied landscapes. Whether to enjoy the heavenly beaches, explore the imposing mountains, discover the historic citadels or savor the local gastronomy, Corsica offers a multitude of possibilities for all tastes.

The region's Relais & Châteaux capture the essence of this diversity and offer their guests unforgettable experiences, combining luxury, comfort and authenticity. Each establishment, with its enchanting setting, its warm welcome, its exceptional gastronomy and its enriching activities, offers a total immersion in the Corsican art of living.

By discovering the Relais & Châteaux of Corsica, you will be transported into a world where every detail is designed to delight the senses and create lasting memories. This chapter presented a detailed overview of the region, integrating geographical, historical, cultural and economic aspects to provide a comprehensive understanding of this unique destination.

- History and Heritage

Corsica, often nicknamed the Island of Beauty, has a rich and complex history that spans several millennia. Its heritage is a fascinating mix of prehistoric remains, medieval fortresses, Genoese and French influences, and well-established local traditions. In this chapter, we will explore key moments in Corsica's history, its iconic monuments and its unique cultural contributions.

Prehistoric Origins and Antiquity

The First Inhabitants

Corsica has been inhabited since prehistoric times, as evidenced by numerous archaeological sites scattered across the island. The oldest traces of human presence date back to around 9,000 BCE.

- Filitosa: This prehistoric site is one of the most important in Corsica. It houses sculpted menhirs dating from the Bronze Age, representing stylized warriors. Filitosa is a unique testimony to the island's megalithic culture.

Greek and Phoenician Influences

Before the arrival of the Romans, Corsica saw the passage of many peoples from the Mediterranean. The Phoenicians and Greeks left their mark on the island, particularly through trade and cultural exchanges.

- Aléria: Founded by the Phocaeans then developed by the Romans, this ancient city is a major archaeological site. The Roman ruins include baths, a forum and a necropolis. The Aléria Archaeological Museum displays Greek and Roman artifacts discovered on site.

The Roman Period

Corsica became a Roman province in 259 BCE. The Romans helped develop the island's infrastructure, building roads, bridges and towns.

- Mariana: This Roman colony, founded in 93 BCE near present-day Bastia, was an important center in the region. Remains include an early Christian basilica and Roman mosaics.

The Middle Ages and the Renaissance

The Medieval Era

After the fall of the Roman Empire, Corsica was invaded by various peoples, including the Vandals, Byzantines and Lombards. The medieval period saw the rise of local lordships and the construction of numerous fortifications to defend against Barbary incursions and internal rivalries.

- The Genoese Towers: During the Genoese period (from the 13th century), more than 90 watchtowers were built along the coast to protect the island from pirates. These towers, still visible today, are emblematic symbols of Genoese heritage in Corsica.

Genoese Domination

The Genoese dominated Corsica from the 13th to the 18th century, leaving a lasting architectural and cultural legacy. The citadels and fortified towns built by the Genoese are still well preserved and bear witness to this era.

- Bonifacio: This citadel perched on limestone cliffs is one of the most impressive in Corsica. The old town, with its narrow streets and medieval houses, offers breathtaking views of the Mediterranean.
- Calvi: Another well-preserved Genoese citadel, Calvi is renowned for its massive fortifications and panoramic views of the bay.

The Corsican Uprising and Pascal Paoli

In the 18th century, the Corsicans revolted against Genoese domination. Pascal Paoli, a Corsican patriot, led the rebellion and established a constitution for the island, making Corsica one of the first modern democracies.

- The House of Pascal Paoli: Located in Morosaglia, this house museum is dedicated to the life and achievements of Pascal Paoli. It offers a fascinating insight into the history of Corsican independence.

The Modern Age and Napoleon Bonaparte

French Annexation

In 1768, the Republic of Genoa ceded Corsica to France. The following year, Napoleon Bonaparte was born in Ajaccio, marking a new era for the island.

- Maison Bonaparte: The birthplace of Napoleon Bonaparte in Ajaccio is today a museum dedicated to the life of the emperor and the history of his family.

The Revolution and the Empire

Corsica played an important role during the French Revolution and under the Napoleonic Empire. The island is a recruitment center for the French army and is undergoing administrative and economic transformations.

The 19th and 20th Century

The Industrial Era

The 19th century saw the development of industry and infrastructure in Corsica, although the island remained predominantly rural. The railway is introduced, facilitating travel and trade.
- The Corsica Train: This picturesque railway connects the island's main towns, offering spectacular views of the mountains and coasts.

World Wars

Corsica played a strategic role during the two world wars. During the Second World War, it was one of the first French regions liberated, in 1943, by the allied forces with the help of Corsican resistance fighters.

- The Resistance Museum in Balagne: Located in Monticello, this museum commemorates the efforts of Corsican resistance fighters during the war and their contribution to the liberation of the island.

Cultural and Architectural Heritage

Villages and Traditional Architecture

Corsica is dotted with picturesque villages, each with its unique character and traditional stone architecture.

- Pigna: This village in Balagne is known for its traditional architecture and cobbled streets. It is also a center for crafts and music.
- Sartène: Nicknamed "the most Corsican of Corsican towns", Sartène is renowned for its granite houses and its cultural traditions, notably the Catenacciu procession during Holy Week.

Churches and Religious Monuments

Corsica has a rich religious heritage, with numerous churches, chapels and convents scattered across the island.

- Sainte-Marie Cathedral in Ajaccio: Built in the 16th century, this baroque cathedral is famous for having been the baptism place of Napoleon Bonaparte.
- The Church of San Michele de Murato: A remarkable example of Romanesque architecture, this church is famous for its polychrome stone bands and decorated interior.

Conclusion

Corsica is a region where history and heritage are omnipresent, shaping the unique character of the island and offering unparalleled cultural wealth. From prehistoric remains to Genoese citadels, including traces of the Roman Empire and places of memory of the world wars, Corsica is a real gold mine for history and heritage lovers.

The Relais & Châteaux of Corsica capture the essence of this historical and cultural wealth, offering their guests unforgettable experiences. Each establishment, with its enchanting setting, warm welcome, exceptional gastronomy and enriching activities, offers total immersion in the history and heritage of the island.

By discovering the Relais & Châteaux of Corsica, you will be transported into a world where every detail is designed to delight the senses and create lasting memories. This chapter explored the multiple facets of Corsica's history and heritage, revealing how each era has helped shape this unique and fascinating destination.

- **Gastronomy and Wine**

Corsica, land of contrasts and flavors, is a true paradise for lovers of gastronomy and wine. Its authentic cuisine, influenced by the sea and the mountains, as well as its unique wines, make this island an exceptional culinary destination. In this chapter, we'll explore the gastronomic delights of Corsica, highlighting the local produce, iconic dishes, renowned chefs, Michelin-starred restaurants and wines that this region is famous for.

Local Products

Products of the Earth

Corsica benefits from a Mediterranean climate favorable to the cultivation of many high-quality agricultural products.

- Chestnuts: Used in many dishes and desserts, chestnuts are a basic ingredient in Corsica. They are found in particular in chestnut flour, used to make breads and cakes.
- Olives and Olive Oil: The production of olives and olive oil is an ancient tradition in Corsica. Corsican olive oil, often of the "Sabine" variety, is renowned for its fruity and slightly spicy flavor.
- Citrus fruits: Corsican clementines, protected by a protected geographical indication (PGI), are particularly tasty.

Seafood

Surrounded by the Mediterranean Sea, Corsica offers an abundance of fresh fish and seafood.

- Sea bass: Known as sea bass in French, this fish is very prized for its delicate flesh.
- Sea urchins: Harvested in winter, they are often eaten fresh, directly on the beach, or incorporated into refined dishes.
- Lobsters and Lobsters: These shellfish are delicacies, often served grilled or in elaborate dishes.

Cheeses and charcuterie

Corsica is also famous for its cheeses and charcuterie, which are essential elements of the local cuisine.

- Brocciu: A fresh cheese made from sheep or goat's whey, used in many Corsican dishes and desserts.
- Niolo and Calinzana : Hard sheep's milk cheeses, known for their pronounced taste.
- Charcuteries: Lonzu (dried pork fillet), figatellu (liver sausage), and prisuttu (cured ham) are essential Corsican specialties.

Traditional dishes

Starters and Soups

Corsican meals often begin with tasty starters and nourishing soups.

- Corsican Soup: A thick soup made from beans, potatoes, cabbage and cold meats.
- Fiadone: A cake made with brocciu, lemon and eggs, often served as a dessert but sometimes also as a light starter.

Main dishes

Corsican main dishes are generous and highlight local products.

- Veal with Olives: A veal stew simmered with olives, tomatoes and aromatic herbs.
- Le Civet de Sanglier: A wild boar stew marinated in red wine with onions, carrots and herbs.
- Cannelloni with Brocciu: Pasta stuffed with brocciu, spinach and herbs, gratinated in the oven.

The desserts

Corsican desserts are often simple but delicious, highlighting local products.

- Canistrelli : Dry biscuits flavored with anise or lemon.
- Pastizzu : A flan made from semolina, milk and lemon.
- Fig Tart: A sweet tart garnished with fresh or candied figs.

Corsican Wines

Red Wines

Corsican red wines are generally robust and full-bodied, with aromas of red fruits and spices.

- Niellucciu : The most emblematic grape variety of Corsica, mainly grown in the Patrimonio appellation. Wines made from Niellucciu are often compared to Sangiovese wines from Tuscany.
- Sciaccarellu : Grown mainly in the Ajaccio region, this grape variety produces light and fruity red wines, with notes of red fruits and pepper.

White Wines

Corsican white wines are fresh and aromatic, often made from native grape varieties.

- Vermentinu: Also known as Vermentino in Italy, this grape variety produces fresh and fragrant white wines, with aromas of white flowers, citrus and exotic fruits.
- Biancu Gentile: An ancient grape variety currently being rehabilitated, producing rich and complex white wines.

Rosé Wines

Corsican rosé wines are renowned for their freshness and elegance, ideal for hot summer days.

- Rosé de Sciaccarellu : Light and fruity, with aromas of strawberry, raspberry and a hint of spice.
- Rosé de Niellucciu : More structured, with notes of red fruits and a beautiful minerality.

Sweet Wines

Corsica also produces natural sweet wines, perfect to accompany desserts or to enjoy on their own.

- Muscat du Cap Corse: A natural sweet wine made from Muscat, with aromas of fresh grapes, honey and flowers.

Star Chefs and Restaurants

The Pioneers of Corsican Haute Cuisine

Corsica has always been a hotbed of culinary creativity, attracting talented chefs who showcase local produce and culinary traditions. Among the pioneers of Corsican haute cuisine, we find Paul Quilès, chef of the U Santa Marina restaurant in Porto-Vecchio, who has redefined regional cuisine with a modern and innovative approach.

Contemporary Chefs

Today, Corsica continues to attract renowned chefs, who perpetuate the tradition of haute cuisine while innovating and experimenting with new flavors. Among the most famous contemporary chefs, we find:

- Jean-Marc Ettori : Chef of the Michelin-starred restaurant La Table de la Ferme in Porto-Vecchio, offering inventive and refined cuisine.
- Hélène Darroze : Chef of the Le Suprême restaurant in Bonifacio, known for her locavore and environmentally friendly cuisine.

Star Restaurants

Corsica is home to many Michelin-starred restaurants, each offering a unique and unforgettable culinary experience. Among the most famous, we find:

- U Santa Marina in Porto-Vecchio: A Michelin-starred restaurant, managed by Paul Quilès, offering modern and creative cuisine in a rustic and elegant setting.
- La Table de la Ferme in Porto-Vecchio: Michelin-starred, this restaurant offers refined and inventive cuisine, highlighting local products from the region.

- Le Suprême in Bonifacio: Another Michelin-starred restaurant by Hélène Darroze , offering high-quality gourmet cuisine.

Oenological and Culinary Experiences

Wine Tastings

Relais & Châteaux de Corsica often offer unique wine and culinary experiences for their guests. From private tastings to vineyard tours, these experiences allow you to discover the region's wines and learn the secrets of their making.

Customers can participate in tasting workshops, led by experts, to learn how to identify the aromas and flavors of Corsican wines. Guided tours of the vineyards allow you to discover the production processes, meet the winegrowers and taste wines directly from the source.

Food and Wine Pairings

Relais & Châteaux also offer food and wine pairings, allowing you to savor Corsican wines in harmony with local cuisine. These pairings highlight the flavors of the dishes and wines, providing a complete and unforgettable gastronomic experience.

Chefs from Michelin-starred restaurants collaborate with sommeliers to create tasting menus that highlight the region's wines. Each dish is carefully paired with a wine, allowing guests to discover new combinations of flavors and textures.

Conclusion

Corsica is a true land of gastronomy and wine, offering unparalleled richness and diversity. Regional cuisine, with its authentic flavors and quality local products, is a pillar of the island's art of living. Corsican wines, renowned for their complexity and elegance, perfectly complement this culinary experience.

The Relais & Châteaux of Corsica capture the essence of this gastronomic richness, offering their guests unique and unforgettable culinary and wine experiences. Each establishment, with its enchanting setting, its warm welcome, its exceptional gastronomy and its enriching activities, offers a total immersion in the Corsican art of living.

By discovering the Relais & Châteaux of Corsica, you will be transported into a world where every detail is designed to delight the senses and create lasting memories. This chapter explored the multiple facets of the region's gastronomy and wines, revealing how each element contributes to making this destination a true oasis of flavors and culinary pleasures.

2. Addresses and Descriptions

Corsica is home to several Relais & Châteaux establishments, each offering a unique experience combining luxury, comfort and island charm. These prestigious hotels and restaurants are located in iconic locations across the island, from idyllic beaches to majestic mountains. In this chapter, we will discover some of the most prestigious addresses and describe in detail what makes them special.

Murtoli Estate

History and Architecture

Domaine de Murtoli, located in Sartène, is a unique location in Corsica, combining traditional stone houses with modern luxury amenities. This area, covering more than 2,500 hectares, offers total immersion in the wild and preserved nature of Corsica.

Culinary Offers

Domaine de Murtoli has several restaurants, each offering a different gastronomic experience. La Table de la Ferme restaurant offers refined cuisine using local produce, while La Table de la Plage offers seaside dining, showcasing fresh seafood. The wine list is carefully selected, highlighting Corsican grands crus and other prestigious wine regions.

Activities and Services

Domaine de Murtoli offers a range of activities for its guests, from relaxation to sport. Guests can enjoy the private beach, hiking trails, fishing and boat tours. Guided tours are also organized to explore the surrounding area, including the town of Sartène and its historic monuments.

Villa Calvi

History and Architecture

Villa Calvi, located in Calvi, is a luxury establishment offering breathtaking views of the Bay of Calvi and the Genoese citadel. This modern and stylish villa combines contemporary design with traditional Corsican touches, creating an atmosphere that is both sophisticated and welcoming.

Culinary Offers

The restaurant at La Villa Calvi, led by a starred chef, offers inventive and refined cuisine, highlighting local and seasonal products. The tasting menu offers dishes such as "Sea Bass Filet" and "Wild Boar Stew". The carefully selected wine list highlights Corsican grands crus and other prestigious wine regions.

Activities and Services

Villa Calvi offers a range of activities for its guests, from relaxation to sport. Guests can enjoy the heated outdoor pool, spa, tennis courts and boat tours. Guided tours are also organized to explore the surrounding area, including the Calvi citadel and the beaches of Balagne.

Scrub

History and Architecture

Le Maquis, located in Porticcio, is a charming hotel offering a spectacular view of the Gulf of Ajaccio. This establishment combines modern luxury with traditional Corsican charm, providing a romantic and peaceful setting for its visitors.

Culinary Offers

The Le Maquis restaurant offers refined cuisine, highlighting local and seasonal products. The tasting menu offers dishes such as "Blue Lobster" and "Veal with Olives". The carefully selected wine list highlights Corsican grands crus and other prestigious wine regions.

Activities and Services

Le Maquis offers a range of activities for its guests, from relaxation to sport. Guests can enjoy the private beach, heated outdoor pool, spa and tennis courts. Guided excursions are also organized to explore the surrounding area, including the city of Ajaccio and its historic monuments.

The Signoria

History and Architecture

La Signoria , located in Calvi, is an old Genoese manor transformed into a luxury hotel. Surrounded by lush gardens, this historic residence offers an elegant and refined setting for its visitors, with breathtaking views of the mountains and the sea.

Culinary Offers

The La Signoria restaurant , led by a starred chef, offers inventive and refined cuisine, highlighting local and seasonal products. The tasting menu offers dishes such as "Filet de Veau de Corse" and "Pigeon de Racan". The carefully selected wine list highlights Corsican grands crus and other prestigious wine regions.

Activities and Services

La Signoria offers a range of activities for its guests, from relaxation to sport. Guests can enjoy the heated outdoor pool, spa, yoga classes and boat tours. Guided tours are also organized to explore the surrounding area, including the Calvi citadel and the beaches of Balagne.

Hotel & Spa des Pêcheurs

History and Architecture

Hôtel & Spa des Pêcheurs, located on the island of Cavallo, is an exclusive establishment offering a luxurious and secluded experience. This private island, between Corsica and Sardinia, offers an idyllic setting with fine sandy beaches and crystal clear waters.

Culinary Offers

The restaurant at the Hôtel & Spa des Pêcheurs offers refined cuisine, highlighting local and seasonal products. The tasting menu offers dishes such as "Langouste de Cavallo" and "Civet de Sanglier". The carefully selected wine list highlights Corsican grands crus and other prestigious wine regions.

Activities and Services

Hôtel & Spa des Pêcheurs offers a range of activities for its guests, from relaxation to sport. Guests can enjoy the private beach, heated outdoor pool, spa, tennis courts and boat tours. Guided tours are also organized to explore the surrounding area, including the island's hidden coves and hiking trails.

Conclusion

The Relais & Châteaux of Corsica offer unique and unforgettable experiences, combining luxury, comfort and island heritage. Each establishment, with its enchanting setting, its warm welcome, its exceptional gastronomy and its enriching activities, offers a total immersion in the Corsican art of living. Whether for a romantic getaway, a peaceful retreat or a cultural exploration, the Relais & Châteaux of the Corsica region are must-see destinations.

By discovering these exceptional establishments, you will be transported to a world where every detail is designed to delight the senses and create lasting memories. This chapter has presented a detailed overview of some of the most prestigious Relais & Châteaux in the region, offering a glimpse of the unique experience that awaits you in each of these enchanting locations.

- Hôtel & Spa des Pecheurs

The Hôtel & Spa des Pêcheurs, located on the island of Cavallo, is an exclusive and luxurious establishment offering a unique experience in Corsica. Nestled between Corsica and Sardinia, this isolated hotel on a private island offers an idyllic setting with sandy beaches, crystal clear waters and high-end services. In this chapter, we will explore the history and architecture of the Hôtel & Spa des Pêcheurs, its culinary offerings, the activities and services offered, and the unique experiences it offers.

History and Architecture

An Exquisite Heritage

The Hôtel & Spa des Pêcheurs was built to provide a luxurious and exclusive retreat on the island of Cavallo. The island, once a fishing spot, has been transformed into a paradise of relaxation and well-being. The hotel embodies elegance and serenity, with architecture that blends harmoniously into the natural landscape of the island.

Elegant Architecture

The architecture of the Hôtel & Spa des Pêcheurs reflects the Mediterranean style with low stone buildings, red tiled roofs and shaded terraces. The interiors are tastefully decorated, combining traditional Corsican elements and contemporary touches to create a warm and sophisticated atmosphere.

The hotel's rooms and suites offer breathtaking views of the sea or gardens. Each room is unique, with distinctive design elements and modern amenities to ensure optimal comfort. The bathrooms, fitted with marble bathtubs and walk-in showers, provide a luxurious setting in which to relax and rejuvenate.

Culinary Offers

The Gourmet Restaurant

The restaurant at the Hôtel & Spa des Pêcheurs, led by a talented chef, offers inventive and refined cuisine, highlighting local and seasonal products. The tasting menu offers dishes such as "Langouste de Cavallo" and "Civet de Sanglier". The carefully selected wine list highlights Corsican grands crus and other prestigious wine regions.

The restaurant's setting is matched by its cuisine, with an elegantly decorated dining room, tables spaced for maximum privacy, and panoramic sea views. Guests can also dine al fresco on the terrace, enjoying the tranquility and beauty of the natural setting.

Regional Cuisine

The chef at the Hôtel & Spa des Pêcheurs places particular emphasis on local products, with a locavore philosophy that favors fresh, seasonal ingredients from local producers. Guests can taste regional specialties such as "Filet de Loup de Mer" and "Tarte aux Figues de Cavallo", accompanied by carefully selected local wines.

The Gourmet Breakfast

The gourmet breakfast at Hôtel & Spa des Pêcheurs is served in the elegantly decorated dining room or on the terrace, with magnificent views of the sea and gardens. Breakfast is composed of fresh, local products, including pastries, fruits, homemade jams, regional cheeses, fresh eggs and pressed fruit juices. Guests can also enjoy hot drinks, such as coffee, tea and hot chocolate.

Activities and Services

The Spa and Wellness Treatments

The Hôtel & Spa des Pêcheurs offers a range of wellness treatments for its guests, from massages to facial treatments, carried out with high quality products. The spa, located in a peaceful and luxurious setting, is a perfect place to relax and unwind after a day exploring the island.

Spa facilities include heated indoor and outdoor swimming pools, saunas, steam rooms, hot tubs and treatment rooms. Professional therapists use advanced techniques and luxury products to ensure optimal results and a luxurious experience.

Outdoor activities

The sandy beaches and crystal clear waters of Cavallo Island provide an ideal setting for water activities such as diving, snorkeling, paddle boarding and sailing. Guests can also take advantage of the hiking trails to explore the island's natural landscapes.

Boat trips are organized to discover the island's hidden coves and historic sites, providing a unique and memorable experience. Guests can also participate in outdoor meditation and yoga sessions, enjoying the tranquility and beauty of the island.

Cultural Activities and Experiences

Hôtel & Spa des Pêcheurs regularly organizes cultural events and unique experiences for its guests. Private concerts, literary readings and art exhibitions are often organized in the establishment's lounges or gardens. These events offer immersion in the local cultural scene and allow guests to meet artists, writers and musicians.

Guests can also participate in cooking workshops, baking classes and wine tastings, led by local chefs. These workshops offer an opportunity to learn regional cooking techniques and taste delicious creations. Hôtel & Spa des Pêcheurs also offers yoga and meditation classes, led by qualified instructors, in the hotel's gardens or wellness areas.

Special Events and Unique Experiences

Weddings and Receptions

The Hôtel & Spa des Pêcheurs is an ideal venue for intimate weddings and private receptions. The property's beaches and lounges provide a romantic and elegant setting for ceremonies and receptions. Hotel staff work closely with couples to create tailor-made events, taking into account every detail, from decor to personalized menus.

The hotel's chefs create wedding menus that reflect the tastes and preferences of the bride and groom, using seasonal ingredients and local produce. The professional and attentive service teams ensure that every event goes off without a hitch. Couples can also enjoy luxurious suites for their wedding night, with special services such as massages, in-room breakfasts and welcome gifts.

Seminars and Business Meetings

The Hôtel & Spa des Pêcheurs offers an exceptional setting for seminars, conferences and business meetings. The property's private lounges, equipped with the latest technology, offer flexible spaces for events of different sizes. Hotel teams work with event organizers to create tailor-made programs, including coffee breaks, business lunches and dinners.

Team-building activities and excursions can also be organized to strengthen team cohesion and provide moments of relaxation outside of work sessions. Guests can take advantage of the hotel's wellness facilities to unwind after a day of meetings, with spa treatments, yoga sessions and massages.

Unique Experiences

The Hôtel & Spa des Pêcheurs offers unique experiences to make each stay memorable. These include private dinners in exclusive locations within the establishment, such as the beach or gardens, offering an intimate and romantic atmosphere. Guests can also participate in wine tasting workshops, led by expert sommeliers, to discover the secrets of the region's wines.

Wellness getaways are also available, including personalized relaxation and relaxation programs, spa treatments, yoga and meditation sessions, as well as healthy and nutritious meals. These programs are designed to help clients recharge their batteries and regain physical and mental balance.

Seasonal and Thematic Offers

The Hôtel & Spa des Pêcheurs regularly offers seasonal and thematic offers to enrich its customers' experience. At Christmas, the establishment is decked out in festive decorations and offers special menus, cookie decorating workshops and Christmas market visits. In summer, gourmet picnics can be organized on the beach or in the gardens.

Romantic getaways are also offered, including candlelit dinners, duo massages and boat rides around the island. For culture lovers, special packages including tickets for exhibitions, shows and concerts are available, offering complete immersion in the cultural life of the region.

Conclusion

The Hôtel & Spa des Pêcheurs is much more than just a luxury hotel; it is a destination in itself, offering a unique and unforgettable experience in the heart of the beautiful island of Cavallo. With its rich history, impressive architecture, refined culinary offerings and a variety of activities and services, this establishment is the ideal place to relax, recharge and discover the French art of living.

Whether for a romantic getaway, a wellness retreat, an intimate wedding or a business meeting, the Hôtel & Spa des Pêcheurs promises an exceptional experience, marked by luxury, comfort and elegance. Guests leave with unforgettable memories, enriched by the unique culture, gastronomy and hospitality of this emblematic establishment of the Corsica region.

- Casadelmar

Casadelmar , located in Porto-Vecchio, is a luxury hotel offering a unique experience combining modernity, comfort and natural beauty. This five-star establishment, nestled on the south-eastern coast of Corsica, is recognized for its contemporary design, spectacular sea views and high-end services. In this chapter, we will explore the history and architecture of Casadelmar , its culinary offerings, the activities and services offered, and the unique experiences it offers.

History and Architecture

A Contemporary Oasis

Casadelmar was designed to offer a luxurious and modern refuge in harmony with the surrounding nature. Opened in 2004, this hotel is distinguished by its bold architecture and minimalist design, perfectly integrating the natural elements of the region.

Elegant and Modern Architecture

The architecture of Casadelmar , designed by architect Jean-François Bodin, uses local materials such as wood, stone and glass to create an atmosphere that is both warm and contemporary. Large floor-to-ceiling windows offer panoramic sea views, while private terraces and landscaped gardens add a touch of serenity and privacy.

The hotel's rooms and suites are decorated with designer furniture and modern artwork. Each room is equipped with luxury amenities, such as king -size beds, marble bathrooms and private balconies with stunning views of the sea or gardens.

Culinary Offers

The Gourmet Restaurant

Casadelmar 's Michelin-starred restaurant is run by talented chef Fabio Bragagnolo . It offers inventive and refined cuisine, highlighting local and seasonal products. The tasting menu offers dishes such as "Red Tuna Tartare" and "Black Truffle Risotto". The carefully selected wine list highlights Corsican grands crus and other prestigious wine regions.

The restaurant's setting is matched by its cuisine, with an elegantly decorated dining room, tables spaced for maximum privacy, and panoramic sea views. Guests can also dine al fresco on the terrace, enjoying the tranquility and beauty of the natural setting.

Regional Cuisine

Chef Fabio Bragagnolo places particular emphasis on local products, with a locavore philosophy that favors fresh, seasonal ingredients from local producers. Guests can taste regional specialties such as "Sea Bass Filet" and "Alta Rocca Suckling Lamb", accompanied by carefully selected local wines.

The Gourmet Breakfast

Casadelmar 's gourmet breakfast is served in the elegantly decorated dining room or on the terrace, with magnificent views of the sea. Breakfast is composed of fresh and local products, including pastries, fruits, jams homemade, regional cheeses, fresh eggs and pressed fruit juices. Guests can also enjoy hot drinks, such as coffee, tea and hot chocolate.

Activities and Services

The Spa and Wellness Treatments

Casadelmar offers a range of wellness treatments for its customers, from massages to facials, performed with high quality products. The spa, located in a peaceful and luxurious setting, is a perfect place to relax and unwind after a day exploring the region.

Spa facilities include heated indoor and outdoor swimming pools, saunas, steam rooms, hot tubs and treatment rooms. Professional therapists use advanced techniques and luxury products to ensure optimal results and a luxurious experience.

Outdoor activities

Casadelmar 's gardens and private beaches provide an ideal setting for outdoor activities such as swimming, snorkeling, paddleboarding and sailing. Guests can also take advantage of the hiking trails to explore the natural landscapes of the area.

Boat trips are organized to discover the hidden coves and historical sites of the region, providing a unique and memorable experience. Guests can also participate in outdoor meditation and yoga sessions, enjoying the tranquility and beauty of the hotel.

Cultural Activities and Experiences

Casadelmar regularly organizes cultural events and unique experiences for its guests. Private concerts, literary readings and art exhibitions are often organized in the establishment's lounges or gardens. These events offer immersion in the local cultural scene and allow guests to meet artists, writers and musicians.

Guests can also participate in cooking workshops, baking classes and wine tastings, led by local chefs. These workshops offer an opportunity to learn regional cooking techniques and taste delicious creations. Casadelmar also offers yoga and meditation classes, led by qualified instructors, in the hotel's gardens or wellness areas.

Special Events and Unique Experiences

Weddings and Receptions

Casadelmar is an ideal venue for hosting intimate weddings and private receptions. The property's gardens and lounges provide a romantic and elegant setting for ceremonies and receptions. Hotel staff work closely with couples to create tailor-made events, taking into account every detail, from decor to personalized menus.

The hotel's chefs create wedding menus that reflect the tastes and preferences of the bride and groom, using seasonal ingredients and local produce. The professional and attentive service teams ensure that every event goes off without a hitch. Couples can also enjoy luxurious suites for their wedding night, with special services such as massages, in-room breakfasts and welcome gifts.

Seminars and Business Meetings

Casadelmar offers an exceptional setting for seminars, conferences and business meetings. The property's private lounges, equipped with the latest technology, offer flexible spaces for events of different sizes. Hotel teams work with event organizers to create tailor-made programs, including coffee breaks, business lunches and dinners.

Team-building activities and excursions can also be organized to strengthen team cohesion and provide moments of relaxation outside of work sessions. Guests can take advantage of the hotel's wellness facilities to unwind after a day of meetings, with spa treatments, yoga sessions and massages.

Unique Experiences

Casadelmar offers unique experiences to make every stay memorable. These include private dinners in exclusive locations within the establishment, such as the beach or gardens, offering an intimate and romantic atmosphere. Guests can also participate in wine tasting workshops, led by expert sommeliers, to discover the secrets of the region's wines.

Wellness getaways are also available, including personalized relaxation and relaxation programs, spa treatments, yoga and meditation sessions, as well as healthy and nutritious meals. These programs are designed to help clients recharge their batteries and regain physical and mental balance.

Seasonal and Thematic Offers

Casadelmar regularly offers seasonal and thematic offers to enrich its customers' experience. At Christmas, the establishment is decked out in festive decorations and offers special menus, cookie decorating workshops and Christmas market visits. In summer, gourmet picnics can be organized on the beach or in the gardens.

Romantic getaways are also offered, including candlelit dinners, duo massages and boat rides around the bay of Porto-Vecchio. For culture lovers, special packages including tickets for exhibitions, shows and concerts are available, offering complete immersion in the cultural life of the region.

Conclusion

Casadelmar is much more than just a luxury hotel; it is a destination in itself, offering a unique and unforgettable experience in the heart of the magnificent Porto-Vecchio region. With its modern design, spectacular sea views, fine culinary offerings and a variety of activities and services, this establishment is the ideal place to relax, recharge and discover the art of living in Corsica.

Whether for a romantic getaway, a wellness retreat, an intimate wedding or a business meeting, Casadelmar promises an exceptional experience, marked by luxury, comfort and elegance. Guests leave with unforgettable memories, enriched by the unique culture, gastronomy and hospitality of this emblematic establishment of the Corsica region.

- Murtoli Estate

The Domaine de Murtoli , located in the Sartène region in Corsica, is an exceptional place offering a unique experience combining nature, luxury and authenticity. Spanning more than 2,500 hectares, this private estate is a true haven of peace where visitors can reconnect with nature while enjoying high-end comfort and services. In this chapter, we will explore the history and architecture of Domaine de Murtoli , its culinary offerings, the activities and services offered, and the unique experiences it offers.

History and Architecture

A Preserved Rural Heritage

The Domaine de Murtoli was founded with the idea of preserving and promoting the natural and cultural heritage of Corsica. The estate includes carefully restored sheepfolds, stone villas and traditional houses, each integrated harmoniously into the surrounding landscape.

Authentic Architecture

The architecture of Domaine de Murtoli respects local traditions, using natural materials such as stone, wood and terracotta. The estate's buildings have been renovated to offer modern comfort while retaining their old-world charm. Each accommodation is unique, with distinctive design elements and modern amenities to ensure optimal comfort.

Interiors are decorated with handcrafted furniture, local artwork and natural textiles, creating a warm and authentic atmosphere. Private terraces and landscaped gardens offer spectacular views of the sea, mountains and wild landscapes of the region.

Culinary Offers

The Gourmet Restaurant

Domaine de Murtoli has several restaurants, each offering a unique dining experience. The main restaurant, La Table de la Ferme, offers inventive and refined cuisine, highlighting local and seasonal products. The tasting menu offers dishes such as "Cabri de Murtoli " and "Fish of the Day grilled over a wood fire". The carefully selected wine list highlights Corsican grands crus and other prestigious wine regions.

Outdoor Cooking

La Table de la Plage and La Table de la Grotte offer outdoor dining in stunning natural settings. La Table de la Plage offers fresh seafood and grills, while La Table de la Grotte offers a unique dining experience in a natural cave, with dishes prepared on site.

The Gourmet Breakfast

Murtoli 's gourmet breakfast is served in each accommodation or outdoors, depending on guest preferences. Breakfast is composed of fresh, local products, including pastries, fruits, homemade jams, regional cheeses, fresh eggs and pressed fruit juices. Guests can also enjoy hot drinks, such as coffee, tea and hot chocolate.

Activities and Services

The Spa and Wellness Treatments

Domaine de Murtoli offers a range of wellness treatments for its guests, ranging from massages to facials, carried out with high quality products. The spa, located in a peaceful and luxurious setting, is a perfect place to relax and unwind after a day exploring the region.

Spa facilities include heated indoor and outdoor swimming pools, saunas, steam rooms, hot tubs and treatment rooms. Professional therapists use advanced techniques and luxury products to ensure optimal results and a luxurious experience.

Outdoor activities

The vast expanses of Domaine de Murtoli provide an ideal setting for outdoor activities such as hiking, horse riding, fishing and golf. Guests can explore hiking trails, take part in mountain biking tours or relax on the estate's private beaches.

Boat trips are organized to discover the hidden coves and historical sites of the region, providing a unique and memorable experience. Guests can also participate in outdoor meditation and yoga sessions, enjoying the tranquility and beauty of the estate.

Cultural Activities and Experiences

Domaine de Murtoli regularly organizes cultural events and unique experiences for its guests. Private concerts, literary readings and art exhibitions are often organized in the establishment's lounges or gardens. These events offer immersion in the local cultural scene and allow guests to meet artists, writers and musicians.

Guests can also participate in cooking workshops, baking classes and wine tastings, led by local chefs. These workshops offer an opportunity to learn regional cooking techniques and taste delicious creations. Domaine de Murtoli also offers yoga and meditation classes, led by qualified instructors, in the hotel's gardens or wellness areas.

Special Events and Unique Experiences

Weddings and Receptions

Domaine de Murtoli is an ideal venue for intimate weddings and private receptions. The property's gardens, beaches and lounges provide a romantic and elegant setting for ceremonies and receptions. Hotel staff work closely with couples to create tailor-made events, taking into account every detail, from decor to personalized menus.

The hotel's chefs create wedding menus that reflect the tastes and preferences of the bride and groom, using seasonal ingredients and local produce. The professional and attentive service teams ensure that every event goes off without a hitch. Couples can also enjoy luxurious suites for their wedding night, with special services such as massages, in-room breakfasts and welcome gifts.

Seminars and Business Meetings

The Domaine de Murtoli offers an exceptional setting for seminars, conferences and business meetings. The property's private lounges, equipped with the latest technology, offer flexible spaces for events of different sizes. Hotel teams work with event organizers to create tailor-made programs, including coffee breaks, business lunches and dinners.

Team-building activities and excursions can also be organized to strengthen team cohesion and provide moments of relaxation outside of work sessions. Guests can take advantage of the hotel's wellness facilities to unwind after a day of meetings, with spa treatments, yoga sessions and massages.

Unique Experiences

The Domaine de Murtoli offers unique experiences to make each stay memorable. These include private dinners in exclusive locations within the establishment, such as the beach or gardens, offering an intimate and romantic atmosphere. Guests can also participate in wine tasting workshops, led by expert sommeliers, to discover the secrets of the region's wines.

Wellness getaways are also available, including personalized relaxation and relaxation programs, spa treatments, yoga and meditation sessions, as well as healthy and nutritious meals. These programs are designed to help clients recharge their batteries and regain physical and mental balance.

Seasonal and Thematic Offers

Domaine de Murtoli regularly offers seasonal and thematic offers to enrich its customers' experience. At Christmas, the establishment is decked out in festive decorations and offers special menus, cookie decorating workshops and Christmas market visits. In summer, gourmet picnics can be organized on the beach or in the gardens.

Romantic getaways are also offered, including candlelit dinners, duo massages and boat trips around the coast of Corsica. For culture lovers, special packages including tickets for exhibitions, shows and concerts are available, offering complete immersion in the cultural life of the region.

Conclusion

The Domaine de Murtoli is much more than just a luxury hotel; it is a destination in itself, offering a unique and unforgettable experience in the heart of the magnificent Sartène region of Corsica. With its rich history, authentic architecture, refined culinary offerings and a variety of activities and services, this establishment is the ideal place to relax, recharge and discover the art of living in Corsica.

Whether for a romantic getaway, a wellness retreat, an intimate wedding or a business meeting, Domaine de Murtoli promises an exceptional experience, marked by luxury, comfort and elegance. Guests leave with unforgettable memories, enriched by the unique culture, gastronomy and hospitality of this emblematic establishment of the Corsica region.

Conclusion

1. The Future of Relais & Châteaux

Relais & Châteaux have always been synonymous with luxury, refinement and traditions. However, like any prestigious institution, they must evolve with the times to meet changing customer expectations and the challenges of the modern world. The future of Relais & Châteaux is based on several essential pillars: sustainability, innovation, authenticity, and commitment to local culture. In this chapter, we will explore how these institutions are preparing to meet these challenges and continue to thrive in the years to come.

Sustainability and Ecology

Ecological Commitment

Environmental awareness has become a priority for many travelers. Relais & Châteaux, keen to preserve the environment, have adopted sustainable practices to minimize their ecological footprint.

- Renewable Energy: Many establishments have invested in renewable energy sources, such as solar and geothermal energy, to reduce their dependence on fossil fuels.
- Waste Management: Waste reduction and recycling are priorities. Some hotels even go so far as to compost their organic waste to use in their gardens.
- Water Conservation: Optimizing water consumption, through modern technologies and responsible practices, is essential to preserve this precious resource.

Sustainable Gastronomy

Gastronomy is at the heart of the Relais & Châteaux experience. The trend towards local, seasonal and organic ingredients continues to grow.

- Local Products: By favoring farm-to-table products, chefs support the local economy and reduce the carbon footprint linked to food transportation.
- Own Crops: Many establishments have their own vegetable gardens, orchards and vineyards, guaranteeing fresh, quality ingredients for their restaurants.
- Sustainable Fishing: Restaurants located by the sea are committed to using sustainable fishing methods and respecting the breeding seasons of marine species.

Innovation and Technology

Connected Experiences

The integration of technology into the customer experience has become essential. Relais & Châteaux strive to find a balance between modern comfort and authenticity.

- Smart Rooms: Smart home technologies allow guests to control lighting, temperature and entertainment systems through mobile apps.
- Personalized Services: The use of artificial intelligence and big data makes it possible to personalize the experience of each customer, by anticipating their needs and preferences.

Well-being and Health

Well-being is an essential component of the Relais & Châteaux experience. Establishments are innovating to offer cutting-edge wellness services.

- High-Tech Spa: The use of advanced technologies for spa treatments, such as cryotherapy, LED light therapies and rejuvenation treatments, attracts a health-conscious clientele.
- Wellness Programs: Yoga retreats, meditation and detox programs are offered to meet the growing demand for wellness-focused stays.

Authenticity and Local Culture

Preservation of Traditions

Authenticity is at the heart of the Relais & Châteaux experience. Establishments are committed to preserving and promoting local culture.

- Traditional Architecture: Renovations and new construction respect local architecture and use traditional materials to maintain the unique character of each region.
- Local Crafts: Hotels highlight local crafts, from handmade furniture to artisanal products available in their boutiques.
- Cultural Experiences: Local cooking classes, guided tours of historic sites and craft workshops allow guests to immerse themselves in regional culture.

Community Support

Relais & Châteaux play an active role in their local communities.

- Local Employment: By recruiting locally, establishments support the regional economy and provide training and development opportunities for residents.
- Local Partnerships: Collaborations with local producers, artisans and artists strengthen ties with the community and enrich the customer experience.

Commitment to Excellence

Continuing Education

Continuing staff training is essential to maintain the standards of excellence of Relais & Châteaux.

- Training Programs: Intensive training programs and regular workshops enable staff to improve their skills and adopt industry best practices.
- International Exchanges: Exchange opportunities between the different Relais & Châteaux establishments make it possible to share knowledge and skills across the world.

Certification and Quality

Relais & Châteaux strive to maintain the highest standards of quality.

- Ecological Certifications: Certifications such as Green Globe and EarthCheck attest to the ecological efforts of establishments.
- Quality Label: The Relais & Châteaux label guarantees an experience of luxury, authenticity and quality on each visit.

Conclusion

The future of Relais & Châteaux is bright, with a clear vision of sustainability, innovation and authenticity. By meeting modern expectations while preserving the traditions and values that have made them famous, these establishments will continue to offer unforgettable experiences. Each Relais & Châteaux, with its enchanting setting, warm welcome, exceptional gastronomy and enriching activities, offers total immersion in the art of living.

By focusing on these pillars, Relais & Châteaux are well placed to meet the challenges of tomorrow and continue to offer exceptional moments to their clients. The commitment to excellence, sustainability and local culture ensures that each stay is not only luxurious but also environmentally friendly and enriching for the local community.

- New Trends

Relais & Châteaux, as bastions of luxury hospitality, continue to evolve to adapt to the changing tastes and needs of modern travelers. New trends in the hotel and restaurant industry strongly influence these establishments, which seek to offer unique and memorable experiences. In this chapter, we will explore the key trends shaping the future of Relais & Châteaux, including holistic wellness, experiential tourism, technological innovation and commitment to sustainability.

Holistic Well-Being

An Integrated Approach to Well-Being

Well-being is no longer limited to traditional spa treatments. Relais & Châteaux adopt a holistic approach, integrating physical, mental and spiritual well-being.

- Yoga and Meditation Retreats: Many establishments offer yoga and meditation programs, often led by internationally renowned instructors, in inspiring natural settings.

- Nutrition and Healthy Cuisine: Menus increasingly include healthy cuisine options, focused on organic, local and seasonal ingredients. Healthy cooking workshops are also offered.
- Alternative Therapies: The integration of alternative therapies such as acupuncture, reflexology and aromatherapy is becoming common, providing clients with varied options to improve their well-being.

Spaces for Relaxation and Reconnection

Relais & Châteaux create spaces specially designed for relaxation and reconnecting with yourself.

- Meditation Gardens: Peaceful gardens, designed for meditation and contemplation, provide a tranquil refuge for guests.
- Forest Baths: Inspired by the Japanese practice of " Shinrin-yoku " or forest bathing, some establishments offer guided walks in the woods to promote relaxation and natural healing.

Experiential Tourism

Cultural Immersion

Travelers are looking for authentic, immersive experiences that allow them to deeply connect with local culture.

- Craft Workshops: Guests can participate in local craft workshops, such as pottery, weaving or jewelry making, led by local artisans.
- Thematic Guided Tours: Guided tours on specific themes, such as history, architecture or local gastronomy, are increasingly popular.

Adventures and Discoveries

Relais & Châteaux offer adventure experiences tailored to the tastes of modern travelers.

- Outdoor Excursions: Activities like hiking, mountain biking, climbing and water sports are organized for outdoor enthusiasts.
- Gastronomic Experiences: Wine tastings, vineyard tours, cooking classes and private dinners in unique locations add a gastronomic dimension to the travel experience.

Technological innovation

Cutting-Edge Technology for Comfort

Technological innovation plays a key role in improving customer comfort and convenience.

- Smart Rooms: Rooms are equipped with smart home technologies, allowing guests to control lighting, temperature and entertainment systems via mobile apps.

- Personalized Services: The use of artificial intelligence and big data makes it possible to personalize the experience of each customer, by anticipating their needs and preferences.

Digitalization of the Customer Experience

Digitalization is transforming the customer experience, making it more fluid and interactive.

- Virtual Check-In and Check-Out: Guests can check-in and check-out via mobile apps, reducing the need to go through the front desk.
- Digital Concierge: Digital concierge services allow guests to book excursions, restaurant tables and spa services directly from their smartphone.

Commitment to Sustainability

Ecological Practices

Relais & Châteaux are increasingly committed to sustainable and ecological practices.

- Reduction of the Carbon Footprint: The use of renewable energies, efficient management of water resources and initiatives to reduce waste contribute to minimizing the carbon footprint of establishments.
- Eco-Responsible Architecture: New construction and renovation projects adopt sustainable architecture principles, using local and recycled materials, and integrating energy-efficient solutions.

Support for the Local Community

Relais & Châteaux are strengthening their commitment to local communities, contributing to economic and social development.

- Local Partnerships: Establishments collaborate with local producers to source food, crafts and services, thus supporting the local economy.
- Community Projects: Many establishments participate in community projects, such as educational programs, conservation initiatives and sustainable development efforts.

Conclusion

Relais & Châteaux, by embracing these new trends, demonstrate their ability to evolve while retaining the fundamental values that define them: luxury, authenticity and excellence. By integrating holistic wellness, experiential tourism, technological innovation and commitment to sustainability, these establishments continue to provide unique and memorable experiences for their guests.

These trends not only evolve the customer experience, they also reaffirm Relais & Châteaux's commitment to quality and authenticity. The future of these establishments looks promising, with a renewed capacity to inspire, delight and offer exceptional moments, while respecting and promoting the cultural and natural riches of their respective environments.

- Innovations and Developments

Relais & Châteaux have always stood out for their ability to offer exceptional and unique experiences to their clients. As the world evolves, these establishments must innovate and grow to meet the new expectations of travelers and the challenges of the modern world. In this chapter, we will explore the key innovations and developments shaping the future of Relais & Châteaux, particularly in the areas of sustainability, technology, gastronomy and well-being.

Innovations in Sustainability

Renewable Energy and Energy Efficiency

Sustainability is a growing priority for Relais & Châteaux, which seeks to reduce its environmental impact while providing optimal comfort to its guests.

- Use of Renewable Energy: Many establishments are investing in renewable energy sources such as solar, wind and geothermal energy to reduce their dependence on fossil fuels.
- Energy Efficient Buildings: New construction and renovations adopt high standards for energy efficiency, with intelligent energy management systems, high-quality insulation and energy-efficient windows.

Waste Management and Circular Economy

Relais & Châteaux implement waste management practices aimed at minimizing their production and maximizing recycling and composting.

- Plastic Reduction: The elimination of single-use plastics and the adoption of biodegradable or reusable materials for bathroom products, food packaging and other common items.
- Composting and Recycling: Composting systems for organic waste and comprehensive recycling programs are put in place to effectively manage waste and reduce its environmental impact.

Technological innovations

Connected Customer Experience

Technological advances allow Relais & Châteaux to personalize and improve the customer experience.

- Smart Rooms: Rooms are equipped with smart home technologies that allow guests to control lighting, temperature, curtains and entertainment systems via mobile apps or voice assistants.
- Personalized Services: The use of artificial intelligence and big data makes it possible to personalize the customer experience by anticipating their needs and preferences, offering tailored recommendations and services.

Digitalization of Services

Digitalization is transforming the interaction between customers and establishments, making services more fluid and accessible.

- Virtual Check-In and Check-Out: Guests can check in and out of the hotel via mobile apps, reducing the need to go through the front desk and speeding up the process.
- Digital Concierge: Digital concierge services allow guests to book excursions, restaurant tables, spa treatments and other services directly from their smartphone.

Innovations in Gastronomy

Sustainable and Locavore Cuisine

Relais & Châteaux emphasize sustainable cuisine that promotes local and seasonal products.

- Locavores Menus: Chefs collaborate with local producers to create menus that highlight regional ingredients, thereby reducing the carbon footprint and supporting the local economy.
- Owned Gardens and Farms: Many establishments grow their own vegetables, fruits and herbs in organic gardens, and some even own farms to raise animals in conditions that respect animal welfare.

Innovative Gastronomic Experiences

Innovation in gastronomy goes beyond simple food preparation, encompassing immersive and educational experiences.

- Culinary Workshops: Cooking classes and workshops are organized to allow guests to learn local cooking techniques and prepare traditional dishes themselves.
- Experiential Dinners: Themed meals, outdoor dinners under the stars and private tastings offer unique and memorable culinary experiences.

Innovations in Well-Being

Holistic Well-Being and Alternative Therapies

Relais & Châteaux adopt a holistic approach to well-being, integrating alternative therapies and relaxation practices.

- Holistic Therapies: The integration of practices such as acupuncture, reflexology, aromatherapy and LED light therapy to offer a complete range of wellness treatments.
- Personalized Wellness Programs: Tailored wellness programs, including yoga, meditation, nutrition and life coaching sessions, are offered to meet clients' specific needs.

Wellness Spaces and Facilities

The wellness facilities at Relais & Châteaux are designed to provide the ultimate relaxing and rejuvenating experience.

- Luxury Spas: Spas equipped with indoor and outdoor swimming pools, saunas, hammams, hot tubs and treatment rooms, offering a wide range of treatments and therapies.
- Spaces for Reconnecting with Nature: Meditation gardens, walking trails and forest baths are created to allow guests to reconnect with nature and enjoy the tranquility of natural environments.

Sustainable Development and Social Responsibility

Community Engagement

Relais & Châteaux are actively engaged in their local communities, contributing to their economic and social development.

- Local Partnerships: Establishments collaborate with local producers, artisans and entrepreneurs to support the regional economy and promote local products.
- Sustainable Development Initiatives: Participation in conservation projects, educational programs and sustainable development initiatives that benefit the local community and the environment.

Ecological Certifications and Standards

To guarantee a positive and lasting impact, Relais & Châteaux strive to obtain ecological certifications and respect high sustainability standards.

- Environmental Certifications: Labels such as Green Globe, EarthCheck and ISO 14001 attest to the efforts made by establishments to reduce their environmental impact.
- Social Responsibility Commitments: The implementation of corporate social responsibility (CSR) policies to promote equity, diversity and sustainable development.

Conclusion

Relais & Châteaux, through their ability to innovate and develop, continue to position themselves as leaders in luxury hotels and gastronomy. By integrating sustainable practices, advanced technologies, innovative gastronomic experiences and a holistic approach to wellness, these establishments offer exceptional experiences that meet the expectations of modern travelers while respecting the core values of authenticity and authenticity. Excellency.

These innovations and developments ensure that Relais & Châteaux will remain popular destinations for those seeking memorable, luxurious and enriching stays. By committing to being at the forefront of trends and providing impeccable service, these establishments will continue to inspire and delight their customers for years to come.

- The Role of Sustainability

Sustainability has become a central pillar for Relais & Châteaux, influencing every aspect of their operations. In a world increasingly aware of environmental and social issues, these prestigious establishments must not only offer luxury experiences but also be models of ecological and social responsibility. This chapter examines how Relais & Châteaux are integrating sustainability into their overall strategy and why this approach is essential for their future.

Commitment to the Environment

Reduction of the Carbon Footprint

Relais & Châteaux are implementing various initiatives to reduce their carbon footprint, by adopting sustainable practices and investing in green technologies.

- Renewable Energy: The use of solar panels, geothermal systems and other renewable energy sources to supply establishments with electricity and heating.
- Energy Efficiency: Installation of LED lighting systems, intelligent energy management devices and low-consumption appliances to minimize energy consumption.

Sustainable Water Management

Water conservation is a priority for Relais & Châteaux, especially in regions where this resource is precious.

- Rainwater Harvesting Systems: Use of rainwater for garden irrigation and cleaning, thereby reducing dependence on drinking water sources.
- Consumption Reduction Technologies: Installation of low-flow faucets, showers and toilets to reduce water consumption in rooms and common areas.

Waste management

Establishments strive to minimize waste and maximize recycling and composting.

- Reduction of Plastics: Removal of single-use plastics, replacement with sustainable alternatives and use of reusable containers.
- Composting and Recycling: Composting programs for food waste and recycling for materials such as glass, paper and metal.

Sustainable Culinary Practices

Local and Seasonal Sourcing

Relais & Châteaux favor local and seasonal products to reduce their carbon footprint and support the local economy.

- Own Farms and Gardens: Many establishments grow their own fruits, vegetables and herbs, guaranteeing the freshness and quality of the ingredients.
- Partnerships with Local Producers: Close collaboration with local farmers, fishermen and breeders to source fresh, high-quality products.

Reduction of Food Waste

The fight against food waste is a major challenge for Relais & Châteaux.
- Tailor-made Menus: Design of menus that use every part of the ingredients to minimize waste.
- Donations: Surplus food is often donated to local organizations to help communities in need.

Social and Economic Commitment

Support for Local Communities

Relais & Châteaux play an active role in supporting and developing local communities.

- Local Employment: Priority to hiring local staff, offering training and professional development opportunities.
- Community Initiatives: Participation in local projects such as the construction of infrastructure, support for education and the promotion of local culture.

Fair and Ethical Trade

Establishments ensure that their business practices meet high ethical standards.

- Fair Trade Products: Use of fair trade products, guaranteeing decent working conditions and fair remuneration for producers.
- Transparency and Traceability: Commitment to transparency in the supply chain, allowing customers to know where the products they consume come from.

Awareness and Education

Customer Education

Relais & Châteaux educate their guests about the importance of sustainability and ecological practices.

- Educational Programs: Organization of seminars, workshops and guided tours to inform guests about the establishment's sustainable initiatives.
- Transparent Communication: Use of communication materials such as brochures, posters and mobile applications to share sustainability efforts with customers.

Staff training

Continuing staff training is essential to maintain sustainable practices and provide quality service.

- Training Programs: Regular courses on environmental best practices, conservation techniques and the importance of sustainability.
- Commitment and Motivation: Encouragement of staff to propose ideas and initiatives to further improve the establishment's sustainable practices.

Conclusion

Commitment to sustainability is essential for Relais & Châteaux, not only to meet the expectations of modern guests but also to ensure the sustainability of the environment and local communities. By integrating sustainable practices into every aspect of their operation, these establishments demonstrate their dedication to preserving the planet and improving people's well-being.

Relais & Châteaux show that luxury and sustainability can go hand in hand, offering exceptional experiences while respecting the principles of environmental and social responsibility. By continuing to innovate and adapt, these properties are well-positioned to inspire and guide the hospitality industry towards a more sustainable and responsible future.